O 1007-50

Mastering Oracle
SQL and SQL*Plus

Apress®

Mastering Oracle SQL and SQL*Plus

Copyright © 2005 by Lex de Haan

ISBN (pbk): 1-59059-448-7

Printed and bound in the United States of America 9 8 7 6 5 4 3 2 1

Trademarked names may appear in this book. Rather than use a trademark symbol with every occurrence of a trademarked name, we use the names only in an editorial fashion and to the benefit of the trademark owner, with no intention of infringement of the trademark.

Lead Editor: Tony Davis
Technical Reviewers: Cary Millsap and Joakim Treugut
Editorial Board: Steve Anglin, Dan Appleman, Ewan Buckingham, Gary Cornell, Tony Davis, John Franklin, Jason Gilmore, Chris Mills, Dominic Shakeshaft, Jim Sumser
Project Manager: Beckie Stones
Copy Edit Manager: Nicole LeClerc
Copy Editor: Marilyn Smith
Production Manager: Kari Brooks-Copony
Production Editor: Kelly Winquist
Compositor: Dina Quan
Proofreader: Liz Welch
Indexer: Michael Brinkman
Artist: Kinetic Publishing
Cover Designer: Kurt Krames
Manufacturing Manager: Tom Debolski

Distributed to the book trade in the United States by Springer-Verlag New York, Inc., 233 Spring Street, 6th Floor, New York, NY 10013, and outside the United States by Springer-Verlag GmbH & Co. KG, Tiergartenstr. 17, 69112 Heidelberg, Germany.

In the United States: phone 1-800-SPRINGER, fax 201-348-4505, e-mail orders@springer-ny.com, or visit http://www.springer-ny.com. Outside the United States: fax +49 6221 345229, e-mail orders@springer.de, or visit http://www.springer.de.

For information on translations, please contact Apress directly at 2560 Ninth Street, Suite 219, Berkeley, CA 94710. Phone 510-549-5930, fax 510-549-5939, e-mail info@apress.com, or visit http://www.apress.com.

The information in this book is distributed on an "as is" basis, without warranty. Although every precaution has been taken in the preparation of this work, neither the author(s) nor Apress shall have any liability to any person or entity with respect to any loss or damage caused or alleged to be caused directly or indirectly by the information contained in this work.

The source code for this book is available to readers at http://www.apress.com in the Downloads section, and also on the author's web site, at http://www.naturaljoin.nl.

Contents at a Glance

Contents

Foreword

It is a true honor to be asked to write an introduction to a book by Lex de Haan. I just hope I can give Lex the credit he deserves for his friendship, knowledge, enthusiasm, carpentry . . . and sheer energy in the many years we've been doing things in the Oracle world.

Lex spent 14 years in Oracle, starting as an instructor in Oracle Netherlands, becoming initiator and coordinator of Oracle's excellent Technical Seminar business, and finally ending up in Oracle's Curriculum Development division as a manager for a bunch of very excellent course developers. He is never afraid to start up something new, to enter new and untried waters... a personal trait he shares with about 0.00001% of the global population.

Then, finally, Lex started up for himself, and, of course, the company name had to reflect his twisted, funny way of thinking: Natural Join. Who else can get away with it, looking stone-faced and with just the slightest twinkle in his eyes, if you look really carefully?

Since then Lex, as always, hasn't looked back but has worked nonstop as instructor all over Europe and the Middle East, and as writer. The book in front of you is, in fact, an update of a book he wrote many moons ago, and which has served as a textbook in various Dutch schools. The upgrade (and translation into English) has been done in an incredibly short time, and as the first one ever, he has kept his deadlines with editor Tony Davis from Apress. Of course. Nothing less should be expected from Lex.

Lex is one of the original members of the OakTable Network, and the man behind the idea of Mini Oak Tables (MOTs), which he produces in his loft, where he has a fair selection of tools to handle most things you'd ever want to do to wood. Lately, he has also produced a bathroom table for me with the universal dimensions 42×4×42 centimeters. After all, 42 is the answer according to the *Hitchhiker's Guide to the Galaxy*. And he has started producing bottle openers in oak. They work.

Before writing this, I had the pleasure of reading the comments made by Cary Millsap and Joakim Treugut (both Oakies as well) on the contents of this book, and they must be the most consistently positive remarks I've seen from those two for a very, very long time.

I think Lex has done it again. At Oracle, he had to excel. As a bass singer, he had to be not just good, but very good. As a carpenter, he has to deliver absolutely perfect MOTs, 42 tables, and bottle openers. As a writer, he has to deliver a standard-setting book. It's really rather irritating to be around him. If, that is, it wasn't for his very nice wife Juliette, who is, I suspect, very much responsible for the energy and good mood always emanating from Lex.

I look forward to many more meetings and late nights with my friend Lex, who shares with several of us a deep affection for the Monty Pythonesque aspects of this world.

Oh, and if you haven't seen Lex in person, I should tell you that he is built exactly like the typical, Dutch house he lives in: tall and narrow, with a lot of good stuff on the upper floor.

Mogens Nørgaard
Technical Director
Miracle A/S

About the Author

 **LEX DE HAAN** studied applied mathematics at the Technical University in Delft, The Netherlands. His experience with Oracle goes back to the mid-1980s, version 4. He worked for Oracle Corporation from 1990 until 2004, in various education-related roles, ending up in Server Technologies (product development) as senior curriculum manager for the advanced DBA curriculum. In that role, he was involved in the development of Oracle9*i* and Oracle Database 10*g*. In March 2004, he decided to go independent and founded Natural Join B.V. (http://www.naturaljoin.nl). Since 1999, he has been involved in the ISO SQL language standardization process, as a member of the Dutch national body.

About the Technical Reviewers

 **CARY MILLSAP** is the principal author of *Optimizing Oracle Performance*, and the lead designer and developer of the Hotsos PD101 course. Prior to cofounding Hotsos in 1999, he served for ten years at Oracle Corporation as one of the company's leading system performance experts. At Oracle, he also founded and served as vice president of the 80-person System Performance Group. He has educated thousands of Oracle consultants, support analysts, developers, and customers in the optimal use of Oracle technology through commitment to writing, teaching, and speaking at public events.

 **JOCKE TREUGUT** started to work with databases at the Stockholm Stock Exchange in 1985. In 1993, he began to use Oracle, and he became very interested in its internals and performance. After attending a wonderful workshop, "How to get information rather than data from the V$ views," by Dave Ensor at the EOUG 1996, Jocke understood that the optimizer and optimization should be his area. In 1997, he started to work for Oracle Support (Sweden) and became their performance expert, remaining there for five years. He then moved to New Zealand, where he worked for Synergy International and created the Oracle Unleashed service; and his presentation about performance tuning at NZOUG 2003 was voted as the best one. He is now working for Aircom International, where he troubleshoots and optimizes database systems around the world. He would like to thank Nancy Yip, Åke Hörnell, Stefan Sundberg, Janne Fälldin, Göran Forsström, Rikard Hedberg, Oracle Support (Sweden), the OakTable Network, and Aircom for their support in fulfilling his dream.

Acknowledgments

I want to thank many friends who contributed to the quality of this book by reviewing it and providing their feedback. Cary Millsap and Jocke Treugut, two good friends and members of the OakTable network, were my main reviewers. Cary helped me with his constant focus on "doing things right" from the very beginning, and Jocke helped me find the right balance between theory and practice. Martin Jensen, one of my good old friends inside Oracle and an Oakie as well, provided precisely the feedback I needed from his impressive Oracle consulting background. Stephen Cannan, my colleague in the Dutch national body for the SQL Standardization and the convenor of the international ISO/IEC/JTC1/SC32/WG3 committee, commented on my draft chapters based on his vast experience in the SQL standardization area.

Kristina Youso, a former colleague and good friend from my years in Global Curriculum Development in Oracle and one of the best content editors I have ever worked with, was so kind to check and improve my English language.

Last, but not least, I must mention the professionalism and enthusiasm of all the Apress folks involved in the production of this book: Tony Davis, Beckie Stones, Marilyn Smith, and Kelly Winquist. Thanks folks . . .

My two daughters are too old to be mentioned here, the cat was not involved in any way, and I leave it up to Mogens Nørgaard to say something nice about my wife, Juliette.

Reactions to this book are more than welcome; send your feedback or questions to the publisher, or via e-mail to the author.

Lex de Haan
http://www.naturaljoin.nl
E-mail: lex.de.haan@naturaljoin.nl

Introduction

This book is a translation and enhancement of the third edition of a book I wrote about SQL in Dutch. The first edition was published in February 1993, the second edition in April 1998, and I finished the third edition to reflect Oracle Database 10*g* in the summer of 2004. I always thought that there were more than enough books in English about the SQL language out there already, but finally, some good friends convinced me to publish an English version of my book.

I hate thick books. I start reading them, put them aside on a certain pile on my desk, from where they are purged every now and then (if the pile becomes too high), without being read to the end. Therefore, in my own book, I have tried to be as concise as possible.

About This Book

This is *not* a book about advanced SQL. It is *not* a book about the Oracle optimizer and diagnostic tools. And it is *not* a book about relational calculus, predicate logic, or set theory. This book is a SQL primer. It is meant to help you learn Oracle SQL by yourself. It is ideal for self-study, but it can also be used as a guide for SQL workshops and instructor-led classroom training.

This is a *practical* book; therefore, you need access to an Oracle environment for hands-on exercises. All the software that you need to install Oracle Database 10*g* on Microsoft Windows and to create an Oracle database is available from the CD-ROM included with this book. This book is based on the following Oracle release:

- Oracle Database 10*g* for Windows (or Red Hat Linux) Release 10.1.0.x

Although this book assumes an Oracle Database 10*g* environment, you can also use it with Oracle9*i* or even with Oracle8*i*. However, Oracle is adding new SQL syntax with every new release; therefore, some SQL syntax examples could fail when issued against these earlier releases. You can check this yourself by querying the online Oracle documentation. *Oracle SQL Reference* offers a section titled "Oracle Database 10*g* New Features in the SQL Reference" at the end of the introduction, preceding Chapter 1.

I follow the ANSI/ISO standard (SQL:2003) as much as possible. Only in cases of useful Oracle-specific SQL extensions do I deviate from this international standard. Therefore, most SQL examples given in this book are probably also valid for other database management system (DBMS) implementations supporting the SQL language. By the way, *Oracle SQL Reference* contains an Appendix B, "Oracle and Standard SQL," discussing the differences between the ANSI/ISO SQL standard and the Oracle SQL implementation.

The SQL and SQL*Plus commands are explained with concrete examples. The examples are presented clearly in a listing format, as in the example shown here.

Listing I-1. *A SQL SELECT Command*

```
SQL> select 'Hello world!'
  2  from    dual;
```

I focus on the main points, avoiding peripheral issues and technical details as much as possible.

This book does not intend (nor pretend) to be complete; the SQL language is too voluminous and the Oracle environment is much too complex. *Oracle SQL Reference* contains about 1,800 pages these days, and even *Oracle SQL Quick Reference* is not really a small document, with its 170 pages. Moreover, the current ANSI/ISO SQL standard documentation has grown to a size that simply is not printable anymore.

The main objective of this book is the combination of *usability* and *affordability*. The official Oracle documentation offers detailed information in case you need it. Therefore, it is a good idea to have the Oracle manuals available while working through the examples and exercises in this book. The Oracle documentation is available online on the Oracle Technology Network (http://www.oracle.com/technology/documentation) and can be downloaded from there (if you don't want to keep an Internet connection open all the time).

The focus of this book is using SQL for data *retrieval*. Data definition and data manipulation are covered in less detail. Security, authorization, and database administration are mentioned only for the sake of completeness in the SQL overview section in Chapter 2.

Throughout the book, we use a case consisting of seven tables. These seven tables contain information about employees, departments, and courses. As Chris Date, a well-known guru in the professional database world (see Appendix E for references to some of the great books he wrote), said during one of his seminars, "There are only three databases: employees and departments, orders and line items, and suppliers and shipments."

The cardinality of the case tables is deliberately kept low. This enables you to check the results of your SQL commands manually, which is nice while you're learning to master the SQL language. In general, checking your results manually is impossible in real information systems, due to the volume of data in such systems. It is not the data volume or query response time that matters in this book. What's important is the database structure complexity and SQL statement correctness. By the way, the two case tables EMPLOYEES and DEPARTMENTS show a striking resemblance to good old SCOTT.EMP and SCOTT.DEPT, two of the Oracle demo tables that have been shipped with Oracle pretty much from the very beginning.

About the Chapters of This Book

Chapter 1 provides a concise introduction to the theoretical background of information systems and some popular database terminology, and then continues with a global overview of the Oracle software and an introduction to the seven case tables. If you really don't like theory and you want to get started with SQL as soon as possible, you could skip this chapter almost entirely and start reading about the case tables in Section 1.9. However, I think Chapter 1 contains a lot of important and useful information. If you skip it, you might want to revisit it later.

Chapter 2 starts with a high-level overview of the SQL language, followed by an introduction to SQL*Plus and *i*SQL*Plus, the two most obvious environments to execute SQL statements interactively. In Chapter 11, we revisit SQL*Plus. That chapter covers some more advanced SQL*Plus features, such as using substitution variables, stored scripts, reporting, and working with HTML.

Data definition is covered in two nonconsecutive chapters: Chapter 3 and Chapter 7. This is done to allow you to start with SQL retrieval as soon as possible. Therefore, Chapter 3 covers only the most basic data-definition concepts (tables, datatypes, and the data dictionary).

Retrieval is also spread over multiple chapters—four chapters, to be precise. Chapter 4 focuses on the SELECT, WHERE, and ORDER BY clauses of the SELECT statement. The most important SQL functions are covered in Chapter 5, which also covers null values and subqueries. In Chapter 8, we start accessing multiple tables at the same time (joining tables) and aggregating query results; in other words, the FROM, the GROUP BY, and the HAVING clauses get our attention in that chapter. To finish the coverage of data retrieval with SQL, Chapter 9 revisits subqueries to show some more advanced subquery constructs. That chapter also introduces windows and analytical functions, hierarchical queries, and flashback features.

■**Note** From Chapter 4 onwards, all chapters except Chapter 6 end with a set of exercises. The answers to these exercises are in Appendix D.

Chapter 6 discusses data manipulation with SQL. The commands INSERT, UPDATE, DELETE, and MERGE are introduced. This chapter also pays attention to some topics related to data manipulation: transaction processing, read consistency, and locking.

In Chapter 7, we revisit data definition, to drill down into constraints, indexes, sequences, and performance. Synonyms are explained in the same chapter. Chapters 8 and 9 continue coverage of data retrieval with SQL.

Chapter 10 introduces views. What are views, when should you use them, and what are their restrictions? This chapter explores the possibilities of data manipulation via views, discusses views and performance, and introduces materialized views.

Chapter 11 is a continuation of Chapter 2, covering more advanced SQL*Plus and *i*SQL*Plus features.

Oracle is an object-relational database management system. Since Oracle8, many object-oriented features have been added to the SQL language. As an introduction to these features, Chapter 12 provides a high-level overview of user-defined datatypes, arrays, nested tables, and multiset operators.

The five appendices at the end of this book offer a SQL*Plus and SQL quick reference, an overview of the Oracle data dictionary, a description of the structure and contents of the seven case tables, the answers to the exercises, and references to other sources of information.

About the CD-ROM

The CD-ROM included with this book contains a Developer License for Oracle Database 10*g*, allowing you to install the Oracle software on a Windows machine and to create a database. The scripts to set up the schema and to create the seven case tables, all examples and answers to the exercises, and various tips about how to set up the right database environment for this book are available from my web site at http://www.naturaljoin.nl, or via the Downloads section of the publisher's web site, http://www.apress.com.

Oracle Technology Network (OTN)

The full Oracle documentation is available online via OTN, the Oracle Technology Network, at http://www.oracle.com/technology/documentation. If you want to install Oracle Database 10*g* on a different operating system, you can download the Oracle software for various platforms from OTN at http://www.oracle.com/technology/software/products/database/oracle10g.

■ ■ ■

CHAPTER 1

Relational Database Systems and Oracle

The focus of this book is writing SQL in Oracle, which is a relational database management system. This first chapter provides a brief introduction to relational database systems in general, followed by an introduction to the Oracle software environment. The main objective of this chapter is to help you find your way in the relational database jungle and to get acquainted with the most important database terminology.

The first three sections discuss the main reasons for automating information systems using databases, what needs to be done to design and build relational database systems, and the various components of a relational database management system. The following sections go into more depth about the theoretical foundation of relational database management systems.

This chapter also gives a brief overview of the Oracle software environment: the components of such an environment, the characteristics of those components, and what can you do with those components.

The last section of this chapter introduces seven sample tables, which are used in the examples and exercises throughout this book to help you develop your SQL skills. In order to be able to formulate and execute the correct SQL statements, you'll need to understand the structures and relationships of these tables.

This chapter does not cover any object-relational database features. Chapter 12 discusses the various Oracle features in that area.

1.1 Information Needs and Information Systems

Organizations have business objectives. In order to realize those business objectives, many decisions must be made on a daily basis. Typically, a lot of *information* is needed to make the right decisions; however, this information is not always available in the appropriate format. Therefore, organizations need formal systems that will allow them to produce the required information, in the right format, at the right time. Such systems are called *information systems*. An information system is a simplified reflection (a *model*) of the real world within the organization.

Information systems don't necessarily need to be automated—the data might reside in card files, cabinets, or other physical storage mechanisms. This data can be converted into the desired information using certain procedures or actions. In general, there are two main reasons to automate information systems:

- **Complexity:** The data structures or the data processing procedures become too complicated.

- **Volume:** The volume of the data to be administered becomes too large.

If an organization decides to automate an information system because of complexity or volume (or both), it typically will need to use some database technology.

The main advantages of using database technology are the following:

- **Accessibility:** Ad hoc data-retrieval functionality, data-entry and data-reporting facilities, and concurrency handling in a multiuser environment

- **Availability:** Recovery facilities in case of system crashes and human errors

- **Security:** Data access control, privileges, and auditing

- **Manageability:** Utilities to efficiently manage large volumes of data

When specifying or modeling information needs, it is a good idea to maintain a clear separation between *information* and *application*. In other words, we separate the following two aspects:

- **What:** The information *content* needed. This is the *logical* level.

- **How:** The desired *format* of the information, the way that the results can be derived from the data stored in the information system, the minimum performance requirements, and so on. This is the *physical* level.

Database systems such as Oracle enable us to maintain this separation between the "what" and the "how" aspects, allowing us to concentrate on the first one. This is because their implementation is based on the *relational model*. The relational model is explained later in this chapter, in Sections 1.4 through 1.7.

1.2 Database Design

One of the problems with using traditional third-generation programming languages (such as COBOL, Pascal, Fortran, and C) is the ongoing maintenance of existing code, because these languages don't separate the "what" and the "how" aspects of information needs. That's why programmers using those languages sometimes spend more than 75% of their precious time on maintenance of existing programs, leaving little time for them to build new programs.

When using database technology, organizations usually need many database applications to process the data residing in the database. These database applications are typically developed using fourth- or fifth-generation application development environments, which significantly enhance productivity by enabling users to develop database applications *faster* while producing applications with *lower maintenance* costs. However, in order to be successful using these fourth- and fifth-generation application development tools, developers must start thinking about the structure of their data first.

It is *very* important to spend enough time on designing the data model *before* you start coding your applications. Data model mistakes discovered in a later stage, when the system is already in production, are very difficult and expensive to fix.

Entities and Attributes

In a database, we store facts about certain objects. In database jargon, such objects are commonly referred to as *entities*. For each entity, we are typically interested in a set of observable and relevant properties, commonly referred to as *attributes*.

When designing a data model for your information system, you begin with two questions:

1. Which entities are relevant for the information system?

2. Which attributes are relevant for each entity, and which values are allowed for those attributes?

We'll add a third question to this list before the end of this chapter, to make the list complete.

For example, consider a company in the information technology training business. Examples of relevant entities for the information system of this company could be course attendee, classroom, instructor, registration, confirmation, invoice, course, and so on. An example of a partial list of relevant attributes for the entity ATTENDEE could be the following:

- Registration number

- Name

- Address

- City

- Date of birth

- Blood group

- Age

- Gender

For the COURSE entity, the attribute list could look as follows:

- Title

- Duration (in days)

- Price

- Frequency

- Maximum number of attendees

■**Note** There are many different terminology conventions for entities and attributes, such as *objects*, *object types*, *types*, *object occurrences*, and so on. The terminology itself is not important, but once you have made a choice, you should use it consistently.

Generic vs. Specific

The difference between *generic* versus *specific* is very important in database design. For example, common words in natural languages such as *book* and *course* have both generic and specific meanings. In spoken language, the precise meaning of these words is normally obvious from the context in which they are used.

When designing data models, you must be very careful about the distinction between generic and specific meanings of the same word. For example, a course has a title and a duration (generic), while a specific course offering has a location, a certain number of attendees, and an instructor. A specific book on the shelf might have your name and purchase date on the cover page, and it might be full of your personal annotations. A generic book has a title, an author, a publisher, and an ISBN code. This means that you should be careful when using words like *course* and *book* for database entities, because they could be confusing and suggest the wrong meaning.

Moreover, we must maintain a clear separation between an entity itself at the generic level and a specific occurrence of that entity. Along the same lines, there is a difference between an entity *attribute* (at the generic level) and a specific *attribute value* for a particular entity occurrence.

Redundancy

There are two types of data: base data and derivable data. *Base data* is data that cannot be derived in any way from other data residing in the information system. It is crucial that base data is stored in the database. *Derivable data* can be deduced (for example, with a formula) from other data. For example, if we store both the age and the date of birth of each course attendee in our database, these two attributes are mutually derivable—assuming that the current date is available at any moment.

Actually, every question issued against a database results in derived data. In other words, it is both undesirable and impossible to store all derivable data in an information system. Storage of derivable data is referred to as *redundancy*. Another way of defining redundancy is storage of the same data more than once.

Sometimes, it makes sense to store redundant data in a database; for example, in cases where response time is crucial and in cases where repeated computation or derivation of the desired data would be too time-consuming. But typically, storage of redundant data in a database should be avoided. First of all, it is a waste of storage capacity. However, that's not the biggest problem, since gigabytes of disk capacity can be bought for relatively low prices these days. The challenge with redundant data storage lies in its ongoing maintenance.

With redundant data in your database, it is difficult to process data manipulation correctly under all circumstances. In case something goes wrong, you could end up with an information system containing internal contradictions. In other words, you would have *inconsistent* data. Therefore, redundancy in an information system results in ongoing consistency problems.

When considering the storage of redundant data in an information system, it is important to distinguish two types of information systems:

- Online transaction processing (OLTP) systems, which typically have a high volume of continuous data changes

- Decision support (DSS) systems, which are mainly, or even exclusively, used for data retrieval and reporting, and are loaded or refreshed at certain frequencies with data from OLTP systems

In DSS systems, it is common practice to store a lot of redundant data to improve system response times. Retrieval of stored data is always faster than data derivation, and the risk of inconsistency is nonexistent because most DSS systems are read-only.

Consistency, Integrity, and Integrity Constraints

Obviously, consistency is a first requirement for any information system, ensuring that you can retrieve reliable information from that system. In other words, you don't want any *contradictions* in your information system.

For example, suppose we derive the following information from our training business information system:

- Attendee 6749 was born on February 13, 2093.

- The same attendee 6749 appears to have gender Z.

- There is another, different attendee with the same number 6749.

- We see a course registration for attendee 8462, but this number does not appear in the administration records where we maintain a list of all persons.

In none of the above four cases is the consistency at stake; the information system is unambiguous in its statements. Nevertheless, there is something wrong because these statements do not conform to common sense.

This brings us to the second requirement for an information system: *data integrity*. We would consider it more in accordance with our perception of reality if the following were true of our information system:

- For any course attendee, the date of birth does not lie in the future.

- The gender attribute for any person has the value M or F.

- Every course attendee (or person in general) has a unique number.

- We have registration information only for existing attendees—that is, attendees known to the information system.

These rules concerning database contents are called *constraints*. You should translate all your business rules into formal integrity constraints. The third example—a unique number for each person—is a primary key constraint, and it implements *entity integrity*. The fourth example—information for only persons known to the system—is a foreign key constraint, implementing *referential integrity*. We will revisit these concepts later in this chapter, in Section 1.5.

Constraints are often classified based on the lowest level at which they can be checked. The following are four constraint types, each illustrated with an example:

- **Attribute constraints:** Checks attributes; for example, "Gender must be M or F."

- **Row constraints:** Checks at the row level; for example, "For salesmen, commission is a mandatory attribute."

- **Table constraints:** Checks at the table level; for example, "Each employee has a unique e-mail address."

- **Database constraints:** Checks at the database level; for example, "Each employee works for an existing department."

In Chapter 7, we'll revisit integrity constraints to see how you can formally specify them in the SQL language.

At the beginning of this section, you learned that information needs can be formalized by identifying which entities are relevant for the information system, and then deciding which attributes are relevant for each entity. Now we can add a third step to the information analysis list of steps to produce a formal data model:

1. Which entities are relevant for the information system?

2. Which attributes are relevant for each entity?

3. Which integrity constraints should be enforced by the system?

Data Modeling Approach, Methods, and Techniques

Designing appropriate data models is not a sinecure, and it is typically a task for IT specialists. On the other hand, it is almost impossible to design data models without the active participation of the future end users of the system. End users usually have the most expertise in their professional area, and they are also involved in the final system acceptance tests.

Over the years, many methods have been developed to support the system development process itself, to generate system documentation, to communicate with project participants, and to manage projects to control time and costs. Traditional methods typically show a strict phasing of the development process and a description of what needs to be done in which order. That's why these methods are also referred to as *waterfall* methods. Roughly formulated, these methods distinguish the following four phases in the system development process:

1. **Analysis:** Describing the information needs and determining the information system boundaries

2. **Logical design:** Getting answers to the three questions about entities, attributes, and constraints, which were presented in the previous section

3. **Physical design:** Translating the logical design into a real database structure

4. **Build phase:** Building database applications

Within the development methods, you can use various *techniques* to support your activities. For example, you can use diagram techniques to represent data models graphically. Some well-known examples of such diagram techniques are Entity Relationship Modeling (ERM) and Unified Modeling Language (UML). In the last section of this chapter, which introduces the sample tables used throughout this book, you will see an ERM diagram that corresponds with those tables.

Another example of a well-known technique is *normalization*, which allows you to remove redundancy from a database design by following some strict rules.

Prototyping is also a quite popular technique. Using prototyping, you produce "quick and dirty" pieces of functionality to simulate parts of a system, with the intention of evoking reactions from the end users. This might result in time-savings during the analysis phase of the development process, and more important, better-quality results, thus increasing the probability of system acceptance at the end of the development process.

Rapid application development (RAD) is also a well-known term associated with data modeling. Instead of the waterfall approach described earlier, you employ an iterative approach.

Some methods and techniques are supported by corresponding computer programs, which are referred to as computer-aided systems engineering (CASE) tools. For example, Oracle offers complete and integral support for system development, from analysis to system generation, with the Oracle Designer software.

Semantics

If you want to use information systems correctly, you must be aware of the *semantics* (the meaning of things) of the underlying data model. A careful choice for table names and column names is a good starting point, followed by applying those names as consistently as possible. For example, the attribute "address" can have many different meanings: home address, work address, mailing address, and so on. The meaning of attributes that might lead to this type of confusion can be stored explicitly in an additional *semantic explanation* to the data model. Although such a semantic explanation is not part of the formal data model itself, you can store it in a *data dictionary*—a term explained in the next section.

Information Systems Terms Review

In this section, the following terms were introduced:

- Entities and attributes

- Generic versus specific

- Occurrences and attribute values

- Base data and derivable data

- Redundancy and consistency

- Integrity and constraints

- Data modeling

- Methods and techniques

- Logical and physical design

- Normalization

- Prototyping and RAD

- CASE tools

- Semantics

1.3 Database Management Systems

The preceding two sections defined the formal concept of an information system. You learned that if an organization decides to automate an information system, it typically uses some database technology. The term database can be defined as follows:

■**Definition** A *database* is a set of data, needed to derive the desired information from an information system and maintained by a separate software program.

This separate software program is called the *database management system* (DBMS). There are many types of database management systems available, varying in terms of the following characteristics:

- Price

- Ability to implement complex information systems

- Supported hardware environment

- Flexibility for application developers

- Flexibility for end users

- Ability to set up connections with other programs

- Speed

- Ongoing operational costs

- User-friendliness

DBMS Components

A DBMS has many components, including a kernel, data dictionary, query language, and tools.

Kernel

The core of any DBMS consists of the code that handles physical data storage, data transport (input and output) between external and internal memory, integrity checking, and so on. This crucial part of the DBMS is commonly referred to as the *kernel*.

Data Dictionary

Another important task of the DBMS is the maintenance of a *data dictionary*, containing all data about the data (the metadata). Here are some examples of information maintained in a data dictionary:

- Overview of all entities and attributes in the database
- Constraints (integrity)
- Access rights to the data
- Additional semantic explanations
- Database user authorization data
- Application data

Query Languages

Each DBMS vendor supports one or more languages to allow access to the data stored in the database. These languages are commonly referred to as *query languages*, although this name is rather confusing. SQL, the language this book is all about, has been the de facto market standard for many years.

DBMS Tools

Most DBMS vendors supply many secondary programs around their DBMS software. I refer to all these programs with the generic term *tools*. These tools allow users to perform tasks such as the following:

- Generate reports
- Build standard data-entry and data-retrieval screens
- Process database data in text documents or in spreadsheets
- Administer the database

Database Applications

Database applications are application programs that use an underlying database to store their data. Examples of such database applications are screen- and menu-driven data-entry programs, spreadsheets, report generators, and so on.

Database applications are often developed using development tools from the DBMS vendor. In fact, most of these development tools can be considered to be database applications themselves, because they typically use the database not only to store regular data, but also to store their application specifications. For example, consider tools such as Oracle Developer and Oracle Designer. With these examples we are entering the relational world, which is introduced in the next section.

DBMS Terms Review

In this section, the following terms were introduced:

- Database

- Database management system (DBMS)

- Kernel

- Data dictionary

- Query language

- Tool

- Database application

1.4 Relational Database Management Systems

The theoretical foundation for a *relational database management system* (RDBMS) was laid out in 1970 by Ted Codd in his famous article "A Relational Model of Data for Large Shared Data Banks" (Codd, 1970). He derived his revolutionary ideas from classical components of mathematics: set theory, relational calculus, and relational algebra.

■**Tip** In general, it certainly is helpful to have some mathematical skills while trying to solve nontrivial problems in SQL.

About ten years after Ted Codd published his article, around 1980, the first RDBMS systems (Relational DBMS systems) aiming to translate Ted Codd's ideas into real products became commercially available. Among the first pioneering RDBMS vendors were Oracle and Ingres, followed a few years later by IBM with SQL/DS and DB2.

We won't go into great detail about this formal foundation for relational databases, but we do need to review the basics in order to explain the term *relational*. The essence of Ted Codd's ideas was two main requirements:

- Clearly distinguish the logical task (the *what*) from the physical task (the *how*) both while designing, developing, and using databases.

- Make sure that an RDBMS implementation fully takes care of the physical task, so the system users need to worry only about executing the logical task.

These ideas, regardless of how evident they seem to be nowadays, were quite revolutionary in the early 1970s. Most DBMS implementations in those days did not separate the logical and physical tasks at all; did not have a solid theoretical foundation of any kind; and offered their users many surprises, ad hoc solutions, and exceptions. Ted Codd's article started a revolution and radically changed the way people think about databases.

What makes a DBMS a *relational* DBMS? In other words: how can we determine how relational a DBMS is? To answer this question, we must visit the theoretical foundation of the relational model. The following two sections discuss two important aspects of the relational model: relational data structures and relational operators. After these two sections, we will address another question: how relational is my DBMS?

1.5 Relational Data Structures

This section introduces the most important relational data structures and concepts:

- Tables, columns, and rows

- The information principle

- Datatypes

- Keys

- Missing information and null values

Tables, Columns, and Rows

The central concept in relational data structures is the *table* or *relation* (from which the relational model derives its name). A table is defined as a set of *rows*, or *tuples*. The rows of a table share the same set of attributes; a row consists of a set of (attribute name; attribute value) pairs. All data in a relational database is represented as *column values* within table rows.

In summary, the basic relational data structures are as follows:

- A database, which is a set of tables

- A table, which is a set of rows

- A row, which is a set of column values

The definition of a row is a little sloppy. A row is not just a set of column values. A more precise definition would be as follows:

A *row* is a set of ordered pairs, where each ordered pair consists of an attribute name with an associated attribute value.

For example, the following is a formal and precise way to represent a row from the DEPARTMENTS table:

```
{(deptno;40),(dname;HR),(location;Boston),(mgr;7839)}
```

This row represents department 40: the HR department in Boston, managed by employee 7839. It would become irritating to represent rows like this; therefore, this book will use less formal notations as much as possible. After all, the concept of tables, rows, and columns is rather intuitive.

In most cases, there is a rather straightforward one-to-one mapping between the entities of the data model and the tables in a relational database. The rows represent the occurrences of the corresponding entity, and the column headings of the table correspond with the attributes of that entity.

The Information Principle

The only way you can associate data in a relational database is by comparing column values. This principle, known as the *information principle*, is applied very strictly, and it is at the heart of the term *relational*.

An important property of sets is the fact that the order of their elements is meaningless. Therefore, the order of the rows in any relational table is meaningless, too, and the order of columns is also meaningless.

Because this is both very fundamental and important, let's rephrase this in another way: in a relational database, there are no pointers to represent relationships. For example, the fact that an employee works for a specific department can be derived only from the two corresponding tables by comparing column values in the two department number columns. In other words, for every retrieval command, you must explicitly specify which columns must be compared. As a consequence, the flexibility to formulate ad hoc queries in a relational database has no limits. The flip side of the coin is the risk of (mental) errors and the problem of the correctness of your results. Nearly every SQL query will return a result (as long as you don't make syntax errors), but is it really the answer to the question you had in mind?

Datatypes

One of the tasks during data modeling is also to decide which values are allowed for each attribute. As a minimum, you could allow only numbers in a certain column, or allow only dates or text. You can impose additional restrictions, such as by allowing only positive integers or text of a certain maximum length.

A set of allowed attribute values is sometimes referred to as a *domain*. Another common term is *datatype* (or just *type*). Each attribute is defined on a certain type. This can be a standard (built-in) type or a user-defined type.

Keys

Each relational table must have at least one *candidate key*. A candidate key is an attribute (or attribute combination) that uniquely identifies each row in that table, with one additional important property: as soon as you remove any attribute from this candidate key attribute combination, the property of unique identification is gone. In other words, a table cannot contain two rows with the same candidate key values at any time.

For example, the attribute combination course code and start date is a candidate key for a table containing information about course offerings. If you remove the start date attribute, the remaining course code attribute is not a candidate key anymore; otherwise, you could offer courses only once. If you remove the course code attribute, the remaining start date attribute is not a candidate key anymore; otherwise, you would never be able to schedule two different courses to start on the same day.

In case a table has multiple candidate keys, it is normal practice to select one of them to become the *primary key*. All components (attributes) of a primary key are mandatory; you must specify attribute values for all of them. Primary keys enforce a very important table constraint: *entity integrity*.

Sometimes, the set of candidate keys doesn't offer a convenient primary key. In such cases, you may choose a *surrogate key* by adding a meaningless attribute with the sole purpose of being the primary key.

■**Note** Using surrogate keys comes with advantages and disadvantages, and fierce debates between database experts. This section is intended to only explain the terminology, without offering an opinion on the use of surrogate keys.

A relational table can also have one or more *foreign keys*. Foreign key constraints are *subset requirements*; the foreign key values must always be a subset of a corresponding set of primary key values. Some typical examples of foreign key constraints are that an employee can work for only an existing department and can report to only an existing manager. Foreign keys implement *referential integrity* in a relational database.

Missing Information and Null Values

A relational DBMS is supposed to treat *missing information* in a systematic and context-insensitive manner. If a value is missing for a specific attribute of a row, it is not always possible to decide whether a certain condition evaluates to *true* or *false*. Missing information is represented by *null values* in the relational world.

The term *null value* is actually misleading, because it does not represent a value; it represents the fact that a value is missing. For example, *null marker* would be more appropriate. However, null value is the term most commonly used, so this book uses that terminology.

Null values imply the need for a *three-valued logic*, such as implemented (more or less) in the SQL language. The third logical value is *unknown*.

■**Note** Null values have had strong opponents and defenders. For example, Chris Date is a well-known opponent of null values and three-valued logic. His articles about this subject are highly readable, entertaining, and clarifying. See Appendix E of this book for some suggested reading.

Constraint Checking

Although most RDBMS vendors support integrity constraint checking in the database these days (Oracle implemented this feature about ten years ago), it is sometimes also desirable to implement constraint checking in client-side database applications. Suppose you have a network between a client-side data-entry application and the database, and the network connection is a bottleneck. In that case, client-side constraint checking probably results in much better response times, because there is no need to access the database each time to check the constraints. Code-generating tools (like Oracle Designer) typically allow you to specify whether constraints should be enforced at the database side, the client side, or both sides.

■**Caution** If you implement certain constraints in your client-side applications only, you risk database users bypassing the corresponding constraint checks by using alternative ways to connect to the database. Client-side constraints are also more difficult to manage.

Predicates and Propositions

To finish this section about relational data structures, there is another interesting way to look at tables and rows in a relational database from a completely different angle, as introduced by Hugh Darwen. This approach is more advanced than the other topics addressed in this chapter, so you might want to revisit this section later.

You can associate each relational table with a table predicate and all rows of a table with corresponding propositions. *Predicates* are logical expressions, typically containing free variables, which evaluate to true or false. For example, this is a predicate:

- There is a course with title T and duration D, price P, frequency F, and a maximum number of attendees M.

If we replace the five variables in this predicate (T, D, P, F, and M) with actual values, the result is a *proposition*. In logic, a proposition is a predicate without free variables; in other words, a proposition is always true or false. This means that you can consider the rows of a relational table as the set of all propositions that evaluate to true.

Relational Data Structure Terms Review

In this section, the following terms were introduced:

- Tables (or relations)

- Rows (or tuples)

- Columns and domains

- Candidate, primary, and foreign keys

- Integrity checking at the database level

- Missing information, null values, and three-valued logic

- Predicates and propositions

1.6 Relational Operators

To manipulate data, you need *operators* that can be applied to that data. Multiplication and addition are typical examples of operators in mathematics; you specify two numbers as input, and the operator produces one output value as a result. Multiplication and addition are examples of *closed operators*, because they produce "things" of the same type you provided as input (numbers). For example, for integers, addition is closed. Add any two integers, and you get another integer. Try it—you can't find two integers that add up to a noninteger. However, division over the integers is *not* closed; for example, 1 divided by 2 is not an integer. Closure is a nice operator property, because it allows you to (re)use the operator results as input for a next operator.

In a database environment, you need operators to derive information from the data stored in the database. In an RDBMS environment, all operators should operate at a high *logical level*. This means, among other things, that they should *not* operate on individual rows, but rather on tables, and that the results of these operators should be tables, too.

Because tables are defined as sets of rows, relational operators should operate on sets. That's why some operators from the classical set theory—such as the union, the difference, and the intersection—also show up as relational operators. See Figure 1-1 for an illustration of these three set operators.

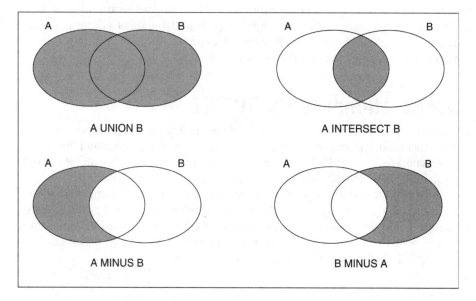

Figure 1-1. *The three most common set operators*

Along with these generic operators from set theory that can be applied to any sets, there are some additional relational operators specifically meant to operate on tables. You can define as many relational operators as you like, but, in general, most of these operators can be reduced to (or built with) a limited number of basic relational operators. The most common relational operators are the following:

- **Restriction:** This operator results in a subset of the rows of the input table, based on a specified restriction condition. This operator is also referred to as *selection*.

- **Projection:** This operator results in a table with fewer columns, based on a specified set of attributes you want to see in the result. In other words, the result is a vertical subset of the input table.

- **Union:** This operator merges the rows of two input tables into a single output table; the result contains all rows that occur in at least one of the input tables.

- **Intersection:** This operator also accepts two input tables; the result consists of all rows that occur in both input tables.

- **Minus:** Again, based on two input tables, this operator produces a result that consists of those rows that occur in the first table but do not occur in the second table. Note that this operator is not symmetric; A MINUS B is not the same as B MINUS A. This operator is also referred to as *difference*.

- **(Cartesian) product:** From two input tables, all possible combinations are generated by concatenating a row from the first table with a row from the second table.

- **(Natural) Join:** From two input tables, one result table is produced. The rows in the result consist of all combinations of a row from the first table with a row from the second table, provided both rows have identical values for the common attributes.

The natural join is an example of an operator that is not strictly necessary, because the effect of this operator can also be achieved by applying the combination of a Cartesian product, followed by a restriction (to check for identical values on the common attributes), and then followed by a projection to remove the duplicate columns.

1.7 How Relational Is My DBMS?

The term *relational* is used (and abused) by many DBMS vendors these days. If you want to determine whether these vendors speak the truth, you are faced with the problem that *relational* is a theoretical concept. There is no simple litmus test to check whether or not a DBMS is relational. Actually, to be honest, there are no pure relational DBMS implementations. That's why it is better to investigate the relational *degree* of a certain DBMS implementation.

This problem was identified by Ted Codd, too; that's why he published 12 rules (actually, there are 13 rules, if you count rule zero, too) for relational DBMS systems in 1986. Since then, these rules have been an important yardstick for RDBMS vendors. Without going into too much detail, Codd's rules are listed here, with brief explanations:

0. **Rule Zero:** For any DBMS that claims to be relational, that system must be able to manage databases entirely through its relational capabilities.

1. **The Information Rule:** All information in a relational database is represented explicitly at the logical level and in exactly one way: by values in tables.

2. **Guaranteed Access Rule:** All data stored in a relational database is guaranteed to be logically accessible by resorting to a combination of a table name, primary key value, and column name.

3. **Systematic Treatment of Missing Information:** Null values (distinct from the empty string, blanks, and zero) are supported for representing missing information and inapplicable information in a systematic way, independent of the datatype.

4. **Dynamic Online Catalog:** The database description is represented at the logical level in the same way as ordinary data, so that authorized users can apply the same relational language to its interrogation as they apply to the regular data.

5. **Comprehensive Data Sublanguage:** There must be at least support for one language whose statements are expressible by some well-defined syntax and comprehensive in supporting all of the following: data definition, view definition, data manipulation, integrity constraints, authorization, and transaction boundaries handling.

6. **Updatable Views:** All views that are theoretically updatable are also updatable by the system.

7. **High-Level Insert, Update, and Delete:** The capability of handling a table or a view as a single operand applies not only to the retrieval of data, but also to the insertion, updating, and deletion of data.

8. **Physical Data Independence:** Application programs remain logically unimpaired whenever any changes are made in either storage representations or access methods.

9. **Logical Data Independence:** Application programs remain logically unimpaired when information-preserving changes that theoretically permit unimpairment are made to the base tables.

10. **Integrity Independence:** Integrity constraints must be definable in the relational data sublanguage and storable in the catalog, not in the application programs.

11. **Distribution Independence:** Application programs remain logically unimpaired when data distribution is first introduced or when data is redistributed.

12. **The Nonsubversion Rule:** If a relational system also supports a low-level language, that low-level language cannot be used to subvert or bypass the integrity rules and constraints expressed in the higher-level language.

Rule 5 refers to transactions. Without going into too much detail here, a *transaction* is defined as a number of changes that should be treated by the DBMS as a single unit of work; a transaction should always succeed or fail completely. For further reading, please refer to *Oracle Insights: Tales of the Oak Table* (Apress, 2004), especially Chapter 1 by Dave Ensor.

1.8 The Oracle Software Environment

Oracle Corporation has its headquarters in Redwood Shores, California. It was founded in 1977, and it was (in 1979) the first vendor to offer a commercial RDBMS.

The Oracle software environment is available for many different platforms, ranging from personal computers (PCs) to large mainframes and massive parallel processing (MPP) systems. This is one of the unique selling points of Oracle: it guarantees a high degree of independence from hardware vendors, as well as various system growth scenarios, without losing the benefits of earlier investments, and it offers extensive transport and communication possibilities in heterogeneous environments.

The Oracle software environment has many components and bundling options. The core component is the DBMS itself: the *kernel*. The kernel has many important tasks, such as handling all physical data transport between memory and external storage, managing concurrency, and providing transaction isolation. Moreover, the kernel ensures that all stored data is represented at the logical level as relational tables. An important component of the kernel is the *optimizer*, which decides how to access the physical data structures in a time-efficient way and which algorithms to use to produce the results of your SQL commands.

Application programs and users can communicate with the kernel by using the SQL language, the main topic of this book. Oracle SQL is an almost fully complete implementation of the ANSI/ISO/IEC SQL:2003 standard. Oracle plays an important role in the SQL standardization process and has done that for many years.

Oracle also provides many tools with its DBMS, to render working with the DBMS more efficient and pleasurable. Figure 1-2 illustrates the cooperation of these tools with the Oracle database, clearly showing the central role of the SQL language as the communication layer between the kernel and the tools, regardless of which tool is chosen.

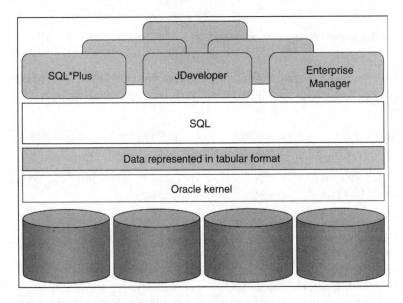

Figure 1-2. *Tools, SQL, and the Oracle database*

■**Note** Besides tools enabling you to build (or generate) application programs, Oracle also sells many ready-to-use application programs, such as the Oracle eBusiness Suite and the Oracle Collaboration Suite.

The following are examples of Oracle software components:

- **SQL*Plus and *i*SQL*Plus:** These two tools stay the closest to the SQL language and are ideal for interactive, ad hoc SQL statement execution and database access. These are the tools we will mainly use in this book. *i*SQL*Plus is a special version of SQL*Plus that runs in a browser such as Mozilla or Microsoft Internet Explorer.

■**Note** Don't confuse SQL with SQL*Plus. SQL is a *language*, and SQL*Plus is a *tool*.

- **Oracle Developer Suite 10*g*:** This is an integrated set of development tools, with the main components Oracle JDeveloper, Oracle Forms, and Oracle Reports.
- **Oracle Enterprise Manager:** This graphical user interface (GUI), which runs in a browser environment, supports Oracle database administrators in their daily work. Regular tasks like startup, shutdown, backup, recovery, maintenance, and performance management can be done with Enterprise Manager.

1.9 Case Tables

This section introduces the seven case tables used throughout this book for all examples and exercises. Appendix C provides a complete description of the tables and also contains some helpful diagrams and reports of the table contents. Chapters 3 and 7 contain the SQL commands to create the case tables (without and with constraints, respectively).

You need some understanding of the structure of the case tables to be able to write SQL statements against the contents of those tables. Otherwise, your SQL statements may be incorrect.

The ERM Diagram of the Case

We start with an ERM diagram depicting the *logical design* of our case, which means that it does not consider any physical (implementation-dependent) circumstances. A *physical design* is the next stage, when the choice is made to implement the case in an RDBMS environment, typically resulting in a table diagram or just a text file with the SQL statements to create the tables and their constraints.

Figure 1-3 shows the ERM diagram for the example used in this book. The ERM diagram shows seven entities, represented by their names in rounded-corner boxes. To maintain readability, most attributes are omitted in the diagram; only the key attributes are displayed.

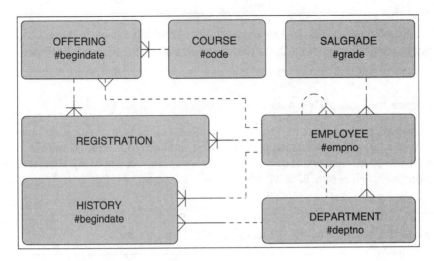

Figure 1-3. *ERM diagram of the case*

We have several relationships between these entities. The ten crow's feet connectors in the diagram represent one-to-many relationships. Each relationship can be read in two directions. For example, the relationship between OFFERING and REGISTRATION should be interpreted as follows:

- Each *registration* is always for exactly one course *offering*.

- A course *offering* may have zero, one, or more *registrations*.

Course offerings without registrations are allowed. All one-to-many relationships in our case have this property, which is indicated in this type of diagram with a dotted line at the optional side of the relationship.

Notice that we have two different relationships between EMPLOYEE and DEPARTMENT: each employee works for precisely one department, and each employee can be the manager of zero, one, or more departments. The EMPLOYEE entity also shows a *recursive relationship* (a relationship of an entity with itself) that implements the hierarchy within the company.

Each entity in the ERM diagram has a *unique identifier*, allowing us to uniquely identify all occurrences of the corresponding entities. This may be a single attribute (for example, EMPNO for the EMPLOYEE entity) or a combination of attributes, optionally combined with relationships. Each attribute that is part of a unique identifier is preceded with a hash symbol (#); relationships that are part of a unique identifier are denoted with a small crossbar. For example, the unique identifier of the OFFERING entity consists of a combination of the BEGINDATE attribute and the relationship with the COURSE entity, and the unique identifier of the entity REGISTRATION consists of the two relationships to the EMPLOYEE and OFFERING entities. By the way, entities like REGISTRATION are often referred to as *intersection entities*; REGISTRATION effectively implements a many-to-many relationship between EMPLOYEE and OFFERING.

An ERM diagram can be transformed into a relational table design with the following steps:

1. Each entity becomes a table.

2. Each attribute becomes a column.

3. Each relationship is transformed into a foreign key (FK) constraint at the crow's foot side.

4. Each unique identifier becomes a component of the primary key (PK).

This mapping results in seven tables: EMPLOYEES, DEPARTMENTS, SALGRADES, COURSES, OFFERINGS, REGISTRATION, and HISTORY.

Table Descriptions

Tables 1-1 through 1-7 describe the structures of the case tables.

Table 1-1. *The EMPLOYEES Table*

Column	Description	Key
EMPNO	Number, unique for every employee	PK
ENAME	Last name	
INIT	Initials (without punctuation)	
JOB	Job description of the employee	
MGR	The employee number of the employee's manager	FK
BDATE	Date of birth	
MSAL	Monthly salary (excluding bonus or commission)	
COMM	Commission component of the yearly salary (only relevant for sales reps)	
DEPTNO	The number of the department for which the employee works	FK

Table 1-2. *The DEPARTMENTS Table*

Column	Description	Key
DEPTNO	Unique department number	PK
DNAME	Department name	
LOCATION	Department location (city)	
MGR	Employee number of the manager of the department	FK

Table 1-3. *The SALGRADES Table*

Column	Description	Key
GRADE	Unique salary grade number	PK
LOWERLIMIT	Lowest salary that belongs to the grade	
UPPERLIMIT	Highest salary that belongs to the grade	
BONUS	Optional (tax-free) bonus on top of the monthly salary	

Table 1-4. *The COURSES Table*

Column	Description	Key
CODE	Course code; unique for each course	PK
DESCRIPTION	Short description of the course contents	
CATEGORY	Course type indicator (allowed values: GEN, BLD, and DSG)	
DURATION	Course duration, expressed in days	

Table 1-5. *The OFFERINGS Table*

Column	Description	Key
COURSE	Course code	PK, FK
BEGINDATE	Start date of the course offering	PK
TRAINER	Employee number of the employee teaching the course	FK
LOCATION	Location (city) where the course is offered	

Table 1-6. *The REGISTRATIONS Table*

Column	Description	Key
ATTENDEE	Employee number of the course attendee	PK, FK1
COURSE	Course code	PK, FK2
BEGINDATE	Start date of the course offering	PK, FK2
EVALUATION	Evaluation of the course by the attendee (positive integer on the scale 1–5)	

Table 1-7. *The HISTORY Table*

Column	Description	Key
EMPNO	Employee number	PK, FK1
BEGINYEAR	Year component (4 digits) of BEGINDATE	
BEGINDATE	Begin date of the time interval	PK
ENDDATE	End date of the time interval	
DEPTNO	The number of the department worked for during the interval	FK2
MSAL	Monthly salary during the interval	
COMMENTS	Allows for free text style comments	

In the description of the EMPLOYEES table, the COMM column deserves some special attention. This commission attribute is relevant only for sales representatives, and therefore contains structurally missing information (for all other employees). We could have created a separate SALESREPS table (with two columns: EMPNO and COMM) to avoid this problem, but for the purpose of this book, the table structure is kept simple.

The structure of the DEPARTMENTS table is straightforward. Note the two foreign key constraints between this table and the EMPLOYEES table: an employee can "work for" a department or "be the manager" of a department. Note also that we don't insist that the manager of a department actually works for that department, and it is not forbidden for any employee to manage more than one department.

The salary grades in the SALGRADES table do not overlap, although in salary systems in the real world, most grades are overlapping. In this table, simplicity rules. This way, every salary always falls into exactly one grade. Moreover, the actual monetary unit (currency) for salaries, commission, and bonuses is left undefined. The optional tax-free bonus is paid monthly, just like the regular monthly salaries.

In the COURSES table, three CATEGORY values are allowed:

- GEN (general), for introductory courses

- BLD (build), for building applications

- DSG (design), for system analysis and design

This means that these three values are the only values allowed for the CATEGORY column; this is an example of an *attribute constraint*. This would also have been an opportunity to design an additional entity (and thus another relational table) to implement course types. In that case, the CATEGORY column would have become a foreign key to this additional table. But again, simplicity was the main goal for this set of case tables.

In all database systems, you need procedures to describe how to handle *historical data* in an information system. This is a very important—and, in practice, far from trivial—component of system design. In our case tables, it is particularly interesting to consider course offerings and course registrations in this respect.

If a scheduled course offering is canceled at some point in time (for example, due to lack of registrations), the course offering is *not* removed from the OFFERINGS table, for statistical/historical reasons. Therefore, it is possible that the TRAINER and/or LOCATION columns are left empty; these two attributes are (of course) relevant only as soon as a scheduled course is going to happen. By the way, this brings up the valid question whether scheduled course offerings and "real" course offerings might be two different entities. Again, an opportunity to end up with more tables; and again, simplicity was the main goal here.

Course *registrations* are considered synonymous with *course attendance* in our example database. This becomes obvious from the EVALUATION column in the REGISTRATIONS table, where the attendee's appreciation of the course is stored at the end of the course, expressed on a scale from 1 to 5; the meaning of these numbers ranges from bad (1) to excellent (5). In case a registration is canceled before a course takes place, we remove the corresponding row from the REGISTRATIONS table. In other words, if the BEGINDATE value of a course registration falls in the past, this means (by definition) that the corresponding course offering took place and was attended.

The HISTORY table maintains information about the working history of all employees. More specifically, it holds data about the departments they have been working for and the salaries they made over the years, starting from the day they were hired. Every change of department and/or monthly salary is recorded in this table. The current values for DEPTNO and MSAL can be stored in this table, too, by keeping the ENDDATE attribute empty until the next change. The COMMENTS column offers room for free text comments, for example, to justify or clarify certain changes.

As noted earlier, the structure and the contents of all seven tables are listed in Appendix C.

CHAPTER 2

■ ■ ■

Introduction to SQL, *i*SQL*Plus, and SQL*Plus

This chapter provides an introduction to the SQL language and two tools for working with it. The first section presents a high-level overview of the SQL language, which will give you an idea of the capabilities of this language. Then some important basic concepts of the SQL language are introduced in the second section, such as constants, literals, variables, expressions, conditions, functions, operators, operands, and so on. Finally, this chapter provides a tour of SQL*Plus and *i*SQL*Plus, the two main tools we will use throughout this book to learn the SQL language. In order to maximize the benefits of any tool, you first must learn how to use it and to identify the main features available in that tool.

This is the first chapter with real SQL statement examples, although no hands-on exercises are included yet. However, for this chapter, it would be beneficial for you to have access to an Oracle database and a schema with the seven case tables introduced in Chapter 1. On my web site (http://www.naturaljoin.nl) or the Downloads section of the Apress web site (http://www.apress.com), you can find the scripts to create this schema, to create and populate the tables in that schema, or to refresh the contents of those tables.

We assume that Oracle is running; database (instance) startup and shutdown are normally tasks of a system or database administrator. Specific startup and shutdown procedures might be in place in your environment. However, if you are working with a stand-alone Oracle environment, and you have enough privileges, you can try the SQL*Plus STARTUP command or use the GUI offered by Oracle Enterprise Manager to start up the database.

2.1 Overview of SQL

SQL (the abbreviation stands for Structured Query Language) is a language you can use in (at least) two different ways: *interactively* or *embedded*. Using SQL interactively means that you enter SQL commands via a keyboard, and you get the command results displayed on a terminal or computer screen. Using embedded SQL involves incorporating SQL commands within a program in a different programming language (such as Java or C). This book deals solely with interactive SQL usage.

Although SQL is called a *query language*, its possibilities go far beyond simply data retrieval. Normally, the SQL language is divided into the following four command categories:

- Data definition (Data Definition Language, or DDL)

- Data manipulation (Data Manipulation Language, or DML)

- Retrieval

- Security and authorization

Data Definition

The SQL data definition commands allow you to create, modify, and remove components of a database structure. Typical database structure components are tables, views, indexes, constraints, synonyms, sequences, and so on. Chapter 1 introduced tables, columns, and constraints; other database object types (such as views, indexes, synonyms, and sequences) will be introduced in later chapters.

Almost all SQL data definition commands start with one of the following three keywords:

- CREATE, to create a new database object

- ALTER, to change an aspect of the structure of an existing database object

- DROP, to drop (remove) a database object

For example, with the CREATE VIEW command, you can create views. With the ALTER TABLE command, you can change the structure of a table (for example, by adding, renaming, or dropping a column). With the DROP INDEX command, you can drop an index.

One of the strengths of an RDBMS is the fact that you can change the structure of a table without needing to change anything in your existing database application programs. For example, you can easily add a column or change its width with the ALTER TABLE command. In modern DBMSs such as Oracle, you can even do this while other database users or applications are connected and working on the database—like changing the wheels of a train at full speed. This property of an RDBMS is known as *logical data independence* (see Ted Codd's rule 9, discussed in Chapter 1).

Data definition is covered in more detail in Chapters 3 and 7.

Data Manipulation and Transactions

Just as SQL data definition commands allow you to change the *structure* of a database, SQL data manipulation commands allow you to change the *contents* of your database. For this purpose, SQL offers three basic data manipulation commands:

- INSERT, to add rows to a table

- UPDATE, to change column values of existing rows

- DELETE, to remove rows from a table

You can add rows to a table with the INSERT command in two ways. One way is to add rows one by one by specifying a list of column values in the VALUES clause of the INSERT statement. The other is to add one or more rows to a table based on a selection (and manipulation) of existing data in the database (called a *subquery*).

■Note You can also load data into an Oracle database with various tools specifically developed for this purpose—such as Data Pump in Oracle Database 10*g*, Export and Import in previous Oracle releases, and SQL*Loader. These tools are often used for high-volume data loads.

Data manipulation commands are always treated as being part of a *transaction*. This means (among other things) that all database changes caused by SQL data manipulation commands get a pending status, until you confirm (commit) or cancel (roll back) the transaction. No one (except the transaction itself) can see the pending changes of a transaction before it is committed. That's why a transaction is often labeled *atomic*: it is impossible for other database users to see parts of a transaction in the database. It is "all or nothing," no matter how many DML operations the transaction comprises.

Sometimes, transactions are committed implicitly; that is, without any explicit request from a user. For example, every data definition command implicitly commits your current transaction. SQL offers two commands to control your transactions explicitly:

- COMMIT, to confirm all pending changes of the current transaction

- ROLLBACK, to cancel all pending changes and restore the original situation

Note the following important differences between data manipulation and data definition:

- DELETE *empties* a table; DROP *removes* a table. TRUNCATE allows you to delete all the rows in a table in an efficient (but irrevocable) way.

- UPDATE changes the *contents* of a table; ALTER changes its *structure*.

- You can undo the consequences of data manipulation with ROLLBACK; data definition commands are irrevocable.

Chapter 6 will revisit data manipulation in more detail. Chapter 7 discusses the TRUNCATE command, which is considered a data definition command.

Retrieval

The only SQL command used to query database data is SELECT. This command acts at the set (or table) level, and always produces a set (or table) as its result. If a certain query returns exactly one row, or no rows at all, the result is still a set: a table with one row or the empty table, respectively.

The SELECT command (as defined in the ANSI/ISO SQL standard) has six main components, which implement all SQL retrieval. Figure 2-1 shows a diagram with these six main components of the SELECT command.

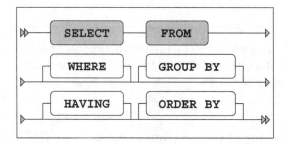

Figure 2-1. *The six main components of the SELECT command*

The lines in this diagram represent all possibilities of the SELECT command, like a railroad map. You can deduce the following three syntax rules from Figure 2-1:

- The order of these six command components is fixed.

- The SELECT and FROM components are mandatory.

- The remaining components (WHERE, GROUP BY, HAVING, and ORDER BY) are optional.

Table 2-1 gives a high-level description of the roles of these six components of the SELECT command.

Table 2-1. *The Six Main Components of the SELECT Command*

Component	Description
FROM	Which table(s) is (are) needed for retrieval?
WHERE	What is the condition to filter the rows?
GROUP BY	How should the rows be grouped/aggregated?
HAVING	What is the condition to filter the aggregated groups?
SELECT	Which columns do you want to see in the result?
ORDER BY	In which order do you want to see the resulting rows?

■Tip The order of the SELECT command components as displayed in Table 2-1 is also a good order to think about them when writing SQL statements. Notice that the SELECT clause is almost the last one.

Components of the SELECT command implement three of the relational operators introduced in Chapter 1 (Section 1.6) as follows:

- The SELECT component acts as the *projection* operator.

- The FROM component implements the *join* operator.

- The *restriction* operator corresponds to the WHERE component.

Now that we are on the subject of relational operators, note that the *union, intersection,* and *difference (minus)* operators are also implemented in SQL. You can use these three set operators to combine the results of multiple SELECT commands into a single result table, as illustrated in Figure 2-2. We will revisit these operators in Chapter 8.

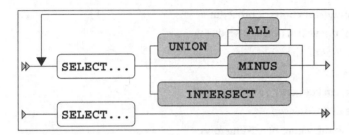

Figure 2-2. *SQL set operators syntax diagram*

Security

SQL offers several commands to implement data security and to restrict data access.

First of all, access to the database must be defined. User authorization is implemented by providing database users a login name and a password, together with some database-wide privileges. These are the most important commands in this area:

- CREATE USER, to define new database users

- ALTER USER, to change properties (privileges and passwords) of existing database users

- DROP USER, to remove user definitions from the database

Privileges and Roles

If users are authorized to access the database, you can implement fine-grained data access by granting specific *privileges*. The Oracle DBMS offers two types of privileges: system privileges and object privileges.

System privileges pertain to the right to perform certain (nonobject-related) actions; for example, you can have the CREATE SESSION privilege (allows you to log on to the database) and the CREATE TABLE privilege. Oracle supports approximately 140 different system privileges.

Object privileges involve the right to access a specific database object in a specific way; for example, the right to issue SELECT, INSERT, and UPDATE commands against the EMPLOYEES table. Table 2-2 lists the most important Oracle object privileges.

■**Note** Granting and revoking system privileges is typically a task for database administrators. See *Oracle SQL Reference* for more details on both system and object privileges.

Table 2-2. *Important Oracle Object Privileges*

Object Privilege	Allowable Action
ALTER	Change the table structure (with ALTER TABLE)
DELETE	Delete rows
EXECUTE	Execute stored functions or procedures
FLASHBACK	Go back in time (with FLASHBACK TABLE)
INDEX	Create indexes on the table
INSERT	Insert new rows
REFERENCES	Create foreign key constraints to the table
SELECT	Query the table (or view)
UPDATE	Change column values of existing rows

The Oracle DBMS allows you to group privileges in *roles*. Roles make user management much easier, more flexible, and also more manageable. The following are the corresponding SQL commands used to administer these privileges and roles:

- GRANT, to grant certain privileges or roles to users or roles

- REVOKE, to revoke certain privileges or roles from users or roles

A typical scenario is the following:

```
CREATE ROLE <role name>
GRANT privileges TO <role name>
GRANT <role name> TO user(s)
```

The first step creates a new (empty) role. The second step (which can be repeated as many times as you like) populates the role with a mix of object and system privileges. The third step grants the role (and thereby all its privileges) to a user in a single step.

Roles have several useful and powerful properties:

- Roles are dynamic; further changes to the role contents automatically affect all users previously granted that role.

- Roles can be enabled or disabled during a session.

- You can protect roles with a password. In that case, only users who know the role password can enable the role.

- The most important advantage of roles is their manageability.

GRANT and REVOKE

Each table has an owner, who is the user who created the table. Table owners are able to grant privileges on their tables to other database users using the GRANT command. As soon as you create a table, you implicitly get all object privileges on that table, WITH GRANT OPTION, as illustrated in Figure 2-3, which shows the syntax of the GRANT command.

■**Note** System privileges and roles are not considered, so the syntax diagram in Figure 2-3 is incomplete.

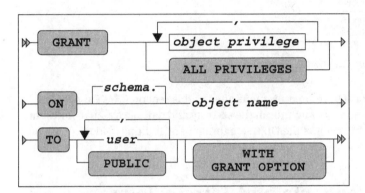

Figure 2-3. *The GRANT command syntax diagram*

Here are some comments about the GRANT command:

- Table owners cannot grant the right to remove a table (DROP TABLE) to other database users. Note, however, that Oracle supports a (rather dangerous) DROP ANY TABLE system privilege.

- If you want to grant all object privileges to someone else, you can use the keyword ALL (see Figure 2-3). (Instead of ALL PRIVILEGES, the Oracle DBMS also allows you to specify ALL.)

- With a single GRANT command, you can grant privileges to a single user, a list of users, a role, or all database users. You can address all database users with the pseudo-user PUBLIC (see Figure 2-3).

- The UPDATE privilege supports an optional refinement: this privilege can also be granted for specific columns, by specifying column names between parentheses.

- In principle, there is no difference between tables and views when granting object privileges; however, the privileges ALTER, INDEX, and REFERENCES are meaningless in the context of views.

- The GRANT OPTION not only grants certain object privileges, but also grants the right to the grantee to spread these privileges further.

The counterpart of GRANT is the REVOKE command. Figure 2-4 shows the syntax diagram for REVOKE.

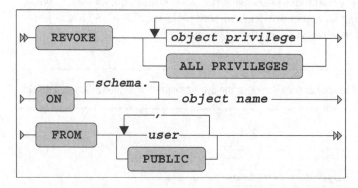

Figure 2-4. *The REVOKE command syntax diagram*

Besides the two standard SQL commands mentioned in this section (GRANT and REVOKE), Oracle supports several additional commands in the security and data access area; for example, to influence the locking behavior of the DBMS, to implement auditing, and to set up more detailed user authorization.

2.2 Basic SQL Concepts and Terminology

This section discusses the following topics:

- Constants (literals)

- Variables

- Operators, operands, conditions, and expressions

- Functions

- Database object names

- Comments

- Reserved words

Constants (Literals)

A *constant* (or *literal*) is something with a fixed value. We distinguish numbers (numeric constants) and text (alphanumeric constants). In database jargon, alphanumeric constants are also referred to as *strings*.

In the SQL language, alphanumeric constants (strings) must be placed between *single quotation marks* (quotes). Note also that strings are case-sensitive in SQL; the difference between lowercase and uppercase characters is significant.

Numbers are also relatively straightforward in SQL; however, don't put them between quotes or they will be interpreted as strings. If you like, you can explicitly indicate that you want SQL to interpret numeric values as *floating point* numbers by adding the suffix f or d to indicate single or double precision, respectively. Be careful with the decimal period and group separators (commas) in numbers, because the correct interpretation of these characters depends on the value of a session parameter (NLS_NUMERIC_CHARACTERS), and there are some cultural differences in this area.

In SQL, dates and time durations (intervals) are special cases. They are typically specified and represented as alphanumeric constants, but they need something else to distinguish them from regular strings. In other words, you must help the DBMS to interpret the strings correctly as date or time-interval constants. Probably the most straightforward (and elegant) method is to prefix the strings with a keyword (DATE, TIMESTAMP, or INTERVAL) and to adhere to a well-defined notation convention. (See the examples in Table 2-3 and the third option in the following list.) These are the three options to specify date and time-related constants in SQL:

- Specify them as alphanumeric constants (strings) and rely on implicit interpretation and conversion by the Oracle DBMS. This is dangerous, because things can go wrong if the actual format parameter for that session is different from the format of the string.

- Specify them as alphanumeric constants (strings) and use a CAST or TO_DATE conversion function to specify explicitly how the strings must be interpreted (see Chapter 5).

- Specify them as alphanumeric constants (strings), prefixed with DATE, TIMESTAMP, or INTERVAL. If you use INTERVAL, you also need a suffix to indicate a dimension, such as DAY, MONTH, or YEAR.

Table 2-3 shows examples of using SQL constants.

Table 2-3. *Examples of SQL Constants (Literals)*

Type	Example
Numeric	42 8.75 8.75F 132
Alphanumeric	'JOneS' 'GEN' '132'
Dates and intervals	DATE '2004-02-09' TIMESTAMP '2004-09-05 11.42.59.00000' INTERVAL '2' SECOND INTERVAL '1-3' YEAR TO MONTH

Note the subtle difference between 132 and '132'. The difference between numbers and strings becomes apparent when considering the operators they support. For example, numbers can be added or multiplied, but you cannot do that with strings. The only operator you can apply to strings is the concatenation operator.

In general, the SQL language is case-insensitive. However, there is one important exception: alphanumeric constants (strings) are case-sensitive. For example, `'JOneS'` is not equal to `'Jones'`. This is sometimes the explanation of getting the message "no rows selected" in cases where you were expecting to see rows in the result.

Variables

A *variable* is something that may have a varying value over time, or even an unknown value. A variable always has a name, so you can refer to it.

SQL supports two types of variables:

- **Column name variables:** The name of a column stays the same, but its value typically varies from row to row while scanning a table.

- **System variables:** These have nothing to do with tables; nevertheless, they can play an important role in SQL. They are commonly referred to as *pseudo columns*. See Table 2-4 for some examples of Oracle system variables.

Table 2-4. *Examples of Oracle System Variables (Pseudo columns)*

Variable	Description
SYSDATE	The current system date in the database
CURRENT_DATE	The current date at the client application side
SYSTIMESTAMP	The system date and exact time, with time zone information
LOCALTIMESTAMP	The system date and exact time, with time zone information, at the client application side
USER	The name used to connect to the database

The difference between dates (and timestamps) at the *database* side and the *client application* side can be relevant if you are connected over a network connection with a database in a remote location.

Users commonly make mistakes by forgetting to include quotes in SQL statements. Consider the following SQL statement fragment:

```
...WHERE LOCATION = UTRECHT...
```

`LOCATION` and `UTRECHT` are both interpreted by Oracle as variable names (column names), although the following was probably the real intention:

```
...WHERE LOCATION = 'UTRECHT'...
```

Operators, Operands, Conditions, and Expressions

An *operator* does something. *Operands* are the "victims" of operations; that is, operands serve as input for operators. Sometimes, operators need only a single operand (in which case, they are also referred to as *monadic* operators), but most operators need two or more operands.

The SQL operators are divided in four categories, where the differentiating factor is the operand datatype:

- Arithmetic operators

- Alphanumeric operators

- Comparison operators

- Logical operators

Arithmetic Operators

The SQL language supports four arithmetic operators, as shown in Table 2-5.

Table 2-5. *SQL Arithmetic Operators*

Operator	Description
+	Addition
-	Subtraction
*	Multiplication
/	Division

You can apply arithmetic operators only on NUMBER values; however, there are some exceptions:

- If you subtract two DATE values, you get the difference between those two dates, expressed in days.

- You can add a DATE and an INTERVAL value, which results in another date.

- If you add a DATE and a NUMBER, the number is interpreted as an interval expressed in days.

The Alphanumeric Operator: Concatenation

SQL offers only one alphanumeric operator, allowing you to concatenate string expressions: ||. This modest number of operators is compensated for by the overwhelming number of alphanumeric *functions* in SQL, which are discussed in Chapter 5. For an example of the use of the concatenation operator, see Table 2-8, later in this chapter.

Comparison Operators

The comparison operators allow you to formulate conditions in SQL. Table 2-6 shows the comparison operators available in SQL.

Table 2-6. *SQL Comparison Operators*

Operator	Description
<	Less than
>	Greater than
=	Equal to
<=	Less than or equal to
>=	Greater than or equal to
<> or !=	Not equal to

Expressions with comparison operators are also referred to as *predicates* or *Boolean expressions*. These expressions evaluate to TRUE or FALSE. Sometimes, the outcome is UNKNOWN, such as when you have rows with missing information. We will revisit this topic in more detail in Chapter 4, when we discuss null values.

Logical Operators

SQL also offers three operators whose operands are conditions: the logical (or Boolean) operators. Table 2-7 lists these operators.

Table 2-7. *SQL Logical Operators*

Operator	Description
AND	Logical AND
OR	Logical OR (the *inclusive* OR)
NOT	Logical negation

Expressions

An *expression* is a well-formed string containing variables, constants, operators, or functions. Just like constants, expressions always have a certain datatype. See Table 2-8 for some examples of expressions.

Table 2-8. *SQL Expression Examples*

Expression	Datatype
3 + 4	Numeric
ENAME || ', ' || INIT	Alphanumeric
LOCATION = 'Utrecht'	Boolean
12*MSAL > 20000 AND COMM >= 100	Boolean
BDATE + INTERVAL '16' YEAR	Date
999	Numeric

The last example in Table 2-8 shows that the simplest expression is just a constant.

When SQL expressions get more complex, operator *precedence* can become an issue; in other words: what are the operator priority rules? Of course, SQL has some precedence rules. For example, arithmetic operators always have precedence over comparison operators, and comparison operators have precedence over logical operators. However, it is highly recommended that you use parentheses in your complex SQL expressions to force a certain expression evaluation order, just as you would do in regular mathematics.

Functions

Oracle has added a lot of functionality to the SQL standard in the area of *functions*. This is definitely one of the reasons why Oracle SQL is so powerful. You can recognize SQL functions by their signature: they have a name, followed by one or more arguments (between parentheses) in a comma-separated list. You can use functions in expressions, in the same way that you can use operators.

These are the six SQL function categories, based on their operand types:

- Numeric functions

- Alphanumeric functions

- Group functions

- Date functions

- Conversion functions

- Other functions

Table 2-9 shows some examples of SQL functions.

Table 2-9. *Examples of SQL Functions*

Function	Explanation
AVG(MSAL)	The average monthly salary
SQRT(16)	The square root of 16
LENGTH(INIT)	The number of characters in the INIT column value
LOWER(ENAME)	ENAME column value, in lowercase
SUBSTR(ENDDATE,4,3)	Three characters of the ENDDATE column value, from the fourth position

Oracle even allows you to create your own SQL functions, by using the PL/SQL or Java languages. Chapter 5 will show a simple example of a user-defined function.

Database Object Naming

All objects in a database need *names*. This applies to tables, columns, views, indexes, synonyms, sequences, users, roles, constraints, functions, and so on. In general, to enhance the readability of your SQL code, it is highly recommended that you restrict yourself to using the characters A through Z, the digits 0 through 9, and optionally the underscore (_).

■**Note** In Oracle, object names are case-insensitive; that is, internally all database object names are converted to uppercase, regardless of how you enter those names.

You may use digits in database object names; however, database object names should always start with a letter. Oracle object names have a maximum length of 30 characters.

Database objects need *different* names to be able to distinguish them, obviously. To be more precise, database objects need unique names within their namespace. On the other hand, different database users may use the same names for their own objects if they like, because the owner/object name combination is used to uniquely identify an object in the database.

If you insist on creating your own object names in Oracle SQL using any characters you like (including, for example, spaces and other strange characters), and you also want your object names to be case-sensitive, you can include those names within double quotes. The only restriction that remains is the maximum name length: 30 characters. Using this "feature" is discouraged, because you will always need to include those names in double quotes again in every interactive SQL statement you want to execute against those objects. On the other hand, you can use this technique *in written applications* to prevent conflicts with reserved words, including reserved words of future DBMS versions not known to you at application development time. Actually, several Oracle database utilities use this technique under the hood for precisely this reason.

Comments

You can add *comments* to SQL commands in order to clarify their intent or to enhance their maintainability. In other words, you can add text that does not formally belong to the SQL statements themselves, and as such should be ignored by the Oracle DBMS. You can add such comments in two ways: between /* and */ or after two consecutive minus signs. Comments after two minus signs are implicitly ended by a newline character; comments between /* and */ can span multiple lines. See Listing 2-1 for two examples.

Listing 2-1. *SQL Comments Examples*

```
/* this text will be considered a comment,
   so the Oracle DBMS will ignore it ... */
-- and this text too, until the end of this line.
```

Listing 2-1 shows how you can add comments to *SQL commands*. Note that you can also add comments to *database objects* with the COMMENT command. See Chapter 7 for details.

Reserved Words

Just like any other language, SQL has a list of *reserved words*. These are words you are not allowed to use, for example, as database object names. If you insist on using a reserved word as an object name, you must enclose the name within double quotes, as explained earlier in the "Database Object Naming" section.

These are some examples of SQL reserved words: AND, CREATE, DROP, FROM, GRANT, HAVING, INDEX, INSERT, MODIFY, NOT, NULL, NUMBER, OR, ORDER, RENAME, REVOKE, SELECT, SYNONYM, SYSDATE, TABLE, UPDATE, USER, VALUES, VIEW, and WHERE.

■**Tip** The Oracle data dictionary contains a V$RESERVED_WORDS view. You can check your object names against this view to avoid using reserved words.

See Appendix A of this book and Chapter 2 of *Oracle SQL Reference* for more details about naming rules for database objects and a more complete listing of SQL reserved words.

2.3 Introduction to *i*SQL*Plus

*i*SQL*Plus is a very convenient tool (or environment) with which to issue SQL commands interactively against an Oracle database. *i*SQL*Plus is automatically configured during an Oracle Database 10*g* software installation, and it runs completely in a browser. In other words, *i*SQL*Plus does not need any Oracle software on a client machine; it needs only a standard browser.

To run *i*SQL*Plus, you just launch your favorite browser and navigate to a specific URL. In most real-world situations, this URL will point to a middle-tier application server or a database server, but you can also use *i*SQL*Plus completely locally on your machine. In the latter case, the URL simply points to the local machine. The exact URL for *i*SQL*Plus may vary in certain environments, but the default format looks like this:

```
http://<name>.<domain>:<portnumber>/isqlplus/
```

In this URL, you should replace <name>.<domain> with a valid machine name or a corresponding physical IP address, and 5560 is the default port number for the *i*SQL*Plus listener process.

This listener process must be active to be able to use *i*SQL*Plus. Under Windows, a typical name for the corresponding service is OracleOraDb10g_home1iSQL*Plus. Consult the Oracle documentation for more information about configuring and troubleshooting *i*SQL*Plus.

In Chapter 11, we will discuss some more advanced features of the *i*SQL*Plus URL address field; for the time being, you now know enough to get started.

At this point, to follow along with the discussion, you need the BOOK schema with the seven case tables created in your database. Refer to my web site (http://www.naturaljoin.nl) or the Apress web site (http://www.apress.com) for guidelines on how to do this.

The *i*SQL*Plus Login screen looks like Figure 2-5.

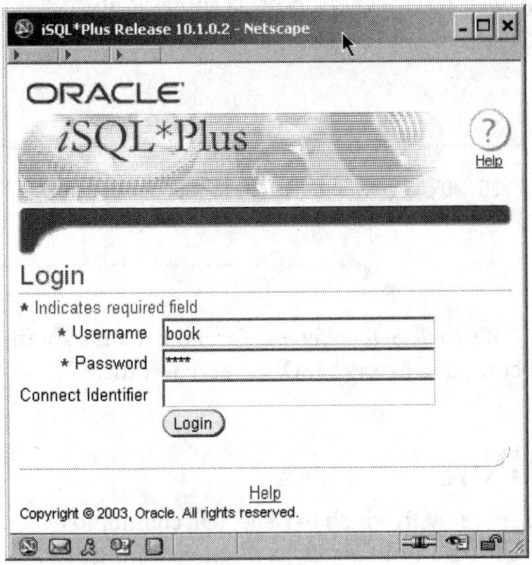

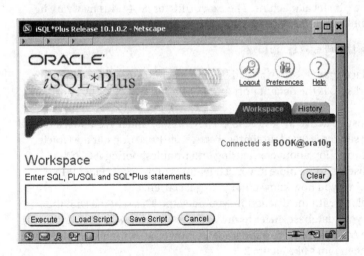

Figure 2-5. *Logging in to iSQL*Plus*

Assuming you have created the user (or schema) BOOK in the database, and assuming you entered the correct password, you can click the Login button. This brings you to the screen shown in Figure 2-6.

Figure 2-6. *iSQL*Plus Workspace screen*

Some interesting features of the Workspace screen are the following:

- In the workspace area, you can enter and edit SQL and SQL*Plus commands. (SQL*Plus commands are introduced in the next section.) You can use the Clear button to clear the workspace, and you can use the Execute button to execute the contents of the workspace.

- You can save and load SQL*Plus scripts with the Save Script and Load Script buttons. (SQL*Plus scripts are introduced in the next section.)

- By clicking the Preferences link in the top-right corner, you can adjust several *i*SQL*Plus settings to change its behavior to your personal taste.

- The History tab lists a history of the current (active) session, enabling you to reload and reexecute certain commands in an efficient way. Note that the history is lost when you exit the *i*SQL*Plus session.

- You can exit the *i*SQL*Plus session by clicking the Logout link.

The *i*SQL*Plus Preferences screen is shown in Figure 2-7. One example of a convenient *i*SQL*Plus option is the Output Location setting, which allows you, for example, to save all results in HTML format in a file. In Chapter 11, we will revisit *i*SQL*Plus and discuss various ways to customize the *i*SQL*Plus environment.

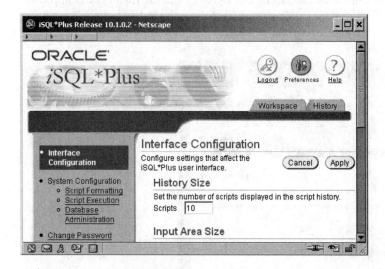

Figure 2-7. *iSQL*Plus Preferences screen*

Figure 2-8 shows the result of a simple SQL statement. To try this out, navigate back to the Workspace tab, enter the SQL command shown in the figure, and click the Execute button.

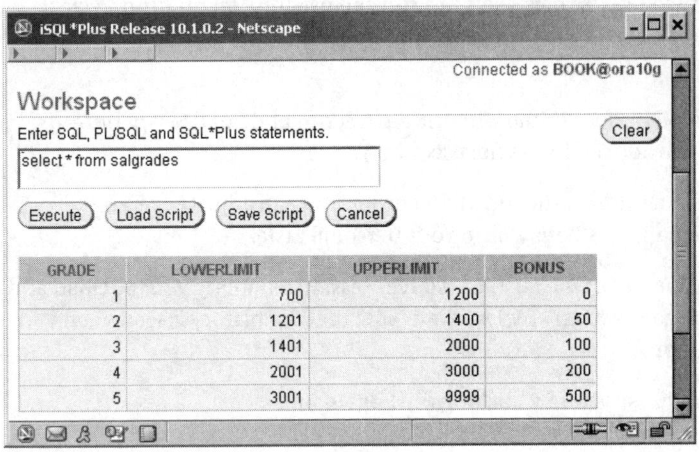

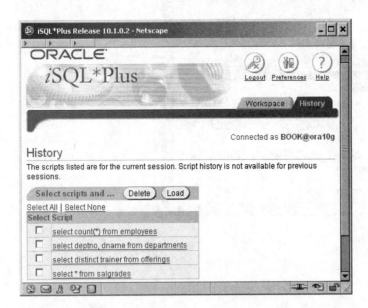

Figure 2-8. *An SQL statement and its result*

If you have already entered various SQL commands during your *i*SQL*Plus session, the contents of the History tab could look something like Figure 2-9. In the History screen, you can select one or more scripts, and then delete them by clicking the Delete button. You can also load scripts in your workspace with the Load button.

Figure 2-9. *i*SQL*Plus History screen*

*i*SQL*Plus also offers extensive online help functionality. Click the Help link (the question mark icon in the upper-right corner of the screen) to reach the screen shown in Figure 2-10.

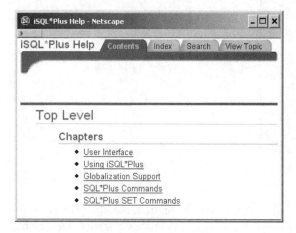

Figure 2-10. *iSQL*Plus Help screen*

For the moment, you know enough about *i*SQL*Plus to start using it as a tool to execute SQL commands.

2.4 Introduction to SQL*Plus

SQL*Plus is very similar to *i*SQL*Plus. The most important difference between them is that SQL*Plus is a "real" client application program, whereas *i*SQL*Plus needs only a local browser to do its work for you.

You can use both SQL*Plus and *i*SQL*Plus for almost all of the examples and exercises in this book. The remaining sections of this chapter are devoted to SQL*Plus, so if you want to start using *i*SQL*Plus, you can skip the remainder of this chapter and continue with Chapter 3. On the other hand, you might want to get familiar with both interfaces.

If Oracle is running, you can start SQL*Plus under Microsoft Windows via the Start menu, by double-clicking the SQL*Plus icon on your desktop, or by executing `sqlplus.exe` or `sqlplusw.exe` from a command window. The difference between the last two executables becomes obvious if you try them; the former is the line-mode version, and the latter offers the GUI.

Under normal circumstances, SQL*Plus responds with a dialog box, prompting you for a username and corresponding password, as shown in Figure 2-11. You can optionally use the Host String field to establish a nondefault connection to a database somewhere else on the network. If your system is correctly configured for a default local connection, you can leave the Host String field empty.

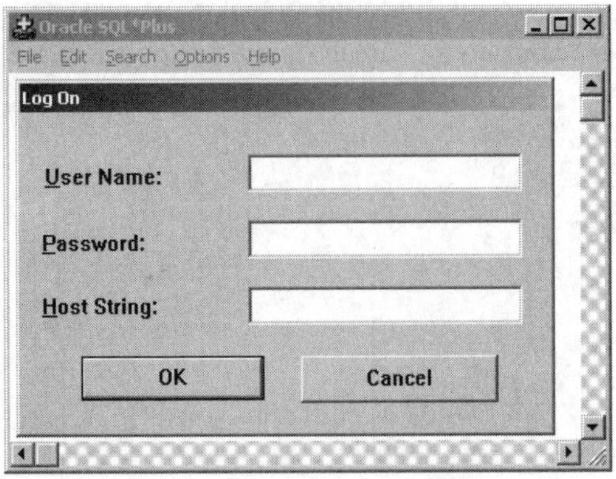

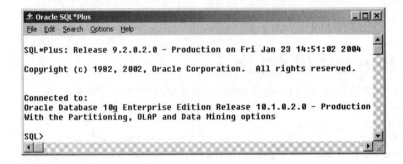

Figure 2-11. *SQL*Plus Log On dialog box*

If you are able to provide a valid username/password combination, the SQL> prompt appears on your screen to indicate that you have successfully established a session, as shown in Figure 2-12. Note that this figure shows that you can establish a connection to a version 10.1.0.2 database with an older version of SQL*Plus (9.2.0.2).

Figure 2-12. *SQL*Plus screen after a successful connection*

You can leave SQL*Plus with the command EXIT or QUIT. See Appendix A for some options of these commands.

Entering Commands

SQL*Plus not only "understands" the SQL language, but it also supports and recognizes several tool-specific SQL*Plus commands. You must make sure to distinguish these SQL*Plus commands from SQL commands, because SQL*Plus treats these two command types differently, as you will see.

Let's start by entering an arbitrary (and rather simple) SQL command in SQL*Plus, as shown in Listing 2-2.

Listing 2-2. *A Basic SQL SELECT Command*

```
SQL> select *
  2  from   employees;
```

Notice that SQL commands are often spread over multiple lines and, by default, SQL*Plus automatically displays line numbers during SQL command entry. If your SQL command is fully entered and you want SQL*Plus to execute it for you, you should finish the last line with a semicolon (;) as a delimiter. If you forget the semicolon (this will probably happen quite often, initially), you can still enter that semicolon on the next (empty) line, as shown here:

```
SQL> select *
  2  from   employees
  3  ;
```

Either way, the command will execute. SQL*Plus will return all columns and all rows of the EMPLOYEES table, since the asterisk character (*) means to show all columns of this table.

EMPNO	ENAME	INIT	JOB	MGR	BDATE	MSAL	COMM	DEPTNO
7369	SMITH	N	TRAINER	7902	17-DEC-65	800		20
7499	ALLEN	JAM	SALESREP	7698	20-FEB-61	1600	300	30
7521	WARD	TF	SALESREP	7698	22-FEB-62	1250	500	30
7566	JONES	JM	MANAGER	7839	02-APR-67	2975		20
7654	MARTIN	P	SALESREP	7698	28-SEP-56	1250	1400	30
7698	BLAKE	R	MANAGER	7839	01-NOV-63	2850		30
7782	CLARK	AB	MANAGER	7839	09-JUN-65	2450		10
7788	SCOTT	SCJ	TRAINER	7566	26-NOV-59	3000		20
7839	KING	CC	DIRECTOR		17-NOV-52	5000		10
7844	TURNER	JJ	SALESREP	7698	28-SEP-68	1500	0	30
7876	ADAMS	AA	TRAINER	7788	30-DEC-66	1100		20
7900	JONES	R	ADMIN	7698	03-DEC-69	800		30
7902	FORD	MG	TRAINER	7566	13-FEB-59	3000		20
7934	MILLER	TJA	ADMIN	7782	23-JAN-62	1300		10

Using the SQL Buffer

SQL*Plus stores your most recent SQL command in an area called the *SQL buffer*. The *SQL buffer* is an important SQL*Plus concept. You can display the content of the SQL buffer using a SQL*Plus command called LIST, as shown in Listing 2-3.

Listing 2-3. *The SQL*Plus LIST Command*

```
SQL> L
  1  select *
  2* from employees

SQL>
```

The ability to retrieve the last SQL statement from the SQL buffer is often very useful when you need to correct errors and reexecute the SQL statement. You will see how to do this in the subsequent sections, where we'll also discuss some other SQL*Plus commands related to the SQL buffer.

If you enter a second SQL command, the SQL buffer is overwritten, and you lose the previous SQL command. In the "Saving Commands" section later in this chapter, you will see an easy method to save SQL commands for reuse in SQL*Plus.

Note from the example in Listing 2-3 that the SQL command returned from the SQL buffer did *not* include a semicolon at the end of it. The semicolon is *not* part of the SQL command itself, and it does not end up in the SQL buffer. If you enter a SQL command (or even a portion of a SQL command) and press the Enter key twice, without first adding a semicolon, the command will not be executed, but it will be saved in the SQL buffer.

The SQL*Plus commands you enter are *not* stored in the SQL buffer. You can run as many SQL*Plus commands as you like, but another SQL*Plus LIST command will display the same SQL command.

From the example in Listing 2-3, you can also note several other things about SQL*Plus commands:

- They are normally executed on a single line, unlike most SQL commands.

- You don't need to enter a semicolon to execute SQL*Plus commands. They execute immediately when you press the Enter key.

- SQL*Plus commands can be abbreviated (L stands for LIST), whereas SQL commands cannot.

Rather than just see what is in the buffer, it is often useful to be able to edit its contents and then reexecute the SQL, so let's now move on to discuss how to do that.

Using an External Editor

You can edit the contents of the SQL buffer in two ways:

- Use an external editor of your choice

- Use the built-in SQL*Plus editor

The main advantage of the SQL*Plus editor is that its functionality is always available in SQL*Plus, and the editor is totally independent of the underlying platform. The disadvantage of the SQL*Plus editor is its lack of user-friendliness and its very limited capabilities. For example, *i*SQL*Plus has a much more intuitive interface to change the contents of the current workspace. This section explains how to use an external editor to edit your SQL commands. The next section will discuss the built-in SQL*Plus editor.

The default external editor under Microsoft Windows is Notepad. SQL*Plus has an Edit ➤ Editor ➤ Define Editor menu option to define your external editor choice, as shown in Figure 2-13.

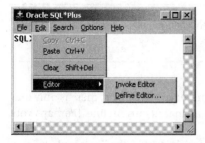

Figure 2-13. *SQL*Plus Define Editor menu option*

You can also change or display the SQL*Plus external editor preference from the command line by using the DEFINE command, as shown in Listing 2-4.

Listing 2-4. *Displaying and Changing the External Editor Preference*

```
SQL> define _editor=Notepad

SQL> define _editor
DEFINE _EDITOR          = "Notepad" (CHAR)

SQL>
```

■**Note** The SQL*Plus variable that holds the name of the external editor is _editor, with a leading under-score in its name.

You can invoke the external editor to change the contents of the SQL buffer. For this purpose, SQL*Plus offers the menu option Invoke Editor (see Figure 2-13) or the SQL*Plus command EDIT. You can invoke the external editor only when your SQL buffer is not empty. An empty buffer results in the error message "nothing to save."

Invoking the external editor starts a subprocess, which means that you cannot return to SQL*Plus until you have closed the external editor window. Alternatively, you may want to start a separate editor session from the operating system (that is, *not* from SQL*Plus) so you can switch between two windows. In that case, you must make sure to save the changes in your editor window before executing the changed SQL command in SQL*Plus.

Using the SQL*Plus Editor

To explore the SQL*Plus editor, we begin with the same simple SQL SELECT command in the SQL buffer (from the "Entering Commands" section earlier in the chapter):

```
SQL> select *
  2  from    employees;
```

■**Note** Please follow all instructions in this section verbatim, even when you think there are some mistakes, because any mistakes are intentional.

It is important to realize that the SQL*Plus editor is line-oriented; that is, there is only one *current line* at any point in time. You can make changes only to that current line. (Perhaps you remember the good old EDLIN editor under MS-DOS?)

SQL*Plus marks the current line on screen with an asterisk (*) after the line number. Normally, it is the line you entered last; in our example, it is the second line.

If you want to change something on the first line, you must first activate that line with the L1 command. Let's try to change the asterisk into two column names. C is an abbreviation for the SQL*Plus command CHANGE. Listing 2-5 shows how to use the LIST and CHANGE commands to make this change. SQL*Plus searches the current line for the first occurrence of an asterisk (*) and changes that character into eename, bdate.

Listing 2-5. *Using the SQL*Plus LIST and CHANGE Commands*

```
SQL> L
  1  select *
  2* from    employees

SQL> L1
  1* select *

SQL> c/*/eename, bdate/
  1* select eename, bdate

SQL> L
  1  select eename, bdate
  2* from    employees

SQL>
```

Instead of slashes (/), you can use any arbitrary character for the string delimiter (separator) in the CHANGE command. Also, a space character between the C and the first separator is not mandatory, and you can omit the last string delimiter too.

Now, let's try to execute the SQL command in the buffer again. The SQL*Plus command to execute the contents of the SQL buffer is RUN, abbreviated to R. Apparently we made a mistake; we get an Oracle error message, as shown in Listing 2-6. Observe the error message. First, it shows a line number indication (ERROR at line 1), and within that line, an asterisk (*) indicates the position where the error was detected. Listing 2-6 also shows a first attempt to correct the error and the erroneous result of our CHANGE command.

Listing 2-6. *Fixing Typos with the SQL*Plus CHANGE Command*

```
SQL> R
  1  select eename, bdate
  2* from   employees
select eename, bdate
       *
ERROR at line 1:
ORA-00904: "EENAME": invalid identifier

SQL> c/e//
  1* slect eename, bdate

SQL>
```

We removed the first occurrence of an e on the first line, instead of the e in eename. This is the default (and only) way the CHANGE command works. This means that you must be careful with this command and be sure to specify appropriate search strings for replacement. In this case, it would have been better to issue the c/ee/e/ command instead.

You can also add text at the end of the current line using the SQL*Plus APPEND command, which is abbreviated A. Listing 2-7 shows how we can first fix the mistake, and then add one more column to the SELECT expression.

Listing 2-7. *Appending Text with the SQL*Plus APPEND Command*

```
SQL> L1
  1* slect eename, bdate

SQL> c/slect ee/select e/
  1* select ename, bdate

SQL> A , deptno
  1* select ename, bdate, deptno

SQL> L
  1  select ename, bdate, deptno
  2* from   employees

SQL>
```

Note that the SQL*Plus APPEND command does not insert a space by default. In this case, we don't need a space, but otherwise you should specify a second space character after the APPEND command.

You can also add one or more additional lines to the SQL buffer with the SQL*Plus INPUT command (abbreviated I), as shown in Listing 2-8. The lines you enter are added *below* the current line. If the current line is the last line in the buffer, the new lines are added at the end of the statement. This also means you need a "special trick" to add lines before the first line, as you'll learn in the next section. Notice the line numbering; SQL*Plus automatically generates appropriate line numbers while entering text. You can stop entering additional lines by pressing the Enter key twice, or by entering a semicolon when you are adding lines at the end of the buffer.

Listing 2-8. *Inserting Text with the SQL*Plus INPUT Command*

```
  1  select ename, bdate, deptno
  2* from   employees

SQL> I
  3  where  deptno = 30;

ENAME     BDATE          DEPTNO
--------  -----------    --------
ALLEN     20-FEB-1961         30
WARD      22-FEB-1962         30
MARTIN    28-SEP-1956         30
BLAKE     01-NOV-1963         30
TURNER    28-SEP-1968         30
JONES     03-DEC-1969         30

SQL>
```

■Note The I is an abbreviation for INPUT, *not* for INSERT. INSERT is a SQL command (to add rows to a table in the database).

The SQL*Plus DEL command deletes the current line from the SQL buffer. You can optionally specify a line number with the DEL command to remove a certain line from the SQL buffer without making that line the current line first, or a range of line numbers to remove several lines with a single DEL command. See Listing 2-9 for an example.

Listing 2-9. *Deleting Lines with the SQL*Plus DEL Command*

```
SQL> L
  1  select ename, bdate, deptno
  2  from   employees
  3* where  deptno = 30

SQL> DEL
```

```
SQL> L
  1  select ename, bdate, deptno
  2* from    employees

SQL>
```

■Note DEL is *not* an abbreviation for DELETE, because DELETE is a SQL command (to remove rows from a table in the database.)

Using SQL Buffer Line Numbers

You can make any line the current one by just entering the line number, without the L (LIST) command, as shown in Listing 2-10.

Listing 2-10. *Using Line Numbers to Change the Current Line*

```
SQL> L
  1  select code, description
  2  from    courses
  3* where   category = 'DSG'

SQL> 2
  2* from    courses

SQL> 42
SP2-0226: Invalid line number

SQL>
```

Using line numbers, you can also *replace* any line in the SQL buffer without needing to use the SQL*Plus DEL command followed by a SQL*Plus INPUT command. Instead, simply enter the desired new line preceded by its line number. Listing 2-11 shows how to replace the first line and add a line at the end of the SQL buffer. Notice that the high line number (42) does not generate an error message, as it does in the example in Listing 2-10.

Listing 2-11. *Using Line Numbers to Change the SQL Buffer*

```
SQL> 1 select *

SQL> L
  1  select *
  2  from    courses
  3* where   category = 'DSG'

SQL> 42 order  by code
```

```
SQL> L
  1  select *
  2  from   courses
  3  where  category = 'DSG'
  4* order  by code

SQL>
```

As explained earlier, the SQL*Plus INPUT command always inserts lines *below* the current line. The trick to insert extra lines *before* the first line is to "overwrite" the artificial line zero, as demonstrated in Listing 2-12. This is a rather trivial example; however, this trick can be quite useful when creating views. Views are discussed in Chapter 10.

Listing 2-12. *Inserting Text Before the First Line of the SQL Buffer*

```
  1  select *
  2  from   courses
  3  where  category = 'DSG'
  4* order  by code

SQL> 0 /* this is just a comment */

SQL> L
  1  /* this is just a comment */
  2  select *
  3  from   courses
  4  where  category = 'DSG'
  5* order  by code

SQL>
```

Using the Ellipsis

If you are using the SQL*Plus CHANGE command, you might benefit from using three consecutive period characters, also known as the *ellipsis*. The examples in Listings 2-13 and 2-14 demonstrate the effect of using the ellipsis. First, we enter a new SQL command into the buffer and deliberately make a mistake.

Listing 2-13. *Entering a SQL Command with a Deliberate Error*

```
SQL> select mgr, department_name
  2  from   departments
  3  where  location = 'SCHIERMONNIKOOG';
select mgr, department_name
            *
ERROR at line 1:
ORA-00904: "DEPARTMENT_NAME": invalid identifier

SQL>
```

Normally, the last command line you entered into the SQL buffer is automatically the current line. However, if an error condition occurs (such as in Listing 2-13), the line where the error is found becomes the current line. This allows you to correct any mistakes with the SQL*Plus CHANGE command immediately, without activating any line with the SQL*Plus LIST command. Listing 2-14 shows this phenomenon; the asterisk in the L* command means to show the current line.

Listing 2-14. *Using the SQL*Plus L* Command and the Ellipsis (...)*

```
SQL> L*
  1* select mgr, department_name

SQL> c/d.../dname
  1* select mgr, dname

SQL> 3
  3* where  location = 'SCHIERMONNIKOOG'

SQL> c/s...g/BOSTON
  3* where  location = 'BOSTON'

SQL>
```

The last example in Listing 2-14 shows that all CHANGE command searches are case-insensitive. As you can see, the ellipsis is powerful, but it's also dangerous. For example, the command c/d.../dname searches for the *first* occurrence of a d on the first line, and then replaces everything to the end of the line.

SQL*Plus Editor Command Review

The SQL*Plus editor is a rather simple editor; nevertheless, it makes sense to spend some time to explore its possibilities. It might come in handy when you need to work with the Oracle DBMS in an environment that is completely unknown to you, or where you are not allowed to launch an external editor from the underlying operating system. The SQL*Plus editor is always available, and it's identical on all platforms supported by Oracle.

Table 2-10 summarizes all the SQL*Plus editor commands covered in this chapter.

Table 2-10. *Some SQL*Plus Editor-Related Commands*

Command	Description
LIST	Show the complete SQL buffer
LIST *n* (or just *n*)	Make line *n* the current line
CHANGE/*old*/*new*/	Change the first occurrence of *old* into *new* on the current line
APPEND *txt*	Append *txt* to the end of the current line
INPUT	Insert line(s) below the current line

Continued

Table 2-10. *Continued*

Command	Description
DEL [x [y]]	Without arguments: remove current line. One argument: remove that line. Two arguments: remove range of lines (x and y can be line numbers, *, or LAST)
RUN (or /)	Execute the contents of the SQL buffer
EDIT	Start an external editor on the current buffer contents
DEFINE _EDITOR	Define your preferred external editor

As Table 2-10 shows, you can use the slash (/) command as an alternative for the SQL*Plus RUN command. The difference between the two is that RUN always displays the SQL command *and* the results, whereas the slash (/) command shows the results only.

Saving Commands

As explained earlier in the chapter, the SQL buffer is overwritten with every new SQL command you enter in SQL*Plus. If you want to save the contents of the SQL buffer, you can use the SQL*Plus SAVE command. The SAVE command creates a script file containing the contents of the SQL buffer.

If a script file already exists, you can specify (with the options APPEND or REPLACE) what you want the SAVE command to do in that case. The APPEND option is useful if you want to save all your SQL commands in one single file; for example, to print that file later.

Under Microsoft Windows, the options for saving the contents of the SQL buffer are also available via the File pull-down menu of SQL*Plus, as shown in Figure 2-14.

Figure 2-14. *The SQL*Plus options for saving the SQL buffer contents*

As an example of saving SQL commands, enter the commands shown in Listing 2-15.

Listing 2-15. *The SQL*Plus SAVE Command*

```
SQL> save BLA

SQL> select * from departments;
```

```
DEPTNO DNAME       LOCATION   MGR
------ ----------  --------  -----
    10 ACCOUNTING NEW YORK   7782
    20 TRAINING   DALLAS     7566
    30 SALES       CHICAGO   7698
    40 HR          BOSTON    7839

SQL> save BLI
Created file BLI.sql

SQL> select * from courses;

CODE DESCRIPTION                     CAT DURATION
---- ------------------------------- --- --------
SQL  Introduction to SQL             GEN     4
OAU  Oracle for application users    GEN     1
JAV  Java for Oracle developers      BLD     4
PLS  Introduction to PL/SQL          BLD     1
XML  XML for Oracle developers       BLD     2
ERM  Data modeling with ERM          DSG     3
PMT  Process modeling techniques     DSG     1
RSD  Relational system design        DSG     2
PRO  Prototyping                     DSG     5
GEN  System generation               DSG     4

10 rows selected.

SQL> save BLA
SP2-0540: File "BLA.sql" already exists.
Use "SAVE filename[.ext] REPLACE".

SQL> save BLA replace
Created file BLA.sql

SQL>
```

Note the error message after the second SAVE BLA attempt; REPLACE (or APPEND) is mandatory if a file already exists.

We have created two script files. These script files get the extension .SQL by default. If you prefer to use a different file name extension, you can change it with the SQL*Plus SUFFIX setting.

Running SQL*Plus Scripts

You can load script files saved with the SAVE command back into the SQL buffer with the GET command, followed by the name of the script. For example, you might reload a script and then edit it. If you want to load a script file and immediately execute it, you can use the START command (to get and run the script), as shown in Listing 2-16.

Listing 2-16. *Using the SQL*Plus GET and START Commands*

```
SQL> GET BLA
  1* select * from courses

SQL> START BLI

DEPTNO DNAME       LOCATION  MGR
------ ---------- --------- -----
    10 ACCOUNTING NEW YORK  7782
    20 TRAINING   DALLAS    7566
    30 SALES      CHICAGO   7698
    40 HR         BOSTON    7839

SQL>
```

Listing 2-17 shows that you can also use the @ shortcut for the SQL*Plus START command.

Listing 2-17. *Using the SQL*Plus @ Command*

```
SQL> L
  1* select * from departments

SQL> @BLA

CODE DESCRIPTION                    CAT DURATION
---- ------------------------------ --- --------
SQL  Introduction to SQL            GEN        4
OAU  Oracle for application users   GEN        1
JAV  Java for Oracle developers     BLD        4
PLS  Introduction to PL/SQL         BLD        1
XML  XML for Oracle developers      BLD        2
ERM  Data modeling with ERM         DSG        3
PMT  Process modeling techniques    DSG        1
RSD  Relational system design       DSG        2
PRO  Prototyping                    DSG        5
GEN  System generation              DSG        4

10 rows selected.

SQL>
```

Specifying Directory Path Specifications

The SQL*Plus commands SAVE, GET, and START can handle full file name specifications, with directory paths. In the absence of a directory path, these commands default to the current directory. In a Microsoft Windows environment, it is relatively simple to define the directory (or folder) in which you want SQL*Plus to start. This is one of the shortcut properties, which you can set in the Start In field of the Properties dialog box, shown in Figure 2-15. Right-click the SQL*Plus icon and select Properties to open this dialog box.

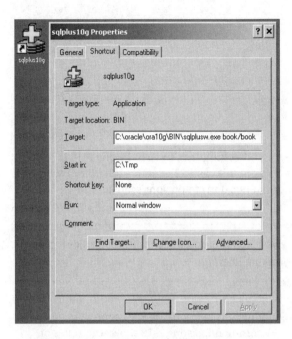

Figure 2-15. *SQL*Plus shortcut properties*

Through the Properties dialog box, you can also simplify the process to start SQL*Plus by specifying your username and password (such as book/book) in the Target field. In that case, the standard Log On dialog box (see Figure 2-11) will be skipped. However, this is a security risk, because anyone with access to your keyboard for more than two seconds will find out your database name and password.

■Tip Under Microsoft Windows, you can also set the SQLPATH Registry setting to define a default search path for all files that cannot be found in the current directory. For example, you could have this Registry setting point to a central directory where you maintain all your generic SQL scripts. Just open the Registry Editor with the REGEDIT command and search for SQLPATH. Under other operating systems, check out the SQLPATH environment variable.

Adjusting SQL*Plus Settings

You can modify the behavior of SQL*Plus in numerous ways, based on SQL*Plus variables or settings. This section provides some simple examples to give you an idea of how this works. Chapter 11 covers the topic in more detail.

Listing 2-18 demonstrates using the SET command to change some SQL*Plus settings.

Listing 2-18. *Changing SQL*Plus Settings with the SET Command*

```
SQL> set pagesize 22
SQL> set pause "Hit [Enter]... "
SQL> set pause on

SQL> run
  1* select * from courses

Hit [Enter]...
```

The effect of changing the PAUSE and PAGESIZE settings as shown in Listing 2-18 is that SQL*Plus now produces screen output per page, in this case, 22 lines at a time. The PAUSE setting is useful if the results of your SQL commands don't fit on your screen.

■Tip When using the PAUSE setting, don't just switch it on or off; make sure to specify a prompt string, too. Otherwise, SQL*Plus will just wait until you press the Enter key.

You can display the current values of SQL*Plus settings with the SHOW command, and you can revert to the default behavior with the SET command. Listing 2-19 shows examples of using these commands.

Listing 2-19. *Displaying SQL*Plus Settings with the SHOW Command*

```
SQL> show pages
pagesize 22

SQL> show pause
PAUSE is ON and set to "Hit [Enter]... "

SQL> set pause off

SQL> show pause
PAUSE is OFF

SQL>
```

Under Microsoft Windows, SQL*Plus offers an Options ➤ Environment menu option, as shown in Figure 2-16. Choosing this option opens the Environment dialog box, where you can view current SQL*Plus settings and modify them, if you wish, as shown in Figure 2-17.

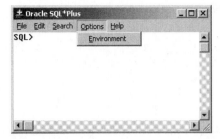

Figure 2-16. *The SQL*Plus Environment option on the Options pull-down menu*

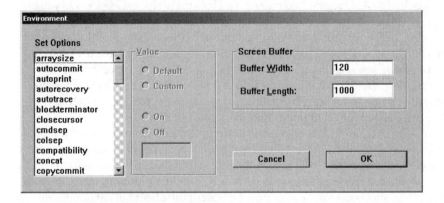

Figure 2-17. *The Environment dialog box*

Although we are discussing the SQL*Plus tool in this section, there is also another (client tool-independent) way to influence your database session behavior: by using the SQL command ALTER SESSION. With this command, you can set several NLS (National Language Support) session parameters, a selection of which are shown in Table 2-11.

Table 2-11. *Examples of NLS Session Parameters*

Parameter	Description
NLS_DATE_FORMAT	Default format to display dates
NLS_TIME_FORMAT	Default format to display timestamps
NLS_LANGUAGE	The language for SQL*Plus feedback and messages
NLS_NUMERIC_CHARACTERS	The decimal point and group separator characters
NLS_CURRENCY	The currency symbol

The most important parameter in this list is probably NLS_DATE_FORMAT, because this parameter influences the way date values are interpreted and displayed by your session, which is often a source of confusion. Listing 2-20 shows an example of using the ALTER SESSION command to set some NLS session parameters.

Listing 2-20. _Changing NLS Parameters with ALTER SESSION_

```
SQL> alter session
  2  set   nls_date_format='dd-mm-yyyy'
  3        nls_language=Dutch
  4        nls_currency='Eur';

Sessie is gewijzigd.

SQL>
```

If you change settings with the ALTER SESSION command, or if you change certain
SQL*Plus settings with the SQL*Plus SET command, you lose these changes as soon as you log
off. On startup, SQL* Plus will use the default values again. If you want to avoid the hassle of
applying the same changes over and over again, you can store these SQL and SQL*Plus commands in a file with the special name login.sql. This file is automatically executed when you
start SQL*Plus, or even when you change connections within a SQL*Plus session with the
CONNECT command. Note that SQL*Plus must be able to find this file in the directory it starts in
(see Figure 2-15) or via the SQLPATH Registry setting. login.sql is an example of a SQL*Plus
script. We will revisit this type of file in more detail in Chapter 11.

If the rows of a result table don't fit on a single line on your screen (and the line wrapping
makes the result rather ugly), a solution might be to narrow the display of one or more
columns with the SQL*Plus COLUMN command. By default, SQL*Plus displays all columns on
the screen with a width derived from the corresponding column definitions found in the data
dictionary. Listing 2-21 shows how you can narrow (or widen) the display of alphanumeric
columns on your screen by using the FORMAT option of the COLUMN command.

Listing 2-21. _Changing the Width of Alphanumeric Columns_

```
SQL> select * from courses
  2  where  category = 'BLD';

CODE DESCRIPTION                       CAT DURATION
---- ------------------------------    --- --------
JAV  Java for Oracle developers        BLD        4
PLS  Introduction to PL/SQL            BLD        1
XML  XML for Oracle developers         BLD        2

SQL> COLUMN description FORMAT a26
SQL> /

CODE DESCRIPTION                CAT DURATION
---- ------------------------   --- --------
JAV  Java for Oracle developers BLD        4
PLS  Introduction to PL/SQL     BLD        1
XML  XML for Oracle developers  BLD        2

SQL>
```

All SQL*Plus commands (and their optional components) can be abbreviated, as long as the abbreviation is unique. For example, the COLUMN command can be abbreviated to COL, and FORMAT can be abbreviated to FOR (see Listing 2-22).

You can influence the width of numeric columns in a similar way, as you can see in Listing 2-22.

Listing 2-22. *Changing the Display of Numeric Columns*

```
SQL> select * from salgrades
  2  where  grade > 3;

GRADE LOWERLIMIT UPPERLIMIT BONUS
----- ---------- ---------- -----
    4       2001       3000   200
    5       3001       9999   500

SQL> COL bonus FOR 9999.99
SQL> /

GRADE LOWERLIMIT UPPERLIMIT     BONUS
----- ---------- ---------- --------
    4       2001       3000    200.00
    5       3001       9999    500.00

SQL>
```

If you want to save all your current SQL*Plus settings in a file (a SQL*Plus script file), use the STORE SET command. See Listing 2-23 for the syntax of this command.

Listing 2-23. *SQL*Plus STORE SET Command Syntax*

```
SQL> STORE SET <filename>[.sql] [REPLACE|APPEND]
```

The brackets in Listing 2-23 (around .sql and REPLACE|APPEND) are part of a common syntax notation convention to denote optional command clauses. This convention is also used in Appendix A of this book. In this convention, a vertical bar (|) can be used to separate optional choices, as in [REPLACE|APPEND]. Uppercase components such as SET and APPEND should be entered verbatim; lowercase components (such as <filename>) should be replaced (in this case) by a file name of your own choice. See Appendix A for more details.

If you have saved all SQL*Plus settings in a script file by using the STORE SET command, you can restore those settings at any time using the START (or @) command. This allows you to write SQL*Plus scripts that capture all SQL*Plus settings at the beginning, change various settings during script execution, and then restore the original settings at the end of the script.

Spooling a SQL*Plus Session

You can record the complete results (as displayed on your screen) of a SQL*Plus session in an operating system file, using the SQL*Plus SPOOL command. Listing 2-24 shows an example.

Listing 2-24. *Using the SQL*Plus SPOOL Command*

```
SQL> spool BLA.TXT [create|replace|append]
SQL> select * from employees;
...
SQL> select * from departments;
...
SQL> spool off
```

The BLA.TXT file, created in the same directory or folder where the SAVE command stores its script files, now contains a complete copy of all screen output. As Listing 2-24 shows, you can influence the behavior of the SPOOL command by specifying one of the following keywords: CREATE, REPLACE, or APPEND. With these three options, you can specify which behavior you want in case the specified file already exists. Just try these options for yourself; the error messages are self-explanatory.

The GUI of SQL*Plus under Microsoft Windows offers a File ➤ Spool menu option to activate or deactivate the SPOOL command, as shown in Figure 2-18.

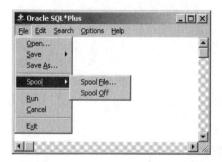

Figure 2-18. *The SQL*Plus File ➤ Spool menu option*

Describing Database Objects

When formulating SQL commands, it is sometimes convenient to get a quick overview of the structure of a table; for example, to see the column names and the datatypes. In such cases, the SQL*Plus DESCRIBE command is what you need. See Listing 2-25 for an example.

Listing 2-25. *The SQL*Plus DESCRIBE Command*

```
SQL> descr employees

Name                           Null?    Type
------------------------------ -------- --------------------
EMPNO                          NOT NULL NUMBER(4)
ENAME                          NOT NULL VARCHAR2(8)
INIT                           NOT NULL VARCHAR2(5)
JOB                                     VARCHAR2(8)
MGR                                     NUMBER(4)
BDATE                          NOT NULL DATE
```

```
MSAL                          NOT NULL NUMBER(6,2)
COMM                                   NUMBER(6,2)
DEPTNO                                 NUMBER(2)

SQL>
```

Executing Commands from the Operating System

The HOST command (most implementations support a platform-specific shortcut, such as $ or !) allows you to execute commands at the underlying operating system; for example, on a Microsoft Windows system, a command window is opened. Depending on the underlying operating system, you can finish the subsession and return to your SQL*Plus session with EXIT, LOGOUT, or a similar command.

Clearing the Buffer and the Screen

With the CLEAR BUFFER command, you can empty the SQL buffer in SQL*Plus. This is something you won't need to do too often, because the SQL buffer is overwritten each time by consecutive commands.

With the CLEAR SCREEN command, you can start at the top of a new, empty SQL*Plus screen.

SQL*Plus Command Review

Table 2-12 shows an overview of all SQL*Plus commands covered in this chapter (including the SQL*Plus editor commands already listed in Table 2-10).

Table 2-12. *Some SQL*Plus Commands*

Command	Description
SAVE	Save the SQL buffer contents in a script file
GET	Read a saved script file back into the SQL buffer
START or @	Execute the contents of a script file
SPOOL	Copy all screen output to a file
SET	Change a SQL*Plus setting
SHOW	Show the current value of SQL*Plus settings
COLUMN ... FORMAT	Change screen display attributes of a column
STORE SET	Save the current SQL*Plus settings in a script file
DESCRIBE	Provide a description of a database object
HOST or $	Start a subsession at the operating system level
CLEAR BUFFER	Empty the SQL buffer
CLEAR SCREEN	Start with an empty SQL*Plus screen

We also introduced the following SQL command in this section:

- ALTER SESSION changes various settings for your session, such as NLS settings.

In Chapter 11, we will revisit SQL*Plus and *i*SQL*Plus to cover some more advanced features of these two tools. In case you are curious about more SQL*Plus features, feel free to visit the Oracle online documentation or refer to the quick reference in Appendix A of this book.

For now, however, you know just enough about the *i*SQL*Plus and SQL*Plus tools to get started with the SQL language in the chapters to follow.

CHAPTER 3

■ ■ ■

Data Definition, Part I

This short chapter is the first one about data definition with SQL. It's intended to get you started using SQL for data retrieval as soon as possible. Therefore, this chapter covers only the data definition basics, such as how to create simple tables using standard datatypes. In Chapter 7, we will revisit data definition with SQL and explore topics such as indexes, synonyms, and constraints.

This chapter is mainly theoretical in nature in that it still offers no hands-on exercises and only a few examples. In the next chapter, you will start writing SQL commands yourself.

The first section introduces the concept of database schemas and database users. In an Oracle database, tables always belong to a schema, and, in general, a schema has a database user as its owner. The second section explains how you can create simple tables, and the most common Oracle datatypes are covered in the third section. To illustrate the contents of the first three sections, the fourth section shows the CREATE TABLE commands to create the sample tables used in the examples in this book (introduced in the previous chapter), without bothering about constraints yet.

The last section of this chapter covers the Oracle data dictionary. It provides a global overview of the data dictionary, lists some typical examples of data dictionary tables, and shows how to execute some simple queries against some of those data dictionary tables.

3.1 Schemas and Users

Before you can start creating and populating tables with SQL, you need to understand how data stored in an Oracle database is organized internally. In the previous chapter, you learned that you cannot do anything in an Oracle database if you do not identify yourself first by specifying a *username* and a *password*. This process identifies you as a certain *database user*.

In an Oracle database there is, in general, a one-to-one relationship between database *users* and database *schemas* with the same name. Briefly, these are the differences between a database user and a database schema:

- A *database user* has a password and certain database privileges.

- A *database schema* is a logical collection of database objects (such as tables, indexes, views, and so on) that is usually owned by the user of the same name.

Normally, when you log on to an Oracle database, you are automatically connected with the corresponding database schema with the same name. However, it is also possible that certain database users don't have their own schema; in other words, they don't have any database objects of their own, and they don't have the privileges to create them either. These "schema-less" users are, for example, authorized only to retrieve or manipulate data in a different database schema.

For example, in SQL*Plus, you can use the CONNECT command to establish a new connection with a different schema, provided you are able to enter a valid combination of a database name and a corresponding password. With the ALTER SESSION SET CURRENT_SCHEMA command, you can "visit" a different schema in SQL*Plus without changing your identity as database user, and therefore without changing any of your privileges.

All of the examples and exercises in this book assume the presence of a database user BOOK, with the password BOOK, and a schema BOOK that contains the seven case tables introduced in the previous chapter. You can find all of the scripts to create the BOOK schema, to create the seven tables, and to insert the rows on my web site at http://www.naturaljoin.nl or the Downloads section of the Apress web site (http://www.apress.com).

3.2 Table Creation

The SQL command to create tables is CREATE TABLE. If you create a table, you must specify a name for the new table, followed by a specification of all table columns. The columns must be specified as a comma-separated list between parentheses.

■**Note** The right to create tables in an Oracle database is not granted to everyone; you need some additional system privileges. If you get error messages when you try to create tables, contact your database administrator or check *Oracle Database Administrator's Guide* in the online documentation.

The basic syntax of the CREATE TABLE command is shown in Figure 3-1.

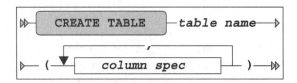

Figure 3-1. *CREATE TABLE basic command syntax diagram*

■**Note** Figure 3-1 does *not* show the complete syntax of the CREATE TABLE command. Just for fun, check out *Oracle SQL Reference* for the amount of documentation describing the CREATE TABLE command. Chapter 7 of this book will revisit this command with the full syntax and more details.

Column specifications normally consist of several components. Figure 3-2 shows the column specification syntax.

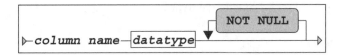

Figure 3-2. *Column specification syntax diagram*

Each column specification starts with a column name, followed by the datatype (discussed in the next section). If you add the optional expression NOT NULL to a column definition, each future row of the table you are creating *must* have a value specified for this column, and you will not be able to update future rows by removing a value for this column. In other words, you define the column to be a mandatory attribute.

The NOT NULL addition is an example of a constraint. You can specify many additional constraints in the CREATE TABLE command, such as UNIQUE, CHECK, PRIMARY KEY, and FOREIGN KEY. Chapter 7 will discuss these options of the CREATE TABLE command.

3.3 Datatypes

Oracle supports many standard datatypes, as you will see if you take a look at the Oracle documentation. Some Oracle datatypes look very similar; some are even synonyms for each other. These datatypes are supported for compatibility purposes of Oracle with other DBMSs or with the ANSI/ISO SQL standard. For example, INT and INTEGER are synonyms for NUMBER(38). Some datatypes are very specific in nature, making them irrelevant for us at this point in time. This section covers only the most common and widely used Oracle datatypes.

In general, there are three categories of column data: numbers (numeric data), text (alphanumeric data), and time-related data. The most important corresponding Oracle datatypes are NUMBER, VARCHAR or VARCHAR2, and DATE, respectively.

Table 3-1 shows some examples of the NUMBER datatype.

Table 3-1. *NUMBER Datatype Examples*

Example	Description
NUMBER(4)	An integer with a maximum length of four digits
NUMBER(6,2)	A number with a maximum precision of six digits; at most two digits behind the decimal point
NUMBER(7,-3)	A multiple of thousand with at most seven digits
NUMBER	Identical to NUMBER(38,*)
NUMBER(*,5)	Identical to NUMBER(38,5)

Oracle offers a number of alphanumeric datatypes. Depending on the Oracle version you are using, there are some differences due to the evolution of the ANSI/ISO SQL standard over the years. For example, since Oracle7, the two datatypes VARCHAR and VARCHAR2 are identical, but this could change in a future Oracle release. If you create a table and you use the VARCHAR datatype, the Oracle DBMS translates VARCHAR to VARCHAR2 on the fly. Therefore, this book refers to only the VARCHAR2 datatype. In cases where the maximum size of the VARCHAR2 datatype (4000) is insufficient for a specific column, you can use the CLOB (Character Large OBject) datatype.

Table 3-2 shows some simple examples of character datatypes.

Table 3-2. *Character Datatype Examples*

Example	Description
VARCHAR2(25)	Alphanumeric, *variable* length, up to 25 characters
CHAR(4)	Alphanumeric, *fixed* length, four characters
CLOB	Alphanumeric, larger than the maximum size of the VARCHAR2 datatype

Table 3-3 lists the maximum size values for the datatypes mentioned so far.

■**Note** The actual units of measure used for the size of CHAR and VARCHAR2 datatypes depend on character semantics (bytes or characters). See Chapter 7 for details.

Table 3-3. *Maximum Datatype Sizes*

Datatype	Maximum Size
NUMBER	38 digits precision
CHAR	2000
VARCHAR2	4000
CLOB	4GB

■**Note** The indicated maximum CLOB size (4GB) is not completely correct. Depending on some configuration parameters, CLOB columns may contain much more than 4GB worth of data. Refer to *Oracle SQL Reference* for details.

The basic datatype for time-related data is DATE. By default, date values are interpreted and displayed according to a standard date format, typically showing only the day, the month, and the last two digits of the year. You can change the default date format for your session or use conversion functions in your SQL commands to display dates in different ways. Internally, Oracle stores dates in such a way that DATE column values are allowed from the year 4712 BC until the year 9999. Oracle dates are internally stored with much more precision than you might expect on first consideration.

■**Caution** DATE columns also contain a time indication (hours, minutes, and seconds), which may cause problems when comparing two dates. For example, seemingly equal dates could be different due to their invisible time components.

Apart from the DATE datatype, Oracle also supports the related datatypes TIMESTAMP (with or without TIME ZONE) and INTERVAL to store other time-related data in table columns. Chapter 7 provides more details on the time-related datatypes.

This book focuses on the usage of the three standard Oracle datatypes: NUMBER, VARCHAR2, and DATE.

3.4 Commands for Creating the Case Tables

This section lists the SQL commands to create the seven case tables introduced in Chapter 1, as an illustration of the concepts covered in the previous three sections, without much additional explanation. Since the BOOK schema consists of seven tables, this section also shows seven CREATE TABLE commands, presented in Listings 3-1 through 3-7.

Note As mentioned earlier, constraint definition (and constraint checking) is not taken into consideration in this chapter; therefore, the following listings do *not* show the complete commands to create the case tables.

Listing 3-1. *The EMPLOYEES Table*

```
SQL> create table  EMPLOYEES
  2  ( empno        number(4)    not null
  3  , ename        varchar2(8)  not null
  4  , init         varchar2(5)  not null
  5  , job          varchar2(8)
  6  , mgr          number(4)
  7  , bdate        date         not null
  8  , msal         number(6,2)  not null
  9  , comm         number(6,2)
 10  , deptno       number(2)                );
```

Listing 3-2. *The DEPARTMENTS Table*

```
SQL> create table  DEPARTMENTS
  2  ( deptno       number(2)    not null
  3  , dname        varchar2(10) not null
  4  , location     varchar2(8)  not null
  5  , mgr          number(4)                );
```

Listing 3-3. *The SALGRADES Table*

```
SQL> create table  SALGRADES
  2  ( grade       number(2)    not null
  3  , lowerlimit  number(6,2)  not null
  4  , upperlimit  number(6,2)  not null
  5  , bonus       number(6,2)  not null );
```

Listing 3-4. *The COURSES Table*

```
SQL> create table  COURSES
  2  ( code        varchar2(6)   not null
  3  , description varchar2(30)  not null
  4  , category    char(3)       not null
  5  , duration    number(2)     not null );
```

Listing 3-5. *The OFFERINGS Table*

```
SQL> create table  OFFERINGS
  2  ( course      varchar2(6)  not null
  3  , begindate   date         not null
  4  , trainer     number(4)
  5  , location    varchar2(8)            );
```

Listing 3-6. *The REGISTRATIONS Table*

```
SQL> create table  REGISTRATIONS
  2  ( attendee    number(4)    not null
  3  , course      varchar2(6)  not null
  4  , begindate   date         not null
  5  , evaluation  number(1)              );
```

Listing 3-7. *The HISTORY Table*

```
SQL> create table  HISTORY
  2  ( empno       number(4)    not null
  3  , beginyear   number(4)    not null
  4  , begindate   date         not null
  5  , enddate     date
  6  , deptno      number(2)    not null
  7  , msal        number(6,2)  not null
  8  , comments    varchar2(60)           );
```

3.5 The Data Dictionary

If you are interested in knowing which tables are present in your database, which columns they have, whether or not those columns are indexed, which privileges are granted to you, and similar information, you should query the *data dictionary*. Another common term for data dictionary is *catalog*. By the way, we already queried the data dictionary implicitly before, in Chapter 2, when using the SQL*Plus DESCRIBE command; this command queries the data dictionary under the hood.

The data dictionary is more or less the internal housekeeping administration of Oracle. The data dictionary stores information about the data, also referred to as *metadata*. The data dictionary is automatically maintained by Oracle; therefore, the data dictionary is always up-to-date.

DBMSs like Oracle store data dictionary data in precisely the same way as they store "regular" data: in tables. This is in compliance with Ted Codd's rule 4 (see Chapter 1). The big advantage of this approach is that you can use the SQL language to query data dictionary data in the same way that you query ordinary data. In other words, if you master the SQL language, you need to know only the names of the data dictionary tables and the names of their columns.

Data dictionary access is a potential security risk. That's why the Oracle DBMS offers system privileges and roles to regulate and protect access to the data dictionary. For example, there is a role SELECT_CATALOG_ROLE, which contains all privileges that you need to be able to access the data dictionary data. Listing 3-8 demonstrates how Oracle controls data dictionary access.

Listing 3-8. *Needing the SELECT_CATALOG_ROLE Role*

```
SQL> describe dba_sys_privs
ERROR:
ORA-04043: object "SYS"."DBA_SYS_PRIVS" does not exist

SQL> connect / as sysdba
Connected.

SQL> grant select_catalog_role to book;
Grant succeeded.

SQL> connect book/book
Connected.

SQL> desc dba_sys_privs
 Name                            Null?    Type
 ------------------------------- -------- ----------------
 GRANTEE                         NOT NULL VARCHAR2(30)
 PRIVILEGE                       NOT NULL VARCHAR2(40)
 ADMIN_OPTION                             VARCHAR2(3)

SQL>
```

Although the information is stored in data dictionary *tables*, most of the time, you access data dictionary *views* instead. On the other hand, views are tables anyway. See Chapter 10 for details about views.

You can refer to *Oracle Server Reference* in the Oracle documentation to get a complete overview of the Oracle data dictionary. Fortunately, the Oracle data dictionary contains a view that lists all Oracle data dictionary views, with a short description of their contents. This view is called DICTIONARY; DICT is a shorter synonym for the same view. Listing 3-9 shows an abbreviated version of the query results. It's abbreviated for a practical reason: the DICT view contains more than 600 rows!

Listing 3-9. *Using the DICT View*

```
SQL> col COLUMN_NAME format a30
SQL> col COMMENTS    format a40 word
SQL>
SQL> select * from dict order by table_name;

TABLE_NAME            COMMENTS
-------------------   ----------------------------------------
ALL_ALL_TABLES        Description of all object and relational
                      tables accessible to the user
ALL_APPLY             Details about each apply process that
                      dequeues from the queue visible to the
                      current user
...
USER_COL_COMMENTS     Comments on columns of user's tables and
                      views
USER_COL_PRIVS        Grants on columns for which the user is
                      the owner, grantor or grantee
...
V$TIMEZONE_NAMES      Synonym for V_$TIMEZONE_NAMES
V$VERSION             Synonym for V_$VERSION

610 rows selected.

SQL>
```

Data dictionary view names typically have prefixes that suggest the existence of four main categories. In Listing 3-9, you can see the ALL, USER, and V$ prefixes. The fourth common prefix is DBA. The idea behind this is that, most of the time, you are interested in information about a certain subcategory of database objects. By using the appropriate views, you automatically suppress information that is not of interest to you. Also, depending on your database privileges, you will not be allowed to use certain categories of data dictionary views. Table 3-4 lists the most common data dictionary view name prefixes. (Note that not all data dictionary views have one of these prefixes.)

Table 3-4. *Common Data Dictionary View Prefixes*

Prefix	Description
USER_...	Information about your own objects
ALL_...	Information about all objects you can access
DBA_...	All information in the database; for database administrators only
[G]V$...	Dynamic performance views; for database administrators only

The *dynamic performance views* (those with a V$ or GV$ name prefix) are a special category. These views are not based on database tables, but rather on information from other sources such as internal memory structures. They are mainly relevant for, and accessible to, database administrators.

Most data dictionary view names give a clear indication of their contents; however, as a consequence, some of these names are very long. That's why some of the most popular data dictionary views also have alternative (shorter) synonyms, such as CAT, OBJ, IND, TABS, and COLS. The CAT view is an especially useful one, because it lists the objects in the current schema. Listing 3-10 shows an example of using the CAT view with our BOOK schema.

Listing 3-10. *Using the CAT View*

```
SQL> select * from cat;

TABLE_NAME                      TABLE_TYPE
------------------------------- -----------
EMPLOYEES                       TABLE
DEPARTMENTS                     TABLE
SALGRADES                       TABLE
COURSES                         TABLE
OFFERINGS                       TABLE
REGISTRATIONS                   TABLE
HISTORY                         TABLE

7 rows selected.

SQL>
```

Suppose you want to query a specific data dictionary view, and you don't know the actual column names of that view. In that case, you can use the SQL*Plus command DESCRIBE, just as you would do for regular tables. As you can see in Listing 3-11, you can use the DESCRIBE command, or you can query the data dictionary view DICT_COLUMNS.

Listing 3-11. *Using the DESCRIBE Command and the DICT_COLUMNS View*

```
SQL> describe DICT_COLUMNS
 Name                    Null? Type
 ----------------------- ----- --------------
 TABLE_NAME                    VARCHAR2(30)
```

```
COLUMN_NAME                    VARCHAR2(30)
COMMENTS                       VARCHAR2(4000)

SQL> select column_name, comments
  2  from   dict_columns
  3  where  table_name = 'ALL_USERS';

COLUMN_NAME                    COMMENTS
--------------------------- -------------------------
USERNAME                       Name of the user
USER_ID                        ID number of the user
CREATED                        User creation date

SQL>
```

Listing 3-12 shows a query against the NLS_SESSION_PARAMETERS view (NLS stands for National Language Support). The result shows, for example, the NLS_DATE_FORMAT value used to display dates.

Listing 3-12. *Using the NLS_SESSION_PARAMETERS View*

```
SQL> select * from nls_session_parameters

PARAMETER               VALUE
----------------------- -----------------------
NLS_LANGUAGE            AMERICAN
NLS_TERRITORY           AMERICA
NLS_CURRENCY            $
NLS_ISO_CURRENCY        AMERICA
NLS_NUMERIC_CHARACTERS  .,
NLS_CALENDAR            GREGORIAN
NLS_DATE_FORMAT         DD-MON-YYYY
NLS_DATE_LANGUAGE       AMERICAN
NLS_SORT                BINARY
NLS_TIME_FORMAT         HH.MI.SSXFF AM
NLS_TIMESTAMP_FORMAT    DD-MON-RR HH.MI.SSXFF AM
NLS_TIME_TZ_FORMAT      HH.MI.SSXFF AM TZR
NLS_TIMESTAMP_TZ_FORMAT DD-MON-RR HH.MI.SSXFF AM TZR
NLS_DUAL_CURRENCY       $
NLS_COMP                BINARY
NLS_LENGTH_SEMANTICS    BYTE
NLS_NCHAR_CONV_EXCP     FALSE

17 rows selected.

SQL>
```

The NLS features in Oracle are documented in great detail in *Globalization Support Guide*.

Table 3-5 lists a selection of useful Oracle data dictionary tables.

Table 3-5. *Some Useful Oracle Data Dictionary Views*

View	Description
DICTIONARY	Description of the data dictionary itself
DICT_COLUMNS	Data dictionary column descriptions
ALL_USERS	Information about all database users
ALL_INDEXES[1]	All indexes
ALL_SEQUENCES[1]	All sequences
ALL_OBJECTS[1]	All objects
ALL_SYNONYMS[1]	All synonyms
ALL_TABLES[1]	All tables
ALL_VIEWS[1]	All views
USER_INDEXES[2]	Indexes
USER_SEQUENCES[2]	Sequences
USER_OBJECTS[2]	Objects
USER_SYNONYMS[2]	Synonyms
USER_TABLES[2]	Tables
USER_TAB_COLUMNS[2]	Columns
USER_VIEWS[2]	Views
USER_RECYCLEBIN	Dropped objects
CAT	Synonym for USER_CATALOG
COLS	Synonym for USER_TAB_COLUMNS
DICT	Synonym for DICTIONARY
DUAL	Dummy table, with one row and one column
IND	Synonym for USER_INDEXES
OBJ	Synonym for USER_OBJECTS
SYN	Synonym for USER_SYNONYMS
TABS	Synonym for USER_TABLES

[1]*Accessible to the user*
[2]*Owned by the user*

Appendix B provides a more complete description of the data dictionary views, and *Oracle Server Reference* provides all the details you need about the Oracle data dictionary.

CHAPTER 4

■ ■ ■

Retrieval: The Basics

In this chapter, you will start to access the seven case tables with SQL. To be more precise, you will learn how to *retrieve* data from your database. For data retrieval, the SQL language offers the SELECT command. SELECT commands are commonly referred to as *queries*.

The SELECT command has six main clauses. Three of them—SELECT, WHERE, and ORDER BY— are discussed in this chapter. Introduction of the remaining three clauses—FROM, GROUP BY, and HAVING—is postponed until Chapter 8.

You can write queries as independent SQL statements, but queries can also occur inside other SQL commands. These are called *subqueries*. This chapter introduces subqueries, and then in Chapter 9, we will revisit subqueries to discuss some of their more advanced features.

Null values and their associated three-valued logic—SQL conditions have the three possible outcomes of TRUE, FALSE, or UNKNOWN—are also covered in this chapter. A thorough understanding of null values and three-valued logic is critical for anyone using the SQL language. Finally, this chapter presents the truth tables of the AND, OR, and NOT operators, showing how these operators handle three-valued logic.

At the end of this chapter, you will find a set of exercises, so you can practice the data-retrieval techniques you learned in the chapter.

4.1 Overview of the SELECT Command

We start this chapter with a short recap of what we already discussed in previous chapters. The six main clauses of the SELECT command are shown in Figure 4-1.

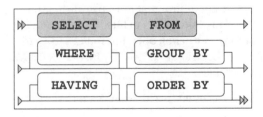

Figure 4-1. *The six main clauses of the SELECT command*

Figure 4-1 is identical to Figure 2-1, and it illustrates the following main syntax rules of the SELECT statement:

- There is a predefined mandatory order of these six clauses.

- The SELECT and FROM clauses are mandatory.

- WHERE, GROUP BY, HAVING, and ORDER BY are optional clauses.

Table 4-1 is identical to Table 2-1, and it shows high-level descriptions of the main SELECT command clauses.

Table 4-1. *The Six Main Clauses of the SELECT Command*

Component	Description
FROM	Which table(s) is (are) needed for retrieval?
WHERE	What is the condition to filter the rows?
GROUP BY	How should the rows be grouped/aggregated?
HAVING	What is the condition to filter the aggregated groups?
SELECT	Which columns do you want to see in the result?
ORDER BY	In which order do you want to see the resulting rows?

According to the ANSI/ISO SQL standard, these six clauses must be processed in the following order: FROM, WHERE, GROUP BY, HAVING, SELECT, ORDER BY. Note that this is *not* the order in which you must specify them in your queries.

As mentioned in the introduction to this chapter, SQL retrieval statements (SELECT commands) are commonly referred to as *queries*. In this chapter, we will focus on queries using three SELECT command clauses:

- **SELECT:** With the SELECT clause of the SELECT command, you specify the columns that you want displayed in the query result and, optionally, which column headings you prefer to see above the result table. This clause implements the relational *projection* operator, explained in Chapter 1.

- **WHERE:** The WHERE clause allows you to formulate conditions that must be true in order for a row to be retrieved. In other words, this clause allows you to filter rows from the base tables; as such, it implements the relational *restriction* operator. You can use various operators in your WHERE clause conditions—such as BETWEEN, LIKE, IN, CASE, NOT, AND, and OR—and make them as complicated as you like.

- **ORDER BY:** With the ORDER BY clause, you specify the order in which you want to see the rows in the result of your queries.

The FROM clause allows you to specify which tables you want to access. In this chapter, we will work with queries that access only a single table, so the FROM clause in the examples in this chapter simply specifies the table name. The FROM clause becomes more interesting when you want to access multiple tables in a single query, as described in Chapter 8.

4.2 The SELECT Clause

Let's start with a straightforward example of a SELECT command, shown in Listing 4-1.

Listing 4-1. *Issuing a Simple SELECT Command*

```
SQL> select * from departments;

 DEPTNO DNAME       LOCATION      MGR
-------- ---------- -------- --------
     10 ACCOUNTING NEW YORK     7782
     20 TRAINING   DALLAS       7566
     30 SALES      CHICAGO      7698
     40 HR         BOSTON       7839

SQL>
```

The asterisk (*) means to show *all* columns of the DEPARTMENTS table. Listing 4-2 shows a slightly more complicated query that selects specific columns from the EMPLOYEES table and uses a WHERE clause to specify a condition for the rows retrieved.

Listing 4-2. *Selecting Specific Columns*

```
SQL> select ename, init, job, msal
  2  from    employees
  3  where   deptno = 30;

ENAME    INIT  JOB          MSAL
-------- ----- -------- --------
ALLEN    JAM   SALESREP     1600
WARD     TF    SALESREP     1250
MARTIN   P     SALESREP     1250
BLAKE    R     MANAGER      2850
TURNER   JJ    SALESREP     1500
JONES    R     ADMIN         800

SQL>
```

Let's look at the *syntax* (the statement construction rules of a language) of this statement more closely. You have a lot of freedom in this area. For example, you can enter an entire SQL command in a single line, spread a SQL command over several lines, and use as many spaces and tabs as you like. New lines, spaces, and tabs are commonly referred to as *white space*. The amount of white space in your SQL statements is meaningless to the Oracle DBMS.

■**Tip** It is a good idea to define some SQL statement layout standards and stick to them. This increases both the readability and the maintainability of your SQL statements. At this point, our SQL statements are short and simple, but in real production database environments, SQL statements are sometimes several pages long.

In the SELECT clause, white space is mandatory after the keyword SELECT. The columns (or *column expressions*) are separated by commas; therefore, white space is not mandatory. However, as you can see in Listing 4-2, spaces after the commas enhance readability.

White space is also mandatory after the keywords FROM and WHERE. Again, any additional white space is not mandatory, but it might enhance readability. For example, you can use spaces around the equal sign in the WHERE clause.

Column Aliases

By default, the column names of the table are displayed above your query result. If you don't like those names—for example, because they do not adequately describe the meaning of the column in the specific context of your query—you can specify different result column headings. You include the heading you want to appear, called a *column alias*, in the SELECT clause of your query, as shown in the example in Listing 4-3.

Listing 4-3. *Changing Column Headings*

```
SQL> select ename, init, msal salary
  2  from    employees
  3  where   deptno = 30;

ENAME     INIT   SALARY
--------  -----  --------
ALLEN     JAM        1600
WARD      TF         1250
MARTIN    P          1250
BLAKE     R          2850
TURNER    JJ         1500
JONES     R           800

SQL>
```

In this example, there is *no* comma between MSAL and SALARY. This small detail has a great effect, as the result in Listing 4-3 shows: SALARY is used instead of MSAL as a column heading (compare this with the result shown in Listing 4-2).

By the way, the ANSI/ISO SQL standard also supports the optional keyword AS between any column name and its corresponding column heading (column alias). Using this keyword enhances readability. In other words, you can also formulate the query in Listing 4-3 as follows:

```
SQL> select ename, init, msal AS salary
  2  from    employees
  3  where   deptno = 30;
```

Note Another way to change the column headings shown in the query results, without changing the SQL command itself, is to give instructions to the tool you are using; that is, SQL*Plus. You can use the HEADING option of the SQL*Plus COLUMN command, as discussed in Chapter 11.

The DISTINCT Keyword

Sometimes, your query results contain duplicate rows. You can eliminate such rows by adding the keyword DISTINCT immediately after the keyword SELECT, as demonstrated in Listing 4-4.

Listing 4-4. *Using DISTINCT to Eliminate Duplicate Rows*

```
SQL> select DISTINCT job, deptno
  2  from    employees;

JOB         DEPTNO
--------    --------
ADMIN           10
ADMIN           30
DIRECTOR        10
MANAGER         10
MANAGER         20
MANAGER         30
SALESREP        30
TRAINER         20

8 rows selected.

SQL>
```

Without the addition of DISTINCT, this query would produce 14 rows, because the EMPLOYEES table contains 14 rows. Remove the keyword DISTINCT from the first line of the query in Listing 4-4, and then execute the query again to see the difference.

Note Using DISTINCT in the SELECT clause might incur some performance overhead, because the Oracle DBMS must sort the result in order to eliminate the duplicate rows.

Column Expressions

Instead of column names, you can also specify column expressions in the SELECT clause. For example, Listing 4-5 shows how you can derive the range of the salary grades in the SALGRADES table, by selecting the difference between upper limits and lower limits.

Listing 4-5. *Using a Simple Expression in a SELECT Clause*

```
SQL> select grade, upperlimit - lowerlimit
  2  from   salgrades;

  GRADE UPPERLIMIT-LOWERLIMIT
-------- ---------------------
       1                   500
       2                   199
       3                   599
       4                   999
       5                  6998

SQL>
```

In the next example, shown in Listing 4-6, we concatenate the employee names with their initials into a single column, and also calculate the yearly salary by multiplying the monthly salary with 12.

Listing 4-6. *Another Example of Using Expressions in a SELECT Clause*

```
SQL> select init||' '||ename name
  2  ,      12 * msal        yearsal
  3  from   employees
  4  where  deptno = 10;

NAME                               YEARSAL
---------------------------------- --------
AB CLARK                             29400
CC KING                              60000
TJA MILLER                           15600

SQL>
```

Now take a look at the rather odd query shown in Listing 4-7.

Listing 4-7. *Selecting an Expression with Literals*

```
SQL> select 3 + 4 from departments;

     3+4
--------
       7
```

```
          7
          7
          7

SQL>
```

The query result might look strange at first; however, it makes sense when you think about it. The outcome of the expression 3+4 is calculated for each row of the DEPARTMENTS table. This is done four times, because there are four departments and we did not specify a WHERE clause. Because the expression 3+4 does not contain any variables, the result (7) is obviously the same for every department row.

The DUAL Table

It makes more sense to execute queries such as the one shown in Listing 4-7 against a dummy table, with only one row and one column. You could create such a table yourself, but the Oracle DBMS supplies a standard dummy table for this purpose, named DUAL, which is stored in the data dictionary. Because the Oracle DBMS *knows* that the DUAL table contains only one single row, you usually get better performance results by using the DUAL table rather than a dummy table that you created yourself.

■**Tip** The Oracle DBMS also provides an X$DUAL table, giving even better performance results than the DUAL table.

Listing 4-8 shows two examples of DUAL table usage. Note that the contents of this DUAL table are totally irrelevant; you use only the property that the DUAL table contains a single row.

Listing 4-8. *Using the DUAL Table*

```
SQL> select 123 * 456 from dual;

 123*456
--------
   56088

SQL> select sysdate from dual;

SYSDATE
-----------
05-SEP-2004

SQL>
```

The second query in Listing 4-8 shows an example of using the system date. You can refer to the system date in Oracle with the keyword SYSDATE. Actually, to be more precise, SYSDATE is a *function* that returns the system date. These functions are also referred to as *pseudo columns*. See Appendix A of this book for examples of other such pseudo columns.

Listing 4-9 shows an example of using SYSDATE to derive the age of an employee, based on the date of birth stored in the BDATE column of the EMPLOYEES table.

Listing 4-9. *Using the System Date*

```
SQL> select ename, (sysdate-bdate)/365
  2  from    employees
  3  where   empno = 7839;

ENAME     (SYSDATE-BDATE)/365
--------  -------------------
KING                 51.83758

SQL>
```

■**Note** The results of your queries using SYSDATE depend on the precise moment the command was run; therefore, when you execute the examples, the results will not be the same as those shown in Listings 4-8 and 4-9.

Null Values in Expressions

You should always consider the possibility of null values occurring in expressions. In case one or more variables in an expression evaluate to a null value, the result of the expression as a whole becomes unknown. We will discuss this area of concern in more detail later in this chapter, in Section 4.9. As an appetizer, look at the result of the query in Listing 4-10.

Listing 4-10. *The Effect of Null Values in Expressions*

```
SQL> select ename, msal, comm, 12*msal + comm
  2  from    employees
  3  where   empno < 7600;

ENAME        MSAL      COMM 12*MSAL+COMM
--------  --------  --------  ------------
SMITH          800
ALLEN         1600       300         19500
WARD          1250       500         15500
JONES         2975

SQL>
```

As you can see, the total yearly salary (including commission) for two out of four employees is unknown, because the commission column of those employees contains a null value.

4.3 The WHERE Clause

With the WHERE clause, you can specify a *condition* to filter the rows for the result. We distinguish *simple* and *compound* conditions.

Simple conditions typically contain one of the SQL comparison operators listed in Table 4-2.

Table 4-2. *SQL Comparison Operators*

Operator	Description
<	Less than
<=	Less than or equal to
>	Greater than
>=	Greater than or equal to
=	Equal to
<>	Not equal to (alternative syntax: !=)

Expressions containing comparison operators constitute statements that can evaluate to TRUE or FALSE. At least, that's how things are in mathematics (logic), as well as in our intuition. (In Section 4.9, you will see that null values make things slightly more complicated in SQL, but for the moment, we won't worry about them.)

Listing 4-11 shows an example of a WHERE clause with a simple condition.

Listing 4-11. *A WHERE Clause with a Simple Condition*

```
SQL> select ename, init, msal
  2  from   employees
  3  where  msal >= 3000;

ENAME    INIT   MSAL
-------- ----- --------
SCOTT    SCJ    3000
KING     CC     5000
FORD     MG     3000

SQL>
```

Listing 4-12 shows another example of a WHERE clause with a simple condition, this time using the <> (not equal to) operator.

Listing 4-12. *Another Example of a WHERE Clause with a Simple Condition*

```
SQL> select dname, location
  2  from   departments
  3  where  location <> 'CHICAGO';
```

```
DNAME       LOCATION
---------- --------
ACCOUNTING NEW YORK
TRAINING   DALLAS
HR         BOSTON

SQL>
```

Compound conditions consist of multiple subconditions, combined with logical operators. In Section 4.5 of this chapter, you will see how to construct compound conditions by using the logical operators AND, OR, and NOT.

4.4 The ORDER BY Clause

The result of a query is a table; that is, a set of rows. The order in which these rows appear in the result typically depends on two aspects:

- The strategy chosen by the optimizer to access the data

- The operations chosen by the optimizer to produce the desired result

This means that it is sometimes difficult to predict the order of the rows in the result. In any case, the order is *not* guaranteed to be the same under all circumstances.

If you insist on getting the resulting rows of your query back in a *guaranteed* order, you must use the ORDER BY clause in your SELECT commands. Figure 4-2 shows the syntax of this clause.

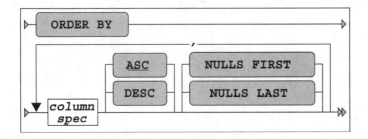

Figure 4-2. *ORDER BY clause syntax diagram*

As Figure 4-2 shows, you can specify multiple sort specifications, separated by commas. Each sort specification consists of a column specification (or column expression), optionally followed by keyword DESC (descending), in case you want to sort in descending order. Without this addition, the default sorting order is ASC (ascending). ASC is underlined in Figure 4-2 to denote that it is the default.

The column specification may consist of a single column name or a column expression. To refer to columns in the ORDER BY clause, you can use any of the following:

- Regular column names

- Column aliases defined in the SELECT clause (especially useful in case of complex expressions in the SELECT clause)

- Column ordinal numbers

Column ordinal numbers in the ORDER BY clause have no relationship with the order of the columns in the database; they are dependent on only the SELECT clause of your query. Try to avoid using ordinal numbers in the ORDER BY clause. Using column aliases instead increases SQL statement readability, and your ORDER BY clauses also become independent of the SELECT clauses of your queries.

Listing 4-13 shows how you can sort query results on column combinations. As you can see, the query result is sorted on department number, and then on employee name for each department.

Listing 4-13. *Sorting Results with ORDER BY*

```
SQL> select deptno, ename, init, msal
  2  from    employees
  3  where   msal < 1500
  4  order   by deptno, ename;

DEPTNO ENAME      INIT     MSAL
-------- --------- ----  --------
    10 MILLER     TJA      1300
    20 ADAMS      AA       1100
    20 SMITH      N         800
    30 JONES      R         800
    30 MARTIN     P        1250
    30 WARD       TF       1250

SQL>
```

Listing 4-14 shows how you can reverse the default sorting order by adding the DESC keyword to your ORDER BY clause.

Listing 4-14. *Sorting in Descending Order with ORDER BY . . . DESC*

```
SQL> select ename, 12*msal+comm as yearsal
  2  from    employees
  3  where   job = 'SALESREP'
  4  order   by yearsal desc;

ENAME      YEARSAL
-------- --------
ALLEN       19500
TURNER      18000
```

```
MARTIN      16400
WARD        15500

SQL>
```

When sorting, null values cause trouble (when don't they, by the way?). How should columns with missing information be sorted? The rows need to go somewhere, so you need to decide. You have four options as to how to treat null values when sorting:

- Always as *first* values (regardless of the sorting order)

- Always as *last* values (regardless of the sorting order)

- As *low* values (lower than any existing value)

- As *high* values (higher than any existing value)

Figure 4-2 shows how you can explicitly indicate how to treat null values in the ORDER BY clause for each individual column expression.

Let's try to find out Oracle's default behavior for sorting null values. See Listing 4-15 for a first test.

Listing 4-15. *Investigating the Ordering of Null Values*

```
SQL> select evaluation
  2  from    registrations
  3  where   attendee = 7788
  4  order   by evaluation;

EVALUATION
----------
         4
         5


SQL>
```

The null value in the result is tough to see; however, it is the third row. If you change the ORDER BY clause to specify a descending sort, the result becomes as shown in Listing 4-16.

Listing 4-16. *Testing the Ordering of Null Values*

```
SQL> select evaluation
  2  from    registrations
  3  where   attendee = 7788
  4  order   by evaluation DESC;

EVALUATION
----------
```

```
          5
          4

SQL>
```

Listings 4-15 and 4-16 show that Oracle treats null values as high values. In other words, the default behavior is as follows:

- NULLS LAST is the default for ASC.

- NULLS FIRST is the default for DESC.

4.5 AND, OR, and NOT

You can combine simple and compound conditions into more complicated compound conditions by using the logical operators AND and OR. If you use AND, you indicate that each row should evaluate to TRUE for both conditions. If you use OR, only one of the conditions needs to evaluate to TRUE. Sounds easy enough, doesn't it?

Well, the fact is that we use the words *and* and *or* in a rather sloppy way in spoken languages. The listener easily understands our precise intentions from the context, intonation, or body language. This is why there is a risk of making mistakes when translating questions from a natural language, such as English, into queries in a formal language, such as SQL.

■**Tip** It is not uncommon to see discussions (mostly after the event) about misunderstandings in the precise wording of the original question in natural language. Therefore, you should always try to sharpen your question in English as much as possible before trying to convert those questions into SQL statements. In cases of doubt, ask clarifying questions for this purpose.

Therefore, in SQL, the meaning of the two keywords AND and OR must be defined very precisely, without any chance for misinterpretation. You will see the formal truth tables of the AND, OR, and NOT operators in Section 4.10 of this chapter, after the discussion of null values. First, let's experiment with these three operators and look at some examples.

The OR Operator

Consider the operator OR. We can make a distinction between the *inclusive* and the *exclusive* meaning of the word. Is it okay if both conditions evaluate to TRUE, or should only one of the two be TRUE? In natural languages, this distinction is almost always implicit. For example, suppose that you want to know when someone can meet with you, and the answer you get is "next Thursday or Friday." In this case, you probably interpret the OR in its exclusive meaning.

What about SQL—is the OR operator inclusive or exclusive? Listing 4-17 shows the answer.

Listing 4-17. *Combining Conditions with OR*

```
SQL> select code, category, duration
  2  from    courses
  3  where   category = 'BLD'
  4  or      duration = 2;

CODE CAT DURATION
---- --- --------
JAV  BLD        4
PLS  BLD        1
XML  BLD        2
RSD  DSG        2

SQL>
```

In this example, you can see that the OR operator in SQL is inclusive; otherwise, the third row wouldn't show up in the result. The XML course belongs to the BLD course category (so the first condition evaluates to TRUE) *and* its duration is two days (so the second condition also evaluates to TRUE).

In the upcoming discussion of the NOT operator, you will see how to construct an exclusive OR.

The AND Operator and Operator Precedence Issues

There is a possible problem if your compound conditions contain a mixture of AND and OR operators. See Listing 4-18 for an experiment with a query against the DUAL table.

Listing 4-18. *Combining Conditions with OR and AND*

```
SQL> select 'is true  ' as condition
  2  from    dual
  3  where   1=1 or 1=0 and 0=1;

CONDITION
---------
is true

SQL>
```

The compound condition in Listing 4-18 consists of three rather trivial, simple conditions, evaluating to TRUE, FALSE, and FALSE, respectively. But what is the outcome of the compound predicate as a whole, and why? Apparently, the compound predicate evaluates to TRUE; otherwise, Listing 4-18 would have returned the message "no rows selected."

In such cases, the result depends on the operator *precedence* rules. You can interpret the condition of Listing 4-18 in two ways, as follows:

1=1 OR ...	If one of the operands of OR is true, the overall result is TRUE.
...AND 0=1	If one of the operands of AND is false, the overall result is FALSE.

Listing 4-18 obviously shows an overall result of TRUE. This implies that the Oracle DBMS evaluates the AND operator first, and then the OR operator:

```
1=1  OR  1=0  AND  0=1  <=>
TRUE OR FALSE AND FALSE <=>
TRUE OR       FALSE     <=>
TRUE
```

With compound conditions, it is always better to use parentheses to indicate the order in which you want the operations to be performed, rather than relying on implicit language precedence rules. Listing 4-19 shows two variants of the query from Listing 4-18, using parentheses in the WHERE clause.

Listing 4-19. *Using Parentheses to Force Operator Precedence*

```
SQL> select 'is true  ' as condition
  2  from    dual
  3  where   (1=1 or 1=0) and 0=1;

no rows selected

SQL> select 'is true  ' as condition
  2  from    dual
  3  where   1=1 or (1=0 and 0=1);

CONDITION
---------
is true

SQL>
```

■**Caution** Remember that you can use white space to beautify your SQL commands; however, *never* allow an attractive SQL command layout (for example, with suggestive indentations) to confuse you. Tabs, spaces, and new lines may increase statement readability, but they don't change the meaning of your SQL statements in any way.

The NOT Operator

You can apply the NOT operator to any arbitrary condition to negate that condition. Listing 4-20 shows an example.

Listing 4-20. *Using the NOT Operator to Negate Conditions*

```
SQL> select ename, job, deptno
  2  from    employees
  3  where   NOT deptno > 10;
```

```
ENAME     JOB        DEPTNO
--------  --------   --------
CLARK     MANAGER         10
KING      DIRECTOR        10
MILLER    ADMIN           10

SQL>
```

In this simple case, you could achieve the same effect by removing the NOT operator and changing the comparison operator > into <=, as shown in Listing 4-21.

Listing 4-21. *Equivalent Query Without Using the NOT Operator*

```
SQL> select ename, job, deptno
  2  from    employees
  3  where   deptno <= 10;

ENAME     JOB        DEPTNO
--------  --------   --------
CLARK     MANAGER         10
KING      DIRECTOR        10
MILLER    ADMIN           10

SQL>
```

The NOT operator becomes more interesting and useful in cases where you have complex compound predicates with AND, OR, and parentheses. In such cases, the NOT operator gives you more control over the correctness of your commands.

In general, the NOT operator should be placed in front of the condition. Listing 4-22 shows an example of illegal syntax and a typical error message when NOT is positioned incorrectly.

Listing 4-22. *Using the NOT Operator in the Wrong Place*

```
SQL> select ename, job, deptno
  2  from    employees
  3  where   deptno NOT > 10;
where   deptno NOT > 10
                    *
ERROR at line 3:
ORA-00920: invalid relational operator

SQL>
```

There are some exceptions to this rule. As you will see in Section 4.6, the SQL operators BETWEEN, IN, and LIKE have their own built-in negation option.

■**Tip** Just as you should use parentheses to avoid confusion with AND and OR operators in complex compound conditions, it is also a good idea to use parentheses to specify the precise scope of the NOT operator explicitly. See Listing 4-23 for an example.

By the way, do you remember the discussion about inclusive and exclusive OR? Listing 4-23 shows how you can construct the exclusive OR in SQL by explicitly excluding the possibility that both conditions evaluate to TRUE (on the fourth line). That's why the XML course is now missing. Compare the result with Listing 4-17.

Listing 4-23. *Constructing the Exclusive OR Operator*

```
SQL> select  code, category, duration
  2  from    courses
  3  where   (category = 'BLD' or  duration = 2)
  4  and not (category = 'BLD' and duration = 2);


CODE CAT DURATION
---- --- --------
JAV  BLD        4
PLS  BLD        1
RSD  DSG        2

SQL>
```

Just as in mathematics, you can eliminate parentheses from SQL expressions. The following two queries are logically equivalent:

```
select * from employees where NOT (ename = 'BLAKE' AND init = 'R')
select * from employees where     ename <> 'BLAKE' OR init <> 'R'
```

In the second version, the NOT operator disappeared, the negation is applied to the two comparison operators, and last, but not least, the AND changes into an OR. You will look at this logical equivalence in more detail in one of the exercises at the end of this chapter.

4.6 BETWEEN, IN, and LIKE

Section 4.3 introduced the WHERE clause, and Section 4.5 explained how you can combine simple and compound conditions in the WHERE clause into more complicated compound conditions by using the logical operators AND, OR, and NOT. This section introduces three new operators you can use in simple conditions: BETWEEN, IN, and LIKE.

The BETWEEN Operator

The BETWEEN operator does not open up new possibilities; it only allows you to formulate certain conditions a bit more easily and more readably. See Listing 4-24 for an example.

Listing 4-24. *Using the BETWEEN Operator*

```
SQL> select ename, init, msal
  2  from   employees
  3  where  msal between 1300 and 1600;

ENAME    INIT    MSAL
-------- -----   --------
ALLEN    JAM     1600
TURNER   JJ      1500
MILLER   TJA     1300

SQL>
```

This example shows that the BETWEEN operator includes both border values (1300 and 1600) of the interval.

The BETWEEN operator has its own built-in negation option. Therefore, the following three SQL expressions are logically equivalent:

```
where msal NOT between 1000 and 2000
where NOT msal between 1000 and 2000
where msal < 1000 OR msal > 2000
```

The IN Operator

With the IN operator, you can compare a column or the outcome of a column expression against a list of values. See Listing 4-25 for an example.

Listing 4-25. *Using the IN Operator*

```
SQL> select empno, ename, init
  2  from   employees
  3  where  empno in (7499,7566,7788);

   EMPNO ENAME    INIT
-------- -------- -----
    7499 ALLEN    JAM
    7566 JONES    JM
    7788 SCOTT    SCJ

SQL>
```

Just like BETWEEN, the IN operator also has its own built-in negation option. The example in Listing 4-26 produces all course registrations that do *not* have an evaluation value of 3, 4, or 5.

Listing 4-26. *Using the NOT IN Operator*

```
SQL> select * from registrations
  2  where evaluation NOT IN (3,4,5);

ATTENDEE COUR BEGINDATE EVALUATION
-------- ---- --------- ----------
    7876 SQL  12-APR-99          2
    7499 JAV  13-DEC-99          2

SQL>
```

Check for yourself that the following four expressions are logically equivalent:

```
where       evaluation NOT in (3,4,5)
where NOT   evaluation     in (3,4,5)
where NOT  (evaluation=3  OR evaluation=4   OR evaluation=5)
where       evaluation<>3 AND evaluation<>4 AND evaluation<>5
```

A rather obvious requirement for the IN operator is that all of the values you specify between the parentheses must have the same (relevant) datatype.

■**TIP** IN operators with long value lists sometimes indicate a poor underlying data model. Adding an attribute can result in SQL code that reads better and executes faster.

The LIKE Operator

You typically use the LIKE operator in the WHERE clause of your queries in combination with a *search pattern*. In the example shown in Listing 4-27, the query returns all courses that have something to do with SQL, using the search pattern %SQL%.

Listing 4-27. *Using the LIKE Operator with the Percent Character*

```
SQL> select * from courses
  2  where description LIKE '%SQL%';

CODE DESCRIPTION                 TYP DURATION
---- --------------------------- --- --------
SQL  Introduction to SQL         GEN        4
PLS  Introduction to PL/SQL      BLD        1

SQL>
```

Two characters have special meaning when you use them in a string (the search pattern) after the LIKE operator. These two characters are commonly referred to as *wildcards*:

- **%:** A percent sign after the LIKE operator means zero, one, or more arbitrary characters (see Listing 4-27).

- **_:** An underscore after the LIKE operator means exactly *one* arbitrary character.

■Note If the LIKE operator (with its two wildcard characters) provides insufficient search possibilities, you can use the REGEXP_LIKE function and regular expressions. See Chapter 5 for information about using regular expressions.

The query shown in Listing 4-28 returns all employees with an uppercase *A* as the second character in their name.

Listing 4-28. *Using the LIKE Operator with the Percent and Underscore Characters*

```
SQL> select empno, init, ename
  2  from    employees
  3  where   ename like '_A%';

  EMPNO INIT  ENAME
-------- ----- --------
   7521 TF    WARD
   7654 P     MARTIN

SQL>
```

Just like the BETWEEN and IN operators, the LIKE operator also features a built-in negation option; in other words, you can use WHERE . . . NOT LIKE . . . .

The following queries show two special cases: one using LIKE without wildcards and one using the % character without the LIKE operator.

```
SQL> select * from employees where ename like 'BLAKE'
SQL> select * from employees where ename = 'BL%'
```

Both queries will be executed by Oracle, without any complaints or error messages. However, in the first example, we could have used the equal sign (=) instead of the LIKE operator to get the same results. In the second example, the percent sign (%) has no special meaning, since it doesn't follow the LIKE operator, so it is very likely we would get back the "no rows selected" message.

If you really want to search for actual percent sign or underscore characters with the LIKE operator, you need to suppress the special meaning of those characters. You can do this with the ESCAPE option of the LIKE operator, as demonstrated in Listing 4-29.

Listing 4-29. *Using the ESCAPE Option of the LIKE Operator*

```
SQL> select empno, begindate, comments
  2  from   history
  3  where  comments like '%0\%%' escape '\';

  EMPNO BEGINDATE   COMMENTS
------- ----------- ---------------------------------------------------------
   7566 01-JUN-1989 From accounting to human resources; 0% salary change
   7788 15-APR-1985 Transfer to human resources; 0% salary raise

SQL>
```

The WHERE clause in Listing 4-29 searches for 0% in the COMMENTS column of the HISTORY table. The backslash (\) suppresses the special meaning of the second percent sign in the search string. Note that you can pick a character other than the backslash to use as the ESCAPE character.

4.7 CASE Expressions

You can tackle complicated procedural problems with CASE expressions. Oracle supports two CASE expression types: *simple* CASE expressions and *searched* CASE expressions.

Figure 4-3 illustrates the syntax of the simple CASE expression. With this type of CASE expression, you specify an *input expression* to be compared with the *values* in the WHEN . . . THEN loop. The implicit comparison operator is always the equal sign. The left operand is always the *input expression*, and the right operand is the *value* from the WHEN clause.

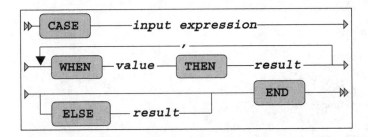

Figure 4-3. *Simple CASE expression syntax diagram*

Figure 4-4 shows the syntax of the searched CASE expression. The power of this type of CASE expression is that you don't specify an input expression, but instead specify complete *conditions* in the WHEN clause. Therefore, you have the freedom to use any logical operator in each individual WHEN clause.

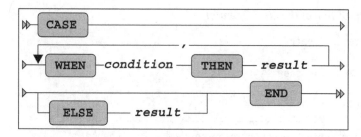

Figure 4-4. *Searched CASE expressions syntax diagram*

CASE expressions are evaluated as follows:

- Oracle evaluates the WHEN expressions in the order in which you specified them, and returns the THEN result of the *first* condition evaluating to TRUE. Note that Oracle does *not* evaluate the remaining WHEN clauses; therefore, the order of the WHEN expressions is important.

- If none of the WHEN expressions evaluates to TRUE, Oracle returns the ELSE expression.

- If you didn't specify an ELSE expression, Oracle returns a null value.

Obviously, you must handle datatypes in a consistent way. The input expressions and the THEN results in the simple CASE expression (Figure 4-3) must have the same datatype, and in both CASE expression types (Figures 4-3 and 4-4), the THEN results should have the same datatype, too.

Listing 4-30 shows a straightforward example of a simple CASE expression, which doesn't require any explanation.

Listing 4-30. *Simple CASE Expression Example*

```
SQL> select attendee, begindate
  2  ,       case evaluation
  3              when 1 then 'bad'
  4              when 2 then 'mediocre'
  5              when 3 then 'ok'
  6              when 4 then 'good'
  7              when 5 then 'excellent'
  8                       else 'not filled in'
  9          end
 10  from   registrations
 11  where  course = 'S02';

ATTENDEE BEGINDATE CASEEVALUATIO
-------- --------- -------------
    7499 12-APR-99 good
    7698 12-APR-99 good
    7698 13-DEC-99 not filled in
```

```
7788 04-OCT-99 not filled in
7839 04-OCT-99 ok
7876 12-APR-99 mediocre
7902 04-OCT-99 good
7902 13-DEC-99 not filled in
7934 12-APR-99 excellent

9 rows selected.

SQL>
```

Listing 4-31 shows an example of a searched CASE expression.

Listing 4-31. *Searched CASE Expression Example*

```
SQL> select ename, job
  2  ,        case when job = 'TRAINER' then '  10%'
  3                when job = 'MANAGER' then '  20%'
  4                when ename = 'SMITH' then '  30%'
  5                                      else '   0%'
  6          end  as raise
  7  from    employees
  8  order by raise desc, ename;


ENAME     JOB        RAISE
--------  ---------  -----

BLAKE     MANAGER    20%
CLARK     MANAGER    20%
JONES     MANAGER    20%
ADAMS     TRAINER    10%
FORD      TRAINER    10%
SCOTT     TRAINER    10%
SMITH     TRAINER    10%
ALLEN     SALESREP    0%
JONES     ADMIN       0%
KING      DIRECTOR    0%
MARTIN    SALESREP    0%
MILLER    ADMIN       0%
TURNER    SALESREP    0%
WARD      SALESREP    0%

14 rows selected.

SQL>
```

In Listing 4-31, note that SMITH gets only a 10% raise, despite the fourth line of the query. This is because he is a trainer, which causes the second line to result in a match; therefore, the remaining WHEN expressions are not considered.

CASE expressions are very powerful and flexible; however, they sometimes become rather long. That's why Oracle offers several functions that you could interpret as abbreviations (or shorthand notations) for CASE expressions, such as COALESCE and NULLIF (both of these functions are part of the ANSI/ISO SQL standard), NVL, NVL2, and DECODE. We will look at these functions in the next chapter.

4.8 Subqueries

Section 4.6 introduced the IN operator. This section introduces the concept of subqueries by starting with an example of the IN operator.

Suppose you want to launch a targeted e-mail campaign, because you have a brand-new course that you want to promote. The target audience for the new course is the developer community, so you want to know who attended one or more build (BLD category) courses in the past. You could execute the following query to get the desired result:

```
select attendee
from   registrations
where  course in ('JAV','PLS','XML')
```

This solution has at least two problems. To start with, you have looked at the COURSES table to check which courses belong to the BLD course category, apparently (evidenced by the JAV, PLS, and XML in the WHERE clause). However, the original question was not referring to any specific courses; it referred to BLD courses. This lookup trick is easy in our demo database, which has a total of only ten courses, but this might be problematic, or even impossible, in real information systems. Another problem is that the solution is rather rigid. Suppose you want to repeat the e-mail promotion one year later for another new course. In that case, you may need to revise the query to reflect the current set of BLD courses.

A much better solution to this problem is to use a *subquery*. This way, you leave it up to the Oracle DBMS to query the COURSES table, by replacing the list of course codes between the parentheses (JAV, PLS, and XML) with a query that retrieves the desired course codes for you. Listing 4-32 shows the subquery for this example.

Listing 4-32. *Using a Subquery to Retrieve All BLD Courses*

```
SQL> select attendee
  2  from   registrations
  3  where  course in (select code
  4                    from   courses
  5                    where  category = 'BLD');

ATTENDEE
--------
    7499
    7566
    7698
    7788
    7839
    7876
```

```
      7788
      7782
      7499
      7876
      7566
      7499
      7900

13 rows selected.

SQL>
```

This eliminates both objections to the initial solution with the hard-coded course codes. Oracle first substitutes the subquery between the parentheses with its result—a number of course codes—and then executes the main query. (Consider "first substitutes . . . and then executes . . ." conceptually; the Oracle optimizer could actually decide to execute the SQL statement in a different way.)

Apparently, 13 employees attended at least one build course in the past (see Listing 4-32). Is that really true? Upon closer investigation, you can see that some employees apparently attended several build courses, or maybe some employees even attended the same build course twice. In other words, the conclusion about the number of employees (13) was too hasty. To retrieve the correct number of employees, you should use SELECT DISTINCT in the main query to eliminate duplicates.

The Joining Condition

It is always your own responsibility to formulate subqueries in such a way that you are not comparing apples with oranges. For example, the next variant of the query shown in Listing 4-33 does not result in an error message; however, the result is rather strange.

Listing 4-33. *Comparing Apples with Oranges*

```
SQL> select attendee
  2  from    registrations
  3  where   EVALUATION in (select DURATION
  4                         from    courses
  5                         where   category = 'BLD');

ATTENDEE
--------
      7900
      7788
      7839
      7900
      7521
      7902
      7698
      7499
```

```
     7499
     7876

10 rows selected.

SQL>
```

This example compares evaluation numbers (from the main query) with course durations from the subquery. Just try to translate this query into an English sentence. . .

Fortunately, the Oracle DBMS does not discriminate between meaningful and meaningless questions. You have only two constraints:

- The datatypes must match, or the Oracle DBMS must be able to make them match with implicit datatype conversion.

- The subquery should not select too many column values per row.

When a Subquery Returns Too Many Values

What happens when a subquery returns too many values? Look at the query in Listing 4-34 and the resulting error message.

Listing 4-34. *Error: Subquery Returns Too Many Values*

```
SQL> select attendee
  2  from   registrations
  3  where  course in
  4       (select course, begindate
  5        from   offerings
  6        where  location = 'CHICAGO');
     (select course, begindate
      *
ERROR at line 4:
ORA-00913: too many values

SQL>
```

The subquery in Listing 4-34 returns (COURSE, BEGINDATE) value pairs, which cannot be compared with COURSE values. However, it is certainly possible to compare attribute combinations with subqueries in SQL. The query in Listing 4-34 was an attempt to find all employees who ever attended a course in Chicago.

In our data model, course offerings are uniquely identified by the combination of the course code and the begin date. Therefore, you can correct the query as shown in Listing 4-35.

Listing 4-35. *Fixing the Error in Listing 4-34*

```
SQL> select attendee
  2  from   registrations
  3  where (course, begindate) in
```

```
4              (select course, begindate
5               from   offerings
6               where  location = 'CHICAGO');

ATTENDEE
--------
    7521
    7902
    7900


SQL>
```

■**Note** Subqueries may, in turn, contain other subqueries. This principle is known as *subquery nesting*, and there is no practical limit to the number of subquery levels you might want to create in Oracle SQL. But be aware that at a certain level of nesting, you will probably lose the overview.

Comparison Operators in the Joining Condition

So far, we have explored subqueries with the IN operator. However, you can also establish a relationship between a main query and its subquery by using one of the comparison operators (=, <, >, <=, >=, <>), as demonstrated in Listing 4-36. In that case, there is one important difference: the subquery *must* return precisely one row. This additional constraint makes sense if you take into consideration how these comparison operators work: they are able to compare only a single left operand with a single right operand.

Listing 4-36. *Using a Comparison Operator in the Joining Condition*

```
SQL> select ename, init, bdate
  2  from    employees
  3  where   bdate > (select bdate
  4                   from    employees
  5                   where   empno = 7876);

ENAME    INIT  BDATE
-------- ----- ---------
JONES    JM    02-APR-67
TURNER   JJ    28-SEP-68
JONES    R     03-DEC-69


SQL>
```

The query in Listing 4-36 shows all employees who are younger than employee 7876. The subquery will never return more than one row, because EMPNO is the primary key of the EMPLOYEES table.

In case there is *no* employee with the employee number specified, you get the "no rows selected" message. You might expect an error message like "single row subquery returns no rows" (actually, this error message once existed in Oracle, many releases ago), but apparently there is no problem. See Listing 4-37 for an example.

Listing 4-37. *When the Subquery Returns No Rows*

```
SQL> select ename, init, bdate
  2  from    employees
  3  where   bdate > (select bdate
  4                   from    employees
  5                   where   empno = 99999);

no rows selected

SQL>
```

The subquery (returning *no* rows, or producing an empty set) is treated like a subquery returning one row instead, containing a null value. In other words, SQL treats this situation as if there *were* an employee 99999 with an unknown date of birth. This may sound strange; however, this behavior is fully compliant with the ANSI/ISO SQL standard.

When a Single-Row Subquery Returns More Than One Row

In case the subquery happens to produce *multiple* rows, the Oracle DBMS reacts with the error message shown in Listing 4-38.

Listing 4-38. *Error: Single-Row Subquery Returns More Than One Row*

```
SQL> select ename, init, bdate
  2  from    employees
  3  where   bdate > (select bdate
  4                   from    employees
  5                   where   ename = 'JONES');
where   bdate > (select bdate
                *
ERROR at line 3:
ORA-01427: single-row subquery returns more than one row

SQL>
```

In this example, the problem is that we have two employees with the same name (Jones). Note that you always risk this outcome, unless you make sure to use an equality comparison against a unique column of the table accessed in the subquery, as in the example in Listing 4-36.

So far, we have investigated subqueries only in the WHERE clause of the SELECT statement. Oracle SQL also supports subqueries in other SELECT statement clauses, such as the FROM clause and the SELECT clause. Chapter 9 will revisit subqueries.

4.9 Null Values

If a column (in a specific row of a table) contains no value, we say that such a column contains a null value. The term *null value* is actually slightly misleading, because it is an indicator of missing information. Null *marker* would have been a better term, because a null value is *not* a value.

There can be many different reasons for missing information. Sometimes, an attribute is *inapplicable*; for example, only sales representatives are eligible for commission. An attribute value can also be *unknown*; for example, the person entering data did not know certain values when the data was entered. And, sometimes, you don't know whether an attribute is applicable or inapplicable; for example, if you don't know the job of a specific employee, you don't know whether a commission value is applicable. The REGISTRATIONS table provides another good example. A null value in the EVALUATION column can mean several things: the course did not yet take place, the attendee had no opinion, the attendee refused to provide her opinion, the evaluation forms are not yet processed, and so on.

It would be nice if you could represent the *reason* why information is missing, but SQL supports only one null value, and according to Ted Codd's rule 3 (see Chapter 1) null values can have only one *context-independent* meaning.

■**Caution** Don't confuse null values with the number zero (0), a series of one or more spaces, or even an empty string. Although an empty string (' ') is formally different from a null value, Oracle sometimes interprets empty strings as null values (see Chapter 6 for some examples). However, you should *never* rely on this (debatable) interpretation of empty strings. You should always use the reserved word NULL to refer to null values in your SQL commands.

Null Value Display

By default, null values are displayed on your computer screen as "nothing," as shown earlier in Listings 4-15 and 4-16. You can change this behavior in SQL*Plus at two levels: the session level and the column level.

You can specify how null values appear at the session level by using the SQL*Plus NULL environment setting, available in the Environment dialog box, shown in Figure 4-5. Select the Options ➤ Environment menu option to open this dialog box.

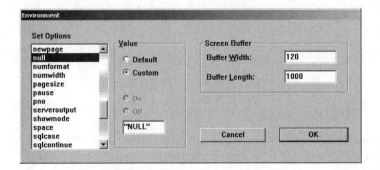

Figure 4-5. *The SQL*Plus Environment dialog box*

You can also influence the way null values are displayed at the column level, by using the SQL*Plus COLUMN command. Listing 4-39 demonstrates adjusting how SQL*Plus displays null values only in the EVALUATION column.

Listing 4-39. *Adjusting the Null Values Display with the COLUMN Command*

```
SQL> column evaluation NULL "unknown!!!"

SQL> select * from registrations
  2  where attendee = 7566;

ATTENDEE COURSE BEGINDATE    EVALUATION
-------- ------ ----------- ----------
    7566 JAV    01-FEB-2000          3
    7566 PLS    11-SEP-2000 unknown!!!

SQL>
```

The Nature of Null Values

Null values sometimes behave counterintuitively. Compare the results of the two queries in Listing 4-40.

Listing 4-40. *Comparing Two "Complementary" Queries*

```
SQL> select empno, ename, comm
  2  from    employees
  3  where   comm > 400;

  EMPNO ENAME         COMM
-------- -------- --------
    7521 WARD          500
    7654 MARTIN       1400

SQL> select empno, ename, comm
  2  from    employees
  3  where   comm <= 400;

  EMPNO ENAME         COMM
-------- -------- --------
    7499 ALLEN         300
    7844 TURNER          0

SQL>
```

The first query in Listing 4-40 returns 2 employees, so you might expect to see the other 12 employees in the result of the second query, because the two WHERE clauses complement each other. However, the two query results actually are *not* complementary.

If Oracle evaluates a condition, there are three possible outcomes: the result can be TRUE, FALSE, or UNKNOWN. In other words, the SQL language is using *three-valued logic*.

Only those rows for which the condition evaluates to TRUE will appear in the result—no problem. However, the EMPLOYEES table contains several rows for which *both* conditions in Listing 4-40 evaluate to UNKNOWN. Therefore, these rows (ten, in this case) will not appear in either result.

Just to stress the nonintuitive nature of null values in SQL, you could say the following:

In SQL, NOT is not "not"

The explanation of this (case-sensitive) statement is left as an exercise at the end of this chapter.

The IS NULL Operator

Suppose you are looking for all employees except the lucky ones with a commission greater than 400. In that case, the second query in Listing 4-40 does not give you the correct answer, because you would expect to see 12 employees instead of 2. To fix this query, you need the SQL IS NULL operator, as shown in Listing 4-41.

Listing 4-41. *Using the IS NULL Operator*

```
SQL> select empno, ename, comm
  2  from    employees
  3  where   comm <= 400
  4  or      comm is null;

  EMPNO ENAME        COMM
-------- -------- --------
   7369 SMITH
   7499 ALLEN         300
   7566 JONES
   7698 BLAKE
   7782 CLARK
   7788 SCOTT
   7839 KING
   7844 TURNER          0
   7876 ADAMS
   7900 JONES
   7902 FORD
   7934 MILLER

12 rows selected.

SQL>
```

Note Oracle SQL provides some functions with the specific purpose of handling null values in a flexible way (such as NVL and NVL2). These functions are covered in the next chapter.

The IS NULL operator—just like BETWEEN, IN, and LIKE—has its own built-in negation option. See Listing 4-42 for an example.

Listing 4-42. *Using the IS NOT NULL Operator*

```
SQL> select ename, job, msal, comm
  2  from    employees
  3  where   comm is not null;

ENAME     JOB          MSAL     COMM
--------  --------  --------  --------
ALLEN     SALESREP      1600       300
WARD      SALESREP      1250       500
MARTIN    SALESREP      1250      1400
TURNER    SALESREP      1500         0

SQL>
```

Note The IS NULL operator *always* evaluates to TRUE or FALSE. UNKNOWN is an impossible outcome.

Null Values and the Equality Operator

The IS NULL operator has only *one* operand: the preceding column name (or column expression). Actually, it is a pity that this operator is not written as IS_NULL (with an underscore instead of a space) to stress the fact that this operator has just a single operand. In contrast, the equality operator (=) has *two* operands: a left operand and a right one.

Watch the rather subtle syntax difference between the following two queries:

```
SQL> select * from registrations where evaluation IS null
SQL> select * from registrations where evaluation  = null
```

If you were to read both queries aloud, you might not even hear any difference. However, the seemingly innocent syntax change has definite consequences for the query results. They don't produce error messages, because both queries are syntactically correct.

If one (or both) of the operands being compared by the equality comparison operator (=) evaluates to a null value, the result is UNKNOWN. In other words, you cannot say that a null value is equal to a null value. The following shows the conclusions:

Expression	Evaluates to
NULL = NULL	UNKNOWN
NULL IS NULL	TRUE

This explains why the query in Listing 4-43 doesn't return all 14 rows of the EMPLOYEES table.

Listing 4-43. *Example of a Counterintuitive WHERE Clause*

```
SQL> select ename, init
  2  from    employees
  3  where   comm = comm;

ENAME     INIT
--------  -----
ALLEN     JAM
WARD      TF
MARTIN    P
TURNER    JJ

SQL>
```

In mathematical logic, we call expressions always evaluating to TRUE a *tautology*. The example in Listing 4-43 shows that certain trivial tautologies from two-valued logic (such as COMM = COMM) don't hold true in SQL.

Null Value Pitfalls

Null values in SQL often cause trouble. You must be aware of their existence in the database *and* their odds of being generated by Oracle in (intermediate) results, and you must continuously ask yourself how you want them to be treated in the processing of your SQL statements. Otherwise, the correctness of your queries will be debatable, to say the least.

You have already seen that null values in expressions generally cause those expressions to produce a null value. In the next chapter, you will learn how the various SQL functions handle null values.

It is obvious that there are many pitfalls in the area of missing information. It may be possible to circumvent at least some of these problems by properly designing your databases. In one of his books, Ted Codd, the "inventor" of the relational model, even proposed introducing *two* types of null values: *applicable* and *inapplicable*. This would imply the need for a four-valued logic (see Ted Codd, 1990).

■**Tip** If you are interested in more details about the trouble of null values (or other theoretical information about relational databases and pitfalls in SQL), the books written by Chris Date are the best starting point for further exploration. In particular, his *Selected Writings* series is brilliant. Chris Date's ability to write in an understandable, entertaining, and fascinating way about these topics far exceeds others in the field.

Here's a brain-twister to finish this section about null values: why does the query in Listing 4-44 produce "no rows selected"? There *are* registrations with evaluation values 4 and 5, for sure. . .

Listing 4-44. *A Brain-Twister*

```
SQL> select * from registrations
  2  where evaluation not in (1,2,3,NULL);


no rows selected

SQL>
```

This problem is left as an exercise at the end of this chapter.

4.10 Truth Tables

Section 4.5 of this chapter showed how to use the AND, OR, and NOT operators to build compound conditions. In that section, we didn't worry too much about missing information and null values, but we are now in a position to examine the combination of three-valued logic and compound conditions. This is often a challenging subject, because three-valued logic is not always intuitive. The most reliable way to investigate compound conditions is to use truth tables.

Table 4-3 shows the truth table of the NOT operator. In truth tables, UNK is commonly used as an abbreviation for UNKNOWN.

Table 4-3. *Truth Table of the NOT Operator*

Op1	NOT (Op1)
TRUE	FALSE
FALSE	TRUE
UNK	UNK

In Table 4-3, Op1 stands for the operand. Since the NOT operator works on a single operand, the truth table needs three rows to describe all possibilities. Note that the negation of UNK is UNK.

Table 4-4 shows the truth table of the AND and OR operators; Op1 and Op2 are the two operands, and the truth table shows all nine possible combinations.

Table 4-4. *Truth Table of the AND and OR Operators*

Op1	Op2	Op1 AND Op2	Op1 OR Op2
TRUE	TRUE	TRUE	TRUE
TRUE	FALSE	FALSE	TRUE
TRUE	UNK	UNK	TRUE
FALSE	TRUE	FALSE	TRUE

Op1	Op2	Op1 AND Op2	Op1 OR Op2
FALSE	FALSE	FALSE	FALSE
FALSE	UNK	FALSE	UNK
UNK	TRUE	UNK	TRUE
UNK	FALSE	FALSE	UNK
UNK	UNK	UNK	UNK

Note that the AND and OR operators are symmetric; that is, you can swap Op1 and Op2 without changing the operator outcome.

If you are facing complicated compound conditions, truth tables can be very useful to rewrite those conditions into simpler, logically equivalent, expressions.

4.11 Exercises

These exercises assume you have access to a database schema with the seven case tables (see Appendix C of this book). You can download the scripts to create this schema from my web site (http://www.naturaljoin.nl) or from the Downloads section of the Apress web site (http://www.apress.com). You may find it helpful to refer to Appendix A of this book for a quick reference to SQL and SQL*Plus. See Appendix D for the answers to the exercise questions.

1. Provide the code and description of all courses with an exact duration of four days.

2. List all employees, sorted by job, and per job by age (from young to old).

3. Which courses have been held in Chicago and/or in Seattle?

4. Which employees attended both the Java course and the XML course? (Provide their employee numbers.)

5. List the names and initials of all employees, except for R. Jones.

6. Find the number, job, and date of birth of all trainers and sales representatives born before 1960.

7. List the numbers of all employees who do not work for the training department.

8. List the numbers of all employees who did not attend the Java course.

9. Which employees have subordinates? Which employees *don't* have subordinates?

10. Produce an overview of all general course offerings (course category GEN) in 1999.

11. Provide the name and initials of all employees who have ever attended a course taught by N. Smith. Hint: Use subqueries, and work "inside out" toward the result; that is, retrieve the employee number of N. Smith, search for the codes of all courses he ever taught, and so on.

12. How could you redesign the EMPLOYEES table to avoid the problem that the COMM column contains null values meaning *not applicable*?

13. In Section 4.9, you saw the following statement: In SQL, NOT is not "not." What is this statement trying to say?

14. Referring to the brain-twister at the end of Section 4.9, what is the explanation of the result "no rows selected" in Listing 4-44?

15. At the end of Section 4.5, you saw the following statement.

   The following two queries are logically equivalent:

```
select * from employees where NOT (ename = 'BLAKE' AND init = 'R')
select * from employees where     ename <> 'BLAKE' OR init <> 'R'
```

   Prove this, using a truth table. Hint: Use P as an abbreviation for ename = 'BLAKE', and use Q as an abbreviation for init = 'R'.

CHAPTER 5

■ ■ ■

Retrieval: Functions

This chapter is a logical continuation of the previous chapter. The main topic is still retrieval. It introduces *functions* and *regular expressions*, which enable you to formulate more powerful and complicated queries in an easy way.

Oracle supports an abundance of functions. Apart from the various ANSI/ISO SQL standard functions, many Oracle-specific functions have been added to Oracle's SQL implementation over the years.

The chapter begins with an overview of the six categories of functions: arithmetic, text, date, general, conversion, and group. The remaining sections discuss each type, with the exception of group functions, which are introduced in Chapter 8. You will also learn about regular expressions, which are used with some text functions to search for certain patterns in text. The last section of this chapter briefly explains how you can define your own SQL functions in Oracle, using the PL/SQL programming language. We conclude this chapter with some exercises.

5.1 Overview of Functions

In Chapter 2, you saw that SQL supports the following standard SQL operators:

- Arithmetic operators: +, -, *, and /

- Alphanumeric operator: || (concatenation)

Besides using these operators, you can also perform many operations on your data using *functions*. You can use functions virtually anywhere within queries: in the SELECT, WHERE, HAVING, and ORDER BY clauses.

You can recognize functions as follows: they have a name, followed by one or more arguments (between parentheses). In general, function arguments can be constants, variables, or expressions, and sometimes function arguments contain functions themselves. Functions inside function arguments are referred to as *nested functions*. In some cases, function arguments are optional. This means that you can omit the optional argument and allow Oracle to use a standard (or default) value.

■**Note** *Oracle SQL Reference* uses different terms for two similar concepts: functions without arguments and pseudo columns. For example, SYSDATE and USER are listed as functions, and ROWNUM, LEVEL, and NEXTVAL are listed as pseudo columns. If you check older versions of the documentation, you will see that Oracle changed terminology over the years. In version 5.1, both SYSDATE and USER were pseudo columns; in version 6.0, SYSDATE was promoted to a function, but USER was still a pseudo column; and in version 7.3, both SYSDATE and USER were documented as functions. You could argue that SYSDATE and USER return the same value for every row, while ROWNUM, LEVEL, and NEXTVAL normally return different values. According to the current *Oracle SQL Reference*, functions take *zero* or more arguments. This book sometimes refers to items as *pseudo columns* where *Oracle SQL Reference* refers to them as *functions*.

Obviously, the function arguments come with some constraints. For example, the datatype of the function arguments must make some logical sense. The Oracle DBMS always tries to perform implicit datatype conversion, and it will generate an error message only if such an attempt fails. In other words, if you specify a number as an argument for a function that expects a string instead, the number will be interpreted alphanumerically. However, if you ask for the square root of an employee name, you will get the error message "ORA-01722: invalid number."

■**Caution** It is *not* a good idea to rely on implicit datatype conversion in your SQL statements. You should always use explicit conversion functions instead. This improves SQL readability, robustness, and possibly performance.

As stated previously, Oracle supports many functions. You can categorize them based on the datatype they expect in their arguments, as shown in Table 5-1.

Table 5-1. *Function Types*

Function Type	Applicable To
Arithmetic functions	Numerical data
Text functions	Alphanumeric data
Date functions	Date/time-related data
General functions	Any datatype
Conversion functions	Datatype conversion
Group functions	Sets of values

The last category in Table 5-1, group functions, is covered in Chapter 8, where we discuss the GROUP BY and HAVING clauses of the SELECT command, since that chapter is a more natural place to introduce them. The other function types are discussed in the following sections.

5.2 Arithmetic Functions

The most popular arithmetic functions of Oracle are listed in Table 5-2.

Table 5-2. *Common Oracle Arithmetic Functions*

Function	Description
ROUND(n[,m])	Round n on m decimal positions
TRUNC(n[,m])	Truncate n on m decimal positions
CEIL(n)	Round n upwards to an integer
FLOOR(n)	Round n downwards to an integer
ABS(n)	Absolute value of n
SIGN(n)	–1, 0, or 1 if n is negative, zero, or positive
SQRT(n)	Square root of n
EXP(n)	e (= 2,7182813…) raised to the nth power
LN(n),LOG(m,n)	Natural logarithm, and logarithm base m
POWER(n,m)	n raised to the mth power
MOD(n,m)	Remainder of n divided by m
SIN(n), COS(n), TAN(n)	Sine, cosine, and tangent of n (n expressed in radians)
ASIN(n), ACOS(n), ATAN(n)	Arcsine, arccosine, and arctangent of n
SINH(n), COSH(n), TANH(n)	Hyperbolic sine, hyperbolic cosine, and hyperbolic tangent of n

As Table 5-2 shows, the ROUND and TRUNC functions have an optional argument m; the default value for m is zero. Note that you can also use negative values for m, as you can see from the second example in Listing 5-1.

Listings 5-1 through 5-4 show some self-explanatory examples of using the following arithmetic functions: ROUND, CEIL, FLOOR, ABS, SIGN, POWER, and MOD.

Listing 5-1. *Using the ROUND, CEIL, and FLOOR Functions*

```
SQL> select round(345.678), ceil(345.678), floor(345.678)
  2  from   dual;

ROUND(345.678) CEIL(345.678) FLOOR(345.678)
-------------- ------------- --------------
           346           346            345

SQL> select round(345.678, 2)
  2  ,       round(345.678,-1)
  3  ,       round(345.678,-2)
  4  from   dual;
```

```
ROUND(345.678,2) ROUND(345.678,-1) ROUND(345.678,-2)
---------------- ------------------ ------------------
          345.68                350                300

SQL>
```

Listing 5-2. *Using the ABS and SIGN Functions*

```
SQL> select  abs(-123),  abs(0),  abs(456)
  2  ,        sign(-123), sign(0), sign(456)
  3  from    dual;

ABS(-123)   ABS(0) ABS(456) SIGN(-123)   SIGN(0) SIGN(456)
--------- -------- -------- ---------- -------- ---------
      123        0      456         -1        0         1

SQL>
```

Listing 5-3. *Using the POWER and MOD Functions*

```
SQL> select power(2,3), power(-2,3)
  2  ,          mod(8,3),    mod(13,0)
  3  from    dual;

POWER(2,3) POWER(-2,3) MOD(8,3) MOD(13,0)
---------- ----------- -------- ---------
         8          -8        2        13

SQL>
```

Listing 5-4. *Using MOD in the WHERE Clause*

```
SQL> select empno as odd_empno
  2  ,        ename
  3  from    employees
  4  where   mod(empno,2) = 1;

ODD_EMPNO ENAME
--------- --------
     7369 SMITH
     7499 ALLEN
     7521 WARD
     7839 KING

SQL>
```

The example in Listing 5-5 calculates the age (expressed in weeks and additional days) of all employees working for department 10. In this example, we use the difference between the BDATE column and the pseudo column SYSDATE. Of course, your results will be different from the results in Listing 5-5, because they depend on the point in time that you execute the query.

Listing 5-5. *Using the FLOOR and MOD Functions*

```
SQL> select ename
  2  ,       floor((sysdate-bdate)/7)    as weeks
  3  ,       floor(mod(sysdate-bdate,7)) as days
  4  from    employees
  5  where   deptno = 10;

ENAME       WEEKS    DAYS
--------    --------  --------
CLARK        2032       5
KING         2688       0
MILLER       2208       6

SQL>
```

Listing 5-6 shows an example using the arithmetic functions SIN, TANH, EXP, LOG, and LN. You probably recognize the number 3.14159265 as an approximation of π (pi), which is used in the SIN function example to convert degrees into radians.

Listing 5-6. *Trigonometric, Exponential, and Logarithmic Functions*

```
SQL> select sin(30*3.14159265/180), tanh(0.5)
  2  ,      exp(4), log(2,32), ln(32)
  3  from   dual;

SIN(30*3.14159265/180) TANH(0.5)    EXP(4) LOG(2,32)    LN(32)
---------------------- --------- -------- --------- --------
                   .5 .4621172 54.59815         5 3.465736

SQL>
```

5.3 Text Functions

The most important Oracle text functions are listed in Table 5-3.

Table 5-3. *Common Oracle Text Functions*

Function	Description
LENGTH(t)	Length (expressed in characters) of t
ASCII(t)	ASCII value of first character of t

Continued

Table 5-3. *Continued*

Function	Description
CHR(*n*)	Character with ASCII value *n*
UPPER(*t*), LOWER(*t*)	*t* in uppercase/lowercase
INITCAP(*t*)	Each word in *t* with initial uppercase; remainder in lowercase
LTRIM(*t*[,*k*])	Remove characters from the left of *t*, until the first character not in *k*
RTRIM(*t*[,*k*])	Remove characters from the right of *t*, after the last character not in *k*
TRIM([[*option*][*c* FROM]]*t*)	Trim character *c* from *t*; *option* = LEADING, TRAILING, or BOTH
LPAD(*t*,*n*[,*k*])	Left-pad *t* with sequence of characters in *k* to length *n*
RPAD(*t*,*n*[,*k*])	Right-pad *t* with *k* to length *n* (the default *k* is a space)
SUBSTR(*t*,*n*[,*m*])	Substring of *t* from position *n*, *m* characters long (the default for *m* is until end)
INSTR(*t*,*k*)	Position of the first occurrence of *k* in *t*
INSTR(*t*,*k*,*n*)	Same as INSTR(*t*,*k*), but starting from position *n* in *t*
INSTR(*t*,*k*,*n*,*m*)	Same as INSTR(*t*,*k*,*n*), but now the *m*th occurrence of *k*
TRANSLATE(*t*,*v*,*w*)	Replace characters from *v* (occurring in *t*) by corresponding character in *w*
REPLACE(*t*,*v*)	Remove each occurrence of *v* from *t*
REPLACE(*t*,*v*,*w*)	Replace each occurrence of *v* in *t* by *w*
CONCAT(*t1*,*t2*)	Concatenate *t1* and *t2* (equivalent to the || operator)

■**Note** Counting positions in strings always start with one, not with zero.

Several text functions have a corresponding function with a B suffix, such as SUBSTRB, INSTRB, and LENGTHB. These special functions express their results in bytes instead of characters. This distinction is relevant only if you are using multibyte character sets. See *Oracle SQL Reference* for more details.

Listing 5-7 shows some examples of the LOWER, UPPER, INITCAP, and LENGTH text functions; the results are self-explanatory.

Listing 5-7. *Using the LOWER, UPPER, INITCAP, and LENGTH Functions*

```
SQL> select lower(job), initcap(ename)
  2  from    employees
  3  where   upper(job) = 'SALESREP'
  4  order   by length(ename);
```

```
LOWER(JOB)  INITCAP(ENAME)
----------  --------------
salesrep    Ward
salesrep    Allen
salesrep    Martin
salesrep    Turner

SQL>
```

Listing 5-8 illustrates the text functions ASCII and CHR. If you compare the third and the fifth columns of the result, you can see that the ASCII function considers only the *first* character of its argument, regardless of the length of the input text (see Table 5-3 for the description of the ASCII text function).

Listing 5-8. *Using the ASCII and CHR Functions*

```
SQL> select ascii('a'), ascii('z')
  2  ,      ascii('A'), ascii('Z')
  3  ,      ascii('ABC'), chr(77)
  4  from   dual;

ASCII('A') ASCII('Z') ASCII('A') ASCII('Z') ASCII('ABC') CHR(77)
---------- ---------- ---------- ---------- ------------ -------
        97        122         65         90           65 M

SQL>
```

The first two column headings in Listing 5-8 are very confusing, because SQL*Plus converts all SELECT clause expressions to uppercase, including your function arguments. If you want lowercase characters in your column headings, you must add column aliases and specify them between double quotes. For example, the first line of Listing 5-8 would look like this:

```
SQL> select ascii('a') as "ASCII('a')", ascii('z') as "ASCII('z')"
```

Listings 5-9 and 5-10 show some self-explanatory examples of using the INSTR, SUBSTR, LTRIM, and RTRIM text functions. (The layout in Listing 5-9 is formatted to increase readability.)

Listing 5-9. *Using the INSTR and SUBSTR Functions*

```
SQL> select dname
  2  ,      substr(dname,4)     as substr1
  3  ,      substr(dname,4,3)   as substr2
  4  ,      instr(dname,'I')    as instr1
  5  ,      instr(dname,'I',5)  as instr2
  6  ,      instr(dname,'I',3,2) as instr3
  7  from   departments;
```

```
DNAME       SUBSTR1 SUBSTR2   INSTR1    INSTR2   INSTR3
----------- ------- -------  --------  --------  --------
ACCOUNTING OUNTING OUN            8         8        0
HR                                0         0        0
SALES      ES      ES             0         0        0
TRAINING   INING   INI            4         6        6

SQL>
```

Listing 5-10. *Using the LTRIM and RTRIM Functions*

```
SQL> select ename
  2  ,       ltrim(ename,'S') as ltrim_s
  3  ,       rtrim(ename,'S') as rtrim_s
  4  from    employees
  5  where   deptno = 20;

ENAME     LTRIM_S   RTRIM_S
--------  --------  --------
ADAMS     ADAMS     ADAM
FORD      FORD      FORD
JONES     JONES     JONE
SCOTT     COTT      SCOTT
SMITH     MITH      SMITH

SQL>
```

Listing 5-11 demonstrates using the LPAD and RPAD functions. Note that they not only *lengthen* strings, as their names suggest, but sometimes they also *shorten* strings; for example, see what happens with ACCOUNTING and TRAINING in Listing 5-11.

Listing 5-11. *Using the LPAD and RPAD Functions*

```
SQL> select dname
  2  ,       lpad(dname,9,'>')
  3  ,       rpad(dname,6,'<')
  4  from    departments;

DNAME       LPAD(DNAM RPAD(D
----------- --------- ------
ACCOUNTING ACCOUNTIN ACCOUN
HR          >>>>>>>HR HR<<<<
SALES       >>>>SALES SALES<
TRAINING    >TRAINING TRAINI

SQL>
```

You can use the LPAD and RPAD functions to produce column-value histograms by providing variable expressions, instead of constant values, as their second argument. For an example, see Listing 5-12, which shows how to create a salary histogram with a granularity of 100.

Listing 5-12. *Producing Histograms with the LPAD and RPAD Functions*

```
SQL> select lpad(msal,4)||' '||
  2         rpad('o',msal/100,'o') as histogram
  3  from   employees
  4  where  deptno = 30;

HISTOGRAM
----------------------------------------------
1600 oooooooooooooooo
1250 oooooooooooo
1250 oooooooooooo
2850 ooooooooooooooooooooooooooooo
1500 000000000000000
 800 00000000

SQL>
```

Listing 5-13 shows the difference between the functions REPLACE and TRANSLATE. TRANSLATE replaces individual characters. REPLACE offers the option to replace words with other words. Note also what happens if you use the REPLACE function with only two arguments, instead of three: the function *removes* words instead of replacing them.

Listing 5-13. *Using the TRANSLATE and REPLACE Functions*

```
SQL> select translate('beer bucket','beer','milk') as translate
  2  ,      replace  ('beer bucket','beer','milk') as replace_1
  3  ,      replace  ('beer bucket','beer')        as replace_2
  4  from   dual;

TRANSLATE   REPLACE_1   REPLACE_2
----------- ----------- ---------
miik muckit milk bucket bucket

SQL>
```

5.4 Regular Expressions

The previous chapter introduced the LIKE operator, and the previous section of this chapter introduced the INSTR, SUBSTR, and REPLACE functions. All of these SQL functions search for text. The LIKE operator offers the two wildcard characters % and _, which allow you to perform more advanced searches. The other three functions accept plain text searches only. This functionality is sometimes insufficient for complicated search operations. Therefore, Oracle SQL also supports four functions: REGEXP_LIKE, REGEXP_INSTR, REGEXP_SUBSTR, and REGEXP_REPLACE. These SQL functions support, as their names suggest, so-called *regular expressions*. Apart from that, they serve the same purpose as their non-REGEXP counterparts.

Regular expressions are well known in all UNIX operating system variants (such as Linux, Solaris, and HP/UX) and are part of the international POSIX standard. They are documented in great detail in *Oracle SQL Reference*, Appendix C. This section provides an introduction to regular expressions, focusing on their use with the Oracle SQL regular expression functions.

Regular Expression Operators and Metasymbols

Table 5-4 shows the most important regular expression metasymbols and their meanings. The Type column in Table 5-4 may contain the following:

- Postfix, which means that the operator *follows* its operand

- Prefix, which means that the operator *precedes* its operand

- Infix, which means that the operator *separates* its operands

- Nothing (empty), which means that the operator has no operands

Table 5-4. *Common Regular Expression Operators and Metasymbols*

Operator	Type	Description
*	Postfix	Zero or more occurrences
+	Postfix	One or more occurrences
?	Postfix	Zero or one occurrence
|	Infix	Operator to separate alternative choices
^	Prefix	Beginning of a string, or position immediately following a newline character
$	Postfix	End of the line
.		Any single character
[[^]*list*]		One character out of a *list*; a circumflex (^) at the beginning works as a negation; a dash (-) between two characters works as a range indicator
( )		Groups a (sub)expression, allowing you to refer to it further down in the expression
{*m*}	Postfix	Precisely *m* times
{*m*,}	Postfix	At least *m* times
{*m*,*n*}	Postfix	At least *m* times, and at most *n* times
n		Refers back to the *n*th subexpression between parentheses (*n* is a digit between 1 and 9)

If the square brackets notation does not give you enough precision or flexibility, you can use multicharacter collation elements, character classes, and equivalence classes, as follows:

- *Multicharacter collation elements* are relevant for certain languages. Valid values are predefined and depend on the NLS_SORT setting. Use [. and .] to enclose collation elements.

- *Character classes* give you more flexibility than the dash symbol between square brackets; for example, you can refer to alphabetic characters, numeric digits, alphanumeric characters, blank spaces, punctuation, and so on. Use [: and :] to enclose character classes.

- *Equivalence classes* allow you to match all accented and unaccented versions of a letter. Use [= and =] to enclose equivalence classes.

Before we look at some examples of how these regular expression operators work with the regular expression functions (in Listings 5-14 through 5-16), we need to discuss the syntax of the functions.

Regular Expression Function Syntax

The four regular expression functions have the following syntax. You can specify regular expressions in their *pattern* argument.

- REGEXP_LIKE(*text, pattern*[, *options*])

- REGEXP_INSTR(*text, pattern*[, *pos*[, *occurrence*[, *return*[, *options*]]]])

- REGEXP_SUBSTR(*text, pattern*[, *pos*[, *occurrence*[, *options*]]])

- REGEXP_REPLACE(*text, pattern*[, *replace* [, *pos*[, *occurrence*[, *options*]]]])

For all four functions, the first two arguments (*text* and *pattern*) are mandatory. These arguments provide the source text and the regular expression to search for, respectively. All of the remaining arguments are optional. However, function arguments can *only* be omitted from the right to the left. For example, if you want to specify a value for the *options* argument of the REGEXP_INSTR function, all six arguments are mandatory and must be specified.

In REGEXP_INSTR, REGEXP_SUBSTR, and REGEXP_REPLACE, you can use the *pos* argument to specify from which position in *text* you want the search to start (the default value is 1), and with *occurrence*, you can specify how often you want to find the search *pattern* (the default value is 1). The *options* argument of all four of the functions and the *return* argument of the REGEXP_INSTR function require a bit more explanation.

Influencing Matching Behavior

You can influence the matching behavior of the regular expression functions with their *options* argument. Table 5-5 shows the values you can specify in the *options* function argument.

Table 5-5. *Regular Expression Option Values*

Option	Description
i	Case-insensitive search (no distinction between uppercase and lowercase)
c	Case-sensitive search
n	Allows the period (.) to match the newline character
m	Treat *text* as multiple lines; ^ and $ refer to the beginning and end of any of those lines

You can specify one or more of these values. If you specify conflicting combinations, such as 'ic', the Oracle DBMS uses the last value (c) and ignores the first one.

Note The default behavior for case-sensitivity depends on the NLS_SORT parameter value.

REGEXP_INSTR Return Value

The *return* option of the REGEXP_INSTR function allows you to influence the return value. By default, the position where the *pattern* was found is returned, but sometimes you want to know the position immediately *after* the found pattern. Of course, you can add the length of the pattern to the result of the function; however, using the *return* option is easier in that case. Table 5-6 shows the values you can specify in the *return* function argument.

Table 5-6. *Regular Expression Return Values*

Return	Description
0	Position of the first character of the pattern found (default)
1	Position of the first character after the pattern found

REGEXP_LIKE

Let's look at an example of the REGEXP_LIKE function, using a SQL*Plus trick that will be explained in a later chapter. The ampersand character (&) in the WHERE clause of the query in Listing 5-14 makes SQL*Plus prompt for a value for *text*; therefore, you can repeat this query in the SQL buffer with the / command as often as you like, specifying different source *text* values to explore the effect of the search pattern.

Listing 5-14. *Using the REGEXP_LIKE Function*

```
SQL> select 'found!' as result from dual
  2  where regexp_like('&text', '^.a{1,2}.+$', 'i');

Enter value for text: bar
```

```
RESULT
------
found!

SQL> /
Enter value for text: BAARF

RESULT
------
found!

SQL> /
Enter value for text: ba

no rows selected

SQL>
```

The results of Listing 5-14 show that the pattern means the following: the first character is arbitrary, followed by at least one and at most two *a* characters, followed by one or more arbitrary characters, while ignoring the differences between uppercase and lowercase. By the way, Listing 5-14 shows that REGEXP_LIKE is a Boolean function; its result is TRUE or FALSE.

REGEXP_INSTR

Listing 5-15 uses the REGEXP_INSTR function to search for history comments with nine or more words. It looks for at least nine nonempty (+) substrings that do not contain spaces ([^]).

Listing 5-15. *Using the REGEXP_INSTR Function*

```
SQL> select comments
  2  from   history
  3  where  regexp_instr(comments, '[^ ]+', 1, 9) > 0;

COMMENTS
------------------------------------------------------------
Not a great trainer; let's try the sales department!
Sales also turns out to be not a success...
Hired as the new manager for the accounting department
Junior sales rep -- has lots to learn... :-)

SQL>
```

Notice that the last row of the result contains only seven actual words. It is found because the text strings -- and :-) are counted as "words."

REGEXP_SUBSTR

Listing 5-16 demonstrates searching for comments between parentheses, using the REGEXP_SUBSTR function. The search pattern looks for a left parenthesis, followed by at least one character not equal to a right parenthesis, followed by a right parenthesis. Note that you need the backslash character (\) to suppress the special meaning of the parentheses.

Listing 5-16. *Using the REGEXP_SUBSTR Function*

```
SQL> select comments
  2  ,       regexp_substr(comments, '\([^\)]+\)') as substring
  2  from    history
  3  where   comments like '%(%';

COMMENTS
-------------------------------------------------------------
SUBSTRING
-------------------------------------------------------------
Project (half a month) for the ACCOUNTING department
(half a month)

SQL>
```

REGEXP_REPLACE

Listing 5-17 shows how you can use the REGEXP_REPLACE function to replace all words starting with an *f* with a question mark.

Listing 5-17. *Using the REGEXP_REPLACE Function*

```
SQL> select regexp_replace(comments, ' f[a-z]* ',' ? ',1,1,'i')
  2  from    history
  3  where   regexp_like(comments, ' f[a-z]* ','i');

REGEXP_REPLACE(COMMENTS,'F[A-Z]*','?',1,1,'I')
-------------------------------------------------------------
Hired as the new manager ? the accounting department
Founder and ? employee of the company
Project (half a month) ? the ACCOUNTING department

SQL>
```

Notice that you must specify values for all function arguments if you want to make the replacement case-insensitive, including default values for *pos* and *occurrence*. The WHERE clause ensures that the query returns only the matching rows.

5.5 Date Functions

Before discussing the various Oracle date functions, let's first review the syntax to specify date/time-related constants (or literals), using predefined ANSI/ISO SQL standard formats. Table 5-7 shows the syntax for the literals and examples.

Table 5-7. *Syntax for Date/Time-Related Constants*

Literal	Example
DATE 'yyyy-mm-dd'	DATE '2004-09-25'
TIMESTAMP 'yyyy-mm-dd hh24:mi:ss.ffffff' [AT TIME ZONE '...']	TIMESTAMP '2004-09-25 23:59:59.99999' AT TIME ZONE 'CET'
TIMESTAMP 'yyyy-mm-dd hh24:mi:ss.ffffff {+|-}hh:mi'	TIMESTAMP '2004-09-25 23:59:59.99 -5:00'
INTERVAL 'expr' <qualifier>	INTERVAL '1' YEAR~ INTERVAL '1 2:3' DAY TO MINUTE

You can experiment with this syntax by entering the following query, using the SQL*Plus ampersand (&) substitution method (as in Listing 5-14):

```
SQL> select &<literal-expression> from dual;
```

If you simply enter an alphanumeric string, such as '21-JUN-04', you must rely on an implicit conversion by Oracle. This implicit conversion succeeds or fails depending on the NLS_DATE_FORMAT and NLS_TIMESTAMP_FORMAT parameter settings for your session. If you want to see an overview of all current NLS parameter settings for your session, you can use the following query:

```
SQL> select * from nls_session_parameters;
```

If you execute this query, you will see the current values for NLS_DATE_FORMAT and NLS_TIMESTAMP_FORMAT.

Table 5-8 shows the most commonly used Oracle date functions.

Table 5-8. *Common Oracle Date Functions*

Function	Description
ADD_MONTHS(d, n)	Date d plus n months
MONTHS_BETWEEN(d, e)	Months between dates d and e
LAST_DAY(d)	Last day of the month containing date d
NEXT_DAY(d, weekday)	The first weekday (mon, tue, etc.) after d
NEW_TIME(d, z1, z2)	Convert date/time d from time zone z1 to z2
ROUND(d[, fmt])	d rounded on fmt (the default for fmt is midnight)
TRUNC(d[, fmt])	d truncated on fmt (the default for fmt is midnight)
EXTRACT(c FROM d)	Extract date/time component c from expression d

We'll start with the last function listed in Table 5-8.

EXTRACT

You can extract various components of a date or timestamp expression with the ANSI/ISO standard EXTRACT function. Depending on the datatype of the argument *d* (DATE, TIMESTAMP, or INTERVAL) the following values for *c* are supported: YEAR, MONTH, DAY, HOUR, MINUTE, SECOND, TIMEZONE_ABBR, and so on. Listing 5-18 shows an example.

Listing 5-18. *Using the EXTRACT Function*

```
SQL> select bdate
  2 ,       extract(year  from bdate) as year_of_birth
  3 ,       extract(month from bdate) as month_of_birth
  4 ,       extract(day   from bdate) as day_of_birth
  5 from    employees
  6 where   ename = 'KING';

BDATE       YEAR_OF_BIRTH MONTH_OF_BIRTH DAY_OF_BIRTH
----------- ------------- -------------- ------------
17-NOV-1952          1952             11           17

SQL>
```

ROUND and TRUNC

Table 5-9 lists the date formats (*fmt*) supported by the date functions ROUND and TRUNC. The default format is 'DD', resulting in rounding or truncating to midnight. For example, TRUNC(SYSDATE) truncates the current system date and time to midnight.

Table 5-9. *ROUND and TRUNC Date Formats*

Format	Description
CC, SCC	Century, with or without minus sign (BC)
[S]YYYY, [S]YEAR, YYY, YY, Y	Year (in various appearances)
IYYY, IYY, IY, I	ISO year
Q	Quarter
MONTH, MON, MM, RM	Month (full name, abbreviated name, numeric, Roman numerals)
IW, WW	(ISO) week number
W	Day of the week
DDD, DD, J	Day (of the year/of the month/Julian day)
DAY, DY, D	Closest Sunday
HH, HH12, HH24	Hours
MI	Minutes

MONTHS_BETWEEN and ADD_MONTHS

Listings 5-19 and 5-20 show examples of using the date functions MONTHS_BETWEEN and
ADD_MONTHS.

Listing 5-19. *Using the MONTHS_BETWEEN Function*

```
SQL> select ename, months_between(sysdate,bdate)
  2  from    employees
  3  where   deptno = 10;

ENAME     MONTHS_BETWEEN(SYSDATE,BDATE)
--------  ----------------------------
CLARK                         467.5042
KING                          618.2461
MILLER                        508.0525

SQL>
```

Listing 5-20. *Using the ADD_MONTHS Function*

```
SQL> select add_months('29-JAN-1996', 1) add_months_1
  2  ,      add_months('29-JAN-1997', 1) add_months_2
  3  ,      add_months('11-AUG-1997',-3) add_months_3
  4  from   dual;

ADD_MONTHS_1 ADD_MONTHS_2 ADD_MONTHS_3
------------ ------------ ------------
29-FEB-1996  28-FEB-1997  11-MAY-1997

SQL>
```

Notice what happens in Listing 5-20 with a non-leap year. There is something else worth
noting about the query in Listing 5-20. As explained earlier, you could get back an error message because you rely on implicit interpretation and conversion of the three strings by Oracle.
It would have been preferable to specify the three date literals in Listing 5-20 using the key
word DATE (see the beginning of this section) or using the TO_DATE conversion function.
(See Section 5.7 later in this chapter for details about conversion functions.)

NEXT_DAY and LAST_DAY

Listing 5-21 shows examples of using the date functions NEXT_DAY, LAST_DAY, ROUND, and TRUNC.
Compare the various function results with the first column, showing the current SYSDATE value.

Listing 5-21. *Using the NEXT_DAY, LAST_DAY, ROUND, and TRUNC Functions*

```
SQL> select sysdate
  2  ,      next_day(sysdate,'SAT') as next_sat
  3  ,      last_day(sysdate)       as last_day
  4  ,      round(sysdate,'YY')     as round_yy
  5  ,      trunc(sysdate,'CC')     as trunc_cc
  6  from   dual;


SYSDATE     NEXT_SAT    LAST_DAY    ROUND_YY    TRUNC_CC
----------- ----------- ----------- ----------- -----------
14-SEP-2004 18-SEP-2004 30-SEP-2004 01-JAN-2005 01-JAN-2001

SQL>
```

5.6 General Functions

The most important general (datatype-independent) functions are shown in Table 5-10.

Table 5-10. *Common General Oracle Functions*

Function	Description
GREATEST(a, b, ...)	Greatest value of the function arguments
LEAST(a, b, ...)	Least value of the function arguments
NULLIF(a, b)	NULL if $a = b$; otherwise a
COALESCE(a, b, ...)	The first not NULL argument (and NULL if all arguments are NULL)
NVL(x, y)	y if x is NULL; otherwise x
NVL2(x, y, z)	y if x is not NULL; otherwise z
DECODE(x, a_1, b_1,	b_1 if $x = a_1$,
a_2, b_2,	b_2 if $x = a_2$, ...
..., a_n, b_n	b_n if $x = a_n$,
[, y])	and otherwise y (or default: NULL)

You can express all of these functions as CASE expressions, too, since they all share a procedural nature. In other words, you don't really need them. Nevertheless, these functions can be useful in your SQL code because, for example, they make your code more compact. Note also that (besides CASE expressions) only the NULLIF and COALESCE functions are part of the ANSI/ISO standard. The remaining five functions (GREATEST, LEAST, NVL, NVL2, and DECODE) are Oracle-specific SQL extensions. In other words, if your goal is to write portable SQL code, you should use only CASE, NULLIF, and COALESCE.

■**Note** Rewriting various command examples in this section using CASE, NULLIF, and COALESCE is left as an exercise to the reader at the end of this chapter, in Section 5.9.

GREATEST and LEAST

The GREATEST and LEAST functions can be useful in certain situations. Don't confuse them with the MAX and MIN group functions (which are covered in detail in Chapter 8). For now, remember the following differences:

- GREATEST and LEAST allow you to make *horizontal* comparisons; they operate at the *row* level.

- MAX and MIN allow you to make *vertical* comparisons; they operate at the *column* level.

Listing 5-22 shows an example of the GREATEST and LEAST functions, selecting three constant expressions against the DUAL table.

Listing 5-22. *Using the GREATEST and LEAST Functions*

```
SQL> select greatest(12*6,148/2,73)
  2  ,       least   (12*6,148/2,73)
  3  from    dual;

GREATEST(12*6,148/2,73) LEAST(12*6,148/2,73)
----------------------- --------------------
                     74                   72

SQL>
```

NVL

The NVL function is useful if you want to prevent certain expressions, or expression components, from evaluating to a null value, as you can see in Listing 5-23.

Listing 5-23. *Using the NVL Function*

```
SQL> select ename, msal, comm
  2  ,       12*msal+nvl(comm,0) as yearsal
  3  from    employees
  4  where   ename like '%T%';

ENAME       MSAL     COMM  YEARSAL
--------  --------  --------  --------
SMITH        800               9600
MARTIN      1250      1400     16400
SCOTT       3000              36000
TURNER      1500         0     18000

SQL>
```

DECODE

The DECODE function is a typical remnant from the days that Oracle SQL did not yet support CASE expressions. There are three good reasons *not* to use DECODE anymore:

- DECODE function expressions are quite difficult to read.

- DECODE is not part of the ANSI/ISO SQL standard.

- CASE expressions are much more powerful.

For completeness, and because you may encounter the DECODE function in legacy Oracle SQL programs, Listing 5-24 shows a query where the DECODE function is used in the SELECT clause and in the ORDER BY clause.

Listing 5-24. *Using the DECODE Function*

```
SQL> select  job, ename
  2  ,        decode(greatest(msal,2500)
  3                  ,2500,'cheap','expensive') as class
  4  from     employees
  5  where    bdate < date '1964-01-01'
  6  order    by decode(job,'DIRECTOR',1,'MANAGER',2,3);

JOB       ENAME    CLASS
--------  -------- ---------
DIRECTOR  KING     expensive
MANAGER   BLAKE    expensive
SALESREP  ALLEN    cheap
SALESREP  WARD     cheap
ADMIN     MILLER   cheap
TRAINER   FORD     expensive
TRAINER   SCOTT    expensive
SALESREP  MARTIN   cheap

SQL>
```

5.7 Conversion Functions

Conversion functions allow you to convert expressions explicitly from one datatype into another datatype. Table 5-11 lists the most common conversion functions in Oracle SQL. See *Oracle SQL Reference* for more conversion functions.

Table 5-11. *Common Oracle Conversion Functions*

Function	Description
TO_CHAR(n[,fmt])	Convert number n to a string
TO_CHAR(d[,fmt])	Convert date/time expression d to a string
TO_NUMBER(t)	Convert string t to a number
TO_BINARY_FLOAT(e[,fmt])	Convert expression e to a floating-point number
TO_BINARY_DOUBLE(e[,fmt])	Convert expression e to a double-precision, floating-point number
TO_DATE(t[,fmt])	Convert string t to a date
TO_YMINTERVAL(t)	Convert string t to a YEAR TO MONTH interval
TO_TIMESTAMP (t[,fmt])	Convert string t to a timestamp
CAST(e AS t)	Convert expression e to datatype t

■**Note** The syntax in Table 5-11 is not complete. Most conversion functions allow you to specify additional NLS parameters after the format (*fmt*) argument. For example, you can influence the currency symbol, the numeric characters (period and comma), and the date language. See *Oracle SQL Reference* and *Globalization Support Guide* for more details.

TO_NUMBER and TO_CHAR

Listing 5-25 shows how you can use the TO_NUMBER and TO_CHAR functions (with or without a format argument) to convert strings to numbers and vice versa.

Listing 5-25. *Using the TO_CHAR and TO_NUMBER Functions*

```
SQL> select 123
  2  ,       to_char(123)
  3  ,       to_char(123,'$09999.99')
  4  ,       to_number('123')
  5  from    dual;

    123 TO_ TO_CHAR(12 TO_NUMBER('123')
-------- --- ---------- ----------------
    123 123 $00123.00               123

SQL>
```

Listing 5-26 shows how you can nest conversion functions. On the third line, you use the TO_DATE function to interpret the string '01/01/2006' as a date value; then, you use the TO_CHAR function to extract the day from the date value, as you can see in the third column of the query result.

Listing 5-26. *Nesting the TO_CHAR and TO_DATE Functions*

```
SQL> select sysdate                              as today
  2  ,         to_char(sysdate,'hh24:mi:ss') as time
  3  ,         to_char(to_date('01/01/2006','dd/mm/yyyy')
  4                    ,'"is on "Day') as new_year_2006
  5  from dual;

TODAY      TIME      NEW_YEAR_2006
---------  --------  ---------------
24-MAY-04 15:05:48 is on Sunday

SQL>
```

In this example, the format Day results in Sunday because the default language is English. You can set the NLS_LANGUAGE parameter to another language to influence this behavior. For example, if you set this session (or system) parameter to DUTCH, the result becomes Zondag (see also Listing 2-20 in Chapter 2). You could also override this default at the statement level, by setting the NLS_DATE_LANGUAGE parameter, as shown in Listing 5-27.

Listing 5-27. *Influencing the Date Language at the Statement Level*

```
SQL> select to_char(sysdate, 'Day')
  2  ,         to_char(sysdate, 'Day', 'nls_date_language=Dutch')
  3  from   dual;

TO_CHAR(S TO_CHAR(S
--------- ---------
Tuesday   Dinsdag

SQL>
```

Conversion Function Formats

Table 5-11 showed that several Oracle conversion functions support an optional format (*fmt*) argument. These format arguments allow you to deviate from the default conversion. Table 5-12 shows most of the possibilities.

Table 5-12. *Conversion Functions: Optional Format Components*

Format	Description
[S]CC	Century; S stands for the minus sign (BC)
[S]YYYY	Year, with or without minus sign
YYY, YY, Y	Last 3, 2, or 1 digits of the year
[S]YEAR	Year spelled out, with or without minus sign (S)
BC, AD	BC/AD indicator

Format	Description
Q	Quarter (1,2,3,4)
MM	Month (01–12)
MONTH	Month name, padded with spaces to length 9
MON	Month name, abbreviated (three characters)
WW, IW	(ISO) week number (01–53)
W	Week number within the month (1–5)
DDD	Day number within the year (1–366)
DD	Day number within the month (1–31)
D	Day number within the week (1–7)
DAY	Day name, padded with spaces to length 9
DY	Day name abbreviation (three characters)
J	Julian date; day number since 01/01/4712 BC
AM, PM	AM/PM indicator
HH[12]	Hour within the day (01–12)
HH24	Hour within the day (00–23)
MI	Minutes within the hour (00–59)
SS	Seconds within the minute (00–59)
SSSSS	Seconds after midnight (0–86399)
/.,	Punctuation characters; displayed verbatim (between date fields)
"..."	String between double quotes displayed within the date expression

■**Note** You can influence several date characteristics, such as the first day of the week, with the
NLS_TERRITORY parameter.

Oracle supports some additions that you can use in conversion function format strings to
further refine the results of those functions. Table 5-13 shows these additions.

Table 5-13. *Conversion Functions: Format Component Additions*

Addition	Description
FM	Fill mode toggle
TH	Ordinal number (e.g., 4th)
SP	Spelled-out number (e.g., four)
THSP, SPTH	Spelled-ordinal number (e.g., fourth)

In *fill mode*, Oracle does not perform padding with spaces, and numbers are not prefixed with leading zeros. You can enable and disable this fill mode mechanism within the same format string as many times as you like, by repeating FM (it is a *toggle*). Ordinal numbers indicate a relative position in a sequence.

The conversion function formats are case-sensitive, as demonstrated in Listing 5-28.

Listing 5-28. *TO_CHAR Formats and Case-Sensitivity*

```
SQL> select to_char(sysdate,'DAY dy Dy') as day
  2  ,        to_char(sysdate,'MONTH mon') as month
  3  from dual;

DAY               MONTH
----------------- -------------
MONDAY    mon Mon MAY         may

SQL>
```

Datatype Conversion

In the area of datatype conversion, you can leave many issues up to the Oracle DBMS. However, for reasons of syntax clarity, it is better to express the datatype conversions explicitly with the appropriate conversion functions. See the query in Listing 5-29 for an example.

Listing 5-29. *Relying on Implicit Datatype Conversion*

```
SQL> select ename, substr(bdate,8)+16
  2  from    employees
  3  where   deptno = 10;

ENAME     SUBSTR(BDATE,8)+16
--------  ------------------
CLARK                     81
KING                      68
MILLER                    78

SQL>
```

This query is internally interpreted and executed by the Oracle DBMS as the following:

```
SQL> select ename, TO_NUMBER(substr(to_char(bdate,'...'),8))+16
  2  from    employees
  3  where   deptno = 10
```

You should have formulated the query that way in the first place.

CAST

The last function to discuss in this section about conversion functions is CAST. This function is part of the ANSI/ISO SQL standard, as opposed to all other conversion functions discussed so far in this section. The CAST function is a *generic* conversion function. It allows you to convert *any* expression to *any* specific datatype, including the option to specify a datatype precision. See Listing 5-30 for some examples.

Listing 5-30. *CAST Function Examples*

```
SQL> select cast(12.98 as number(2)) example1
  2  ,      cast('oak' as char(10) ) example2
  3  ,      cast(null  as date     ) example3
  4  from   dual;

EXAMPLE1 EXAMPLE2   EXAMPLE3
-------- ---------- ---------
      13 oak

SQL>
```

5.8 Stored Functions

Although you might argue that Oracle already offers more than enough functions, you may find that you need a specific capability that isn't already provided. In that case, you can develop your own functions (using PL/SQL) and add them to the SQL language.

PL/SQL is the standard procedural programming language for Oracle databases. PL/SQL is a superset of SQL, adding several procedural capabilities to the nonprocedural SQL language. Here, we will investigate one simple example of PL/SQL language usage in relation to custom functions. For more information about PL/SQL, refer to *Oracle PL/SQL User's Guide and Reference*.

Listing 5-31 shows how to define a function to determine the number of employees for a given department.

Listing 5-31. *Creating a Stored Function Using PL/SQL*

```
SQL> create or replace function emp_count(p_deptno in number)
  2  return number is
  3         cnt number(2) := 0;
  4  begin
  5         select count(*) into cnt
  6         from   employees e
  7         where  e.deptno = p_deptno;
  8         return (cnt);
```

```
 9  end;
10  /

Function created.

SQL>
```

Now it becomes relatively easy to produce an overview of all departments, with their (correct) number of employees, as you can see in Listing 5-32. This query would be more complicated without this function. In particular, department 40 (the well-known department without employees) would not show up in your query results without some extra work. Without the stored function, you would need a so-called OUTER JOIN (see Chapter 8) or you would need a subquery in the SELECT clause (see Chapter 9).

Listing 5-32. *Using the Stored Function*

```
SQL> select deptno, dname, location
  2  ,       emp_count(deptno)
  3  from    departments;

  DEPTNO DNAME       LOCATION EMP_COUNT(DEPTNO)
-------- ---------- -------- -----------------
      10 ACCOUNTING NEW YORK                 3
      20 TRAINING   DALLAS                   5
      30 SALES      CHICAGO                  6
      40 HR         BOSTON                   0

SQL>
```

Listing 5-33 shows how the SQL*Plus DESCRIBE command treats these stored functions.

Listing 5-33. *Describing a Stored Function*

```
SQL> describe emp_count

FUNCTION emp_count RETURNS NUMBER

Argument Name            Type             In/Out Default?
------------------------ ---------------- ------ --------
P_DEPTNO                 NUMBER           IN

SQL>
```

5.9 Exercises

Use a database schema with the seven case tables (see Appendix C of this book) to perform the following exercises. The answers are presented in Appendix D.

1. For all employees, provide their last name, a comma, followed by their initials.

2. For all employees, list their last name and date of birth, in a format such as April 2nd, 1967.

3. On which day are (or were) you exactly 10,000 days old?
   On which day of the week is (was) this?

4. Rewrite the example in Listing 5-23 using the NVL2 function.

5. Rewrite the example in Listing 5-24 to remove the DECODE functions using CASE expressions, both in the SELECT clause and in the ORDER BY clause.

6. Rewrite the example in Listing 5-20 using DATE and INTERVAL constants, in such a way that they become independent of the NLS_DATE_FORMAT setting.

7. Investigate the difference between the date formats WW and IW (week number and ISO week number) using an arbitrary date, and explain your findings.

8. Look at Listing 5-15, where we use the REGEXP_INSTR function to search for words. Rewrite this query using REGEXP_LIKE. Hint: You can use {$n,$} to express "at least n times."

5.8 Exercises

CHAPTER 6

■ ■ ■

Data Manipulation

In this chapter, you will learn how to change the contents of an Oracle database. The SQL commands to change the database contents are commonly referred to as Data Manipulation Language (DML) commands.

The first four sections of this chapter cover the DML commands INSERT, UPDATE, DELETE, and MERGE. The first three commands have names that are self-explanatory. The fourth one, MERGE, allows you to perform a mixture of insertions, updates, and deletions in a single statement, which is especially useful in data warehousing environments.

In production environments, especially when dealing with high-volume transactions, data manipulation is mostly performed via database applications. In general, these database applications are built (or generated) with application development tools such as Oracle Forms and Oracle JDeveloper. Such applications offer a pleasant user-friendly interface to the database; however, they still use the basic INSERT, UPDATE, and DELETE commands under the hood to communicate with the database, so you should understand how these commands work. Additionally, sometimes "manual" data manipulation via SQL*Plus can be very efficient. For example, you may want to perform global updates (such as to change a certain column for all rows of a table at the same time) or to remove all rows of a table.

Section 6.5 explains the concept of *transactions* and introduces three transaction-related SQL commands: COMMIT, SAVEPOINT, and ROLLBACK.

This chapter is also the most obvious place in this book to pay some attention to *read consistency* and *locking*. So, the last section discusses how the Oracle DBMS guarantees transaction isolation in a multiuser environment. It provides an introduction to the concepts involved, without going into too many technical details.

6.1 The INSERT Command

You can use the INSERT command to add rows to a table. Along with the standard INSERT command, Oracle SQL also supports a multitable version.

Standard INSERT Commands

The standard INSERT command supports the following two ways to insert rows:

- Use the VALUES clause, followed by a list of column values (between parentheses). This method allows you to insert only *one* row at a time per execution of the INSERT command.

- Formulate a subquery, thus using existing data to generate new rows.

141

Both alternatives are shown in the syntax diagram in Figure 6-1.

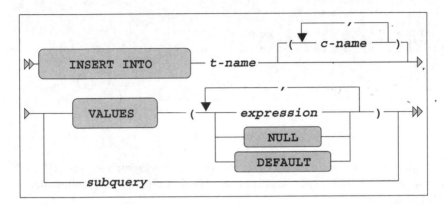

Figure 6-1. *INSERT command syntax diagram*

If you know all of the table columns, including the internal physical order in which they are presented by the SQL*Plus DESCRIBE command, you don't need to specify column names after the table name in the INSERT command. If you omit column names, you must provide *precisely enough* values and specify them in the correct order.

Caution Leaving out column names is rather dangerous, because your INSERT statement may become invalid after nondestructive table reorganizations (such as changing the column order). Column names also improve the readability of your SQL statements.

In the VALUES clause, you can specify a comma-separated list of literals or an expression. You can use the reserved word NULL to specify a null value for a specific column. You can also specify the reserved word DEFAULT to instruct the Oracle DBMS to insert the default value associated with the corresponding column. These default values are part of the table definition, stored in the data dictionary. If you don't specify a value for a specific column in your INSERT statement, there are two possibilities:

- If the column has an associated DEFAULT value, the Oracle DBMS will insert that value.

- If you did not define a DEFAULT value for the column, the Oracle DBMS inserts a null value (provided, of course, that the column allows null values).

Note Because the Oracle DBMS will automatically insert the default value when another value isn't specified, the DEFAULT keyword isn't really necessary for INSERT statements. However, the DEFAULT keyword can be quite useful when writing UPDATE statements, which are discussed in Section 6.2.

The second way of using the INSERT command fills a table with a subquery. There are no special constraints for these subqueries, as long as you make sure they produce the right number of values of the right datatype. You can even use a subquery against the table into which you are inserting rows. This sounds like a strange approach; however, INSERT INTO X SELECT * FROM X is one of the fastest methods to fill a table, provided you don't have unique or primary key constraints.

Note The fact that you are able to query and insert into the same table at the same time is due to Oracle's read consistency implementation. See Section 6.6 for details.

Listing 6-1 shows four INSERT statement examples: three using the VALUES clause and one using the subquery method.

Listing 6-1. *Four INSERT Command Examples*

```
SQL> insert into departments                              -- Example 1
  2  values (90,'SUPPORT','SEATTLE', NULL);

1 row created.

SQL> insert into employees(empno,ename,init,bdate,msal,deptno) -- Example 2
  2  values (7001,'ZOMBIE','ZZ',trunc(sysdate), 0, DEFAULT);

1 row created.

SQL> select * from employees where empno = 7001;

EMPNO ENAME   INIT JOB MGR BDATE       MSAL COMM DEPTNO
----- ------- ---- --- --- ----------- ---- ---- ------
 7001 ZOMBIE  ZZ           15-SEP-2004    0        10

SQL> insert into departments(dname,location,deptno)       -- Example 3
  2  values('CATERING','ORLANDO', 10);
insert into departments(dname,location,deptno)
*
ERROR at line 1:
ORA-00001: unique constraint (BOOK.D_PK) violated

SQL> insert into salgrades                                -- Example 4
  2  select grade + 5
  3  ,      lowerlimit + 2300
  4  ,      least(9999, upperlimit + 2300)
  5  ,      500
  6  from   salgrades;
```

```
5 rows created.

SQL> rollback;
Rollback complete.

SQL>
```

The examples work as follows:

- The first example inserts a new department 90 without specifying column names. It also shows how you can insert a null value with the reserved word NULL.

- The second example shows how you can use DEFAULT to assign the default department number to a new employee. (Chapter 7 explains how to assign such default values). The default value for the DEPTNO column of the EMPLOYEES table is 10, as you can see in Listing 6-1.

- The third example shows a violation of a primary key constraint; department 10 already exists.

- The fourth example shows how you can use a subquery to insert rows with the INSERT command. It uses the LEAST function (introduced in Chapter 5) to avoid constraint violations. The first argument (9999) ensures that the upper limit will never become greater than 9999.

At the end of Listing 6-1, we use ROLLBACK to undo our changes. The ROLLBACK command is explained in Section 6.5.

■**Note** After this chapter, we need all tables again in their unmodified state. Make sure to undo all changes you apply in this chapter, or re-create the tables before proceeding with Chapter 7.

Multitable INSERT Commands

Along with the two standard ways to use the INSERT command, Oracle SQL also supports *multitable inserts*. Using this method, you can specify multiple INTO clauses in a single INSERT command, with or without corresponding conditions.

The syntax of the multitable INSERT command without conditions is shown in Figure 6-2. The subquery retrieves a set of rows. For each row returned by the subquery, the Oracle DBMS executes each INTO clause once.

You can also make the INTO clauses conditional, using a WHEN ... THEN ... ELSE construct, as shown in the syntax diagram in Figure 6-3. In this case, you must choose between ALL or FIRST. If you specify ALL, Oracle evaluates each WHEN clause for every row from the subquery. If you specify FIRST, Oracle skips subsequent WHEN clauses after the first one that evaluates to true. Each expression in the WHEN condition must refer to columns returned by the SELECT list of the subquery.

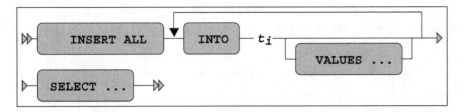

Figure 6-2. *Unconditional multitable INSERT command syntax diagram*

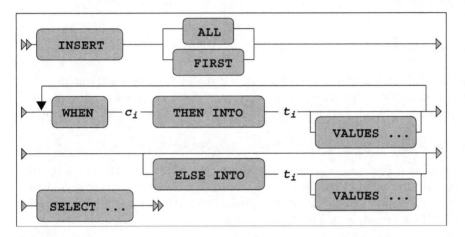

Figure 6-3. *Conditional multitable INSERT command syntax diagram*

For further details and examples of conditional and unconditional multitable inserts, refer to *Oracle SQL Reference*.

One more comment, before we move on to the UPDATE command: as you will see in Chapter 10, you can also perform data manipulation via inline views. For example, you can specify a subquery instead of a table name in INSERT commands.

6.2 The UPDATE Command

You can change column values of existing rows in your tables with the UPDATE command. As shown in the syntax diagram in Figure 6-4, the UPDATE command has three main components:

- **UPDATE:** The table you want to update

- **SET:** The change you want to apply

- **WHERE:** The rows to which you want to apply the change

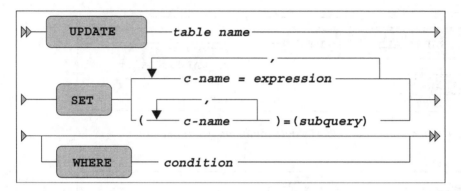

Figure 6-4. *UPDATE command syntax diagram*

If you omit the optional WHERE clause, the change is applied to all rows of the table. This illustrates the fact that the UPDATE command operates at the table level, so you need the WHERE clause as the relational restriction operator to limit the scope of the UPDATE command to a subset of the table.

As you can see from Figure 6-4, the SET clause offers two alternatives:

- You can specify a comma-separated list of single-column changes. With this approach, you can use the DEFAULT keyword as an expression. This allows you to change column default values in the data dictionary at any point in time without the need to change the UPDATE commands in your applications.

- You can drive the change with a subquery. The subquery must provide the right number of values for the list of column names specified between the parentheses. Of course, the datatypes should also match, or the Oracle DBMS should at least be able to convert values to the appropriate datatypes on the fly.

The first approach is illustrated in Listing 6-2, and the second approach is shown in Listing 6-3.

Listing 6-2. *UPDATE Command Example*

```
SQL> update employees
  2  set    job   = 'SALESREP'
  3  ,      msal  = msal - 500
  4  ,      comm  = 0
  5  ,      deptno = 30
  6  where  empno = 7876;

1 row updated.

SQL> rollback;
Rollback complete.

SQL>
```

Listing 6-3. *UPDATE Command Example Using a Subquery*

```
SQL> update registrations
  2  set    evaluation = 1
  3  where (course,begindate)
  4     in (select course,begindate
  5         from   offerings
  6         where  location = 'CHICAGO');

3 rows updated.

SQL> rollback;
Rollback complete.

SQL>
```

As with the INSERT examples in Listing 6-1, in both of these listings, we use the ROLLBACK command to undo any changes made.

6.3 The DELETE Command

The simplest data manipulation command is DELETE, as shown in the syntax diagram in Figure 6-5. This command also operates at the table level, and you use the WHERE clause to restrict the set of rows you want to delete from the table. If you omit the WHERE clause, the DELETE command results in an empty table.

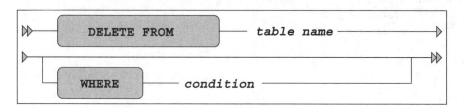

Figure 6-5. *DELETE command syntax diagram*

Note the difference between the following two commands:

```
SQL> drop  table departments;
SQL> delete from departments;
```

The DROP TABLE command not only removes the contents of the table, but also the table itself, including all dependent objects/structures such as indexes and privileges. DROP TABLE is a *data definition* (DDL) command. The DELETE command does not change the database structure, but only the contents—it is a *data manipulation* (DML) command. Moreover, the effects of a DROP TABLE command cannot be undone with a ROLLBACK command, as opposed to the effects of a DELETE command, which can. (The ROLLBACK command is introduced in Section 6.5.)

■**Note** In Chapter 7, you will see that there is a different way to get a table back after a DROP TABLE statement.

Listing 6-4 shows how you can delete a salary grade.

Listing 6-4. *Example of a DELETE Command*

```
SQL> delete from salgrades
  2  where  grade = 5;

1 row deleted.

SQL> rollback;
Rollback complete.

SQL>
```

To illustrate the fact that you can also use subqueries in the FROM clause of the DELETE statement, Listing 6-5 shows an alternative formulation for the same DELETE statement. Again, we use the ROLLBACK command to undo our changes.

Listing 6-5. *Alternative DELETE Command, Using a Subquery*

```
SQL> delete from (select *
  2                 from   salgrades
  3                 where  grade = 5);

1 row deleted.

SQL> rollback;
Rollback complete.

SQL>
```

In this case, there are no obvious advantages to using a subquery over using a regular DELETE statement. However, the subquery syntax also works (under certain conditions) with more complicated subqueries, opening up some very interesting possibilities.

Deleting rows may seem rather straightforward, but you might encounter complications due to constraint violations. The same is true for the UPDATE and INSERT commands, by the way. Constraints are discussed in the next chapter.

Because this section is about deleting rows, there is another SQL command that deserves mention here: TRUNCATE. The TRUNCATE command allows you to delete *all rows* of a table in a more efficient way than with the DELETE command. The TRUNCATE command belongs to the category of the data definition (DDL) commands, and so it is covered in the next chapter.

6.4 The MERGE Command

The MERGE command is a rather strange one. It is able to perform insertions, updates, and deletions in a single statement. This makes the MERGE command very efficient in data warehouse environments, where the tables are often populated/updated from external sources. The MERGE command is able to react appropriately to the existence (or nonexistence) of certain rows in the tables you are updating.

This book is not about data warehousing, so we will look at only a rather simple example of the MERGE command to see how it operates. For more details, see *Oracle SQL Reference* and *Oracle Data Warehousing Guide*.

Listing 6-6 shows the first step of our example, where we create and populate two small tables. Both tables have three columns: a product ID, a cumulative quantity sold, and a product status.

Listing 6-6. *Preparation for the MERGE Example*

```
SQL> create table delta_tab
  2 (pid number, sales number, status varchar2(6));
Table created.

SQL> create table master_tab
  2 (pid number, sales number, status varchar2(6));
Table created.

SQL> insert into master_tab values(1,12,'CURR');
1 row created.

SQL> insert into master_tab values(2,13,'NEW' );
1 row created.

SQL> insert into master_tab values(3,15,'CURR');
1 row created.

SQL> insert into delta_tab  values(2,24,'CURR');
1 row created.

SQL> insert into delta_tab  values(3, 0,'OBS' );
1 row created.

SQL> insert into delta_tab  values(4,42,'CURR');
1 row created.

SQL> commit;
Commit complete.

SQL>
```

Listing 6-7 shows the starting point of our example, before we execute a MERGE command. In the master table, we have three rows, for products 1, 2, and 3. In the delta table, we also have three rows, for products 2, 3, and 4.

Listing 6-7. *Situation Before Executing the MERGE Command*

```
SQL> select * from master_tab;

    PID    SALES STATUS
-------- -------- ------
      1       12 CURR
      2       13 NEW
      3       15 CURR

SQL> select * from delta_tab;

    PID    SALES STATUS
-------- -------- ------
      2       24 CURR
      3        0 OBS
      4       42 CURR

SQL>
```

Now we use the MERGE command, as shown in Listing 6-8.

Listing 6-8. *The MERGE Command and Its Effect on the MASTER_TAB Table*

```
SQL> merge into master_tab m
  2        using delta_tab d
  3        on (m.pid = d.pid)
  4  when  matched
  5  then  update set   m.sales  = m.sales+d.sales
  6                ,     m.status = d.status
  7        delete where m.status = 'OBS'
  8  when  not matched
  9  then  insert values (d.pid,d.sales,'NEW');

3 rows merged.

SQL> select * from master_tab;

    PID    SALES STATUS
-------- -------- ------
      1       12 CURR
      2       37 CURR
      4       42 NEW

SQL>
```

In Listing 6-8, the first three command lines specify the roles of the two tables involved and the joining condition between the two tables. Lines 5, 6, and 7 specify what must be done when processing a row from the DELTA_TAB table if there is a matching row in the MASTER_TAB table. Line 9 specifies what must be done when such a matching row does not exist.

Do you see what happened with the contents of the MASTER_TAB table?

- The first row is not touched, because the DELTA_TAB contains no row for product 1.

- The second row is updated: the SALES value is incremented with 24, and the STATUS is set to CURR.

- The third (original) row is deleted, because after applying the UPDATE clause, the DELETE condition became TRUE.

- The fourth row is inserted, because there was no row for product 4.

6.5 Transaction Processing

All DML changes (INSERT, UPDATE, DELETE, and MERGE) that you apply to the contents of the database initially get a "pending" status. This means (among other things) that you can see the changed rows, but other database users will see *the original data* when they query the same table rows. Moreover, as long as your changes are in this pending state, other database users will not be able to change those rows, until you confirm or abandon your pending changes.

The SQL command to confirm pending changes to the database is COMMIT, and the command to cancel them is ROLLBACK. This allows you to perform a number of changes, then confirm them with a COMMIT or cancel them with ROLLBACK, then perform another number of changes, and so on.

COMMIT and ROLLBACK close a current *transaction* and open a new one. A transaction is considered to be a *logical unit of work*. In other words, a transaction is a set of changes that will succeed or fail as a whole.

■**Note** The Oracle DBMS also allows you to define *autonomous transactions* using PL/SQL. These are subtransactions that you can COMMIT or ROLLBACK independently from their main transactions. See *PL/SQL User's Guide and Reference* for details.

For example, account transfer transactions in a banking system normally consist of (at least) two updates: a debit to account A and a credit to account B. In such situations, it makes a lot of sense to COMMIT after each debit/credit combination, and *not* in between each update. What if something went wrong (for example, the system crashed) after the debit update was committed but the credit update had not been processed yet? You would end up with corrupted administration records. Moreover, even in the absence of any disasters, a different database user could start a reporting application precisely at the "wrong" moment in between the two updates, which would result in inconsistent financial reports.

On the other hand, if you wait too long before committing your changes, you risk losing your work when the system crashes. During system recovery, all pending transactions will be rolled back to guarantee database consistency. This may be annoying, but it's necessary.

By the way, this illustrates the fact that not only database users are able to issue *explicit* COMMIT and ROLLBACK commands. Oracle tools can also issue those commands *implicitly*. For example, if you leave SQL*Plus in a normal way with the EXIT or QUIT command, or if you create a new session with the SQL*Plus CONNECT command, SQL*Plus first sends a COMMIT command to the database.

Another consequence of a delayed committing of your changes is that you block other database users who want to update or delete the same rows. Section 6.6 discusses this locking behavior in a little more detail.

All DDL commands (such as CREATE, ALTER, DROP, GRANT, and REVOKE) always imply an *implicit* COMMIT. To put it another way, each single DDL command is executed as a transaction in itself, consisting of a single command, and is committed immediately.

The SQL*Plus AUTOCOMMIT Option

SQL*Plus supports an AUTOCOMMIT option. To access this option under Microsoft Windows, select Options ➤ Environment and choose the autocommit category in the Set Options list box, as shown in Figure 6-6. You can choose to commit DML commands immediately by selecting the On radio button, or to commit each time after a certain number of successful DML commands by entering a number in the Value field.

▪**Caution** You should use the AUTOCOMMIT feature with caution and only under special conditions. First of all, you lose the opportunity to issue the ROLLBACK command to undo your changes in case of mistakes. Moreover, you lose the transaction principle that some mutations belong to the same logical unit of work.

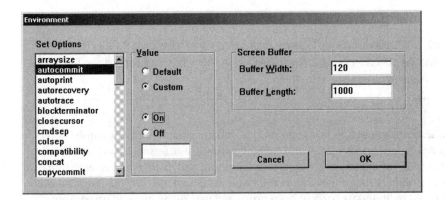

Figure 6-6. *The SQL*Plus AUTOCOMMIT setting in the Environment dialog box*

As Listing 6-9 shows, you can also manipulate and retrieve the SQL*Plus AUTOCOMMIT setting in character mode, using the SQL*Plus SET command.

Listing 6-9. *The SQL*Plus AUTOCOMMIT Setting (Character Mode)*

```
SQL> set  autocommit on
SQL> show autocommit
autocommit IMMEDIATE

SQL> set  autocommit 42
SQL> show autocommit
AUTOCOMMIT ON for every 42 DML statements

SQL> set  autocommit off
SQL>
```

Transaction Design

Now that you have an idea of the transaction concept, let's give transaction design a little
more attention. As stated previously, transactions should be considered as *logical* units of
work. So, you should decide which set of database changes should always succeed or fail in
its entirety. However, you should also take some *physical* aspects into consideration, because
your transaction design may incur undesirable side effects.

The following three transaction designs may cause performance problems or other
unnecessary overhead in high-load system environments:

- Committing too frequently

- Committing too infrequently

- Letting a lot of time elapse between DML changes and COMMIT

The last two designs (committing too infrequently and letting a lot of time elapse) force
the Oracle DBMS to keep transaction undo information available for an unnecessarily long
time, and they also block other transactions from changing the same data. The first design
(committing too frequently) could cause unnecessary contention on certain system resources.
See also Section 6.6 for more about read consistency and locking.

Savepoints

You can define "interim points," known as *savepoints*, within your transactions. During a
transaction, you can roll back to such savepoints *without* rolling back the transaction as a
whole, thus maintaining the changes you made before the savepoint. Listing 6-10 shows an
example where we issue four DELETE commands in total, and we define a savepoint between
the second and the third DELETE command. With the ROLLBACK TO SAVEPOINT command, we
undo the last two DELETE commands, but the first two changes maintain their pending status.

Listing 6-10. *Using Savepoints Within a Transaction*

```
SQL> delete from history    where empno=7654;
2 rows deleted.

SQL> delete from employees where empno=7654;
1 row deleted.

SQL> savepoint ONE;
Savepoint created.

SQL> delete from offerings where course='ERM';
1 row deleted.

SQL> delete from courses   where code   ='ERM';
1 row deleted.

SQL> rollback to savepoint ONE;
Rollback complete.

SQL> select description
  2  from    courses
  3  where   code='ERM';

DESCRIPTION
---------------------------------------------
Data modeling with ERM

SQL> rollback;
Rollback complete.

SQL>
```

■**Note** You can define as many savepoints per transaction as you like. Actually, the Oracle DBMS uses implicit savepoints internally to implement statement-level rollback.

6.6 Locking and Read Consistency

Normally, many users and applications access database systems at the same time. This is known as *concurrency*. The DBMS must make sure that concurrency is handled properly. The most drastic approach for a DBMS would be to handle all user transactions one by one, blocking all data exclusively until the end of each transaction. Such a transaction serialization approach would result in unnecessary and unacceptable wait times; the overall system *throughput* would be very poor.

Normally, DBMSs like Oracle control concurrent data access with *locking*. For example, locking is necessary to prevent database users from updating rows with pending (uncommitted) changes from other database users. This section gives some information about how the Oracle DBMS handles locking and concurrency.

Locking

To understand how the Oracle DBMS handles locking, we need to identify a difference between two categories of database users:

- **Readers:** Users *retrieving* data (issuing SELECT statements)

- **Writers:** Users *changing* data (issuing INSERT, UPDATE, DELETE, and MERGE commands)

The Oracle DBMS does not lock any data for retrieval. This means that *readers* never block *readers*. Moreover, this also means that *writers* never need to wait for *readers*, and vice versa.

■**Note** The Oracle DBMS's handling of data locking does *not* mean that readers and writers do not hinder each other in any way. Readers and writers can cause delays for each other by contending for certain system resources.

Multiple database users trying to change the same rows need to wait for each other, so *writers* may block other *writers*. Each attempt to change a row tries to acquire the corresponding *row-level lock* first. If the lock cannot be acquired, you must wait until the pending change is committed or rolled back. All row-level locks are released upon a COMMIT (explicit or implicit) or ROLLBACK. This means that the Oracle DBMS tries to minimize locking overhead and tries to maximize throughput and concurrency.

Read Consistency

In a database environment, *read consistency* is an important concept. Read consistency is a first requirement to guarantee correct query results. Regardless of how long it runs *and* regardless what else happens simultaneously in the database, the Oracle DBMS must make sure that each SQL query maintains access to a consistent *snapshot* of the data at the point in time when the query started. It needs this snapshot because a query should *never* see any uncommitted changes. Moreover, a query should not see changes that were committed *after* the query started. This means that the Oracle DBMS must be able to reconstruct previous versions of the data in order to process queries. We will not go into technical details here, but the Oracle DBMS accomplishes this (without using locking) by using information stored in undo segments.

Believe it or not, read consistency is even important in a *single-user* environment. Suppose that upper management has decided to grant a salary raise of 50% to all employees who currently earn less than the average salary of their department. You might want your salary to be checked last by the UPDATE statement, hoping that earlier salary raises have influenced your department's average salary in such a way that you became entitled to a raise, too. In an Oracle environment, this hope is in vain, because the read consistency mechanism will ensure that the subquery in the UPDATE statement (to derive the average salary of your department) returns the same result, regardless of how often the subquery is reexecuted for the same department, within the scope of that single UPDATE command.

By default, read consistency is implemented at the *statement* level. In case you need read consistency at the *transaction* level—for example, for a report that consists of multiple queries—you must do something to override this default behavior to guarantee consistent report results. In such a situation, you could decide to manually lock all tables with the LOCK TABLE command. However, locking data prevents concurrent transactions from changing that data, resulting in wait situations and reducing throughput. Therefore, locking the data manually is not a recommended approach.

There is a better solution in this situation, without the disadvantages of using locking: the SQL command SET TRANSACTION. This command allows you to specify the desired transaction isolation level (in compliance with the ANSI/ISO SQL standard). See Figure 6-7 for the (partial) syntax of this command.

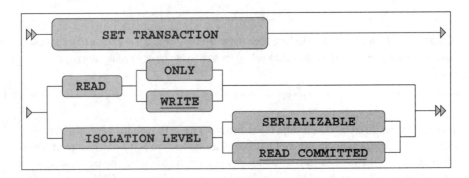

Figure 6-7. *SET TRANSACTION command syntax diagram*

The components of the SET TRANSACTION command work as follows:

- READ WRITE is the Oracle default, implementing statement-level read consistency.

- READ ONLY implements transaction-level read consistency.

- ISOLATION LEVEL READ COMMITTED is the Oracle default behavior.

- ISOLATION LEVEL SERIALIZABLE implies the failure of DML statements that attempt to update rows that already had pending changes when the serializable transaction started.

In the situation of the report consisting of multiple queries, issuing the SET TRANSACTION READ ONLY command at the beginning of the transaction would be the right choice. But note that because the Oracle DBMS does *not* use any locking or other obstructive techniques when you do this, you incur the risk that, at a certain point in time, the Oracle DBMS will not be able to reconstruct the desired original data anymore, especially if your read-only transaction is running a long time. You get the following error message in such situations:

```
ORA-01555: Snapshot too old
```

See *Oracle Concepts* for more details about transaction isolation levels.

This completes your introduction to data manipulation commands and concepts. You learned about the four DML commands of the SQL language: INSERT, UPDATE, DELETE, and MERGE. Then we discussed transaction processing, using the commands COMMIT, SAVEPOINT, and ROLLBACK. Finally, we briefly discussed read consistency and locking, and introduced the SET TRANSACTION command, which you can use to influence the default read consistency behavior of the Oracle DBMS.

Before continuing with Chapter 7, which returns to the topic of data definition, make sure that all of your case tables are in their unmodified state. You should have rolled back all of the changes you applied in this chapter. Alternatively, you can re-create the tables before proceeding.

CHAPTER 7

■ ■ ■

Data Definition, Part II

Chapter 3 introduced just enough data definition (DDL) syntax to enable you to create the seven case tables for this book, using simple CREATE TABLE commands without any constraint specifications. This second DDL chapter goes into more detail about some data definition aspects, although it is still not intended as a complete reference on the topic. (Discussion of the CREATE TABLE command alone covers more than 100 pages in the Oracle Database 10*g* documentation.)

The first two sections revisit the CREATE TABLE command and the datatypes supported by Oracle Database 10*g*. Section 7.3 introduces the ALTER TABLE command, which allows you to change the structure of an existing table (such as to add columns or change datatypes), and the RENAME command, which allows you to rename a table or view. You will learn how to define and handle constraints in Section 7.4.

Section 7.5 covers indexes. The main purpose of indexes is to improve performance (response time) by providing more efficient access paths to table data. Thus, Section 7.6 provides a brief introduction to performance, mainly in the context of checking if the optimizer is using your indexes.

The most efficient method to generate sequence numbers (for example, for order numbers) in an Oracle environment is by using sequences, which are introduced in Section 7.7.

We continue with synonyms, in Section 7.8. By creating synonyms you can work with abbreviations for table names, hide the schema name prefix of table names, or even hide the remote database where the table resides. Section 7.9 explains the CURRENT_SCHEMA session parameter.

Section 7.10 discusses the DROP TABLE command and the recycle bin, a concept introduced in Oracle Database 10*g*. By default, all dropped tables go to the recycle bin, allowing you to recover from human errors.

The next two sections cover some other SQL commands related to data definition: TRUNCATE and COMMENT. The final section contains some review exercises.

7.1 The CREATE TABLE Command

Chapter 3 introduced the CREATE TABLE command and showed a basic command syntax diagram. This section explores the CREATE TABLE command in a little more detail. Figure 7-1 shows a more (but still far from) complete syntax diagram.

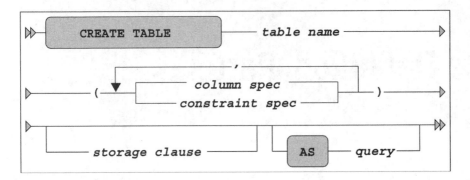

Figure 7-1. *CREATE TABLE command syntax diagram*

Figure 7-1 shows that the CREATE TABLE command supports two component types: *column* specifications and *constraint* specifications.

You can provide an optional STORAGE clause, with various physical storage specifications for the table you are creating. This is an important means to optimize and spread the physical storage of your data on disk. For more information about the STORAGE clause and handling physical storage, see *Oracle SQL Reference*.

According to the syntax diagram in Figure 7-1, you can also create new tables based on a subquery with the AS clause. The CREATE TABLE ... AS SELECT ... command (also known as CTAS) is comparable to one of the possibilities of the INSERT command shown in Figure 6-1 (in Chapter 6), where you insert rows into an existing table using a subquery. The only difference is that with CTAS, you create *and* populate the table in a single SQL command. In this case, you can omit the column specifications between the parentheses. If you want to use column specifications anyway, you are not allowed to specify datatypes. In CTAS commands, the new table always inherits the datatypes from the results of the subquery.

The syntax for column specifications in a CREATE TABLE command is detailed in Figure 7-2.

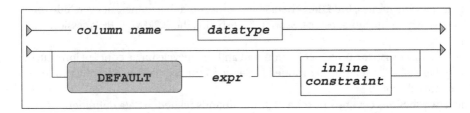

Figure 7-2. *CREATE TABLE column specification syntax*

Figure 7-2 shows that you can specify constraints in two ways:

• As independent (*out-of-line*) components of the CREATE TABLE command (see Figure 7-1)

• As *inline constraints* inside a column specification (see Figure 7-2)

We will discuss both types of constraints in Section 7.4.

You can use the DEFAULT option to specify a value (or an expression) to be used for INSERT commands that don't contain an explicit value for the corresponding column.

7.2 More on Datatypes

Datatypes were introduced in Chapter 3. Table 7-1 provides a more complete overview of the most important Oracle datatypes.

Table 7-1. *Important Oracle Datatypes*

Datatype	Description
CHAR[(n)]	Character string with fixed length n (default 1)
VARCHAR2(n)	Variable-length string; maximum n characters
DATE	Date (between 4712 BC and 9999 AD)
TIMESTAMP	Timestamp, with or without time zone information
INTERVAL	Date/time interval
BLOB	Unstructured binary data (Binary Large Object)
CLOB	Large text (Character Large Object)
RAW(n)	Binary data; maximum n bytes
NUMBER	Integer; maximum precision 38 digits
NUMBER(n)	Integer; maximum n digits
NUMBER(n,m)	Total of n digits; maximum m digits right of the decimal point
BINARY_FLOAT	32-bit floating-point number
BINARY_DOUBLE	64-bit floating-point number

■Note If you insert values into a NUMBER(n,m) column and you exceed precision n, you get an error message. If you exceed scale m, the Oracle DBMS rounds the value.

The Oracle DBMS supports many datatype synonyms for portability with other DBMS implementations and for compliance with the ANSI/ISO standard. For example, CHARACTER is identical to CHAR; DECIMAL(n,m) is identical to NUMBER(n,m); and NUMBER even has multiple synonyms, such as INTEGER, REAL, and SMALLINT.

Each Oracle datatype has its own precision or length limits, as shown in Table 7-2.

Table 7-2. *Oracle Datatype Limits*

Datatype	Limit
NUMBER	38 digits
CHAR	2000
VARCHAR2	4000
RAW	2000 bytes
BLOB	(4GB – 1) × (database block size)
CLOB	(4GB – 1) × (database block size)

Character Datatypes

Since Oracle7 (released more than ten years ago), VARCHAR and VARCHAR2 have exactly the same meaning. However, Oracle recommends using the VARCHAR2 datatype, because a future Oracle release might treat those two datatypes differently.

If you go a little further back in time (Oracle version 6 and earlier), the datatypes CHAR and VARCHAR were synonyms, both representing *variable*-length character strings; the Oracle DBMS didn't support fixed-length strings. The change in behavior in Oracle7 caused a lot of problems, although it was announced in advance. This is one of the reasons why we now have VARCHAR and VARCHAR2.

You may have noticed that Table 7-2 shows 2000 and 4000 for the CHAR and VARCHAR2 datatype limits, respectively. You might wonder in which unit these numbers are expressed. That depends on the value of the NLS_LENGTH_SEMANTICS parameter. The default for the Oracle DBMS is to use BYTE length semantics. If you want to make your SQL code independent of this parameter, you can override its value by using explicit BYTE and CHAR suffixes in your datatype specifications. Here are a couple examples:

- CHAR(42 BYTE): Fixed string, 42 bytes

- VARCHAR2(2000 CHAR): Variable string, maximum of 2000 characters

Comparison Semantics

If VARCHAR2 and VARCHAR do diverge in the future, the VARCHAR2 datatype will be guaranteed to be backward-compatible. The eventual difference between these two datatypes could be the treatment of comparisons involving strings of different lengths, or maybe the interpretation of empty strings as null values. There are two different semantics to compare strings of different lengths: padded comparison (padding with spaces) and nonpadded comparison.

If you compare two strings, character by character, and all of the characters are identical until the point where the shortest string is processed, nonpadded comparison semantics automatically "declares" the longest string as being greater than the shorter string. On the other hand, padded comparison semantics extends the shortest string with spaces until the length of the longest string, and continues comparing characters. This means that trailing spaces in strings don't influence padded comparison results. Here are examples of the comparison types:

- Padded comparison: 'RAID5' = 'RAID5   '

- Nonpadded comparison: ' RAID5' < ' RAID5   '

By using the VARCHAR2 datatype instead of the VARCHAR datatype, especially in all your SQL script files, you are guaranteed to get *nonpadded* comparison semantics, regardless of the development and implementation of the VARCHAR datatype in any future release of the Oracle DBMS.

Column Data Interpretation

There is an important difference between the RAW and VARCHAR2 datatypes. RAW column data (like BLOB data) is never interpreted by the DBMS in any way. For example, VARCHAR2 column data is converted automatically during transport from an ASCII to an EBCDIC environment. You typically use the RAW and BLOB datatypes for columns containing binary data, such as scanned documents, sound tracks, and movie fragments.

Numbers Revisited

Before we move on to the ALTER TABLE command in the next section, let's briefly revisit numbers. The Oracle DBMS has always stored NUMBER values in a proprietary internal format, to maintain maximum *portability* to the impressive list of different platforms (operating systems) that it supports. The NUMBER datatype is still the best choice for most columns containing numeric data. However, the internal storage of this datatype implies some processing overhead, especially when you are performing many nontrivial numerical computations in your SQL statements.

Since Oracle Database 10*g* you can also store *floating-point* numbers in your table columns. Floating-point numbers don't offer the same precision as NUMBER values, but they may result in better response times for numerical computations. You can choose between two floating-point datatypes:

- BINARY_FLOAT: 32-bit, single precision

- BINARY_DOUBLE: 64-bit, double precision

You can also specify floating-point constants (literals) in your SQL statements with a suffix f (single precision) or d (double precision), as shown in Listing 7-1.

Listing 7-1. *Floating-Point Literals*

```
SQL> select 5.1d, 42f from dual;

      5.1D        42F
---------- ----------
  5.1E+000   4.2E+001

SQL>
```

We won't use these two floating-point datatypes in this book. See *Oracle SQL Reference* for more details.

7.3 The ALTER TABLE and RENAME Commands

Sometimes, it is necessary to change the structure of existing tables. For example, you may find that the maximum width of a certain column is defined too low, you might want to add an extra column to an existing table, or you may need to modify a constraint. In these situations, you can use the ALTER TABLE command. Figure 7-3 shows the syntax diagram for this command.

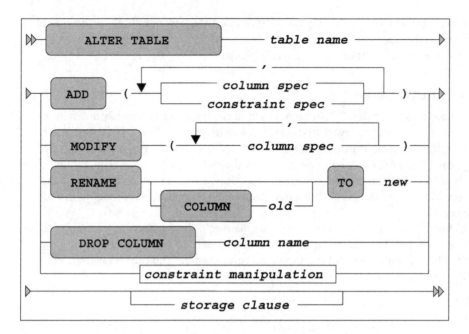

Figure 7-3. *ALTER TABLE command syntax diagram*

■Note The ALTER TABLE command is much more complicated and extended than Figure 7-3 suggests. See *Oracle SQL Reference* for more details.

You can add columns or constraint definitions to an existing table with the ADD option. The MODIFY option allows you to change definitions of existing columns. For example, you can widen a column, allow null values with NULL, or prohibit null values with NOT NULL.

You can drop columns from tables with the DROP COLUMN option. You can also set columns to "unused" with the ALTER TABLE ... SET UNUSED command, and physically remove them from the database later with the ALTER TABLE ... DROP UNUSED COLUMNS command. This may be useful when you want to drop multiple columns in a single scan (accessing the rows only once). The RENAME COLUMN option allows you to change the name of a column.

■Caution You should be careful with the "destructive" DROP COLUMN option. Some database applications may depend on the existence of the column you are dropping.

With the *constraint manipulation* option, you can remove, enable, or disable constraints. Figure 7-4 shows the syntax details of this ALTER TABLE command option. For more details about constraint handling, see the next section.

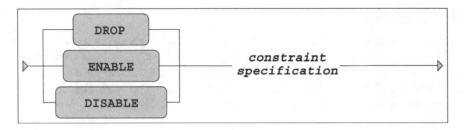

Figure 7-4. *ALTER TABLE constraint manipulation syntax*

Just like the CREATE TABLE command, the ALTER TABLE command also allows you to influence various physical table storage attributes.

In general, you can apply any structure change to existing tables, even when they contain rows. However, there are some exceptions. For example, for obvious reasons you cannot add a NOT NULL column to a nonempty table, unless you immediately specify a DEFAULT value in the same ALTER TABLE command. Listing 7-2 shows an example.

Listing 7-2. *ALTER TABLE Command Examples*

```
SQL> alter table registrations
  2   add  (entered_by number(4) default 7839 not null);

Table altered.

SQL> alter table registrations
  2   drop  column entered_by;

Table altered.

SQL>
```

■**Note** The ALTER TABLE statement is probably the best illustration of the power of the relational model. Think about this: you can change a table definition while the table contains data and applications are running.

The RENAME command is rather straightforward. It allows you to change the name of a table or view (views are discussed in Chapter 10). Figure 7-5 shows the syntax diagram for the RENAME command.

Figure 7-5. *RENAME command syntax diagram*

7.4 Constraints

As you saw in the previous sections, you can specify constraint definitions in the CREATE TABLE and ALTER TABLE commands. As noted earlier in the description of the CREATE TABLE command, you can treat constraints as independent table components (for example, at the end of your CREATE TABLE command after all column definitions) or as part of a column definition. A common terminology to distinguish these two ways to specify constraints is *out-of-line* versus *inline* constraints.

For each constraint definition, you can optionally specify a constraint name. It is highly recommended that you do so for all your constraint definitions. If you don't specify a constraint name yourself, the Oracle DBMS generates a far from informative name for you: SYS_C*nnnnn*, where *nnnnn* is an arbitrary sequence number. Once constraints are created, you need their names to manipulate (enable, disable, or drop) them. Moreover, constraint names show up in constraint violation error messages. Therefore, well-chosen constraint names make error messages more informative. See Listing 7-3 later in this section for an example, showing a foreign key constraint violation.

Out-of-Line Constraints

Figure 7-6 shows the syntax details for out-of-line constraints. This syntax is slightly different from the inline constraint syntax.

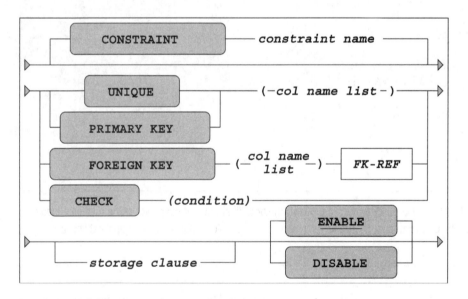

Figure 7-6. *Out-of-line constraint syntax diagram*

In the syntax diagram, *col name list* refers to a comma-separated list of one or more column names. The type of constraint can be UNIQUE, PRIMARY KEY, FOREIGN KEY, and CHECK. By default, constraints become active immediately, unless you specify the DISABLE option; in other words, the default option is ENABLE.

The four types of constraints work as follows:

- UNIQUE allows you to prevent duplicate values in a column or a column combination.

- PRIMARY KEY and FOREIGN KEY allow you to implement *entity integrity* and *referential integrity*. See Chapter 1 for a detailed discussion of these concepts.

- CHECK allows you to specify any arbitrary *condition* as a constraint.

Figure 7-7 shows the syntax details of a foreign key constraint reference (*FK-REF* in Figure 7-6).

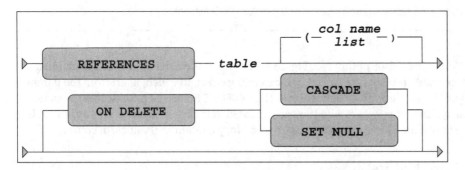

Figure 7-7. *Foreign key reference syntax diagram*

You can omit the comma-separated list of column names (*col name list* in Figure 7-7) in the foreign key reference. In that case, the foreign key constraint automatically refers to the primary key of the referenced table.

■**Tip** In general, it is considered good practice to have foreign keys always refer to primary keys, although foreign keys may also reference unique keys.

To understand the **ON DELETE** option of the foreign key reference, consider the example of a foreign key constraint violation shown in Listing 7-3. Normally, it is impossible to remove parent (master) rows if the database still contains child (detail) rows. In Listing 7-3, we try to remove the XML course while the database still apparently contains XML course offerings.

Listing 7-3. *Example of a Foreign Key Constraint Violation*

```
SQL> delete from courses
  2  where  code = 'XML';

delete from courses
*
ERROR at line 1:
ORA-02292: integrity constraint (BOOK.O_COURSE_FK) violated -
          child record found

SQL>
```

Note Listing 7-10 shows the definition of the O_COURSE_FK constraint.

The ON DELETE CASCADE option (see Figure 7-7) changes the behavior in such situations. The master/detail problems are solved by a cascading effect, in which, apart from the parent row, all child rows are implicitly deleted, too. The ON DELETE SET NULL option solves the same problem in a different way: the child rows are updated, rather than deleted. This approach is applicable only if the foreign key columns involved may contain null values, of course.

Inline Constraints

The *inline* constraint syntax is shown in Figure 7-8. There are some subtle differences from the syntax for out-of-line constraints:

- You don't specify column names in inline constraints, because inline constraints always belong to the column definition in which they are embedded.

- The foreign key constraint reference (FK-REF) is the same for both constraint types (see Figure 7-7), but you don't specify the keywords FOREIGN KEY for an inline constraint—REFERENCES is enough.

- In the context of inline constraints, a NOT NULL constraint is allowed. In out-of-line constraints, this is impossible, unless you rewrite it as a CHECK constraint.

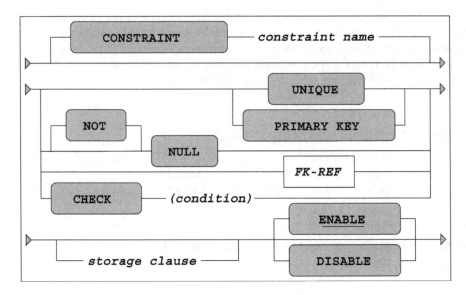

Figure 7-8. *Inline constraint syntax diagram*

Constraint Definitions in the Data Dictionary

Constraint definitions are stored in the data dictionary. The two most important views are
USER_CONSTRAINTS and USER_CONS_COLUMNS. Listing 7-4 shows how you can produce an
overview of all referential integrity constraints for the current user.

Listing 7-4. *Foreign Key Constraints in the Data Dictionary*

```
SQL> select table_name
  2  ,       constraint_name
  3  ,       status
  4  ,       r_constraint_name as references
  5  from    user_constraints
  6  where   constraint_type = 'R';

TABLE_NAME           CONSTRAINT_NAME      STATUS    REFERENCES
-------------------- -------------------- --------  ----------
EMPLOYEES            E_MGR_FK             ENABLED   E_PK
DEPARTMENTS          D_MGR_FK             ENABLED   E_PK
EMPLOYEES            E_DEPT_FK            ENABLED   D_PK
OFFERINGS            O_TRAIN_FK           ENABLED   E_PK
OFFERINGS            O_COURSE_FK          ENABLED   C_PK
REGISTRATIONS        R_OFF_FK             ENABLED   O_PK
REGISTRATIONS        R_ATT_FK             ENABLED   E_PK
HISTORY              H_DEPT_FK            ENABLED   D_PK
HISTORY              H_EMPNO_FK           ENABLED   E_PK

SQL>
```

Tools like Oracle Forms and Oracle Designer can use constraint definitions from the data dictionary; for example, to generate code for constraint checking in database applications.

Last, but not least, the Oracle optimizer uses knowledge about constraint information from the data dictionary to decide about efficient execution plans for SQL statements. To reiterate what we discussed in Chapter 1, constraints are very important, and they *must* be defined in the database.

Case Table Definitions with Constraints

Listings 7-5 through 7-12 show the CREATE TABLE commands for the seven case tables of this book. The constraints in these CREATE TABLE commands are meant to be self-explanatory, showing various examples of PRIMARY KEY, FOREIGN KEY, UNIQUE, CHECK, and NOT NULL constraints.

■**Note** For more details about the seven case tables, refer to Appendix C of this book.

Listing 7-5. *The EMPLOYEES Table*

```
create table employees
( empno      NUMBER(4)    constraint E_PK          primary key
                          constraint E_EMPNO_CHK check (empno > 7000)
, ename      VARCHAR2(8)  constraint E_NAME_NN   not null
, init       VARCHAR2(5)  constraint E_INIT_NN   not null
, job        VARCHAR2(8)
, mgr        NUMBER(4)    constraint E_MGR_FK      references employees
, bdate      DATE         constraint E_BDAT_NN   not null
, msal       NUMBER(6,2)  constraint E_MSAL_NN   not null
, comm       NUMBER(6,2)
, deptno     NUMBER(2)    default 10
,                         constraint E_SALES_CHK check
                                     (decode(job,'SALESREP',0,1)
                                      + nvl2(comm,        1,0) = 1)
) ;
```

Listing 7-6. *The DEPARTMENTS Table*

```
create table departments
( deptno NUMBER(2)      constraint D_PK          primary key
                        constraint D_DEPTNO_CHK check (mod(deptno,10) = 0)
, dname  VARCHAR2(10)   constraint D_DNAME_NN   not null
                        constraint D_DNAME_UN   unique
                        constraint D_DNAME_CHK  check (dname = upper(dname))
, location VARCHAR2(8)  constraint D_LOC_NN     not null
                        constraint D_LOC_CHK    check (location = upper(location))
```

```
, mgr     NUMBER(4)        constraint D_MGR_FK        references employees
) ;
```

Listing 7-7. *Adding a Foreign Key Constraint*

```
alter table employees add
(constraint E_DEPT_FK foreign key (deptno) references departments);
```

Listing 7-8. *The SALGRADES Table*

```
create table salgrades
( grade      NUMBER(2)   constraint S_PK        primary key
, lowerlimit NUMBER(6,2) constraint S_LOWER_NN  not null
                         constraint S_LOWER_CHK check (lowerlimit >= 0)
, upperlimit NUMBER(6,2) constraint S_UPPER_NN  not null
, bonus      NUMBER(6,2) constraint S_BONUS_NN  not null
,                        constraint S_LO_UP_CHK check
                                               (lowerlimit <= upperlimit)
) ;
```

Listing 7-9. *The COURSES Table*

```
create table courses
( code        VARCHAR2(6)  constraint C_PK      primary key
, description VARCHAR2(30) constraint C_DESC_NN not null
, category    CHAR(3)      constraint C_CAT_NN  not null
, duration    NUMBER(2)    constraint C_DUR_NN  not null
,                          constraint C_CODE_CHK check
                                               (code = upper(code))
,                          constraint C_CAT_CHK check
                                               (category in ('GEN','BLD','DSG'))
) ;
```

Listing 7-10. *The OFFERINGS Table*

```
create table offerings
( course    VARCHAR2(6) constraint O_COURSE_NN not null
                        constraint O_COURSE_FK references courses
, begindate DATE        constraint O_BEGIN_NN  not null
, trainer   NUMBER(4)   constraint O_TRAIN_FK  references employees
, location  VARCHAR2(8)
,                       constraint O_PK        primary key
                                               (course,begindate)
) ;
```

Listing 7-11. *The REGISTRATIONS Table*

```
create table registrations
( attendee    NUMBER(4)   constraint R_ATT_NN     not null
                          constraint R_ATT_FK     references employees
, course      VARCHAR2(6) constraint R_COURSE_NN  not null
, begindate   DATE        constraint R_BEGIN_NN   not null
, evaluation  NUMBER(1)   constraint R_EVAL_CHK   check (evaluation in (1,2,3,4,5))
,                         constraint R_PK         primary key
                                                  (attendee,course,begindate)
,                         constraint R_OFF_FK     foreign key (course,begindate)
                                                  references offerings
) ;
```

Listing 7-12. *The HISTORY Table*

```
create table history
( empno      NUMBER(4)    constraint H_EMPNO_NN   not null
                          constraint H_EMPNO_FK   references employees
                                                  on delete cascade
, beginyear  NUMBER(4)    constraint H_BYEAR_NN   not null
, begindate  DATE         constraint H_BDATE_NN   not null
, enddate    DATE
, deptno     NUMBER(2)    constraint H_DEPT_NN    not null
                          constraint H_DEPT_FK    references departments
, msal       NUMBER(6,2)  constraint H_MSAL_NN    not null
, comments   VARCHAR2(60)
,                         constraint H_PK         primary key (empno,begindate)
,                         constraint H_BEG_END    check (begindate < enddate)
) ;
```

A Solution for Foreign Key References: CREATE SCHEMA

While we are on the topic of creating multiple tables, Oracle SQL also supports the ANSI/ISO standard CREATE SCHEMA command. This command allows you to create a complete schema (consisting of tables, views, and grants) with a single DDL command/transaction. One advantage of the CREATE SCHEMA command is that it succeeds or fails as an atomic transaction. It also solves the problem of two tables having foreign key references to each other (see Listings 7-5, 7-6, and 7-7), where you normally need at least one ALTER TABLE command, because foreign keys can reference only existing tables.

Listing 7-13 shows how you could have created the case tables with the CREATE SCHEMA command.

Listing 7-13. *The CREATE SCHEMA Command*

```
SQL> create schema authorization BOOK
  2        create table employees      (...)
  3        create table departments    (...)
  4        create table salgrades      (...)
  5        create table courses        (...)
  6        create table offerings      (...)
  7        create table registrations  (...)
  8        create table history        (...)
  9        create view ... as select ... from ...
 10        grant select on ... to public;
```

■**Note** The name of this command (as implemented by Oracle) is confusing, because it does not actually create a schema. Oracle schemas are created with the CREATE USER command. The command succeeds only if the schema name is the same as your Oracle database username.

You can specify the CREATE SCHEMA command components in any order. Within each component definition, you can refer to other (earlier or later) schema components.

Deferrable Constraints

The Oracle DBMS also supports *deferrable constraints*, allowing you to specify *when* you want the constraints to be checked. These are the two possibilities:

- IMMEDIATE checks at the statement level.
- DEFERRED checks at the end of the transaction.

Before you can use this distinction, you must first allow a constraint to be deferrable. The default option for all constraints that you create is NOT DEFERRABLE. If you want your constraints to be deferrable, add the DEFERRABLE option in the constraint definition, as shown in Figure 7-9, just before the *storage clause* specification (see Figures 7-6 and 7-8).

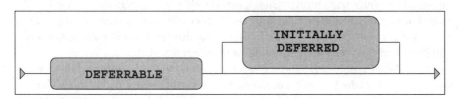

Figure 7-9. *DEFERRABLE option for constraint definitions*

If you allow constraints to be deferrable using the DEFERRABLE option, they still have a default behavior of INITIALLY IMMEDIATE. The INITIALLY option allows you to specify the desired default constraint checking behavior, using IMMEDIATE or DEFERRED.

You can dynamically change or override the default behavior of deferrable constraints at the transaction level with the SET CONSTRAINTS command, as shown in Figure 7-10.

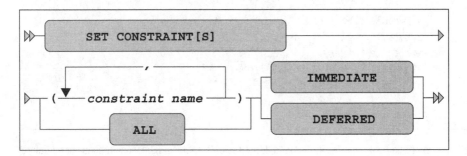

Figure 7-10. *SET CONSTRAINTS command syntax diagram*

At first sight, the complexity of all this constraint-checking syntax may look overwhelming. The following summary may help clarify how it works:

- By default, the Oracle DBMS *always* uses immediate constraint checking.

- You must explicitly allow a constraint to be deferrable. By default, constraints are *not* deferrable.

- If constraints are deferrable, you can choose how they should be checked *by default*: immediate or deferred.

- If constraints are deferrable, you can influence their behavior with the SET CONSTRAINTS command.

7.5 Indexes

In general, rows within a regular table are unordered. Although the Oracle DBMS offers many different ways to physically organize tables on disk (heap tables, index clusters, hash clusters, index-organized tables, and sorted hash clusters), you should never expect the rows to be physically stored in a certain order. Even if a particular order exists today, there is no guarantee that it will be the same tomorrow. This is a fundamental property of relational databases (see Ted Codd's rule 8 in Chapter 1 about physical data independence).

Suppose the EMPLOYEES table contains 50,000 rows (instead of the 14 rows we have), and suppose you want to know which employees have a name starting with a *Q*. Normally, the Oracle DBMS can use only one method to produce the results for this query: by accessing all 50,000 rows (with a full table scan) and checking the name for each of those rows. This could take quite some time, and perhaps there would be no employees at all with such a name.

An *index* on employee names would be very useful in this situation. When you create an index, the Oracle DBMS creates, and starts to maintain, a separate database object containing a sorted list of column values (or column combination values) with row identifiers referring to the corresponding rows in the table. To further optimize access, indexes are internally organized in a tree structure. (See *Oracle Concepts* for more details on physical index structures.) If there were such an index on employee names, the optimizer could decide to abandon the full table scan approach and perform an index search instead. The index offers a very efficient access path to all names, returning all row identifiers of employees with a name starting with a *Q*. This probably would result in a huge performance improvement, because there are only a few database blocks to be visited to produce the query result.

For some of your other queries, indexes on department numbers or birth dates could be useful. You can create as many indexes per table as you like.

In summary, the performance of your SQL statements can often be improved significantly by creating indexes. Sometimes, it is obvious that an index will help, such as when your tables contain a lot of rows and your queries are very selective (only retrieving a few rows). On the other hand, though, you may find that your application benefits from an index on a single-row, single-column table.

Indexes may speed up queries, but the other side of the index picture is the maintenance overhead. Every additional index slows down data manipulation further, because every INSERT/UPDATE/DELETE statement against a table must immediately be processed against all corresponding indexes to keep the indexes synchronized with the table. Also, indexes occupy additional space in your database. This means that you should carefully consider which columns should be indexed and which ones should not be indexed.

These are some suggestions for index candidates:

- Foreign key columns

- Columns often used in WHERE clauses

- Columns often used in ORDER BY and GROUP BY clauses

Here, we'll look at the commands for index creation and management.

Index Creation

Figure 7-11 shows the (simplified) syntax of the CREATE INDEX command.

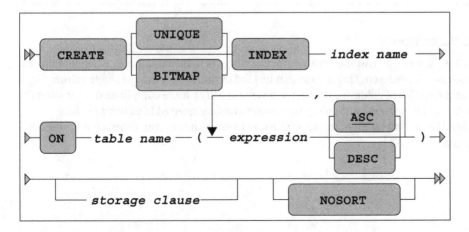

Figure 7-11. *CREATE INDEX command syntax diagram*

The *storage clause* allows you to influence various physical index storage attributes, such as the storage location and the space allocation behavior. See *Oracle SQL Reference* for more details. If the table rows happen to be inserted and stored in index order, you can specify the NOSORT option to speed up index creation. The Oracle DBMS will skip the sort phase (normally needed during index creation), but if the rows turn out to be in the wrong order, the CREATE INDEX command will fail with an error message.

Unique Indexes

Unique indexes serve two purposes: they provide additional access paths to improve response times (like nonunique indexes), and they also prevent duplicate values. You create unique indexes by specifying the UNIQUE option of the CREATE INDEX command (see Figure 7-11).

Note, however, that it is recommended to ensure uniqueness in your tables using the PRIMARY KEY and UNIQUE constraints, leaving it up to the Oracle DBMS to choose an appropriate physical implementation of those constraints.

Bitmap Indexes

Regular indexes work the best if the corresponding columns contain many different values, resulting in better selectivity. Unique indexes offer the best selectivity, because they contain only different values. This means that every equality search (... WHERE COL = ...) results in at most one row. At the other side of the spectrum, if a column contains only a few values (typical examples are gender, status, and yes/no columns), a regular index is not very useful, because the average selectivity of equality searches will be poor.

For such low-cardinality columns, the Oracle DBMS supports *bitmap indexes*. Bitmap indexes also outperform regular indexes if your WHERE clause is complicated, using many AND, OR, and NOT connectives. You create bitmap indexes by specifying the BITMAP option (see Figure 7-11).

■**Caution** Indexes slow down data manipulation, and bitmap indexes are the most expensive index type in terms of maintenance. Don't create bitmap indexes on tables with a lot of DML activity.

Function-Based Indexes

As Figure 7-11 shows, you can specify an *expression* between the parentheses when defining the table columns to be indexed. That means that instead of simply specifying a single column or a comma-separated list of columns, you can choose to specify a more complicated expression in an index definition. Indexes containing such expressions are referred to as *function-based indexes*. See Listing 7-14 for an example, where we create an index on an expression for the yearly salary.

Listing 7-14. *Creating a Function-Based Index*

```
SQL> create index year_sal_idx
  2  on employees (12*msal + coalesce(comm,0));
Index created.

SQL>
```

The index we created in Listing 7-14 can provide an efficient access path for the Oracle DBMS to produce the result of the following query:

```
SQL> select * from employees where 12*msal+coalesce(comm,0) > 18000;
```

Function-based indexes can be used in combination with various NLS features to enable linguistic sorting and searching. See *Oracle SQL Reference* and *Oracle Globalization Support Guide* for more details. One of the exercises at the end of this chapter will ask you to create a function-based index for another specific purpose.

Index Management

Since indexes are maintained by the Oracle DBMS, each table change is immediately propagated to the indexes. In other words, indexes are always up-to-date. However, if your tables incur continuous and heavy DML activity, you might want to consider rebuilding your indexes. Of course, you could simply drop them and then re-create them. However, using the ALTER INDEX ... REBUILD or ALTER INDEX ... COALESCE command is more efficient. Figure 7-12 shows the (partial) syntax diagram for the ALTER INDEX command.

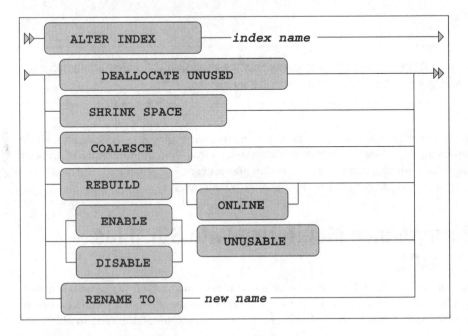

Figure 7-12. *ALTER INDEX command syntax diagram*

The various ALTER INDEX command options in Figure 7-12 (which is far from complete) show that this command belongs to the purview of database administrators, so we will not discuss them here.

Note The ENABLE and DISABLE options of the ALTER INDEX command (see Figure 7-12) apply only to function-based indexes. If you set indexes to UNUSABLE, you must REBUILD (or DROP and CREATE) them before they can be used again.

You can remove indexes with the DROP INDEX command. Figure 7-13 shows the syntax diagram for DROP INDEX.

Figure 7-13. *DROP INDEX command syntax diagram*

Here is an example of removing an index:

```
SQL> drop index year_sal_idx;
Index dropped.

SQL>
```

Tip In periods of heavy data-manipulation activity, without a lot of reporting (retrieval) activity, you may consider dropping indexes temporarily, and re-creating them later.

When you're working with indexes, keep in mind that although you can decide about index *existence* with the CREATE INDEX and DROP INDEX commands, the Oracle optimizer decides about index *usage*. The optimizer chooses the execution plan for each SQL statement. The next section explains how you can see if the optimizer is using your indexes.

7.6 Performance Monitoring with SQL*Plus AUTOTRACE

This is *not* a book about SQL performance tuning. However, in a chapter where we talk about creating indexes, it makes sense to at least show how you can see whether the indexes you create are actually used. What you need for that purpose is a way to see SQL execution plans.

Oracle provides many *diagnostic tools* (such as the SQL trace facility, TKPROF, and EXPLAIN PLAN) to help you with your performance-tuning efforts. However, discussion of these useful Oracle tools is not appropriate here; see *Oracle Performance Tuning Guide* for more details. Fortunately, SQL*Plus offers a limited but user-friendly alternative for those diagnostic tools: the AUTOTRACE facility.

If you want to use all of the options of the AUTOTRACE setting, you may need to prepare your Oracle environment:

- SQL*Plus assumes the existence of a PLAN_TABLE table to store execution plans. If necessary, you can create a local copy in your own schema with the utlxplan.sql script. Oracle Database 10*g* has a public synonym PLAN_TABLE, pointing to a global temporary table. Creating a local PLAN_TABLE is necessary only in earlier releases.

- You must have sufficient privileges for certain AUTOTRACE features. You need the PLUS_TRACE role, created by the plustrce.sql script. The plustrce.sql script must be executed from the SYSTEM database user account. If you don't have access to that privileged account, contact your local database administrator.

Both the utlxplan.sql and plustrce.sql scripts are shipped with the Oracle software. Listing 7-15 shows how you would run these scripts under Microsoft Windows. The question marks in these commands are interpreted as the directory where the Oracle software is installed on your machine.

Listing 7-15. *Preparing for SQL*Plus AUTOTRACE Usage*

```
SQL> connect system/manager
Connected.

SQL> @?\sqlplus\admin\plustrce
Role created.

SQL> grant plustrace to book;
Grant succeeded.

SQL> connect book/book
Connected.

SQL> @?\rdbms\admin\utlxplan
Table created.

SQL>
```

After you have prepared your environment, you can use AUTOTRACE. Figure 7-14 shows the syntax diagram for using AUTOTRACE.

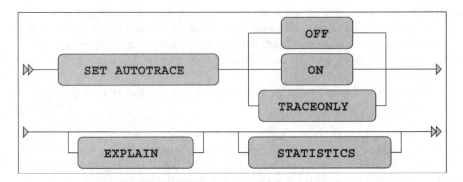

Figure 7-14. *SQL*Plus AUTOTRACE setting syntax diagram*

Listing 7-16 shows an example of using the ON EXPLAIN option. SQL*Plus executes the query, shows the query results, and displays the execution plan.

Listing 7-16. *Showing Query Results and Execution Plans*

```
SQL> set autotrace on explain
SQL> select ename from employees where empno < 7500;

ENAME
---------------
SMITH
ALLEN

Execution Plan
----------------------------------------------------------------
0      SELECT STATEMENT Optimizer=ALL_ROWS
       (Cost=2 Card=2 Bytes=20)
1    0    TABLE ACCESS (BY INDEX ROWID) OF 'EMPLOYEES' (TABLE)
          (Cost=2 Card=2 Bytes=20)
2    1      INDEX (RANGE SCAN) OF 'E_PK' (INDEX (UNIQUE))
            (Cost=1 Card=2)

SQL>
```

From Listing 7-16, you can see that the optimizer decided to use the unique index E_PK for a range scan, and it chose to access the EMPLOYEES table using the row identifiers resulting from the index range scan.

Listing 7-17 shows how you can use the TRACEONLY STATISTICS option to suppress the query results (you don't see the rows) and how you can produce a list of performance-related statement execution statistics. A detailed discussion of these statistics is not appropriate here, but you can see (for example) that no sorting was needed for this query, no data was read from disk (physical reads), and eight buffer cache block visits (consistent gets and db block gets) were needed.

Listing 7-17. *Showing Statistics Only*

```
SQL> set autotrace traceonly statistics
SQL> select * from employees;

14 rows selected.

Statistics
-----------------------------------------------------------
          0  recursive calls
          0  db block gets
          8  consistent gets
          0  physical reads
          0  redo size
       1488  bytes sent via SQL*Net to client
        508  bytes received via SQL*Net from client
          2  SQL*Net roundtrips to/from client
          0  sorts (memory)
          0  sorts (disk)
         14  rows processed

SQL> set autotrace off
SQL>
```

Note If you use AUTOTRACE TRACEONLY EXPLAIN, the SQL statement is *not* executed. This is because you ask for only an execution plan, *not* for statement results and *not* for execution statistics.

7.7 Sequences

Information systems often use monotonically increasing sequence numbers for primary key columns, such as for orders, shipments, registrations, or invoices. You could implement this functionality with a small secondary table to maintain the last/current value for each primary key, but this approach is guaranteed to create performance problems in a multiuser environment. It is much better to use *sequences* in such cases.

Before we continue, there is one important thing you should know about sequences: sequence values can show gaps. That means that certain sequence values may disappear and never make it into the column they were meant for. The Oracle DBMS *cannot guarantee* sequences without gaps (we won't go into the technical details of why this is true). Normally, this should not be a problem. Primary key values are supposed to be unique, and increasing values are nice for sorting purposes, but there is no reason why you shouldn't allow gaps in the values. However, if the absence of gaps is a business requirement, you have no choice other than using a small secondary table to maintain these values.

■**Note** If "absence of gaps" is one of your business requirements, then you probably have a poorly conceived business requirement. You should consider investing some time into reforming your business requirements.

Sequences can be created, changed, and dropped with the following three SQL commands:

```
SQL> create sequence <sequence name> ...
SQL> alter sequence <sequence name> ...
SQL> drop sequence <sequence name>;
```

Figure 7-15 shows the syntax diagram of the CREATE SEQUENCE command. The ALTER SEQUENCE command has a similar syntax.

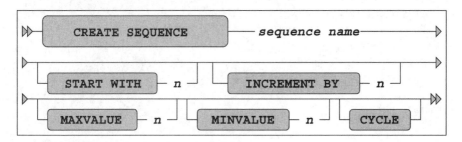

Figure 7-15. *CREATE SEQUENCE command syntax diagram*

A sequence definition may consist of a start value, increment value, minimum value, and maximum value. You can also specify whether the sequence generator should stop when reaching a boundary value, or CYCLE the sequence numbers within the minimum/maximum range. All sequence attributes are optional, as Figure 7-15 shows; they all have default values.

Each sequence has two pseudo columns: NEXTVAL and CURRVAL. The meaning of each of these columns is self-explanatory. Listing 7-18 shows how you can create and use a sequence DEPTNO_SEQ to generate department numbers, using the DUAL table. (Note that normally you would use sequence values in INSERT statements.)

Listing 7-18. *Creating and Using a Sequence*

```
SQL> create sequence deptno_seq
  2  start with 50 increment by 10;

Sequence created.

SQL> select deptno_seq.nextval, deptno_seq.currval from dual;

  NEXTVAL  CURRVAL
-------- --------
      50       50
```

```
SQL> select deptno_seq.currval from dual;

 CURRVAL
--------
      50

SQL> select deptno_seq.currval, deptno_seq.nextval from dual;

 CURRVAL   NEXTVAL
-------- --------
      60        60

SQL>
```

You can use CURRVAL multiple times, in different SQL statements, once you have selected NEXTVAL in an earlier statement, as shown in Listing 7-18. For example, in an order-entry system, you might select a sequence value with NEXTVAL to insert a new order, and then use the same value (CURRVAL) several times to insert multiple line items for that order.

Note the result of the last query in Listing 7-18. Since you select CURRVAL *before* NEXTVAL in the SELECT clause, you might expect to see the current value (50), followed by the next value (60), but apparently that is not the case. This behavior is based on the consistency principle that it doesn't matter in which order you specify the expressions in the SELECT clause of your queries, because you actually select those expressions *at the same time*. Try selecting NEXTVAL multiple times in the same SELECT clause and see what happens (the explanation is the same).

7.8 Synonyms

You can use the CREATE SYNONYM command to create synonyms for tables or views. Once created, you can use synonyms in all your SQL commands instead of "real" table (and view) names. For example, you could use synonyms for tables with very long table names.

Synonyms are especially useful if you are accessing tables from different schemas, not owned by yourself. Without synonyms, you must explicitly prefix those object names with the schema name and a period. The Oracle data dictionary is a perfect example of synonym usage. You can simply specify the data dictionary view names in your queries, without any prefix, although you obviously don't own those data dictionary objects.

Synonyms are a "convenience" feature. They don't provide any additional privileges, and they don't create security risks. They just save you some typing, and they also allow you to make your applications schema-independent.

Schema-independence is important. By using synonyms, your applications don't need to contain explicit schema names. This makes your applications more flexible and easier to maintain, because the mapping to physical schema and object names is in the synonym definitions, separated from the application code.

Figure 7-16 shows the syntax diagram for the CREATE SYNONYM command.

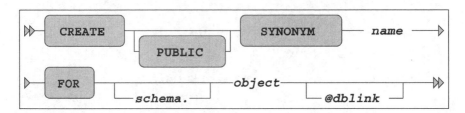

Figure 7-16. *CREATE SYNONYM command syntax diagram*

Oracle supports public and private synonyms, as you can see in Figure 7-16. By default, synonyms are private. You need to specify the PUBLIC keyword to create public synonyms. All database users can *use* public synonyms, but you need DBA privileges to be able to *create* them. The synonyms for the data dictionary objects are examples of public synonyms. Anyone can create private synonyms, but only their owners can use them.

Caution Although synonyms are useful, they can also cause performance problems. In particular, public synonyms are known to cause such problems. For further details, go to Steve Adams's web site (http://www.ixora.com.au) and search for "avoiding public synonyms."

Listing 7-19 shows how you can create a synonym, how the synonym shows up in the data dictionary views CAT and USER_SYNONYMS, and how you can drop a synonym.

Listing 7-19. *Creating and Dropping a Synonym*

```
SQL> create synonym e for employees;
Synonym created.

SQL> describe e
 Name                     Null?    Type
 ------------------------ -------- ------------
 EMPNO                    NOT NULL NUMBER(4)
 ENAME                    NOT NULL VARCHAR2(8)
 INIT                     NOT NULL VARCHAR2(5)
 JOB                               VARCHAR2(8)
 MGR                               NUMBER(4)
 BDATE                    NOT NULL DATE
 MSAL                     NOT NULL NUMBER(6,2)
 COMM                              NUMBER(6,2)
 DEPTNO                            NUMBER(2)

SQL> select * from cat;
```

```
TABLE_NAME            TABLE_TYPE
--------------------  -----------
EMPLOYEES             TABLE
DEPARTMENTS           TABLE
SALGRADES             TABLE
COURSES               TABLE
OFFERINGS             TABLE
REGISTRATIONS         TABLE
HISTORY               TABLE
DEPTNO_SEQ            SEQUENCE
E                     SYNONYM

SQL> select synonym_name, table_owner, table_name
  2  from    user_synonyms;

SYNONYM_NAME          TABLE_OWNER TABLE_NAME
--------------------  ----------- ----------------
E                     BOOK        EMPLOYEES

SQL> drop synonym e;
Synonym dropped.

SQL>
```

Synonyms are often used in distributed database environments to implement full data independence. The user (or database application) does not need to know where (in which database) tables or views are located. Normally, you need to specify explicit database links using the at sign (@) in the object name, but synonyms can hide those database link references.

7.9 The CURRENT_SCHEMA Setting

The ALTER SESSION command provides another convenient way to save you the effort of prefixing object names with their schema name, but without using synonyms. This is another "convenience" feature, just like synonyms.

Suppose the demo schema SCOTT (with the EMP and DEPT tables) is present in your database, and suppose you are currently connected as database user BOOK. In that situation, you can use the ALTER SESSION command as shown in Listing 7-20.

Listing 7-20. *The CURRENT_SCHEMA Setting*

```
SQL> alter session set current_schema=scott;
Session altered.

SQL> show user
USER is "BOOK"

SQL> select * from dept;
```

```
DEPTNO DNAME              LOC
-------- -------------- -------------
      10 ACCOUNTING      NEW YORK
      20 RESEARCH        DALLAS
      30 SALES           CHICAGO
      40 OPERATIONS      BOSTON

SQL> alter session set current_schema=book;
Session altered.

SQL>
```

You can compare the CURRENT_SCHEMA setting in the database with the change directory (cd) command at the operating system level. In a similar way, it allows you to address all objects locally.

Again, this does not change anything with regard to security and privileges. If you really want to assume the identity of a schema owner, you must use the SQL*Plus CONNECT command, and provide the username/schema name and the corresponding password.

7.10 The DROP TABLE Command

You can drop your tables with the DROP TABLE command. Figure 7-17 shows the syntax diagram for the DROP TABLE command.

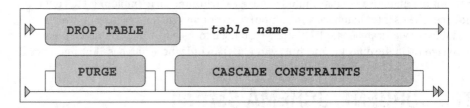

Figure 7-17. *DROP TABLE command syntax diagram*

Unless you have specific system privileges, you cannot drop tables owned by other database users. Also, you cannot roll back a DROP TABLE command. As you've learned in previous chapters, this is true for all DDL statements (CREATE, ALTER, and DROP).

"*Errare humanum est,*" as the Romans said. Because human errors occur occasionally, Oracle Database 10*g* introduced the concept of the database *recycle bin*. By default, all dropped tables (and their dependent objects) initially end up in the recycle bin. You can query the recycle bin using the [USER_]RECYCLEBIN view, as shown in Listing 7-21. To make sure we start with an empty recycle bin, we begin the experiment with a PURGE command.

Listing 7-21. *Dropping Tables and Querying the Recycle Bin*

```
SQL> purge recyclebin;
Recyclebin purged.

SQL> drop table history;
Table dropped.

SQL> select object_name, original_name, droptime
  2  from   recyclebin;

OBJECT_NAME                        ORIGINAL_NAME         DROPTIME
--------------------------------   -------------------   -------------------
BIN$mlRH1je9TBOeVEUhukIpCw==$0 H_PK                      2004-07-01:20:22:23
BIN$EETkZCYORSKCR3BhtF9cJw==$0 HISTORY                  2004-07-01:20:22:23

SQL>
```

As you can see, the objects are renamed, but the original names are kept as well. There is one entry for the HISTORY table and one entry for the primary key index. You can recover tables (and optionally rename them) from the recycle bin by using the FLASHBACK TABLE command:

```
SQL> flashback table history to before drop
  2  [rename to <new name>];
Flashback complete.

SQL>
```

■**Caution** There is no guarantee the FLASHBACK TABLE command always succeeds. The recycle bin can be purged explicitly (by a database administrator) or implicitly (by the Oracle DBMS).

If you want to drop a table and bypass the recycle bin, you can use the PURGE option of the DROP TABLE command, as shown in Figure 7-17.

If you drop a table, you implicitly drop certain dependent database objects, such as indexes, triggers, and table privileges granted to other database users. You also invalidate certain other database objects, such as views and packages. Keep this in mind during database reorganizations. To re-create a table, it is *not* enough to simply issue a CREATE TABLE command after a DROP TABLE command. You need to reestablish the full environment around the dropped table.

If you issue a DROP TABLE command, you may get the following error message if other tables contain foreign key constraints referencing the table that you are trying to drop:

```
ORA-02449: unique/primary keys in table referenced by foreign keys
```

Try to drop the EMPLOYEES table, and see what happens. You can solve this problem by using the CASCADE CONSTRAINTS option, as shown in Figure 7-17. Note, however, that this means that all offending foreign key constraints are dropped, too.

7.11 The TRUNCATE Command

The TRUNCATE command allows you to delete all rows from a table. Figure 7-18 shows the syntax diagram for the TRUNCATE command.

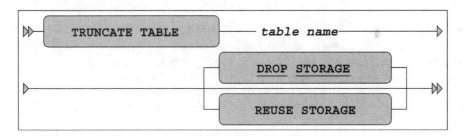

Figure 7-18. *TRUNCATE command syntax diagram*

The default behavior is DROP STORAGE, as indicated by the underlining in Figure 7-18.

Compared with DROP TABLE (followed by a CREATE TABLE), the big advantage of TRUNCATE is that all related indexes and privileges survive the TRUNCATE operation.

This command has two possible advantages over the DELETE command: the performance (response time) is typically better for large tables, and you can optionally reclaim the allocated space. However, there is a price to pay for these two advantages: you cannot perform a ROLLBACK to undo a TRUNCATE, because TRUNCATE is a DDL command. The Oracle DBMS treats DDL commands as single-statement transactions and commits them immediately.

7.12 The COMMENT Command

The COMMENT command allows you to add clarifying (semantic) explanations about tables and table columns to the data dictionary. Figure 7-19 shows the syntax diagram for this command.

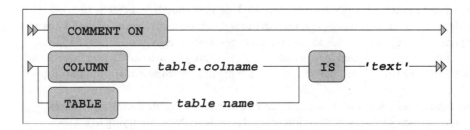

Figure 7-19. *COMMENT command syntax diagram*

Listing 7-22 shows how you can use the COMMENT command to add comments to the data dictionary for a table (SALGRADES) and a column (EMPLOYEES.COMM), and how you can retrieve that information from the data dictionary.

Listing 7-22. *Adding Comments to Columns and Tables*

```
SQL> comment on table salgrades
  2  is       'Salary grades and net bonuses';
Comment created.

SQL> comment on column employees.comm
  2  is       'For sales reps only';
Comment created.

SQL> select comments
  2  from    user_tab_comments
  3  where   table_name = 'SALGRADES';

COMMENTS
-------------------------------------------
Salary grades and net bonuses

SQL> select comments
  2  from    user_col_comments
  3  where   table_name  = 'EMPLOYEES'
  4  and     column_name = 'COMM';

COMMENTS
-------------------------------------------
For sales reps only

SQL>
```

7.13 Exercises

The following exercises will help you to better understand the concepts described in this chapter. The answers are presented in Appendix D.

1. Listing 7-5 defines the constraint E_SALES_CHK in a rather cryptic way. Formulate the same constraint without using DECODE and NVL2.

2. Why do you think the constraint E_DEPT_FK (in Listing 7-7) is created with a separate ALTER TABLE command?

3. Although this is not covered in this chapter, try to come up with an explanation of the following phenomenon: when using sequences, you cannot use the pseudo column CURRVAL in your session without first calling the pseudo column NEXTVAL:

```
SQL> select deptno_seq.currval from dual;
select deptno_seq.currval from dual
       *
ERROR at line 1:
ORA-08002: sequence DEPTNO_SEQ.CURRVAL is not yet defined in this session

SQL>
```

4. Why is it better to use sequences in a multiuser environment, as opposed to maintaining a secondary table with the last/current sequence values?

5. How is it possible that the EVALUATION column of the REGISTRATIONS table accepts null values, in spite of the constraint R_EVAL_CHK (see Listing 7-11)?

6. If you define a PRIMARY KEY or UNIQUE constraint, the Oracle DBMS normally creates a unique index under the covers (if none of the existing indexes can be used) to check the constraint. Investigate and explain what happens if you define such a constraint as DEFERRABLE.

7. You can use function-based indexes to implement "conditional uniqueness" constraints. Create a unique function-based index on the REGISTRATIONS table to check the following constraint: employees are allowed to attend the OAU course only once. They may attend other courses as many times as they like. Test your solution with the following command (it should fail):

```
SQL> insert into registrations values (7900,'OAU',trunc(sysdate),null);
```

Hint: You can use a CASE expression in the index expression.

CHAPTER 8

■ ■ ■

Retrieval: Multiple Tables and Aggregation

This chapter resumes the discussion of the retrieval possibilities of the SQL language. It is a logical continuation of Chapters 4 and 5.

The first section introduces the concept of *row* or *tuple variables*. We did not discuss them so far, because we haven't needed them up to now. By the way, most SQL textbooks don't mention tuple variables at all—at least not the way this book does. When you start specifying multiple tables in the FROM clause of your SELECT statements, it is a good idea to start using tuple variables (also referred to as *table aliases* in Oracle) in a consistent way.

Section 8.2 explains *joins*, which specify a comma-separated list of table names in the FROM clause and filter the desired row combinations with the WHERE clause. Section 8.3 shows the ANSI/ISO standard syntax to produce joins (supported since Oracle9*i*), and Section 8.4 goes into more details about *outer joins*.

In large information systems (containing huge amounts of detailed information), it is quite common to be interested in *aggregated* (condensed) information. For example, you may want to get a course overview for a specific year, showing the number of attendees per course, with the average evaluation scores. You can formulate the underlying queries you need for such reports by using the GROUP BY clause of the SELECT command. *Group functions* (such as COUNT, AVG, MIN, and MAX) play an important role in such queries. If you have aggregated your data with a GROUP BY clause, you can optionally use the HAVING clause to filter query results at the group level. Topics surrounding basic aggregation are covered in Sections 8.5, 8.6, and 8.7. Section 8.8 continues the discussion of aggregation to introduce some more advanced features of the GROUP BY clause, such as CUBE and ROLLUP. Section 8.9 introduces the concept of *partitioned outer joins*.

Section 8.10 discusses the three set operators of the SQL language: UNION, MINUS, and INTERSECT. Finally, the chapter finishes with exercises.

8.1 Tuple Variables

Until now, we have formulated our SQL statements as follows:

```
SQL> select ename, init, job
  2  from    employees
  3  where   deptno = 20
```

Actually, this statement is rather incomplete. In this chapter, we must be a little more precise, because the SQL commands are getting slightly more complicated. To be complete and accurate, we should have written this statement as shown in Listing 8.1.

Listing 8-1. *Using Tuple Variables in a Query*

```
SQL> select e.ename, e.init, e.job
  2  from    employees e
  3  where   e.deptno = 20
```

In this example, e is a *tuple variable*. Tuple is just a "dignified" term for row, derived from the relational theory. In Oracle, tuple variables are referred to as *table aliases* (which is actually rather confusing), and the ANSI/ISO standard talks about *correlation names*.

Note the syntax in Listing 8-1: you "declare" the tuple variable in the FROM clause, immediately following the table name, separated by white space only.

A tuple variable always ranges over a table, or a table expression. In other words, in the example in Listing 8-1, e is a variable representing *one* row from the EMPLOYEES table at any time. Within the context of a specific row, you can refer to specific column (or attribute) values, as shown in the SELECT and WHERE clauses of the example in Listing 8-1. The tuple variable precedes the column name, separated by a period. Figure 8-1 shows the column reference e.JOB and its value ADMIN for employee 7900.

	EMPNO	ENAME	INIT	JOB	...	DEPTNO
	...					
	7876	ADAMS	AA			
e	7900	JONES	R	ADMIN	...	30
	7902	FORD	...			
	7934	...				
	...					

Figure 8-1. *The EMPLOYEES table with a tuple variable*

Do you remember those old-fashioned calendars with one page per month, with a transparent strip that could move up and down to select a certain week, and a little window that could move on that strip from the left to the right to select a specific day of the month? If not, Figure 8-2 shows an example of such a calendar. The transparent strip would be the tuple variable in that metaphor.

Figure 8-2. *Calendar with sliding day indicator window*

Using the concept of tuple variables, we can describe the execution of the SQL command in Listing 8-1 as follows:

1. The tuple variable e ranges (row by row) over the EMPLOYEES table (the row order is irrelevant).

2. Each row e is checked against the WHERE clause, and it is passed to an intermediate result set if the WHERE clause evaluates to TRUE.

3. For each row in the intermediate result set, the expressions in the SELECT clause are evaluated to produce the final query result.

As long as you are writing simple queries (as we have done so far in this book), you don't need to worry about tuple variables. The Oracle DBMS understands your SQL intentions anyway. However, as soon as your SQL statements become more complicated, it might be wise (or even mandatory) to start using tuple variables. Tuple variables always have at least one advantage: they enhance the readability and maintainability of your SQL code.

8.2 Joins

You can specify multiple tables in the FROM component of a query. We start this section with an intended mistake, to evoke an Oracle error message. See what happens in Listing 8-2 where our intention is to discover which employees belong to which departments.

Listing 8-2. *Ambiguously Defined Columns*

```
SQL> select deptno, location, ename, init
  2  from   employees, departments;
select deptno, location, ename, init
       *
ERROR at line 1:
ORA-00918: column ambiguously defined

SQL>
```

The message, including the asterisk (*), reveals the problem here. The Oracle DBMS cannot figure out which DEPTNO column we are referring to. Both tables mentioned in the FROM clause have a DEPTNO column, and that's why we get an error message.

Cartesian Products

See Listing 8-3 for a second attempt to find which employees belong to which departments. Because we fixed the ambiguity issue, we get query results, but these results don't meet our expectations. The tuple variables e and d range *freely* over both tables, because there is no constraining WHERE clause; therefore, the query result we get is the *Cartesian product* of both tables, resulting in 56 rows. We have 14 employees and 4 departments, and 14 times 4 results in 56 possible combinations.

Listing 8-3. *The Cartesian Product of Two Tables*

```
SQL> select d.deptno, d.location, e.ename, e.init
  2  from   employees e, departments d;

  DEPTNO LOCATION ENAME    INIT
-------- -------- -------- -----
      10 NEW YORK SMITH    N
      10 NEW YORK ALLEN    JAM
      10 NEW YORK WARD     TF
      10 NEW YORK JONES    JM
      10 NEW YORK MARTIN   P
      10 NEW YORK BLAKE    R
      10 NEW YORK CLARK    AB
      10 NEW YORK SCOTT    SCJ
...
```

```
    40 BOSTON    ADAMS    AA
    40 BOSTON    JONES    R
    40 BOSTON    FORD     MG
    40 BOSTON    MILLER   TJA

56 rows selected.

SQL>
```

Equijoins

The results in Listing 8-3 reveal the remaining problem: the query lacks a WHERE clause. In Listing 8-4, we fix the problem by adding a WHERE clause, and we also add an ORDER BY clause to get the results ordered by department, and within each department, by employee name.

Listing 8-4. *Joining Two Tables*

```
SQL> select  d.deptno, d.location, e.ename, e.init
  2  from    employees e, departments d
  3  where   e.deptno = d.deptno
  4  order   by d.deptno, e.ename;

 DEPTNO LOCATION ENAME    INIT
-------- -------- -------- -----
     10 NEW YORK CLARK    AB
     10 NEW YORK KING     CC
     10 NEW YORK MILLER   TJA
     20 DALLAS   ADAMS    AA
     20 DALLAS   FORD     MG
     20 DALLAS   JONES    JM
     20 DALLAS   SCOTT    SCJ
     20 DALLAS   SMITH    N
     30 CHICAGO  ALLEN    JAM
     30 CHICAGO  BLAKE    R
     30 CHICAGO  JONES    R
     30 CHICAGO  MARTIN   P
     30 CHICAGO  TURNER   JJ
     30 CHICAGO  WARD     TF

14 rows selected.

SQL>
```

Listing 8-4 shows a *join* or, to be more precise, an *equijoin*. This is the most common join type in SQL.

INTERMEZZO: SQL LAYOUT CONVENTIONS

Your SQL statements should be correct in the first place, of course. As soon as SQL statements get longer and more complicated, it becomes more and more important to adopt a certain layout style. Additional white space (spaces, tabs, and new lines) has no meaning in the SQL language, but it certainly enhances code readability and maintainability. You could have spread the query in Listing 8-4 over multiple lines, as follows:

```
SQL> select   d.deptno
  2 ,          d.location
  3 ,          e.ename
  4 ,          e.init
  5 from       employees  e
  6 ,          departments d
  7 where      e.deptno = d.deptno
  8 order by d.deptno
  9 ,          e.ename
```

This SQL layout convention has proved itself to be very useful in practice. Note the placement of the commas at the beginning of the next line as opposed to the end of the current line. This makes adding and removing lines easier, resulting in fewer unintended errors. Any other standard is fine, too. This is mostly a matter of taste. Just make sure to adopt a style and use it consistently.

Non-equijoins

If you use a comparison operator other than an equal sign in the WHERE clause in a join, it is called a *non-equijoin* or *thetajoin*. For an example of a thetajoin, see Listing 8-5, which calculates the total annual salary for each employee.

Listing 8-5. *Thetajoin Example*

```
SQL> select e.ename          employee
  2 ,        12*e.msal+s.bonus total_salary
  3 from     employees e
  4 ,        salgrades s
  5 where    e.msal between s.lowerlimit
  6                    and s.upperlimit;

EMPLOYEE TOTAL_SALARY
-------- ------------
SMITH            9600
JONES            9600
ADAMS           13200
WARD            15050
MARTIN          15050
MILLER          15650
TURNER          18100
```

```
ALLEN            19300
CLARK            29600
BLAKE            34400
JONES            35900
SCOTT            36200
FORD             36200
KING             60500

14 rows selected.

SQL>
```

By the way, you can choose any name you like for your tuple variables. Listing 8-5 uses e and s, but any other names would work, including longer names consisting of any combination of letters and digits. Enhanced readability is the only reason why this book uses (as much as possible) the first characters of table names as tuple variables in SQL statements.

Joins of Three or More Tables

Let's try to enhance the query of Listing 8-5. In a third column, we also want to see the name of the department that the employee works for. Department names are stored in the DEPARTMENTS table, so we add three more lines to the query, as shown in Listing 8-6.

Listing 8-6. *Joining Three Tables*

```
SQL> select e.ename           employee
  2  ,       12*e.msal+s.bonus total_salary
  3  ,       d.dname           department
  4  from    employees  e
  5  ,       salgrades  s
  6  ,       departments d
  7  where   e.msal between s.lowerlimit
  8                     and s.upperlimit
  9  and     e.deptno = d.deptno;

EMPLOYEE TOTAL_SALARY DEPARTMENT
-------- ------------ ----------
SMITH            9600 TRAINING
JONES            9600 SALES
ADAMS           13200 TRAINING
WARD            15050 SALES
MARTIN          15050 SALES
MILLER          15650 ACCOUNTING
TURNER          18100 SALES
ALLEN           19300 SALES
CLARK           29600 ACCOUNTING
BLAKE           34400 SALES
JONES           35900 TRAINING
```

```
SCOTT            36200 TRAINING
FORD             36200 TRAINING
KING             60500 ACCOUNTING

14 rows selected.

SQL>
```

The main principle is simple. We now have three free tuple variables (e, s, and d) ranging over three tables. Therefore, we need (at least) two conditions in the WHERE clause to get the correct row combinations in the query result.

For the sake of completeness, you should note that the SQL language supports table names as default tuple variables, without the need to declare them explicitly in the FROM clause. Look at the following example:

```
SQL> select employees.ename, departments.location
  2  from    employees, departments
  3  where   employees.deptno = departments.deptno;
```

This SQL statement is syntactically correct. However, we will avoid using this SQL "feature" in this book. It is rather confusing to refer to a table in one place and to refer to a specific row from a table in another place with the same name, without making a clear distinction between row and table references. Moreover, the names of the tables used in this book are long enough to justify declaring explicit tuple variables in the FROM clause and using them everywhere else in the SQL statement, thus reducing the number of keystrokes.

Self-Joins

In SQL, you can also join a table to itself. Although this join type is essentially the same as a regular join, it has its own name: *autojoin* or *self-join*. In other words, autojoins contain tables being referenced more than once in the FROM clause. This provides another good reason why you should use explicit tuple variables (as opposed to relying on table names as implicit tuple variables) in your SQL statements. In autojoins, the table names result in ambiguity issues. So why not use tuple variables consistently in all your SQL statements?

Listing 8-7 shows an example of an autojoin. The query produces an overview of all employees born after January 1, 1965, with a second column showing the name of their managers. (You may want to refer to Figure C-3 in Appendix C, which shows a diagram of the hierarchy of the EMPLOYEES table.)

Listing 8-7. *Autojoin (Self-Join) Example*

```
SQL> select e.ename as employee
  2  ,       m.ename as manager
  3  from    employees m
  4  ,       employees e
  5  where   e.mgr = m.empno
  6  and     e.bdate > date '1965-01-01';
```

```
EMPLOYEE MANAGER
-------- --------
TURNER   BLAKE
JONES    BLAKE
ADAMS    SCOTT
JONES    KING
CLARK    KING
SMITH    FORD

6 rows selected.

SQL>
```

Because we have two tuple variables e and m, both ranging freely over the same table, we get 14 × 14 = 196 possible row combinations. The WHERE clause filters out the correct combinations, where row m reflects the manager of row e.

8.3 Alternative ANSI/ISO Standard Join Syntax

The join examples shown in the previous section use the Cartesian product operator (the comma in the FROM clause) as a starting point, and then filter the rows using an appropriate WHERE clause. There's absolutely nothing wrong with that approach, and the syntax is fully compliant with the ANSI/ISO SQL standard, but the ANSI/ISO SQL standard also supports alternative syntax to specify joins. This alternative join syntax is covered in this section.

First, let's look again at the join statement in Listing 8-7. You could argue that the WHERE clause of that query contains two different condition types: line 5 contains the *join condition* to make sure you combine the right rows, and line 6 is a "real" (nonjoin) condition to filter the employees based on their birth dates.

Listing 8-8 shows an equivalent query, producing the same results, using a different join syntax. Note the keywords JOIN and ON. Also note also that this join syntax doesn't use any commas in the FROM clause.

Listing 8-8. *JOIN . . . ON Example*

```
SQL> select e.ename as employee
  2  ,      m.ename as manager
  3  from   employees m
  4         JOIN
  5         employees e
  6         ON e.mgr = m.empno
  7  where  e.bdate > date '1965-01-01'
  8  order  by employee;

EMPLOYEE MANAGER
-------- --------
ADAMS    SCOTT
CLARK    KING
```

```
JONES     BLAKE
JONES     KING
SMITH     FORD
TURNER    BLAKE

6 rows selected.

SQL>
```

The syntax of Listing 8-8 is more elegant than the syntax in Listing 8-7, because the join is fully specified in the FROM clause and the WHERE clause contains only the nonjoin condition.

Natural Joins

You can also use the NATURAL JOIN operator in the FROM clause. Listing 8-9 shows an example that joins the EMPLOYEES table with the HISTORY table.

Question: Before reading on, how is it possible that Listing 8-9 produces 15 rows in the result, instead of 14?

Listing 8-9. *Natural Join Example*

```
SQL> select ename, beginyear, msal, deptno
  2  from   employees
  3         natural join
  4         history;

ENAME    BEGINYEAR    MSAL    DEPTNO
-------- --------- -------- --------
SMITH         2000      800       20
ALLEN         1999     1600       30
WARD          1992     1250       30
WARD          2000     1250       30
JONES         1999     2975       20
MARTIN        1999     1250       30
BLAKE         1989     2850       30
CLARK         1988     2450       10
SCOTT         2000     3000       20
KING          2000     5000       10
TURNER        2000     1500       30
ADAMS         2000     1100       20
JONES         2000      800       30
FORD          2000     3000       20
MILLER        2000     1300       10

15 rows selected.

SQL>
```

Explanation: To understand what's happening in Listing 8-9, you must know how the NATURAL JOIN operator is defined in the SQL language. Listing 8-9 illustrates the behavior of the NATURAL JOIN operator:

1. The NATURAL JOIN operator determines which columns the two tables (EMPLOYEES and HISTORY) have in common. In this case, these are the three columns EMPNO, MSAL, and DEPTNO.

2. It joins the two tables (using an equijoin) over *all columns* they have in common.

3. It suppresses the duplicate columns resulting from the join operation in the previous step. This is why you don't get an error message about MSAL and DEPTNO in the SELECT clause being ambiguously defined.

4. Finally, the NATURAL JOIN operator evaluates the remaining query clauses. In Listing 8-9, the only remaining clause is the SELECT clause. The final result shows the desired four columns.

Apparently, every employee occurs only once in the result, except WARD. This means that this employee has been employed by the same department (30) for the same salary (1250) during two distinct periods of his career. This is a pure coincidence. If the query had returned 14 rows instead of 15, we would probably not have been triggered to investigate the query for correctness. Remember that some *wrong* queries may give "correct" results by accident.

This example shows that you should be very careful when using the NATURAL JOIN operator. Probably the biggest danger is that a natural join may "suddenly" start producing strange and undesirable results if you add new columns to your tables, or you rename existing columns, thus accidentally creating matching column names.

■**Caution** Natural joins are safe only if you practice a very strict column-naming standard in your database designs.

Equijoins on Columns with the Same Name

SQL offers an alternative way to specify equijoins, allowing you to explicitly specify the columns you want to participate in the equijoin operation. As you saw in Listing 8-8, you can use the ON clause followed by fully specified join predicates. You can also use the USING clause, specifying column names instead of full predicates. See Listing 8-10 for an example.

Listing 8-10. *JOIN … USING Example*

```
SQL> select e.ename, e.bdate
  2  ,       h.deptno, h.msal
  3  from    employees e
  4          join
  5          history h
  6          using (empno)
  7  where   e.job = 'ADMIN';
```

```
ENAME      BDATE          DEPTNO    MSAL
--------   -----------    --------  --------
JONES      03-DEC-1969        30       800
MILLER     23-JAN-1962        10      1275
MILLER     23-JAN-1962        10      1280
MILLER     23-JAN-1962        10      1290
MILLER     23-JAN-1962        10      1300

SQL>
```

Note that you need tuple variables again, because you join over only the EMPNO column; the columns h.DEPTNO and e.DEPTNO are now different.

Figure 8-3 shows the syntax diagram of the ANSI/ISO join syntax, including the NATURAL JOIN operator, the ON clause, and the USING clause.

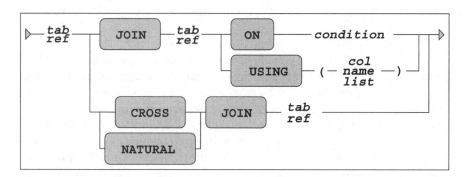

Figure 8-3. *ANSI/ISO join syntax diagram*

Note that you can also use a CROSS JOIN syntax. The result is identical to the effect of the comma operator in the FROM clause: the Cartesian product.

The examples in the remainder of this book will show a mixture of "old-fashioned" joins (as introduced in Section 8.2) and the alternative ANSI/ISO SQL join syntax explained in this section.

8.4 Outer Joins

Earlier in the chapter, in Listing 8-4, we executed a regular join (an equijoin) similar to the one shown in Listing 8-11.

Listing 8-11. *Regular Join*

```
SQL> select d.deptno, d.location
  2  ,       e.ename, e.init
  3  from    employees e, departments d
  4  where   e.deptno = d.deptno
  5  order   by d.deptno, e.ename;
```

```
DEPTNO LOCATION ENAME     INIT
-------- -------- --------  -----
    10 NEW YORK CLARK     AB
    10 NEW YORK KING      CC
    10 NEW YORK MILLER    TJA
    20 DALLAS   ADAMS     AA
    20 DALLAS   FORD      MG
    20 DALLAS   JONES     JM
    20 DALLAS   SCOTT     SCJ
    20 DALLAS   SMITH     N
    30 CHICAGO  ALLEN     JAM
    30 CHICAGO  BLAKE     R
    30 CHICAGO  JONES     R
    30 CHICAGO  MARTIN    P
    30 CHICAGO  TURNER    JJ
    30 CHICAGO  WARD      TF

14 rows selected.

SQL>
```

The result in Listing 8-11 shows no rows for department 40, for an obvious reason: that department does exist in the DEPARTMENTS table, but it has no corresponding employees. In other words, if tuple variable d refers to department 40, there is not a single row e in the EMPLOYEES table to make the WHERE clause evaluate to TRUE.

If you want the fact that department 40 exists to be reflected in your join results, you can make that happen with an *outer join*. For outer joins in Oracle, you can choose between two syntax options:

- The "old" outer join syntax, supported by Oracle since many releases, and implemented many years before the ANSI/ISO standard defined a more elegant outer join syntax

- The ANSI/ISO standard outer join syntax

We will discuss an example of both outer join syntax variants, based on the regular join in Listing 8-11.

Old Oracle-Specific Outer Join Syntax

First, change the fourth line of the command in Listing 8-11 and add a plus sign between parentheses, as shown in Listing 8-12.

Listing 8-12. *The (+) Outer Join Syntax*

```
SQL> select d.deptno, d.location
  2  ,       e.ename, e.init
  3  from    employees e, departments d
  4  where   e.deptno(+) = d.deptno
  5  order   by d.deptno, e.ename;
```

```
DEPTNO LOCATION ENAME     INIT
-------- -------- --------- -----
    10 NEW YORK CLARK     AB
    10 NEW YORK KING      CC
    10 NEW YORK MILLER    TJA
    20 DALLAS   ADAMS     AA
    20 DALLAS   FORD      MG
    20 DALLAS   JONES     JM
    20 DALLAS   SCOTT     SCJ
    20 DALLAS   SMITH     N
    30 CHICAGO  ALLEN     JAM
    30 CHICAGO  BLAKE     R
    30 CHICAGO  JONES     R
    30 CHICAGO  MARTIN    P
    30 CHICAGO  TURNER    JJ
    30 CHICAGO  WARD      TF
    40 BOSTON

15 rows selected.

SQL>
```

As you can see, department 40 now also appears in the result. The effect of the addition (+) in the WHERE clause has combined department 40 with two null values for the employee data. The main disadvantage of this outer join syntax is that you must make sure to add the (+) operator in the right places in your SQL command. Failing to do so normally results in disabling the outer join effect. Another disadvantage of this outer join syntax is its lack of readability.

New Outer Join Syntax

The new ANSI/ISO outer join syntax is much more elegant and readable. Listing 8-13 shows the version to get the same results as in Listing 8-12.

Listing 8-13. *ANSI/ISO Outer Join Example*

```
SQL> select deptno, d.location
  2  ,       e.ename, e.init
  3  from    employees e
  4          right outer join
  5          departments d
  6          using (deptno)
  7  order   by deptno, e.ename;

DEPTNO LOCATION ENAME     INIT
-------- -------- --------- -----
    10 NEW YORK CLARK     AB
    10 NEW YORK KING      CC
    10 NEW YORK MILLER    TJA
```

```
      20  DALLAS    ADAMS    AA
      20  DALLAS    FORD     MG
      20  DALLAS    JONES    JM
      20  DALLAS    SCOTT    SCJ
      20  DALLAS    SMITH    N
      30  CHICAGO   ALLEN    JAM
      30  CHICAGO   BLAKE    R
      30  CHICAGO   JONES    R
      30  CHICAGO   MARTIN   P
      30  CHICAGO   TURNER   JJ
      30  CHICAGO   WARD     TF
      40  BOSTON

15 rows selected.

SQL>
```

In Listing 8-13 we used a RIGHT OUTER JOIN, because we suspect the presence of rows at the right-hand side (the DEPARTMENTS table) without corresponding rows at the left-hand side (the EMPLOYEES table). If you switched the two table names in the FROM clause, you would need the LEFT OUTER JOIN operator. Oracle also supports the FULL OUTER JOIN syntax, where both tables participating in the join operation handle rows without corresponding rows on the other side in a special way. Figure 8-4 shows all three outer join syntax possibilities.

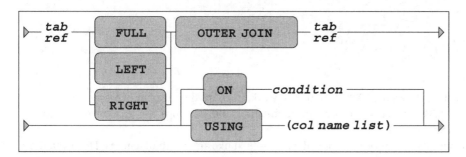

Figure 8-4. *ANSI/ISO outer join syntax diagram*

The outer join operator is especially useful if you want to aggregate (summarize) data; for example, when you want to produce a course overview showing the number of attendees for each scheduled course. In such an overview, you obviously also want to see all scheduled courses for which no registrations are entered yet, so you might consider canceling or post-poning those courses. This type of query (with aggregation) is the topic of Section 8.5.

Outer Joins and Performance

Although outer joins obviously imply some additional processing for the DBMS, there is no reason to avoid outer joins for performance reasons. The Oracle optimizer knows how to handle outer joins efficiently. Moreover, given a certain data model, you sometimes *need* outer joins.

Don't try to invent your own workarounds in such cases, and don't believe unfounded statements like "outer joins are bad."

In Section 8.9, we will revisit outer joins to discuss *partitioned* outer joins.

8.5 The GROUP BY Component

Until now, we have considered queries showing information about only individual rows. Each row in our query results so far had a one-to-one correspondence with some row in the database. However, in real life, you often want to produce aggregated information from a database, where the rows in the query results represent information about a set of database rows. For example, you might want to produce an overview showing the number of employees (the head count) per department. For this type of query, you need the GROUP BY clause of the SELECT command, as shown in Listing 8-14.

Listing 8-14. *The GROUP BY Clause*

```
SQL> select e.deptno       as "department"
  2  ,        count(e.empno) as "number of employees"
  3  from    employees e
  4  group  by e.deptno;

department number of employees
---------- -------------------
        10                   3
        20                   5
        30                   6

SQL>
```

Listing 8-14 shows the COUNT function at work, to count the number of employees per department. COUNT is an example of a *group function*, and we'll look at it and the other group functions in Section 8.6.

The result of this query is a table, of course—just like any result of a query. However, there is no one-to-one mapping anymore between the rows of the EMPLOYEES table and the three rows of the result. Instead, you aggregate employee data per department.

To explain how the GROUP BY operator works, and how the SQL language handles aggregation, Listing 8-15 shows an imaginary representation of an intermediate result. Listing 8-15 shows a pseudo-table, with three rows and six columns. For readability, some columns of the EMPLOYEES table are omitted. In the last column, you see the three different department numbers, and the other five columns show *sets* of attribute values. These sets are represented by enumerating their elements in a comma-separated list between braces. Some of these sets contain null values only, such as e.COMM for departments 10 and 20.

■**Note** The representation in Listing 8-15 is purely fictitious and only serves educational purposes. Data structures as shown in Listing 8-15 do not occur in reality.

Listing 8-15. *The Effect of GROUP BY e.DEPTNO*

e.EMPNO	e.JOB	e.MGR	e.MSAL	e.COMM	e.DEPTNO
=======	=============	======	======	======	========
{7782	{'MANAGER'	{7839	{2450	{NULL	10
,7839	,'DIRECTOR'	,NULL	,5000	,NULL	
,7934}	,'ADMIN' }	,7782}	,1300}	,NULL}	
{7369	{'TRAINER'	{7902	{ 800	{NULL	20
,7566	,'MANAGER'	,7839	,2975	,NULL	
,7788	,'TRAINER'	,7566	,3000	,NULL	
,7876	,'TRAINER'	,7788	,1100	,NULL	
,7902}	,'TRAINER'}	,7566}	,3000}	,NULL}	
{7499	{'SALESREP'	{7698	{1600	{ 300	30
,7521	,'SALESREP'	,7698	,1250	, 500	
,7654	,'SALESREP'	,7698	,1250	,1400	
,7698	,'MANAGER'	,7839	,2850	,NULL	
,7844	,'SALESREP'	,7698	,1500	, 0	
,7900}	,'ADMIN' }	,7698}	, 800}	,NULL}	

Going back to Listing 8-14, it now becomes clear what the COUNT(e.EMPNO) function does: it returns the number of elements of each e.EMPNO set.

You could argue that (as an effect of the GROUP BY e.DEPTNO clause) the last column in Listing 8-15 (e.DEPTNO) contains "regular" values, and the other five columns become "set-valued" attributes. You can use only e.DEPTNO in the SELECT clause. If you want to see data from the other columns in your query result, you must use group functions (such as COUNT) to aggregate those sets into a single value. See the next section for a discussion of group functions.

■**Note** To be more precise, we should refer to *multisets* instead of *sets* in this context. Duplicate values are maintained, as you can see in Listing 8-15. We will discuss multisets in Chapter 12.

Multiple-Column Grouping

You can also group on multiple-column expressions, separated by commas. For example, the query in Listing 8-16 produces an overview of the number of registrations per course.

Listing 8-16. *Grouping on Two Columns*

```
SQL> select   r.course, r.begindate
  2 ,         count(r.attendee) as attendees
  3 from      registrations r
  4 group  by r.course, r.begindate;
```

```
COURSE BEGINDATE    ATTENDEES
------ ----------- ----------
JAV    13-DEC-1999         5
JAV    01-FEB-2000         3
OAU    10-AUG-1999         3
OAU    27-SEP-2000         1
PLS    11-SEP-2000         3
SQL    12-APR-1999         4
SQL    04-OCT-1999         3
SQL    13-DEC-1999         2
XML    03-FEB-2000         2

9 rows selected.

SQL>
```

This result shows one row for each different (COURSE, BEGINDATE) combination found in the REGISTRATIONS table.

Note As you can see, the rows in Listing 8-16 are ordered on the columns of the GROUP BY clause. However, if you want a certain ordering of your query results, you should *never* rely on implicit DBMS behavior and *always* specify an ORDER BY clause.

GROUP BY and Null Values

If a column expression on which you apply the GROUP BY clause contains null values, these null values end up together in a separate group. See Listing 8-17 for an example.

Listing 8-17. *GROUP BY and Null Values*

```
SQL> select e.comm, count(e.empno)
  2  from    employees e
  3  group   by e.comm;

    COMM COUNT(E.EMPNO)
-------- --------------
       0              1
     300              1
     500              1
    1400              1
                     10

SQL>
```

Apparently, we have ten employees without commission.

8.6 Group Functions

In the previous section, we used the COUNT function to count the number of employees per department and the number of registrations per course. COUNT is an example of a *group function*. All group functions have two important properties in common:

- They can be applied only to *sets* of values.

- They return a single aggregated value, derived from that set of values.

That's why group functions often occur in combination with GROUP BY (and optionally the HAVING clause, covered in Section 8.7) in SQL commands. The most important Oracle group functions are listed in Table 8-1.

Table 8-1. *Common Oracle Group Functions*

Function	Description	Applicable To
COUNT()	Number of values	All datatypes
SUM()	Sum of all values	Numeric data
MIN()	Minimum value	All datatypes
MAX()	Maximum value	All datatypes
AVG()	Average value	Numeric data
MEDIAN()	Median (middle value)	Numeric or date (time) data
STATS_MODE()	Modus (most frequent value)	All datatypes
STDDEV()	Standard deviation	Numeric data
VARIANCE()	Statistical variance	Numeric data

The last column in Table 8-1 shows the applicable datatypes for all group functions. The functions MIN and MAX are applicable to any datatype, including dates and alphanumeric strings. MIN and MAX need only an ordering (sorting) criterion for the set of values. Note also that you can apply the AVG function only to numbers, because the average is defined as the SUM divided by the COUNT, and the SUM function accepts only numeric data.

Let's look at some group function examples in Listing 8-18.

Listing 8-18. *Some Examples of Group Functions*

```
SQL> select e.deptno
  2  ,       count(e.job)
  3  ,       sum(e.comm)
  4  ,       avg(e.msal)
  5  ,       median(e.msal)
  6  from    employees e
  7  group   by e.deptno;
```

```
DEPTNO COUNT(E.JOB) SUM(E.COMM) AVG(E.MSAL) MEDIAN(E.MSAL)
-------- ------------ ----------- ----------- --------------
    10            3               2916.667           2450
    20            5                   2175           2975
    30            6        2200     1541.667           1375

SQL>
```

Group Functions and Duplicate Values

If you apply a group function to a set of column values, that set of values may contain duplicate values. By default, these duplicate values are all treated as individual values, contributing
to the end result of all group functions applied to the set of values. For example, we have five
employees in department 20, but we have only two different jobs in that department. Nevertheless, Listing 8-18 shows 5 as the result of COUNT(e.JOB) for department 20.

If you want SQL group functions to ignore duplicate values (except one, of course), you
must specify the keyword DISTINCT immediately after the first parenthesis. Although it is syntactically correct, the addition of DISTINCT is meaningless for the MIN and MAX functions. Look
at Listing 8-19 for some examples.

Listing 8-19. *Using the DISTINCT Option for Group Functions*

```
SQL> select count(deptno), count(distinct deptno)
  2  ,      avg(comm),  avg(coalesce(comm,0))
  3  from   employees;

COUNT(DEPTNO) COUNT(DISTINCTDEPTNO) AVG(COMM) AVG(COALESCE(COMM,0))
------------- --------------------- --------- ---------------------
           14                     3       550              157.1429

SQL>
```

Note that Listing 8-19 also shows that you can use group functions in the SELECT clause of
a query *without* a GROUP BY clause. The absence of a GROUP BY clause in combination with the
presence of group functions in the SELECT clause always results in a single-row result. In other
words, the full table is aggregated into a single row. You can achieve precisely the same result
by grouping on a constant expression. Try this yourself; for example, see what happens if you
add GROUP BY 'x' to the query in Listing 8-19.

Group Functions and Null Values

The ANSI/ISO SQL standard postulates group functions to ignore null values completely.
There is only one exception to this rule: the COUNT(*) function. This special case is discussed
later in this section. This is a reasonable compromise. The only other consistent behavior for
group functions would be to return a null value as soon as the input contains a null value.

This would imply that all your SQL statements (containing group functions) should contain additional code to handle null values explicitly. So, ignoring null values completely is not a bad idea. Just make sure that you understand the consequences of this behavior. See Table 8-2 for some typical examples.

Table 8-2. *Behavior of Group Functions and Null Values*

Set X	SUM(X)	MIN(X)	AVG(X)	MAX(X)
{1,2,3,NULL}	6	1	2	3
{1,2,3,0}	6	0	1.5	3
{1,2,3,2}	8	1	2	3

The SUM function does not make any distinction between {1,2,3,NULL} and {1,2,3,0}. The MIN and AVG functions don't make any distinction between {1,2,3,NULL} and {1,2,3,2}. The MAX function gives the same result on all three sets.

Looking back at Listing 8-19, you see an example of function *nesting*: the AVG function operates on the result of the COALESCE function. This is a typical method to handle null values explicitly. As you can see from Listing 8-19, the results of AVG(COMM) and AVG(COALESCE(COMM,0)) are obviously different. In this case, the Oracle DBMS replaces all null values by zeros before applying the AVG function, because the null values in the COMM column actually mean "not applicable."

The next query, shown in Listing 8-20, tells us how many *different* courses are scheduled for each trainer and the total number of scheduled courses.

Listing 8-20. *GROUP BY and DISTINCT*

```
SQL> select  trainer
  2  ,        count(distinct course)
  3  ,        count(*)
  4  from     offerings
  5  group  by trainer;

TRAINER COUNT(DISTINCTCOURSE) COUNT(*)
-------- --------------------- --------
   7369                      2        3
   7566                      2        2
   7788                      2        2
   7876                      1        1
   7902                      2        2
                            3        3

SQL>
```

Apparently, we have three course offerings without a trainer being assigned.

Grouping the Results of a Join

The query in Listing 8-21 shows the average evaluation ratings for each trainer, over all courses delivered.

Listing 8-21. *GROUP BY on a Join*

```
SQL> select o.trainer, avg(r.evaluation)
  2  from   offerings o
  3         join
  4         registrations r
  5         using (course,begindate)
  6  group  by o.trainer;

 TRAINER AVG(R.EVALUATION)
-------- -----------------
    7369                 4
    7566              4.25
    7788
    7876                 4
    7902                 4

SQL>
```

Notice the USING clause in line 5, with the COURSE and BEGINDATE columns. This USING clause with two columns is needed to get the correct join results.

The COUNT(*) Function

As mentioned earlier, group functions operate on a set of values, with one important exception. Besides column names, you can specify the asterisk (*) as an argument to the COUNT function. This widens the scope of the COUNT function from a specific column to the full row level. COUNT(*) returns the number of rows in the entire group.

■**Note** If you think that SELECT COUNT(1) is faster than SELECT COUNT(*), try a little experiment and prepare to be surprised—you will find out that there is no difference. Don't trust opinions...

Listing 8-20 already showed an example of using the COUNT(*) function, to get the total number of scheduled courses for each trainer from the OFFERINGS table. Listing 8-22 shows another example of using the COUNT(*) function, this time applied against the EMPLOYEES table.

Listing 8-22. *Count Employees Per Department (First Attempt)*

```
SQL> select e.deptno, count(*)
  2  from   employees e
  3  group  by e.deptno;
```

```
DEPTNO COUNT(*)
-------- --------
      10        3
      20        5
      30        6

SQL>
```

Obviously, department 40 is missing in this result. If you want to change the query into an outer join in order to show department 40 as well, you must be careful. What's wrong with the query in Listing 8-23? Apparently, we suddenly have one employee working for department 40.

Listing 8-23. *Count Employees Per Department (Second Attempt)*

```
SQL> select deptno, count(*)
  2  from   employees e
  3         right outer join
  4         departments d
  5         using (deptno)
  6  group  by deptno;

DEPTNO COUNT(*)
-------- --------
      10        3
      20        5
      30        6
      40        1

SQL>
```

Compare the results in Listing 8-23 with the results in Listing 8-24. The only difference is the argument of the COUNT function. Listing 8-24 obviously shows the correct result, because department 40 has no employees. By counting over the primary key e.EMPNO, you are sure that all "real" employees are counted, while the null value introduced by the outer join is correctly ignored. You could have used any other NOT NULL column as well.

Listing 8-24. *Count Employees Per Department (Third Attempt)*

```
SQL> select deptno, count(e.empno)
  2  from   employees e
  3         right outer join
  4         departments d
  5         using (deptno)
  6  group  by deptno;

DEPTNO COUNT(E.EMPNO)
-------- --------------
      10              3
```

```
        20              5
        30              6
        40              0

SQL>
```

At the end of Chapter 5, you saw an example of a PL/SQL stored function to count all employees per department (Section 5.8, Listing 5-31). In that chapter, I mentioned that this counting problem is not trivial to solve in standard SQL. In Listings 8-22, 8-23, and 8-24, you see that you should indeed be careful. You need an outer join, and you should make sure to specify the correct argument for the COUNT function to get correct results.

■ **Caution** You should be careful with the COUNT function, especially if null values might cause problems (since group functions ignore them) and you want to count row occurrences.

Valid SELECT and GROUP BY Clause Combinations

If your queries contain a GROUP BY clause, some syntax combinations are invalid and result in Oracle error messages, such as the following:

```
ORA-00937: not a single-group group function.
```

This always means that there is a mismatch between your SELECT clause and your GROUP BY clause.

To demonstrate valid versus invalid syntax, Table 8-3 shows one invalid and three valid syntax examples. Table 8-3 assumes you have a table T with four columns A, B, C, and D.

Table 8-3. *Valid and Invalid GROUP BY Syntax Examples*

Syntax	Valid?
select a, b, max(c) from t ... group by a	No
select a, b, max(c) from t ... group by a,b	Yes
select a, count(b), min(c) from t ... group by a	Yes
select count(c) from t ... group by a	Yes

The examples in Table 8-3 illustrate the following two general rules:

- You do not *need* to select the column expression you group on (see the last example).

- Any column expression that is *not* part of the GROUP BY clause can occur *only* in the SELECT clause as an argument to a group function. That's why the first example is invalid.

By the way, all GROUP BY examples so far showed only column names, but you can also group on column expressions, such as in the example shown in Listing 8-25.

Listing 8-25. *Grouping on Column Expressions*

```
SQL> select case mod(empno,2)
  2            when 0 then 'EVEN '
  3                   else 'ODD '
  4         end  as empno
  5  ,      sum(msal)
  6  from   employees
  7  group  by mod(empno,2);

EMPNO SUM(MSAL)
----- ---------
EVEN      20225
ODD        8650

SQL>
```

This query shows the salary sums for employees with even and odd employee numbers.

8.7 The HAVING Clause

If you aggregate rows into groups with GROUP BY, you might also want to filter your query result further by allowing only certain groups into the final query result. You can achieve this with the HAVING clause. Normally, you use the HAVING clause only following a GROUP BY clause. For example, Listing 8-26 shows information about departments with more than four employees.

Listing 8-26. *HAVING Clause Example*

```
SQL> select deptno, count(empno)
  2  from   employees
  3  group  by deptno
  4  having count(*) >= 4;

DEPTNO COUNT(EMPNO)
------- ------------
    20            5
    30            6

SQL>
```

However, the SQL language allows you to write queries with a HAVING clause without a preceding GROUP BY clause. In that case, Oracle assumes an implicit GROUP BY on a constant expression, just as when you use group functions in the SELECT clause without specifying a GROUP BY clause; that is, the full table is treated as a single group.

The Difference Between WHERE and HAVING

It is important to distinguish the WHERE clause from the HAVING clause. To illustrate this difference, Listing 8-27 shows a WHERE clause added to the previous query.

Listing 8-27. *HAVING vs. WHERE*

```
SQL> select   deptno, count(empno)
  2  from      employees
  3  where     bdate > date '1960-01-01'
  4  group by deptno
  5  having    count(*) >= 4;

  DEPTNO COUNT(EMPNO)
-------- ------------
      30            5

SQL>
```

The WHERE condition regarding the day of birth (line 3) can be checked against *individual rows* of the EMPLOYEES table. On the other hand, the COUNT(*) condition (line 5) makes sense only at the *group* level. That's why group functions should never occur in a WHERE clause. They typically result in the following Oracle error message:

```
ORA-00934: group function is not allowed here.
```

You'll see this error message in Listing 8-29, caused by a classic SQL mistake, as discussed shortly.

HAVING Clauses Without Group Functions

On the other hand, valid HAVING clauses without group functions are very rare, and they should be rewritten. In Listing 8-28, the second query is much more efficient than the first one.

Listing 8-28. *HAVING Clause Without a Group Function*

```
SQL> select deptno, count(*)
  2  from      employees
  3  group  by deptno
  4  having deptno <= 20;

  DEPTNO COUNT(*)
-------- --------
      10        3
      20        5

SQL> select deptno, count(*)
  2  from      employees
```

```
  3  where  deptno <= 20
  4  group  by deptno;

DEPTNO COUNT(*)
-------- --------
      10        3
      20        5

SQL>
```

A Classic SQL Mistake

Take a look at the query in Listing 8-29. It looks very logical, doesn't it? Who earns more than the average salary?

Listing 8-29. *Error Message: Group Function Is Not Allowed Here*

```
SQL> select empno
  2  from    employees
  3  where   msal > avg(msal);
where  msal > avg(msal)
                *
ERROR at line 3:
ORA-00934: group function is not allowed here

SQL>
```

However, if you think in terms of tuple variables, the problem becomes obvious: the WHERE clause has only a *single row* as its context, turning the AVG function into something impossible to derive.

You can solve this problem in many ways. Listings 8-30 and 8-31 show two suggestions.

Listing 8-30. *One Way to Find Who Earns More Than the Average Salary*

```
SQL> select e.empno
  2  from    employees e
  3  where   e.msal > (select avg(x.msal)
  4                    from    employees x);

  EMPNO
--------
   7566
   7698
   7782
   7788
   7839
```

```
    7902

SQL>
```

Listing 8-31. *Another Way to Find Who Earns More Than the Average Salary*

```
SQL> select    e1.empno
  2  from       employees e1
  3  ,          employees e2
  4  group by e1.empno
  5  ,          e1.msal
  6  having     e1.msal > avg(e2.msal);

    MNR
--------
    7566
    7698
    7782
    7788
    7839
    7902

SQL>
```

The solution in Listing 8-31 would probably not win an SQL beauty contest, but it is certainly worth further examination. This solution is based on the Cartesian product of the EMPLOYEES table with itself. Notice that it doesn't have a WHERE clause. Notice also that you group on e1.EMPNO and e1.MSAL, which allows you to refer to this column in the HAVING clause.

Grouping on Additional Columns

You sometimes need this (apparently) superfluous grouping on additional columns. For example, suppose you want to see the employee number and the employee name, followed by the total number of course registrations. The query in Listing 8-32, which could be a first attempt to solve this problem, produces an Oracle error message.

Listing 8-32. *Error Message: Not a GROUP BY Expression*

```
SQL> select    e.empno, e.ename, count(*)
  2  from       employees e
  3             join
  4             registrations r
  5             on (e.empno = r.attendee)
  6  group by e.empno;
select    e.empno, e.ename, count(*)
                *
```

```
ERROR at line 1:
ORA-00979: not a GROUP BY expression

SQL>
```

The pseudo-intermediate result in Listing 8-33 explains what went wrong here, and why you must also group on e.ENAME.

Listing 8-33. *Pseudo-Intermediate GROUP BY Result*

```
GROUP BY e.EMPNO                    GROUP BY e.EMPNO,e.ENAME

e.EMPNO     e.ENAME    e.INIT  ...  e.EMPNO    e.ENAME    e.INIT  ...
=======  ==========  ======       =======  ========  ======
   7369  {'SMITH'}  {'N'}           7369  'SMITH'   {'N'}
   7499  {'ALLEN'}  {'JAM'}         7499  'ALLEN'   {'JAM'}
   7521  {'WARD' }   ...            7521    ...        ...
   7566   ...                        ...
```

The two results look similar; however, there is an important difference between sets consisting of a single element, such as {'SMITH'}, and a literal value, such as 'SMITH'. In mathematics, sets with a single element are commonly referred to as singleton sets, or just *singletons*.

Listing 8-34 shows another instructive mistake.

Listing 8-34. *Error Message: Not a Single-Group Group Function*

```
SQL> select deptno
  2  ,       sum(msal)
  3  from    employees;
select deptno
       *
ERROR at line 1:
ORA-00937: not a single-group group function

SQL>
```

In the absence of a GROUP BY clause, the SUM function would return a single row, while DEPTNO would produce 14 department numbers. Two columns with different row counts cannot be presented side-by-side in a single result. After the correction in Listing 8-35, the error message disappears, and you get the desired results.

Listing 8-35. *Correction of the Error Message in Listing 8-34*

```
SQL> select    deptno
  2  ,          sum(msal)
  3  from       employees
  4  group by deptno;
```

```
DEPTNO     SUM(MSAL)
-------- -------------
      10          8750
      20         10875
      30          9250

SQL>
```

In summary, if your query contains a GROUP BY clause, the SELECT clause is allowed to contain only group expressions. A group expression is a column name that is part of the GROUP BY clause, or a group function applied to any other column expression. See also Table 8-3 at the end of Section 8.6.

8.8 Advanced GROUP BY Features

The previous sections showed examples of using "standard" GROUP BY clauses. You can also use some more advanced features of the GROUP BY clause. Here, we will look at GROUP BY CUBE and GROUP BY ROLLUP.

Let's start with a regular GROUP BY example, shown in Listing 8-36.

Listing 8-36. *Regular GROUP BY Example*

```
SQL> select    deptno, job
  2  ,          count(empno) headcount
  3  from       employees
  4  group by deptno, job;

DEPTNO JOB          HEADCOUNT
-------- ----------- ----------
      10 MANAGER            1
      10 DIRECTOR           1
      10 ADMIN              1
      20 MANAGER            1
      20 TRAINER            4
      30 MANAGER            1
      30 SALESREP           4
      30 ADMIN              1

8 rows selected.

SQL>
```

You get an overview with the number of employees per department, and within each department per job. To keep things simple, let's forget about department 40, the department without employees.

GROUP BY ROLLUP

Notice what happens if you change the GROUP BY clause and add the keyword ROLLUP, as shown in Listing 8-37.

Listing 8-37. *GROUP BY ROLLUP Example*

```
SQL> select   deptno, job
  2  ,         count(empno) headcount
  3  from      employees
  4  group by ROLLUP(deptno, job);

  DEPTNO JOB       HEADCOUNT
-------- -------- ---------
      10 ADMIN            1
      10 MANAGER          1
      10 DIRECTOR         1
>>>   10                  3 <<<
      20 MANAGER          1
      20 TRAINER          4
>>>   20                  5 <<<
      30 ADMIN            1
      30 MANAGER          1
      30 SALESREP         4
>>>   30                  6 <<<
>>>                      14 <<<

12 rows selected.

SQL>
```

The ROLLUP addition results in four additional rows, marked with >>> and <<< in Listing 8-37 for readability. Three of these four additional rows show the head count per department over all jobs, and the last row shows the total number of employees.

GROUP BY CUBE

You can also use the CUBE keyword in the GROUP BY clause. Listing 8-38 shows an example.

Listing 8-38. *GROUP BY CUBE Example*

```
SQL> select   deptno, job
  2  ,         count(empno) headcount
  3  from      employees
  4  group by CUBE(deptno, job);
```

```
   DEPTNO JOB      HEADCOUNT
   -------- -------- ----------
                          14
>>>         ADMIN        2 <<<
>>>         MANAGER      3 <<<
>>>         TRAINER      4 <<<
>>>         DIRECTOR     1 <<<
>>>         SALESREP     4 <<<
       10                3
       10 MANAGER        1
       10 DIRECTOR       1
       10 ADMIN          1
       20                5
       20 MANAGER        1
       20 TRAINER        4
       30                6
       30 MANAGER        1
       30 SALESREP       4
       30 ADMIN          1

17 rows selected.

SQL>
```

This time, you get five more rows in the query result, marked in the same way with >>> and <<<, showing the number of employees per job, regardless of which department employs them.

Tip Both GROUP BY CUBE and GROUP BY ROLLUP are two special cases of the GROUP BY GROUPING SETS syntax, offering more flexibility. You can also merge the results of different grouping operations into a single GROUP BY clause by specifying them in a comma-separated list. For more details, see *Oracle SQL Reference.*

CUBE, ROLLUP, and Null Values

The CUBE and ROLLUP keywords generate many null values in query results, as you can see in Listings 8-37 and 8-38. You can distinguish these system-generated null values from other null values; for example, to replace them with some explanatory text. You can use the GROUPING and GROUPING_ID functions for that purpose.

The GROUPING Function

Listing 8-39 shows an example of the GROUPING function.

Listing 8-39. *GROUPING Function Example*

```
SQL> select    deptno
  2 ,          case GROUPING(job)
  3                 when 0 then job
  4                 when 1 then '**total**'
  5             end job
  6 ,          count(empno) headcount
  7 from       employees
  8 group by rollup(deptno, job);

DEPTNO JOB         HEADCOUNT
-------- ---------- ---------
      10 ADMIN              1
      10 MANAGER            1
      10 DIRECTOR           1
      10 **total**          3
      20 MANAGER            1
      20 TRAINER            4
      20 **total**          5
      30 ADMIN              1
      30 MANAGER            1
      30 SALESREP           4
      30 **total**          6
         **total**         14

12 rows selected.

SQL>
```

Unfortunately, the GROUPING function can return only two results: 0 or 1. That's why the last two lines both show '**total**'.

The GROUPING_ID Function

The GROUPING_ID function is more flexible that the GROUPING function, because it can return several different results, as you can see in Listing 8-40.

Listing 8-40. *GROUPING_ID Function Example with ROLLUP*

```
SQL> select    deptno
  2 ,          case GROUPING_ID(deptno, job)
  3                 when 0 then job
  4                 when 1 then '**dept **'
  5                 when 3 then '**total**'
  6             end  job
  7 ,          count(empno) headcount
  8 from       employees
  9 group by rollup(deptno, job);
```

```
DEPTNO JOB        HEADCOUNT
-------- --------- ---------
    10 ADMIN             1
    10 MANAGER           1
    10 DIRECTOR          1
    10 **dept **         3
    20 MANAGER           1
    20 TRAINER           4
    20 **dept **         5
    30 ADMIN             1
    30 MANAGER           1
    30 SALESREP          4
    30 **dept **         6
       **total**        14

12 rows selected.

SQL>
```

You may be puzzled by the value 3 being used on the fifth line in Listing 8-40. Things become clear when you convert 3 to a binary representation, which results in the binary number 11. The two ones in this number act as a flag to trap the situation in which both columns contain a null value. GROUP BY ROLLUP can produce only 1 (binary 01) and 3 (binary 11), but GROUP BY CUBE can also generate 2 (binary 10). Look at the results in Listing 8-41. Obviously, GROUPING_ID produces a 0 (zero) for all "regular" rows in the result.

Listing 8-41. *GROUPING_ID Function Example with CUBE*

```
SQL> select   deptno, job
  2  ,         GROUPING_ID(deptno, job) gid
  3  from      employees
  4  group by cube(deptno, job);

DEPTNO JOB          GID
-------- -------- --------
                      3
       ADMIN          2
       MANAGER        2
       TRAINER        2
       DIRECTOR       2
       SALESREP       2
    10                1
    10 ADMIN          0
    10 MANAGER        0
    10 DIRECTOR       0
    20                1
```

```
     20 MANAGER        0
     20 TRAINER        0
     30                1
     30 ADMIN          0
     30 MANAGER        0
     30 SALESREP       0

17 rows selected.

SQL>
```

8.9 Partitioned Outer Joins

We discussed outer joins in Section 8.4. This section introduces partitioned outer joins.
To explain what partitioned outer joins are, let's start with a regular (right) outer join in
Listing 8-42.

Listing 8-42. *Regular Right Outer Join Example*

```
SQL> break on department skip 1 on job

SQL> select d.dname as department
  2  ,       e.job   as job
  3  ,       e.ename as employee
  4  from    employees e
  5          right outer join
  6          departments d
  7          using (deptno)
  8  order   by department, job;

DEPARTMENT JOB      EMPLOYEE
---------- -------- --------
ACCOUNTING ADMIN    MILLER
           DIRECTOR KING
           MANAGER  CLARK


HR                       <<<


SALES      ADMIN    JONES
           MANAGER  BLAKE
           SALESREP ALLEN
                    WARD
                    TURNER
                    MARTIN
```

```
TRAINING   MANAGER  JONES
           TRAINER  SMITH
                    FORD
                    ADAMS
                    SCOTT

15 rows selected.

SQL>
```

The SQL*Plus BREAK command allows you to enhance the readability of query results. In Listing 8-42, we use the BREAK command to suppress repeating values in the DEPARTMENT and JOB columns, and to insert an empty line between the departments. (See Chapter 11 for details about BREAK.) The result shows 15 rows, as expected. We have 14 employees, and the additional row (marked with <<<) is added by the outer join for the HR department without employees.

Look at Listing 8-43 to see what happens if we add one extra clause, just before the RIGHT OUTER JOIN operator.

Listing 8-43. *Partitioned Outer Join Example*

```
SQL> select  d.dname as department
  2  ,        e.job   as job
  3  ,        e.ename as employee
  4  from     employees e
  5           PARTITION BY (JOB)
  6           right outer join
  7           departments d
  8           using (deptno)
  9  order  by department, job;

DEPARTMENT JOB      EMPLOYEE
---------- -------- --------
ACCOUNTING ADMIN    MILLER
           DIRECTOR KING
           MANAGER  CLARK
           SALESREP          <<<
           TRAINER           <<<

HR         ADMIN             <<<
           DIRECTOR          <<<
           MANAGER           <<<
           SALESREP          <<<
           TRAINER           <<<
```

```
SALES      ADMIN     JONES
           DIRECTOR            <<<
           MANAGER   BLAKE
           SALESREP  ALLEN
                     WARD
                     TURNER
                     MARTIN
           TRAINER             <<<

TRAINING   ADMIN               <<<
           DIRECTOR            <<<
           MANAGER   JONES
           SALESREP            <<<
           TRAINER   SMITH
                     FORD
                     ADAMS
                     SCOTT

26 rows selected.

SQL>
```

Listing 8-43 shows at least one row for each combination of a department and a job. Compared with Listing 8-42, the single row for the HR department is replaced with 12 additional rows, highlighting all nonexisting department/job combinations. A *regular* outer join considers full tables when searching for matching rows in the other table. The *partitioned* outer join works as follows:

1. Split the driving table in partitions based on a column expression (in Listing 8-43, this column expression is JOB).

2. Produce separate outer join results for each partition with the other table.

3. Merge the results of the previous step into a single result.

Partitioned outer joins are especially useful when you want to aggregate information over the time dimension, a typical requirement for data warehouse reporting. See *Oracle SQL Reference* for more details and examples.

8.10 Set Operators

You can use the SQL set operators UNION, MINUS, and INTERSECT to combine the results of two independent query blocks into a single result. As you saw in Chapter 2, the set operators have the syntax shown in Figure 8-5.

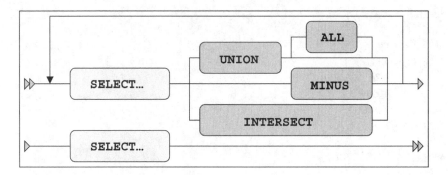

Figure 8-5. *Set operators syntax diagram*

These SQL operators correspond with the union, minus, and intersect operators you know from mathematics. Don't we all have fond memories of our teachers drawing those Venn diagrams on the whiteboard (or blackboard, for you older readers)? See also Figure 1-1. The meanings of these set operators in SQL are listed in Table 8-4.

Table 8-4. *Set Operators*

Operator	Result
Q1 UNION Q2	All rows occurring in Q1 *or* in Q2 (or in both)
Q1 UNION ALL Q2	As UNION, retaining duplicate rows
Q1 MINUS Q2	The rows from Q1, *without* the rows from Q2
Q1 INTERSECT Q2	The rows occurring in Q1 *and* in Q2

By default, all three set operators suppress duplicate rows in the query result. The only exception to this rule is the UNION ALL operator, which does *not* eliminate duplicate rows. One important advantage of the UNION ALL operator is that the Oracle DBMS does not need to sort the rows. Sorting is needed for all other set operators to trace duplicate rows.

The UNION, MINUS, and INTERSECT operators cannot be applied to any arbitrary set of two queries. The intermediate (separate) results of queries Q1 and Q2 must be "compatible" in order to use them as arguments to a set operator. In this context, compatibility means the following:

- Q1 and Q2 must select the same number of column expressions.

- The datatypes of those column expressions must match.

Some other rules and guidelines for SQL set operators are the following:

- The result table inherits the column names (or aliases) from Q1.

- Q1 cannot contain an ORDER BY clause.

- If you specify an ORDER BY clause at the end of the query, it doesn't refer to Q2, but rather to the total result of the set operator.

Set operators are very convenient when building new queries by combining the multiple query blocks you wrote (and tested) before, without writing completely new SQL code. This simplifies testing, because you have more control over correctness.

Listing 8-44 answers the following question: "Which locations host course offerings without having a department?"

Listing 8-44. *MINUS Set Operator Example*

```
SQL> select o.location from offerings o
  2  MINUS
  3  select d.location from departments d;

LOCATION
--------
SEATTLE

SQL>
```

You can also try to solve this problem without using the MINUS operator. See Listing 8-45 for a suggestion.

Listing 8-45. *Alternative Solution Without Using the MINUS Operator*

```
SQL> select DISTINCT o.location
  2  from    offerings o
  3  where   o.location not in
  4          (select d.location
  5           from    departments d)
```

Note that you must add a DISTINCT operator, to handle situations where you have multiple course offerings in the same location. As explained before, the MINUS operator automatically removes duplicate rows.

Are the two queries in Listing 8-44 and 8-45 logically equivalent? Further investigations are left to the readers in one of the exercises at the end of this chapter.

You can also produce outer join results by using the UNION operator. You will see how to do this in Listings 8-46 and 8-47.

We start with a regular join in Listing 8-46. In Listing 8-47 you add the additional department(s) needed for the outer join with a UNION operator, while assigning the right number of employees for those departments: zero.

Listing 8-46. *Regular Join*

```
SQL> select   d.deptno
  2  ,         d.dname
  3  ,         count(e.empno) as headcount
  4  from      employees e
  5  ,         departments d
  6  where     e.deptno = d.deptno
```

```
  7  group by d.deptno
  8  ,        d.dname;

DEPTNO DNAME      HEADCOUNT
-------- ---------- ---------
      10 ACCOUNTING         3
      20 TRAINING           5
      30 SALES              6

SQL>
```

Listing 8-47. *Expansion to an Outer Join with a UNION Operator*

```
SQL> select  d.deptno
  2  ,        d.dname
  3  ,        count(e.empno) as headcount
  4  from     employees e
  5  ,        departments d
  6  where    e.deptno = d.deptno
  7  group by d.deptno
  8  ,        d.dname
  9  union
 10  select   x.deptno
 11  ,        x.dname
 12  ,        0        as headcount
 13  from     departments x
 14  where    x.deptno not in (select y.deptno
 15                           from    employees y);

DEPTNO DNAME      HEADCOUNT
-------- ---------- ---------
      10 ACCOUNTING         3
      20 TRAINING           5
      30 SALES              6
      40 HR                 0

SQL>
```

8.11 Exercises

The following exercises will help you to better understand the topics covered in this chapter. The answers are presented in Appendix D.

1. Produce an overview of all course offerings. Provide the course code, begin date, course duration, and name of the trainer.

2. Provide an overview, in two columns, showing the names of all employees who ever attended an SQL course, with the name of the trainer.

3. For all employees, list their name, initials, and yearly salary (including bonus and commission).

4. For all course offerings, list the course code, begin date, and number of registrations. Sort your results on the number of registrations, from high to low.

5. List the course code, begin date, and number of registrations for all course offerings in 1999 with at least three registrations.

6. Provide the employee numbers of all employees who ever taught a course as a trainer, but never attended a course as an attendee.

7. Which employees attended a specific course more than once?

8. For all trainers, provide their name and initials, the number of courses they taught, the total number of students they had in their classes, and the average evaluation rating. Round the evaluation ratings to one decimal.

9. List the name and initials of all trainers who ever had their own manager as a student in a general course (category GEN).

10. Did we ever use two classrooms at the same time in the same course location?

11. Produce a matrix report (one column per department, one row for each job) where each cell shows the number of employees for a specific department and a specific job. In a single SQL statement, it is impossible to dynamically derive the number of columns needed, so you may assume you have three departments only: 10, 20, and 30.

12. Listing 8-26 produces information about all departments with *more* than four employees. How can you change the query to show information about all departments with *fewer* than four employees?

13. Look at Listings 8-44 and 8-45. Are those two queries logically equivalent? Investigate the two queries and explain the differences, if any.

CHAPTER 9

■ ■ ■

Retrieval: Some Advanced Features

This is the fourth chapter in a series about retrieval features of SQL. It is a logical continuation of Chapters 4, 5, and 8.

First, we revisit subqueries, beginning with an introduction to the three operators ANY, ALL, and EXISTS. These operators allow you to create a special relationship between main queries and subqueries, as opposed to using the IN operator or standard comparison operators. You will also learn about *correlated subqueries*, which are subqueries where some subquery clauses refer to column expressions from the main query.

In Sections 9.2 and 9.3, we will look at subqueries in query components other than the WHERE clause: the SELECT and the FROM clauses. One special case of using subqueries in the FROM clause is the *Top-N SQL* feature. In Section 9.4 we will discuss the WITH clause, also referred to as *subquery factoring*, which allows you to define one or more subqueries in the beginning of your SQL commands, and then to reference them by name in the remainder of your SQL command.

We continue with *hierarchical queries*. Relational tables are essentially flat structures, but they can represent hierarchical data structures; for example, by using foreign key constraints referring to the primary key of the same table. The MGR column of the EMPLOYEES table is a classic example of such a hierarchical relationship. Oracle SQL supports explicit syntax to simplify retrieval of hierarchical data structures.

The next subject we investigate is *windowing*. Within the context of a single row (or tuple variable), you can define a dependent window of rows, with an optional ordering within that window. Once you have defined such windows, you can apply various powerful *analytical functions* to derive aggregate information about the rows in that window.

Finally, this chapter discusses a helpful Oracle SQL feature allowing you to travel back in time: *flashback queries*. The chapter ends with some exercises.

9.1 Subqueries Continued

Chapter 4 discussed various examples of subqueries, using the IN operator or standard logical comparison operators. As a refresher, let's start with two standard subquery examples.

The subquery in Listing 9-1 shows all 13 registrations we have for build courses; that is, for course category 'BLD'.

Listing 9-1. *Subquery Using the IN Operator*

```
SQL> select  r.attendee, r.course, r.begindate
  2  from    registrations r
  3  where   r.course in (select c.code
  4                       from   courses c
  5                       where  c.category = 'BLD');

ATTENDEE COURSE BEGINDATE
-------- ------ -----------
    7499 JAV    13-DEC-1999
    7566 JAV    01-FEB-2000
    7698 JAV    01-FEB-2000
    7788 JAV    13-DEC-1999
    7839 JAV    13-DEC-1999
    7876 JAV    13-DEC-1999
    7788 JAV    01-FEB-2000
    7782 JAV    13-DEC-1999
    7499 PLS    11-SEP-2000
    7876 PLS    11-SEP-2000
    7566 PLS    11-SEP-2000
    7499 XML    03-FEB-2000
    7900 XML    03-FEB-2000

13 rows selected.

SQL>
```

Listing 9-2 shows how you can retrieve all employees who are younger than colleague 7566.

Listing 9-2. *Single-Row Subquery Using a Comparison Operator*

```
SQL> select e.empno, e.ename, e.init, e.bdate
  2  from    employees e
  3  where   e.bdate > (select x.bdate
  4                     from   employees x
  5                     where  x.empno = 7566);

   EMPNO ENAME    INIT  BDATE
-------- -------- ----- -----------
    7844 TURNER   JJ    28-SEP-1968
    7900 JONES    R     03-DEC-1969

SQL>
```

Listing 9-2 shows an example of a *single-row subquery*. The subquery *must* return a single row, because the comparison operator (>) in the third line would fail otherwise. If subqueries of this type nevertheless return more than a single row, you get an Oracle error message, as you discovered in Chapter 4 (see Listing 4-38).

This section continues the discussion of subqueries by explaining the possibilities of the ANY, ALL, and EXISTS operators. You'll also learn about correlated subqueries.

The ANY and ALL Operators

SQL allows you to combine standard comparison operators (<, >, =, and so on) with subqueries returning any number of rows. You can do that by specifying ANY or ALL between the comparison operator and the subquery. Listing 9-3 shows an example of using the ANY operator.

Listing 9-3. *ANY Operator Example*

```
SQL> select e.empno, e.ename, e.job, e.msal
  2  from    employees e
  3  where   e.msal > ANY (select x.msal
  4                        from    employees x
  5                        where   x.job = 'MANAGER');

   EMPNO ENAME     JOB          MSAL
-------- -------- -------- --------
    7839 KING      DIRECTOR    5000
    7788 SCOTT     TRAINER     3000
    7902 FORD      TRAINER     3000
    7566 JONES     MANAGER     2975
    7698 BLAKE     MANAGER     2850

SQL>
```

Listing 9-3 shows all employees with a monthly salary that is higher than *at least one* manager. Listing 9-4 shows the "happy few" with a higher salary than *all* managers.

Listing 9-4. *ALL Operator Example*

```
SQL> select e.empno, e.ename, e.job, e.msal
  2  from    employees e
  3  where   e.msal > ALL (select x.msal
  4                        from    employees x
  5                        where   x.job = 'MANAGER');

   EMPNO ENAME     JOB          MSAL
-------- -------- -------- --------
    7788 SCOTT     TRAINER     3000
    7839 KING      DIRECTOR    5000
    7902 FORD      TRAINER     3000

SQL>
```

Defining ANY and ALL

As the examples illustrate, the ANY and ALL operators work as follows:

- ANY ... means the result is true for *at least one value* returned by the subquery.

- ALL ... means the result is true *for all values* returned by the subquery.

Table 9-1 formulates the definitions of ANY and ALL a bit more formally, using iterated OR and AND constructs. In the table, # represents any standard comparison operator: <, >, =, >=, <=, or <>. Also, V1, V2, V3, and so on represent the values returned by the subquery.

Table 9-1. *Definition of ANY and ALL*

X # ANY(*subquery*)	X # ALL(*subquery*)
(X # V1) OR	(X # V1) AND
(X # V2) OR	(X # V2) AND
(X # V3) OR ...	(X # V3) AND ...

Rewriting SQL Statements Containing ANY and ALL

In most cases, you can rewrite your SQL statements in such a way that you don't need the ANY and ALL operators. For example, we could have used a group function in Listing 9-4 to rebuild the subquery into a single-row subquery, as shown in Listing 9-5.

Listing 9-5. *Using the MAX Function in the Subquery, Instead of ALL*

```
SQL> select e.ename, e.job, e.msal
  2  from    employees e
  3  where   e.msal > (select max(x.msal)
  4                     from    employees x
  5                     where   x.job = 'MANAGER');

ENAME     JOB        MSAL
--------  --------   --------
SCOTT     TRAINER    3000
KING      DIRECTOR   5000
FORD      TRAINER    3000

SQL>
```

In Exercise 6 of Section 9.8 we will look at the queries of Listings 9-4 and 9-5 in more detail. Note that the following SQL constructs are logically equivalent:

- X = ANY(*subquery*) <=> X IN (*subquery*)

- X <> ALL(*subquery*) <=> X NOT IN (*subquery*)

Look at the following two rather special cases of ANY and ALL:

- X = ALL(*subquery*)

- X <> ANY(*subquery*)

If the *subquery* returns two or more different values, the first expression is *always* FALSE, because X can never be equal to two different values at the same time. Likewise, if the *subquery* returns two or more different values, the second expression is *always* TRUE, because any X will be different from at least one of those two values from the subquery.

Before we go on with the next topic, consider the case with ANY and ALL when the subquery returns no rows at all. What do you think happens? We'll investigate this as one of the exercises at the end of this chapter.

Correlated Subqueries

SQL also supports *correlated subqueries*. Look at the example in Listing 9-6, and you will find out why these subqueries are referred to as being *correlated*.

Listing 9-6. *Correlated Subquery Example*

```
SQL> select e.ename, e.init, e.msal
  2  from    employees e
  3  where   e.msal > (select avg(x.msal)
  4                     from    employees x
  5                     where   x.deptno = e.deptno   -- Note the reference to e
  6                    );

ENAME      INIT    MSAL
--------   -----   --------
ALLEN      JAM     1600
JONES      JM      2975
BLAKE      R       2850
SCOTT      SCJ     3000
KING       CC      5000
FORD       MG      3000

SQL>
```

You might want to compare this query with Listing 8-30 in the previous chapter, because they are similar. This query shows all employees who earn a higher salary than the average salary of their own department. There is one thing that makes this subquery special: it contains a reference to the tuple variable e (see e.DEPTNO in the fifth line) from the main query. This means that you cannot execute this subquery independently, in isolation, because that would result in an Oracle error message. You must interpret this subquery within the context of a specific row from the main query.

The Oracle DBMS processes the query in Listing 9-6 as follows:

- The tuple variable e ranges over the EMPLOYEES table, thus assuming 14 different values.

- For *each* row e, the subquery is executed after replacing e.DEPTNO by the literal department value of row e.

■**Caution** Reexecuting a subquery for every single row of the main query may have a significant performance impact. The Oracle optimizer will try to produce an efficient execution plan, and there are some smart optimization algorithms for correlated subqueries; nevertheless, it is always a good idea to consider (and test) performance while writing SQL statements for production systems.

In mathematics, a distinction is made between *free* and *bound* variables. In the subquery of Listing 9-6, x is the free variable and e is bound by the main query.

Let's look at another example in Listing 9-7. This query provides the fourth youngest employee of the company or, to be more precise, all employees for which there are three younger colleagues. Note that the result isn't necessarily a set containing a single employee.

Listing 9-7. *Another Example of a Correlated Subquery*

```
SQL> select e.*
  2  from    employees e
  3  where (select count(*)
  4         from    employees x
  5         where  x.bdate > e.bdate) = 3;

 EMPNO ENAME     INIT  JOB        MGR BDATE        MSAL  COMM DEPTNO
 ------ --------- ----- -------- ------ ----------- ------ ------ ------
  7876 ADAMS     AA    TRAINER   7788 30-DEC-1966  1100          20

SQL>
```

You can also formulate these types of queries using windows and analytical functions, as described in Section 9.6 of this chapter.

The EXISTS Operator

Correlated subqueries often occur in combination with the EXISTS operator. Again, let's start with an example. The query in Listing 9-8 shows all course offerings without registrations.

Listing 9-8. *Correlated Subquery with EXISTS Operator*

```
SQL> select o.*
  2  from    offerings o
  3  where  not exists
  4         (select r.*
```

```
  5        from    registrations r
  6        where   r.course    = o.course
  7        and     r.begindate = o.begindate);


COURSE BEGINDATE    TRAINER LOCATION
------ -----------  -------- --------
ERM    15-JAN-2001
PRO    19-FEB-2001          DALLAS
RSD    24-FEB-2001     7788 CHICAGO
XML    18-SEP-2000          BOSTON

SQL>
```

The EXISTS operator is not interested in the actual rows (and column values) resulting from the subquery, if any. This operator checks for only the *existence* of subquery results. If the subquery returns at least one resulting row, the EXISTS operator evaluates to TRUE. If the subquery returns no rows at all, the result is FALSE.

Subqueries Following an EXISTS Operator

You could say that the EXISTS and NOT EXISTS operators are kind of empty set checkers. This implies that it doesn't matter which expressions you specify in the SELECT clause of the subquery. For example, you could also have written the query of Listing 9-8 as follows:

```
SQL> select o.*
  2  from    offerings o
  3  where   not exists
  4          (select 'x'
  5           from    registrations r ...
```

■**Note** The ANSI/ISO SQL standard defines * as being an arbitrary literal in this case.

Subqueries that follow an EXISTS operator are often *correlated*. Think about this for a moment. If they are *uncorrelated*, their result is precisely the same for each row from the main query. There are only two possible outcomes: the EXISTS operator results in TRUE for all rows or FALSE for all rows. In other words, EXISTS followed by an uncorrelated subquery becomes an "all or nothing" operator.

■**Caution** A subquery returning a null value (that is, a single row) is *not* the same as a subquery returning nothing (that is, the empty set).

EXISTS, IN, and Three-Valued Logic

Another important point is that the result of the EXISTS operator is always TRUE or FALSE, and never UNKNOWN. Especially in queries where null values and negations are involved, this may lead to counterintuitive and surprising results.

See Listing 9-9 for another EXISTS example, to finish this section. The query is intended to provide the personal details of all employees who ever taught an SQL course.

Listing 9-9. *Another Correlated Subquery with EXISTS Operator*

```
SQL> select e.*
  2  from    employees e
  3  where   exists (select o.*
  4                  from    offerings o
  5                  where   o.course = 'SQL'
  6                  and     o.trainer = e.empno);
```

EMPNO	ENAME	INIT	JOB	MGR	BDATE	MSAL	COMM	DEPTNO
7369	SMITH	N	TRAINER	7902	17-DEC-1965	800		20
7902	FORD	MG	TRAINER	7566	13-FEB-1959	3000		20

```
SQL>
```

This problem can also be solved with an IN operator, as shown in Listing 9-10. The query results are omitted.

Listing 9-10. *Alternative Formulation for Listing 9-9*

```
SQL> select e.*
  2  from    employees e
  3  where   e.empno in (select o.trainer
  4                      from    offerings o
  5                      where   o.course = 'SQL')
```

You can also use a join to solve the problem, as shown in Listing 9-11. This is probably the most obvious approach, although the choice between writing joins or subqueries is highly subjective. Some people think "bottom up" and prefer subqueries; others think "top down" and prefer to write joins.

Listing 9-11. *Another Alternative Formulation for Listing 9-9*

```
SQL> select DISTINCT e.*
  2  from    employees e
  3          join
  4          offerings o
  5          on e.empno = o.trainer
  6  where   o.course = 'SQL'
```

Notice the DISTINCT option in the SELECT clause. Investigate what happens if you remove the DISTINCT option in Listing 9-11. You'll find that the query result will consist of *three* rows, instead of two.

So far, we have considered only subqueries in the WHERE clause. However, you can use subqueries in other SQL statement components, such as the SELECT and FROM clauses. In the next sections, we will look at subqueries in these other clauses.

9.2 Subqueries in the SELECT Clause

Check out Listings 5-31 and 5-32 in Chapter 5, which demonstrate determining the number of employees in each department. The ANSI/ISO SQL standard offers an alternative approach for that problem, using a subquery in the SELECT clause, as shown in Listing 9-12.

Listing 9-12. *Example of a Subquery in the SELECT Clause*

```
SQL> select d.deptno, d.dname, d.location
  2  ,      (select count(*)
  3          from   employees e
  4          where  e.deptno = d.deptno) as emp_count
  5  from   departments d;

DEPTNO DNAME      LOCATION EMP_COUNT
-------- ---------- -------- ---------
     10 ACCOUNTING NEW YORK         3
     20 TRAINING   DALLAS           5
     30 SALES      CHICAGO          6
     40 HR         BOSTON           0

SQL>
```

You could argue that this is not only a *correct* solution, but it also is a very *elegant* solution. It's elegant, because the driving table for this query (see the FROM clause) is the DEPARTMENTS table. After all, we are looking for information about departments, so the DEPARTMENTS table is the most intuitive and obvious table to start our search for the result. The first three attributes (DEPTNO, DNAME, and LOCATION) are "regular" attributes that can be found from the corresponding columns of the DEPARTMENTS table; however, the fourth attribute (the number of employees) is not stored as a column value in the database. See Chapter 1 for a discussion of database design and normalization as a technique to reduce redundancy.

Because the department head count is not physically stored in a column of the DEPARTMENTS table, we derive it by using a subquery in the SELECT clause. This is precisely how you can read this query: in the FROM clause, you visit the DEPARTMENTS table, and in the SELECT clause you select four expressions. Without using an outer join, regular join, or GROUP BY, you still get the correct number of employees (zero) for department 40.

> ■**Note** You could argue that the GROUP BY clause of the SQL language is redundant. You can solve most (if not all) aggregation problems using a correlated subquery in the SELECT clause, without using GROUP BY at all.

As noted, the subquery in Listing 9-12 is correlated. d.DEPTNO has a different value for each row d of the DEPARTMENTS table, and the subquery is executed four times for those different values: 10, 20, 30, and 40. Although it is not strictly necessary, it is a good idea to assign a column alias (EMP_COUNT in Listing 9-12) to the subquery expression, because it enhances the readability for both the query itself and for its results.

So far, we have distinguished only single-row queries and subqueries returning any number of rows. At this point, it makes sense to identify a third subquery type, which is a subtype of the single-row subquery type: *scalar subqueries*. The name indicates an important property of this type of subqueries: the result not only consists of precisely one row, but also with precisely one column value. You can use scalar subqueries almost everywhere in your SQL commands in places where a column expression or literal value is allowed and makes sense. The scalar subquery generates the literal value.

In summary, you can say that SQL supports the following subquery hierarchy:

- **Multirow subqueries:** No restrictions

- **Single-row subqueries:** Result must contain a single row

- **Scalar subqueries:** Result must be a single row and a single column

9.3 Subqueries in the FROM Clause

The next clause we investigate is the FROM clause. Actually, the FROM clause is one of the most obvious places to allow subqueries in SQL. Instead of specifying "real" table names, you simply provide subqueries (or table expressions) to take their place as a derived table.

Inline Views

Listing 9-13 shows an example of a subquery in the FROM clause. The Oracle documentation refers to these subqueries as *inline views*, as does this book; however, this is not a commonly accepted term. The name *inline view* will become clearer in Chapter 10, when we discuss views in general.

Listing 9-13. *Inline View Example*

```
SQL> select  e.ename, e.init, e.msal
  2  from    employees e
  3          join
  4          (select   x.deptno
  5          ,         avg(x.msal) avg_sal
  6          from      employees x
  7          group by x.deptno           ) g
```

```
   8         using (deptno)
   9 where   e.msal > g.avg_sal;

ENAME      INIT    MSAL
--------   -----   --------
ALLEN      JAM       1600
JONES      JM        2975
BLAKE      R         2850
SCOTT      SCJ       3000
KING       CC        5000
FORD       MG        3000

SQL>
```

A big difference between a "real" table and a subquery is that the real table has a name. Therefore, if you use subqueries in the FROM clause, you must define a tuple variable (or *table alias*, in Oracle terminology) over the result of the subquery. At the end of line 7 in Listing 9-13, we define tuple variable g. This tuple variable allows us to refer to column expressions from the subquery, as shown by g.AVG_SAL in the last line of the example. By the way, the query in Listing 9-13 is an alternative solution for the query in Listing 9-6.

ROWNUM and Top-N SQL

Suppose you just want to know the three top salaries of the HISTORY table. You can solve this problem with a complicated query, using GROUP BY and HAVING, but there is a simpler solution. Oracle SQL offers a nice feature for this type of problem, called *Top-N SQL*. Top-N SQL is based on using a subquery in the FROM clause, and offers very good performance and a syntax that is more readable than equivalent alternative solutions.

You can imagine that sorting all employee history rows, just to retrieve the three highest salary values, is a rather expensive operation, especially if the HISTORY table contains many rows. You might as well use three placeholders, and scan all rows (without sorting them), while maintaining the highest three values in those placeholders. That's exactly what Top-N SQL does. See Listing 9-14 for an example.

Listing 9-14. *Top-N SQL Example*

```
SQL> select *
  2  from   (select empno, msal
  3          from   history
  4          order  by msal desc)
  5  where  rownum <= 3;

   EMPNO     MSAL
--------  --------
    7839      5000
    7839      4900
    7839      4800

SQL>
```

Notice that Listing 9-14 uses the ROWNUM pseudo column. You can use this pseudo column in every query. It represents the order in which the rows arrived in the query result. In Exercise 12, Section 9.8, we will look at the ROWNUM pseudo column in more detail.

■**Caution** You should be careful with the ROWNUM pseudo column, because its value depends on the actual execution plan chosen by the optimizer.

In Listing 9-14, the subquery contains an ORDER BY clause. That is rather unusual for a subquery. Normally, you always sort your results in the *main query*; you never specify an ORDER BY clause in subqueries. However, the Top-N SQL feature is relying on the fact that the subquery is sorted. You could argue that the ROWNUM <= 3 condition is merged into the subquery.

Note that the following SQL statement will *not* give you the same performance as the query in Listing 9-14, because it performs a full sort before even looking at the WHERE clause:

```
SQL> select empno, sal
  2  from    history
  3  where   rownum <= 3
  4  order   by msal desc;
```

For further details about the ROWNUM pseudo column and the Top-N SQL feature, refer to *Oracle SQL Reference*.

So far, this chapter expanded your knowledge about subqueries with the ANY, ALL, and EXISTS operators. Moreover, we looked at correlated subqueries and subqueries in other places than the WHERE clause. The next section about subqueries introduces the WITH clause.

9.4 The WITH Clause

Listing 9-13 showed an example of using a subquery in a FROM clause. We could have written the same query with a slightly different syntax, as shown in Listing 9-15.

Listing 9-15. *WITH Clause Example*

```
SQL> WITH g AS
  2       (select   x.deptno
  3       ,         avg(x.msal) avg_sal
  4       from      employees x
  5       group by x.deptno)
  6  select e.ename, e.init, e.msal
  7  from    employees e
  8       join      g
  9       using (deptno)
 10  where   e.msal > g.avg_sal;
```

```
ENAME    INIT    MSAL
-------- -----  --------
ALLEN    JAM     1600
JONES    JM      2975
BLAKE    R       2850
SCOTT    SCJ     3000
KING     CC      5000
FORD     MG      3000

SQL>
```

As you can see, we have isolated the subquery definition, in lines 1 through 5, from the actual query, in lines 6 through 10. This makes the structure of the main query clearer. Using the WITH clause syntax becomes even more attractive if you refer multiple times to the same subquery from the main query. You can define as many subqueries as you like in a single WITH clause, separated by commas.

```
SQL> WITH    v1 AS (select ... from ...)
  2  ,       v2 AS (select ... from ...)
  3  ,       v3 AS ...
  4  select ...
  5  from    ...
```

If you define multiple subqueries in the WITH clause, you are allowed to refer to any subquery name that you defined earlier in the same WITH clause; that is, the definition of subquery V2 can refer to V1 in its FROM clause, and the definition of V3 can refer to both V1 and V2.

Under the hood, the Oracle DBMS has two ways to execute queries with a WITH clause:

- Merge the subquery definitions into the main query. This makes the subqueries behave just like inline views.

- Execute the subqueries, store the results in a temporary table, and access the temporary tables from the main query.

See *Oracle SQL Reference* for more details and examples. The common name for the WITH clause syntax is *subquery factoring*.

9.5 Hierarchical Queries

Relational tables are flat structures. All rows of a table are equally important, and the order in which the rows are stored is irrelevant. However, some data structures have hierarchical relationships. A famous example in most books about relational database design is the "bill of materials (BOM)" problem, where you are supposed to design an efficient relational database structure to store facts about which (sub)components are needed to build more complicated components, up to highly complicated objects such as cars and airplanes. Figure 9-1 shows an ERM diagram with a typical solution. On the left, you see the most generic solution with a many-to-many relationship, and on the right you see a typical solution using two entities.

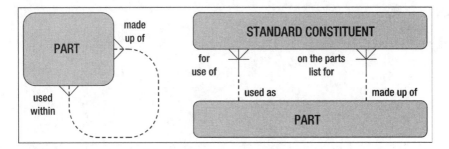

Figure 9-1. *A solution for the "bill of materials" problem*

Notice that for the solution on the left-hand side, if you replaced the entity name PART with THING, and you replaced the two relationship descriptions with "related to," then you would you have the ultimate in generic data models! Although this book is not about database design, consider this joke as a serious warning: don't make your data models overly generic.

Even if hierarchical data structures are correctly translated into relational tables, the retrieval of such structures can still be quite challenging. We have an example of a simple hierarchical relationship in our sample tables: the management structure in the EMPLOYEES table is implemented with the MGR column and its foreign key constraint to the EMPNO column of the same table.

■**Note** In hierarchical structures, it is common practice to refer to *parent* rows and *children* rows. Another common (and self-explanatory) terminology is using a tree metaphor by referring to *root*, *branch*, and *leaf* rows.

START WITH and CONNECT BY

Oracle SQL supports a number of operators—and pseudo columns populated by those operators—to facilitate queries against hierarchical data. Let's look at a simple example first, shown in Listing 9-16.

Listing 9-16. *Hierarchical Query Example*

```
SQL> select  ename, LEVEL
  2  from    employees
  3  START   WITH mgr is null
  4  CONNECT BY NOCYCLE PRIOR empno = mgr;


ENAME       LEVEL
--------  --------
KING           1
JONES          2
SCOTT          3
ADAMS          4
FORD           3
```

```
SMITH            4
BLAKE            2
ALLEN            3
WARD             3
MARTIN           3
TURNER           3
JONES            3
CLARK            2
MILLER           3

14 rows selected.

SQL>
```

The START WITH and CONNECT BY clauses allow you to do the following:

- Identify a starting point (root) for the tree structure.

- Specify how you can walk up or down the tree structure from any row.

The START WITH and CONNECT BY clauses must be specified *after* the WHERE clause (if any) and *before* the GROUP BY clause (if any).

■Note It is your own responsibility to indicate the correct starting point (or root) for the hierarchy. Listing 9-16 uses MGR IS NULL as a condition, because we know that the null value in the MGR column has a special meaning. The Oracle DBMS treats *each* row for which the START WITH condition evaluates to TRUE as root for a separate tree structure; that is, you can define multiple tree structures within the context of a single query.

The NOCYCLE keyword in the CONNECT BY clause is optional; however, if you omit NOCYCLE, you risk ending up in a loop. If that happens, the Oracle DBMS returns the following error message:

```
ORA-01436: CONNECT BY loop in user data
```

Our EMPLOYEES table doesn't contain any cyclic references, but specifying NOCYCLE never hurts.

Pay special attention to the placement of the PRIOR operator. The PRIOR operator always points to the parent row. In Listing 9-16, PRIOR is placed before EMPNO, so we are able to find parent rows by starting from the MGR column value of the current row and then searching the EMPNO column values in all other rows for a match. If you put PRIOR in the wrong place, you define hierarchical relationships in the opposite direction. Just see what happens in Listing 9-16 if you change the fourth line to CONNECT BY PRIOR MGR = EMPNO or to CONNECT BY EMPNO = PRIOR MGR.

At first sight, the result in Listing 9-16 is not very impressive, since you just get a list of employee names, followed by a number. And if we had omitted LEVEL from the SELECT clause, the result would have been completely trivial. However, many things happened behind the scenes. We just have not exploited the full benefits yet.

LEVEL, CONNECT_BY_ISCYCLE, and CONNECT_BY_ISLEAF

As a consequence of using START WITH and CONNECT BY, the Oracle DBMS assigns several pseudo column values to every row. Listing 9-16 showed a first example of such a pseudo column: LEVEL. You can use these pseudo column values for many purposes; for example, to filter specific rows in the WHERE clause or to enhance the readability of your results in the SELECT clause.

The following are the hierarchical pseudo columns:

- **LEVEL:** The level of the row in the tree structure.

- **CONNECT_BY_ISCYCLE:** The value is 1 for each row with a *child* that is also a *parent* of the same row (that is, you have a cyclic reference); otherwise, the value is 0.

- **CONNECT_BY_ISLEAF:** The value is 1 if the row is a *leaf*; otherwise, the value is 0.

Listing 9-17 shows an example using the LEVEL pseudo column combined with the LPAD function, adding indentation to highlight the hierarchical query results.

Listing 9-17. *Enhancing Readability with the LPAD Function*

```
SQL> select  lpad(' ',2*level-1)||ename as ename
  2  from    employees
  3  start   with mgr is null
  4  connect by nocycle prior empno = mgr;

ENAME
-----------------
 KING
   JONES
     SCOTT
       ADAMS
     FORD
       SMITH
   BLAKE
     ALLEN
     WARD
     MARTIN
     TURNER
     JONES
   CLARK
     MILLER

14 rows selected.

SQL>
```

CONNECT_BY_ROOT and SYS_CONNECT_BY_PATH

If you use START WITH and CONNECT BY to define a hierarchical query, you can use two interesting hierarchical operators in the SELECT clause:

- **CONNECT_BY_ROOT:** This operator allows you to connect each row (regardless of its level in the tree structure) with its own root.

- **SYS_CONNECT_BY_PATH:** This function allows you to display the full path from the current row to its root.

See Listing 9-18 for an example of using both operators. Note that the START WITH clause in Listing 9-18 creates three separate tree structures: one for each manager.

Listing 9-18. *Using CONNECT_BY_ROOT and SYS_CONNECT_BY_PATH*

```
SQL> select   ename
  2  ,         connect_by_root ename          as manager
  3  ,         sys_connect_by_path(ename,' > ') as full_path
  4  from     employees
  5  start    with job = 'MANAGER'
  6  connect by prior empno = mgr;

ENAME     MANAGER  FULL_PATH
--------  -------- ---------------------------
JONES     JONES    > JONES
SCOTT     JONES    > JONES > SCOTT
ADAMS     JONES    > JONES > SCOTT > ADAMS
FORD      JONES    > JONES > FORD
SMITH     JONES    > JONES > FORD > SMITH
BLAKE     BLAKE    > BLAKE
ALLEN     BLAKE    > BLAKE > ALLEN
WARD      BLAKE    > BLAKE > WARD
MARTIN    BLAKE    > BLAKE > MARTIN
TURNER    BLAKE    > BLAKE > TURNER
JONES     BLAKE    > BLAKE > JONES
CLARK     CLARK    > CLARK
MILLER    CLARK    > CLARK > MILLER

13 rows selected.

SQL>
```

You can specify additional conditions in the CONNECT BY clause, thus eliminating entire subtree structures. Note the important difference with conditions in the WHERE clause: those conditions filter only individual rows. See *Oracle SQL Reference* for more details and examples.

Hierarchical Query Result Sorting

If you want to sort the results of hierarchical queries, and you use a regular ORDER BY clause, the carefully constructed hierarchical tree gets disturbed in most cases. In such cases, you can use the SIBLINGS option of the ORDER BY clause. This option doesn't destroy the hierarchy of the rows in the result. See Listing 9-19 for an example, and watch what happens with the query result if we remove the SIBLINGS option.

Listing 9-19. *ORDER SIBLINGS BY Example*

```
SQL> select  ename
  2 ,        sys_connect_by_path(ename,'|') as path
  3 from     employees
  4 start    with mgr is null
  5 connect  by prior empno = mgr
  6 order    SIBLINGS by ename;

ENAME    PATH
-------- ------------------------------
KING     |KING
BLAKE    |KING|BLAKE
ALLEN    |KING|BLAKE|ALLEN
JONES    |KING|BLAKE|JONES
MARTIN   |KING|BLAKE|MARTIN
TURNER   |KING|BLAKE|TURNER
WARD     |KING|BLAKE|WARD
CLARK    |KING|CLARK
MILLER   |KING|CLARK|MILLER
JONES    |KING|JONES
FORD     |KING|JONES|FORD
SMITH    |KING|JONES|FORD|SMITH
SCOTT    |KING|JONES|SCOTT
ADAMS    |KING|JONES|SCOTT|ADAMS

14 rows selected.

SQL> c/siblings//
  6* order    by ename

SQL> /

ENAME    PATH
-------- ------------------------------
ADAMS    |KING|JONES|SCOTT|ADAMS
ALLEN    |KING|BLAKE|ALLEN
BLAKE    |KING|BLAKE
CLARK    |KING|CLARK
FORD     |KING|JONES|FORD
```

```
JONES      |KING|JONES
JONES      |KING|BLAKE|JONES
KING       |KING
MARTIN     |KING|BLAKE|MARTIN
MILLER     |KING|CLARK|MILLER
SCOTT      |KING|JONES|SCOTT
SMITH      |KING|JONES|FORD|SMITH
TURNER     |KING|BLAKE|TURNER
WARD       |KING|BLAKE|WARD

14 rows selected.

SQL>
```

9.6 Analytical Functions and Windows

This section introduces the concept of *analytical functions* and *windows*, which make up a very powerful part of the ANSI/ISO SQL standard syntax. Analytical functions enable you to produce derived attributes that would otherwise be very complicated to achieve in SQL.

Earlier in this chapter, in Section 9.2, you saw how subqueries in the SELECT clause allow you to add derived attributes to the SELECT clause of your queries. Analytical functions and windows provide similar functionality.

Figure 9-2 illustrates the concept of a window and its corresponding (current) row. Analytical functions allow you to derive aggregated information about the window corresponding to the current row.

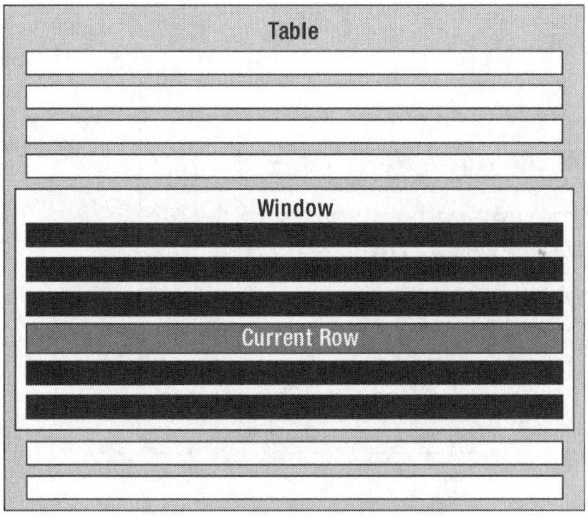

Figure 9-2. *Table, window, and current row*

You specify windows in the SELECT clause of your queries, as a component of an analytical function. The (simplified) syntax of analytical functions looks like the following:

```
SQL> select analytical-function(col-expr) OVER (window-spec) [AS col-alias]
  2  ,     ...
  3  from  ...
```

Analytical Window Specification

You specify windows with the OVER clause of analytical functions. Figure 9-3 shows the syntax details of a window specification, to be entered between parentheses.

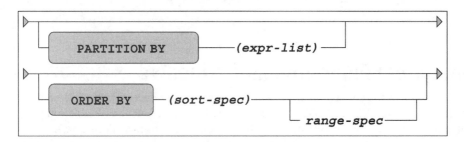

Figure 9-3. *Window specification syntax diagram*

Note that the syntax in Figure 9-3 allows for an *empty* window specification—all components are optional. The default window is the entire (nonpartitioned and unordered) table. The details about the PARTITION BY and ORDER BY components of a window specification will be discussed soon. First, let's drill down a little further into how you can specify a range of rows for your analytical window. The corresponding syntax is shown in Figure 9-4.

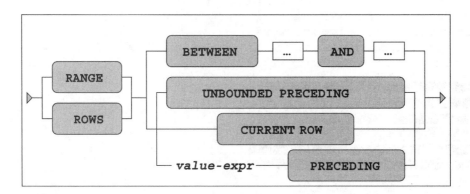

Figure 9-4. *Range specification syntax diagram*

You can choose between RANGE and ROWS; they are synonyms. If you don't use the BETWEEN ... AND ... syntax and you specify only one point, the Oracle DBMS considers it the starting point, and the ending point defaults to the current row.

Figure 9-5 shows the BETWEEN ... AND ... syntax details. Note that UNBOUNDED FOLLOWING is invalid as a starting point, and UNBOUNDED PRECEDING is invalid as an ending point.

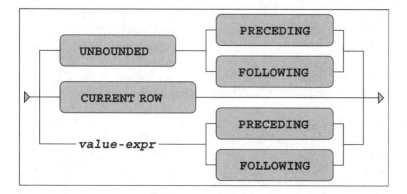

Figure 9-5. *BETWEEN ... AND ... Syntax Diagram*

Here are some typical examples of valid range specifications:

- ROWS UNBOUNDED PRECEDING

- ROWS BETWEEN CURRENT ROW AND UNBOUNDED FOLLOWING

- RANGE BETWEEN 3 PRECEDING AND 3 FOLLOWING

Analytical Window Ordering

The Oracle DBMS applies the analytical function to the window rows. Some analytical function expressions don't need any ordering, but they are the exceptions. For example, as soon as you use keywords like PRECEDING and FOLLOWING, you need to specify a certain row ordering within your window, to give those keywords their meaning. If you make a mistake and forget to specify an ORDER [SIBLINGS] BY window component, the Oracle error message is self-explanatory. SIBLINGS is valid only in hierarchical queries, as explained in the previous section.

If you want predictable query results, you should choose the *correct* window ordering. More specifically, if you sort on a column (or column combination) that isn't unique within your window, concepts like "previous row" and "following row" become rather slippery. Let's look at the example in Listing 9-20.

Listing 9-20. *Nondeterministic Window Sorting*

```
SQL> select mgr, ename, msal
  2  ,        sum(msal) over
  3           ( order by mgr, msal
  4             range unbounded preceding
  5           ) as cumulative
  6  from     employees
  7  order    by mgr, msal;
```

```
    MGR ENAME        MSAL CUMULATIVE
-------- -------- -------- ----------
    7566 SCOTT        3000       6000   <<<
    7566 FORD         3000       6000   <<<
    7698 JONES         800       6800
    7698 WARD         1250       9300   <<<
    7698 MARTIN       1250       9300   <<<
    7698 TURNER       1500      10800
    7698 ALLEN        1600      12400
    7782 MILLER       1300      13700
    7788 ADAMS        1100      14800
    7839 CLARK        2450      17250
    7839 BLAKE        2850      20100
    7839 JONES        2975      23075
    7902 SMITH         800      23875
         KING         5000      28875

14 rows selected.

SQL>
```

As you can see in Listing 9-20, the fourth column shows a cumulative monthly salary, because we define a window per employee from the beginning of the table (UNBOUNDED PRECEDING) until the current row. The current row is (in this case) the default upper boundary of the window, so you don't need to specify this explicitly.

As you can also see in Listing 9-20, the cumulative salary doesn't "behave" properly. Look at the four highlighted rows (<<<). This is *not* a bug; there is something wrong with the query. The window sorting specification (MGR, MSAL) is not precise enough. Employees SCOTT and FORD happen to have the same manager *and* the same monthly salary, and the same is true for WARD and MARTIN. You can solve this problem by changing the ORDER BY clause in line 3, to make it deterministic, as shown in Listing 9-21.

Listing 9-21. *Deterministic Window Sorting*

```
SQL> select mgr, ename, msal
  2  ,      sum(msal) over
  3         ( order by mgr, msal, EMPNO
  4           range unbounded preceding
  5         ) as cumulative
  6  from   employees
  7  order  by mgr, msal;

    MGR ENAME        MSAL CUMULATIVE
-------- -------- -------- ----------
    7566 SCOTT        3000       3000
    7566 FORD         3000       6000
    7698 JONES         800       6800
    7698 WARD         1250       8050
```

```
     7698 MARTIN      1250       9300
     7698 TURNER      1500      10800
     7698 ALLEN       1600      12400
     7782 MILLER      1300      13700
     7788 ADAMS       1100      14800
     7839 CLARK       2450      17250
     7839 BLAKE       2850      20100
     7839 JONES       2975      23075
     7902 SMITH        800      23875
          KING        5000      28875

14 rows selected.

SQL>
```

By adding EMPNO (which is the primary key), you ensure that the window ordering is deterministic.

Partitioned Analytical Windows

Now let's enhance this example a little further. As shown in Figure 9-3, you can optionally partition analytical windows, just as you can partition outer joins (as discussed in Section 8.9 of the previous chapter). This makes the analytical functions start again for each partition. If you look at the results in Listing 9-21, you can see that the cumulative salary increases with every row, up to 28875.

In Listing 9-22, we add a PARTITION BY clause to the window specification, before the ORDER BY clause. This makes the cumulative salary start again from zero for every manager.

Listing 9-22. *PARTITION BY Example*

```
SQL> break on MGR

SQL> select mgr, ename, msal
  2  ,      sum(msal) over
  3         ( PARTITION BY mgr
  4           order by mgr, msal, empno
  5           range unbounded preceding
  6         ) as cumulative
  7  from   employees
  8  order  by mgr, msal;

  MGR ENAME       MSAL CUMULATIVE
-------- -------- -------- ----------
 7566 SCOTT       3000       3000
      FORD        3000       6000
 7698 JONES        800        800
      WARD        1250       2050
      MARTIN      1250       3300
```

```
        TURNER      1500      4800
        ALLEN       1600      6400
   7782 MILLER      1300      1300
   7788 ADAMS       1100      1100
   7839 CLARK       2450      2450
        BLAKE       2850      5300
        JONES       2975      8275
   7902 SMITH        800       800
        KING        5000      5000

14 rows selected.

SQL>
```

Analytical Functions

For analytical functions, you can use all of the regular group functions, such as SUM, MAX, MIN, AVG, and COUNT (see Section 8.6 of Chapter 8). On top of that, Oracle SQL offers an impressive list of additional analytical functions that can be used only for window queries. Two of these are LAG and LEAD, which are demonstrated in Listing 9-23.

Listing 9-23. *LAG and LEAD Analytical Functions*

```
SQL> break on empno

SQL> select empno, begindate, msal
  2  ,      LAG(msal) over
  3         ( partition by empno
  4           order by empno, begindate
  5         ) as prev_sal
  6  ,      LEAD(msal) over
  7         ( partition by empno
  8           order by empno, begindate
  9         ) as next_sal
 10  from   history
 11  order  by empno, begindate;

   EMPNO BEGINDATE        MSAL PREV_SAL NEXT_SAL
-------- ----------- -------- -------- --------
    7369 01-JAN-2000      950               800
         01-FEB-2000      800      950
    7499 01-JUN-1988     1000              1300
         01-JUL-1989     1300     1000     1500
         01-DEC-1993     1500     1300     1700
         01-OCT-1995     1700     1500     1600
         01-NOV-1999     1600     1700
```

```
...
     7902 01-SEP-1998      1400                    1650
          01-OCT-1998      1650       1400         2500
          15-MAR-1999      2500       1650         3000
          01-JAN-2000      3000       2500         3000
          01-AUG-2000      3000       3000
     7934 01-FEB-1998      1275                    1280
          01-MAY-1998      1280       1275         1290
          01-FEB-1999      1290       1280         1300
          01-JAN-2000      1300       1290

79 rows selected.

SQL>
```

Applying these analytical functions to the HISTORY table, we get an historic overview per employee/begin date period, showing the monthly salary, the previous monthly salary, and the next monthly salary. If a previous or next value for the salary is inapplicable or unavailable, you get a null value instead.

See *Oracle SQL Reference* for more details and examples of analytical functions. To begin with, along with LAG and LEAD, check out RANK and DENSE_RANK.

9.7 Flashback Features

This section covers some Oracle-specific extensions of the SQL language. Although they might appear slightly off topic, the flashback features are simply too valuable to remain uncovered in this book.

In Chapter 6, we talked about the concept of *read consistency*. Read consistency means that your SQL statements always get a consistent view of the data, regardless of what other database users or applications do with the same data at the same time. The Oracle DBMS provides a *snapshot* of the data at the point in time when the statement execution started. In the same chapter, you also saw that you can change your session to be READ ONLY, so that your query results depend on the data as it was at the beginning of your session.

The Oracle DBMS has its methods to achieve this, without using any locking techniques affecting other database users or applications. How this is done is irrelevant for this book. This section shows some interesting ways to use the same technique, by stating explicitly in your queries that you want to go back in time.

■**Note** The flashback query feature may need some configuration efforts before you can use it. This is the task of a database administrator. Therefore, it is not covered in this book. See the Oracle documentation for more details.

Before we start our flashback query experiments, we first create a temporary copy of the EMPLOYEES table, as shown in Listing 9-24. This allows us to perform various experiments without destroying the contents of the real EMPLOYEES table. We also change the NLS_TIMESTAMP_FORMAT parameter with the ALTER SESSION command, to influence how timestamp values are displayed on the screen.

Listing 9-24. *Preparing for the Flashback Examples*

```
SQL> create table e as select * from employees;
Table created.

SQL> alter session set nls_timestamp_format='DD-MON-YYYY HH24:MI:SS.FF3';
Session altered.

SQL> select localtimestamp as table_created from dual;
TABLE_CREATED
-----------------------------------------------------------
01-OCT-2004 10:53:42.746

SQL> update e set msal = msal + 10;
14 rows updated.
SQL> commit;
Commit complete.

SQL> select localtimestamp as after_update_1 from dual;
AFTER_UPDATE_1
-----------------------------------------------------------
01-OCT-2004 10:54:26.138

SQL> update e set msal = msal - 20 where  deptno = 10;
3 rows updated.
SQL> commit;
Commit complete.

SQL> select localtimestamp as after_update_2 from dual;
AFTER_UPDATE_2
-----------------------------------------------------------
01-OCT-2004 10:54:42.602

SQL> delete from e where  deptno <= 20;
8 rows deleted.
SQL> commit;
Commit complete.

SQL> select localtimestamp as now            from dual;
NOW
-----------------------------------------------------------
01-OCT-2004 10:55:25.623

SQL>
```

■**Tip** Don't execute these four steps too quickly in a row. You should take some time in between the steps. This makes it much easier during your experiments to go back to a specific point in time.

AS OF

Listing 9-25 shows a first example of a flashback query. First, we select the current situation with a regular query. Then we use the AS OF TIMESTAMP option in the FROM clause to go back in time. As in examples in earlier chapters, we use the SQL*Plus ampersand (&) substitution trick, which allows us to repeat the query conveniently with different timestamp values.

Listing 9-25. *Flashback Example: AS OF Syntax*

```
SQL> select empno, ename, deptno, msal
  2  from   e;

  EMPNO ENAME      DEPTNO     MSAL
-------- -------- -------- --------
   7499 ALLEN         30     1610
   7521 WARD          30     1260
   7654 MARTIN        30     1260
   7698 BLAKE         30     2860
   7844 TURNER        30     1510
   7900 JONES         30      810

SQL> select empno, ename, deptno, msal
  2  from   e
  3         AS OF TIMESTAMP to_timestamp('&timestamp');

Enter value for timestamp: 01-OCT-2004 10:53:47.000

  EMPNO ENAME      DEPTNO     MSAL
-------- -------- -------- --------
   7369 SMITH         20      800
   7499 ALLEN         30     1600
   7521 WARD          30     1250
   7566 JONES         20     2975
   7654 MARTIN        30     1250
   7698 BLAKE         30     2850
   7782 CLARK         10     2450
   7788 SCOTT         20     3000
   7839 KING          10     5000
   7844 TURNER        30     1500
   7876 ADAMS         20     1100
   7900 JONES         30      800
   7902 FORD          20     3000
   7934 MILLER        10     1300
```

```
14 rows selected.

SQL> /
Enter value for timestamp: 01-OCT-2004 10:53:42.000
from    e
        *
ERROR at line 2:
ORA-01466: unable to read data - table definition has changed

SQL>
```

Of course, the timestamps to be used in Listing 9-25 depend on the timing of your experiments. Choose appropriate timestamps if you want to test these statements yourself. If you executed the steps of Listing 9-24 with some decent time intervals (as suggested), you have enough appropriate candidate values to play with.

The Oracle error message at the bottom of Listing 9-25 indicates that this query is trying to go back too far in time. In this case, table E didn't even exist. Data definition changes (ALTER TABLE E ...) may also prohibit flashback queries, as suggested by the error message text.

VERSIONS BETWEEN

In Listing 9-26, we go one step further, using the VERSIONS BETWEEN operator. Now we get the complete history of the rows—that is, as far as the Oracle DBMS is able reconstruct them.

Listing 9-26. *Flashback Example: VERSIONS BETWEEN Syntax*

```
SQL> break on empno

SQL> select empno, msal
  2  ,       versions_starttime
  3  ,       versions_endtime
  4  from    e
  5          versions between timestamp minvalue and maxvalue
  6  where   deptno = 10
  7  order   by empno, versions_starttime nulls first;

  EMPNO    MSAL VERSIONS_STARTTIME       VERSIONS_ENDTIME
-------- -------- ------------------------ ------------------------
   7782    2450                           01-OCT-2004 10:54:23.000
           2460 01-OCT-2004 10:54:23.000  01-OCT-2004 10:54:41.000
           2440 01-OCT-2004 10:54:41.000  01-OCT-2004 10:55:24.000
           2440 01-OCT-2004 10:55:24.000
   7839    5000                           01-OCT-2004 10:54:23.000
           5010 01-OCT-2004 10:54:23.000  01-OCT-2004 10:54:41.000
           4990 01-OCT-2004 10:54:41.000  01-OCT-2004 10:55:24.000
           4990 01-OCT-2004 10:55:24.000
   7934    1300                           01-OCT-2004 10:54:23.000
           1310 01-OCT-2004 10:54:23.000  01-OCT-2004 10:54:41.000
```

```
       1290 01-OCT-2004 10:54:41.000  01-OCT-2004 10:55:24.000
       1290 01-OCT-2004 10:55:24.000

12 rows selected.

SQL>
```

By using the VERSIONS BETWEEN operator in the FROM clause, you introduce several additional pseudo columns, such as VERSIONS_STARTTIME and VERSIONS_ENDTIME. You can use these pseudo columns in your queries.

By using the correct ORDER BY clause (watch the NULLS FIRST clause in Listing 9-26), you get a complete historical overview. You don't see a start time for the three oldest salary values because you created the rows too long ago, and you don't see an end time for the last value because it is the current salary value.

FLASHBACK TABLE

In Chapter 7, you learned that you can rescue an inadvertently dropped table from the recycle bin with the FLASHBACK TABLE command. Listing 9-27 shows another example of this usage.

Listing 9-27. *Using FLASHBACK TABLE ... TO BEFORE DROP*

```
SQL> drop table e;
Table dropped.

SQL> flashback table e to before drop;
Flashback complete.

SQL> select * from e;

EMPNO ENAME     INIT  JOB        MGR  BDATE        MSAL  COMM  DEPTNO
------ --------- ----- --------- ------ ----------- ------ ------ ------
  7499 ALLEN     JAM   SALESREP   7698 20-FEB-1961  1610   300     30
  7521 WARD      TF    SALESREP   7698 22-FEB-1962  1260   500     30
  7654 MARTIN    P     SALESREP   7698 28-SEP-1956  1260  1400     30
  7698 BLAKE     R     MANAGER    7839 01-NOV-1963  2860           30
  7844 TURNER    JJ    SALESREP   7698 28-SEP-1968  1510     0     30
  7900 JONES     R     ADMIN      7698 03-DEC-1969   810           30

SQL>
```

You can go back to any point in time with the FLASHBACK TABLE command, as you can see in Listing 9-28. Note the following important difference: Listings 9-25 and 9-26 show *queries* against table E where you go back in time, but the FLASHBACK TABLE example in Listing 9-28 *changes* the database and restores table E to a given point in time.

Listing 9-28. *Another FLASHBACK TABLE Example*

```
SQL> select count(*) from e;

COUNT(*)
--------
       6

SQL> flashback table e to timestamp to_timestamp('&timestamp');
Enter value for timestamp: 01-OCT-2004 10:54:00.000

Flashback complete.

SQL> select count(*) from e;

COUNT(*)
--------
      14

SQL>
```

It is not always possible to go back in time with one table using the FLASHBACK TABLE command. For example, you could have constraints referring to other tables prohibiting such a change. See *Oracle SQL Reference* for more details about the FLASHBACK TABLE command.

9.8 Exercises

You can practice applying the advanced retrieval functions covered in this chapter in the following exercises. The answers are presented in Appendix D.

1. It is normal practice that (junior) trainers always attend a course taught by a senior colleague before teaching that course themselves. For which trainer/course combinations did this happen?

2. Actually, if the junior trainer teaches a course for the first time, that senior colleague (see the previous exercise) sits in the back of the classroom in a supporting role. Try to find these course/junior/senior combinations.

3. Which employees never taught a course?

4. Which employees attended all build courses (category BLD)?
   They are entitled to get a discount on the next course they attend.

5. Provide a list of all employees having the same monthly salary and commission as (at least) one employee of department 30. You are interested in only employees from other departments.

6. Look again at Listings 9-4 and 9-5. Are they really logically equivalent? Just for testing purposes, search on a nonexisting job and execute both queries again. Explain the results.

7. You saw a series of examples in this chapter about all employees that ever taught an SQL course (in Listings 9-9 through 9-11). How can you adapt these queries in such a way that they answer the negation of the same question (… all employees that *never* …)?

8. Check out your solution for exercise 4 in Chapter 8: "For all course offerings, list the course code, begin date, and number of registrations. Sort your results on the number of registrations, from high to low." Can you come up with a more elegant solution now, without using an outer join?

9. Who attended (at least) the same courses as employee 7788?

10. Give the name and initials of all employees at the bottom of the management hierarchy, with a third column showing the number of management levels above them.

11. Look at the query result in Listing 9-22. The last two rows are:

7902	SMITH	800	800
	KING	5000	5000

Looking at the other rows in Listing 9-22, you might expect the following results instead:

7902	SMITH	800	800
	KING	5000	5800

What is the correct result, and why?

12. Why don't you get any result from the following query?

```
SQL> select * from employees where rownum = 2;

no rows selected

SQL>
```

■ ■ ■

CHAPTER 10

Views

This chapter covers views, a very important component of the relational model (see Ted Codd's rule 6, in Chapter 1). The first section explains the concept of views. The second section discusses how to use the `CREATE VIEW` command to create views. In the next section, you'll learn about the various ways you can use views in SQL, in the areas of retrieval, logical data independency, and security.

Then we explore the (im)possibilities of data manipulation via views. How does it work, which are the constraints, and what should we consider? You'll learn about updatable views, nonupdatable views, and the `WITH CHECK OPTION` clause of the `CREATE VIEW` command.

Section 10.5 discusses data manipulation via inline views. This name is slightly confusing, because inline views are not "real" views. Rather, they are subqueries in the `FROM` clause, as discussed in the previous chapter. Data manipulation via inline views allows you to perform various complicated and creative data manipulation operations, which would otherwise be very complex (or impossible) via the underlying base tables.

Section 10.6 covers views and performance. Following that is a section about materialized views. Materialized views are very popular in data warehousing environments, which have relatively high data volumes with mainly read-only access. Materialized views allow you to improve query response times with some form of controlled redundancy. The chapter ends with some exercises.

10.1 What Are Views?

The result of a query is always a table, or more precisely, a *derived* table. Compared with "real" tables in the database, the result of a query is volatile, but nevertheless, the result *is* a table. The only thing that is missing for the query result is a name. Essentially, a view is nothing more than a query with a given name. A more precise definition is as follows:

■**DEFINITION**   A *view* is a virtual table with the result of a stored query as its "contents," which are derived each time you access the view.

The first part of this definition states two things:

- **A view is a virtual *table*:** That is, you can treat a view (in almost all circumstances) as a table in your SQL statements. Every view has a name, and that's why views are also referred to as *named queries*. Views have columns, each with a name and a datatype, so you can execute queries against views, and you can manipulate the "contents" of views (with some restrictions) with INSERT, UPDATE, DELETE, and MERGE commands.

- **A view is a *virtual* table:** In reality, when you access a view, it only *behaves* like a table. Views don't have any rows; that's why the view definition says "contents" (within quotation marks). You define views as named queries, which are stored in the data dictionary; that's why another common term for views is *stored queries*. Each time you access the "contents" of a view, the Oracle DBMS retrieves the view query from the data dictionary and uses that query to produce the virtual table.

Data manipulation on a view sounds counterintuitive; after all, views don't have any rows. Nevertheless, views are supposed to behave like tables as much as possible. If you issue data manipulation commands against a view, the DBMS is supposed to translate those commands into corresponding actions against the underlying base tables. Note that some views are not updatable; that's why Ted Codd's rule 6 (see Chapter 1) explicitly refers to views being *theoretically updatable*. We'll discuss data manipulation via views in Section 10.4 of this chapter.

Views are not only dependent on changes in the *contents* of the underlying base tables, but also on certain changes in the *structure* of those tables. For example, a view doesn't work anymore if you drop or rename columns of the underlying tables that are referenced in the view definition.

10.2 View Creation

You can create views with the CREATE VIEW command. Figure 10-1 shows the corresponding syntax diagram.

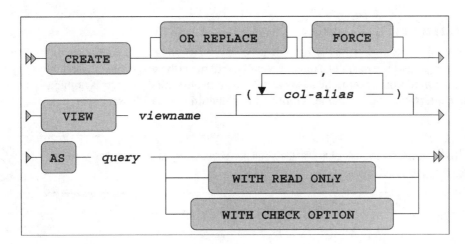

Figure 10-1. *CREATE VIEW syntax diagram*

The OR REPLACE option allows you to replace an existing view definition. This is especially useful if you have granted various privileges on your views. View privileges are not retained when you use the DROP VIEW / CREATE VIEW command sequence (as explained later in this section), but a CREATE OR REPLACE VIEW command does preserve them. The FORCE option doesn't check whether the underlying base tables (used in the view definition) exist or whether you have sufficient privileges to access those base tables. Obviously, these conditions must eventually be met at the time you start using your view definition.

Normally, views inherit their column names from the defining query. However, you should be aware of some possible complications. For example, you might have a query result on your screen showing multiple columns with the same name, and you may have column headings showing functions or other arbitrary column expressions. Obviously, you cannot use query results with these problems as the basis for a view definition. Views have the same column naming rules and constraints as regular tables: column names must be different, and they cannot contain characters such as brackets and arithmetic operators. You can solve such problems in two ways:

- You can specify column aliases in the SELECT clause of the defining query, in such a way that the column headings adhere to all column naming rules and conventions. In this book's examples, we use this method as much as possible.

- You can specify explicit column aliases in the CREATE VIEW command between the view name and the AS clause (see Figure 10-1).

The WITH CHECK OPTION and WITH READ ONLY options influence view behavior under data manipulation activity, as described later in this chapter, in Section 10.4.

Listing 10-1 shows two very similar SQL statements. However, note the main difference; the first statement creates a *view*, and the second statement creates a *table*.

Listing 10-1. *Views vs. Tables*

```
SQL> create view dept20_v as
  2  select * from employees where deptno = 20;

View created.

SQL> create table dept20_t as
  2  select * from employees where deptno = 20;

Table created.

SQL>
```

The "contents" of the view DEPT20_V will always be fully dependent on the EMPLOYEES table. The table DEPT20_T uses the current EMPLOYEES table as only a starting point. Once created, it is a fully independent table with its own contents.

Creating a View from a Query

Listing 10-2 shows an example of a regular query with its result. The query is a join over three tables, providing information about all employees and their departments. Note that we use an alias in the SELECT clause (see line 6) to make sure that all columns in the query result have different names. See line 2, where you select the ENAME column, too.

Listing 10-2. *A Regular Query, Joining Three Tables*

```
SQL> select e.empno
  2  ,        e.ENAME
  3  ,        e.init
  4  ,        d.dname
  5  ,        d.location
  6  ,        m.ENAME     as MANAGER
  7  from     employees   e
  8           join
  9           departments d using (deptno)
 10           join
 11           employees   m on (e.empno = d.mgr);

  EMPNO ENAME     INIT  DNAME       LOCATION MANAGER
-------- -------- ----- ----------- -------- -------
   7369 SMITH     N     TRAINING    DALLAS   JONES
   7499 ALLEN     JAM   SALES       CHICAGO  BLAKE
   7521 WARD      TF    SALES       CHICAGO  BLAKE
   7566 JONES     JM    TRAINING    DALLAS   JONES
   7654 MARTIN    P     SALES       CHICAGO  BLAKE
   7698 BLAKE     R     SALES       CHICAGO  BLAKE
   7782 CLARK     AB    ACCOUNTING  NEW YORK CLARK
   7788 SCOTT     SCJ   TRAINING    DALLAS   JONES
   7839 KING      CC    ACCOUNTING  NEW YORK CLARK
   7844 TURNER    JJ    SALES       CHICAGO  BLAKE
   7876 ADAMS     AA    TRAINING    DALLAS   JONES
   7900 JONES     R     SALES       CHICAGO  BLAKE
   7902 FORD      MG    TRAINING    DALLAS   JONES
   7934 MILLER    TJA   ACCOUNTING  NEW YORK CLARK

14 rows selected.

SQL>
```

Listing 10-3 shows how you can transform this query into a view definition, by inserting one additional line at the beginning of the command.

Listing 10-3. *Creating a View from the Query in Listing 10-2*

```
SQL> create view empdept_v as      -- This line is added
  2  select e.empno
  3  ,       e.ENAME
  4  ,       e.init
  5  ,       d.dname
  6  ,       d.location
  7  ,       m.ENAME    as MANAGER
  8  from    employees   e
  9          join
 10          departments d using (deptno)
 11          join
 12          employees   m on (m.empno = d.mgr);

View created.

SQL>
```

This view is now a permanent part of your collection of database objects. However, note that if we had not used an alias for m.ENAME, Listing 10-3 would give the following Oracle error message:

```
ORA-00957: duplicate column name
```

Getting Information About Views from the Data Dictionary

Listing 10-4 queries the OBJ data dictionary view. As you can see, you now have two views in your schema: DEPT20_V and EMPDEPT_V.

Listing 10-4. *Querying the Data Dictionary to See Your Views*

```
SQL> select object_name, object_type
  2  from    obj
  3  where   object_type in ('TABLE','VIEW')
  4  order   by object_type, object_name;

OBJECT_NAME                     OBJECT_TYPE
------------------------------- -----------
COURSES                         TABLE
DEPARTMENTS                     TABLE
DEPT20_T                        TABLE
E                               TABLE
EMPLOYEES                       TABLE
HISTORY                         TABLE
OFFERINGS                       TABLE
REGISTRATIONS                   TABLE
SALGRADES                       TABLE
```

```
DEPT20_V                        VIEW
EMPDEPT_V                       VIEW

11 rows selected.

SQL>
```

Listing 10-5 shows that you can use the SQL*Plus DESCRIBE command on a view, just as you can on regular tables, and it also shows an example of a query against a view.

Listing 10-5. *Using DESCRIBE and Writing Queries Against Views*

```
SQL> describe empdept_v
Name                            Null?     Type
------------------------------- --------- -------------
EMPNO                           NOT NULL  NUMBER(4)
ENAME                           NOT NULL  VARCHAR2(8)
INIT                            NOT NULL  VARCHAR2(5)
DNAME                           NOT NULL  VARCHAR2(10)
LOCATION                        NOT NULL  VARCHAR2(8)
MANAGER                         NOT NULL  VARCHAR2(8)

SQL> select * from empdept_v where manager = 'CLARK';

   EMPNO ENAME      INIT  DNAME       LOCATION MANAGER
-------- ---------- ----- ----------- -------- --------
    7934 MILLER     TJA   ACCOUNTING  NEW YORK CLARK
    7839 KING       CC    ACCOUNTING  NEW YORK CLARK
    7782 CLARK      AB    ACCOUNTING  NEW YORK CLARK

SQL>
```

You can query the USER_VIEWS data dictionary view to retrieve your view definitions, as shown in Listing 10-6.

■**Note** The two leading SQL*Plus commands in Listing 10-6 are used only to make the results more readable. Chapter 11 discusses these (and many other) SQL*Plus commands in more detail.

Listing 10-6. *Retrieving View Definitions from the Data Dictionary*

```
SQL> set     long 999
SQL> column text format a42 word wrapped

SQL> select view_name, text
  2  from    user_views;
```

```
VIEW_NAME                     TEXT
----------------------------  ----------------------------------------
DEPT20_V                      select "EMPNO","ENAME","INIT","JOB",
                              "MGR","BDATE","MSAL","COMM","DEPTNO"
                              from employees where deptno=20

EMPDEPT_V                     select e.empno
                              ,       e.ENAME
                              ,       e.init
                              ,       d.dname
                              ,       d.location
                              ,       m.ENAME     as MANAGER
                              from    employees   e
                                      join
                                      departments d using (deptno)
                                      join
                                      employees   m on (m.empno = d.mgr)

SQL>
```

Apparently, if you define a view with a query starting with SELECT * FROM ..., the asterisk (*) gets expanded (and stored) as a comma-separated list of column names. Compare the query in Listing 10-1, where you created the DEPT20_V view, with the TEXT column contents in Listing 10-6.

Replacing and Dropping Views

You cannot *change* the definition of an existing view. Oracle SQL offers an ALTER VIEW command, but you can use that command only to recompile views that became invalid. You can *drop* a view definition only, with the DROP VIEW command.

The DROP VIEW command is very straightforward, and doesn't need additional explanation:

```
SQL> drop view <view_name>;
```

Alternatively, you can *replace* the definition of an existing view with the CREATE OR REPLACE VIEW command, as described earlier in this section.

10.3 What Can You Do with Views?

You can use views for many different purposes. This section lists and explains the most important ones: to simplify database retrieval, to maintain logical data independence, and to implement data security.

Simplifying Data Retrieval

Views can *simplify* database retrieval significantly. You can build up (and test) complex queries step by step, for more control over the correctness of your queries. In other words, you will be more confident that your queries return the right results.

You can also store (hide) frequently recurring *standard queries* in a view definition, thus reducing the number of unnecessary mistakes. For example, you might define views based on frequently joined tables, UNION constructs, or complex GROUP BY statements.

Suppose we are interested in an overview showing all employees who have attended more course days than the average employee. This is not a trivial query, so let's tackle it in multiple phases. As a first step toward the final solution, we ask the question, "How many course days did everyone attend?" The query in Listing 10-7 provides the answer.

Listing 10-7. *Working Toward a Solution: Step 1*

```
SQL> select    e.empno
  2 ,          e.ename
  3 ,          sum(c.duration) as days
  4  from      registrations  r
  5            join courses   c on (c.code  = r.course)
  6            join employees e on (e.empno = r.attendee)
  7  group by e.empno
  8 ,          e.ename;

    EMPNO ENAME         DAYS
-------- --------- --------
    7900 JONES            3
    7499 ALLEN           11
    7521 WARD             1
    7566 JONES            5
    7698 BLAKE           12
    7782 CLARK            4
    7788 SCOTT           12
    7839 KING             8
    7844 TURNER           1
    7876 ADAMS            9
    7902 FORD             9
    7934 MILLER           4

12 rows selected.

SQL>
```

This is not the solution to our problem yet, but it is already quite complicated. We have a join and a GROUP BY clause over a combination of two columns. If the result in Listing 10-7 were a real table, our original problem would be much easier to solve. Well, we can simulate that situation by defining a view. So we add one extra line to the query in Listing 10-7, as shown in Listing 10-8.

Listing 10-8. *Working Toward a Solution: Step 2*

```
SQL> create or replace view course_days as
  2  select    e.empno
  3  ,         e.ename
  4  ,         sum(c.duration) as days
  5  from      registrations  r
  6            join courses   c on (c.code = r.course)
  7            join employees e on (e.empno = r.attendee)
  8  group by e.empno
  9  ,        e.ename;

View created.

SQL> select *
  2  from    course_days
  3  where   days > 10;

   EMPNO ENAME        DAYS
-------- -------- --------
    7499 ALLEN          11
    7698 BLAKE          12
    7788 SCOTT          12

SQL>
```

Now, the original problem is rather easy to solve. Listing 10-9 shows the solution.

Listing 10-9. *Working Toward a Solution: The Final Step*

```
SQL> select *
  2  from    course_days
  3  where   days > (select avg(days)
  4                  from    course_days);

   EMPNO ENAME        DAYS
-------- -------- --------
    7499 ALLEN          11
    7698 BLAKE          12
    7788 SCOTT          12
    7839 KING            8
    7876 ADAMS           9
    7902 FORD            9

SQL>
```

Of course, you could argue that you could solve this query directly against the two base tables, but it is easy to make a little mistake. Moreover, your solution will probably be difficult to interpret. We could have used an inline view as well, or we could have separated the query in Listing 10-7 into a WITH clause, as described in Section 9.4 of Chapter 9. Inline views and subquery factoring (using the WITH clause) are good alternatives if you don't have the right system privileges to create views. A big advantage of using views, compared with inline views and subquery factoring, is the fact that view definitions are persistent; that is, you might benefit from the same view for more than one problem. Views occupy very little space (the DBMS stores the query text only), and there is no redundancy at all.

Maintaining Logical Data Independence

You can use views to change the (logical) external interface of the database, as exposed to database users and applications, without the need to change the underlying database structures themselves. In other words, you can use views to implement *logical data independency*. For example, different database users can have different views on the same base tables. You can rearrange columns, filter on rows, change table and column names, and so on.

Distributed databases often use views (or synonyms) to implement logical data independency and hide complexity. For example, you can define (and store) a view as a "local" database object. Behind the scenes, the view query accesses data from other databases on the network, but this is completely transparent to database users and applications.

You can also provide *derivable information* via views; that is, you implement *redundancy* at the *logical* level. The COURSE_DAYS view we created in Listing 10-8 is an example, because that view derives the number of course days.

Implementing Data Security

Last, but not least, views are a powerful means to implement data *security*. Views allow you to hide certain data from database users and applications. The view query precisely determines which rows and columns are exposed via the view. By using the GRANT and REVOKE commands on your views, you specify in detail which actions against the view data are allowed. In this approach, you don't grant any privileges at all on the underlying base tables, since you obviously don't want database users or applications to bypass the views and access the base tables directly.

10.4 Data Manipulation via Views

As you've learned in this chapter, views are virtual tables, and they are supposed to behave like tables as much as possible. For retrieval, that's no problem. However, data manipulation via views is not always possible. A view is *theoretically updatable* if the DML command against the view can be unambiguously decomposed into corresponding DML commands against rows and columns of the underlying base tables.

Let's consider the three views created in Listings 10-10 and 10-11.

Listing 10-10. *CRS_OFFERINGS View, Based on a Join*

```
SQL> create or replace view crs_offerings as
  2  select o.course as course_code, c.description, o.begindate
  3  from   offerings o
  4         join
  5         courses   c
  6         on (o.course = c.code);

View created.

SQL>
```

Listing 10-11. *Simple EMP View and Aggregate AVG_EVALUATIONS View*

```
SQL> create or replace view emp as
  2  select empno, ename, init
  3  from   employees;

View created.

SQL> create or replace view avg_evaluations as
  2  select course
  3  ,      avg(evaluation) as avg_eval
  4  from   registrations
  5  group  by course;

View created.

SQL>
```

First, let's look at the most simple view: the EMP view. The Oracle DBMS should be able to delete rows from the EMPLOYEES table via this view, or to change any of the three column values exposed by the view. However, inserting new rows via this view is impossible, because the EMPLOYEES table has NOT NULL columns without a default value (such as the date of birth) outside the scope of the EMP view. See Listing 10-12 for some DML experiments against the EMP view.

Listing 10-12. *Testing DML Commands Against the EMP View*

```
SQL> delete from emp
  2  where  empno = 7654;

1 row deleted.

SQL> update emp
  2  set    ename = 'BLACK'
  3  where  empno = 7698;
```

```
1 row updated.

SQL> insert into emp
  2  values (7999,'NEWGUY','NN');
insert into e
*
ERROR at line 1:
ORA-01400: cannot insert NULL into ("BOOK"."EMPLOYEES"."BDATE")

SQL> rollback;
Rollback complete.

SQL>
```

Note that the ORA-01400 error message in Listing 10-12 actually reveals several facts about the underlying (and supposedly hidden) table:

- The schema name (BOOK)

- The table name (EMPLOYEES)

- The presence of a mandatory BDATE column

Before you think you've discovered a security breach in the Oracle DBMS, I should explain that you get this informative error message only because you are testing the EMP view while connected as BOOK. If you are connected as a different database user with INSERT privilege against the EMP view only, the error message becomes as follows:

```
ORA-01400: cannot insert NULL into (???)
```

Updatable Join Views

The CRS_OFFERINGS view (see Listing 10-10) is based on a join of two tables: OFFERINGS and COURSES. Nevertheless, you are able to perform some data manipulation via this view, as long as the data manipulation can be translated into corresponding actions against the two underlying base tables. CRS_OFFERINGS is an example of an *updatable join view*. The Oracle DBMS is getting closer and closer to the full implementation of Ted Codd's rule 6 (see Chapter 1). Listing 10-13 demonstrates testing some DML commands against this view.

Listing 10-13. *Testing DML Commands Against the CRS_OFFERINGS View*

```
SQL> delete from crs_offerings where course_code = 'ERM';

1 row deleted.

SQL> insert into crs_offerings (course_code, begindate)
  2          values ('OAU' , trunc(sysdate));
```

```
1 row created.

SQL> rollback;
Rollback complete.

SQL>
```

There are some rules and restrictions that apply to updatable join views. Also, the concept of *key-preserved tables* plays an important role in this area. As the name indicates, a key-preserved table is an underlying base table with a one-to-one row relationship with the rows in the view, via the primary key or a unique key.

These are some examples of updatable join view restrictions:

- You are allowed to issue DML commands against updatable join views only if you change a *single* underlying base table.

- For INSERT statements, all columns into which values are inserted must belong to a key-preserved table.

- For UPDATE statements, all columns updated must belong to a key-preserved table.

- For DELETE statements, if the join results in more than one key-preserved table, the Oracle DBMS deletes from the first table named in the FROM clause.

- If you created the view using WITH CHECK OPTION, some additional DML restrictions apply, as explained a little later in this section.

As you can see in Listing 10-13, the DELETE and INSERT statements against the CRS_OFFERINGS updatable join view succeed. Feel free to experiment with other data manipulation commands. The Oracle error messages are self-explanatory if you hit one of the restrictions:

```
ORA-01732: data manipulation operation not legal on this view
ORA-01752: cannot delete from view without exactly one key-preserved table
ORA-01779: cannot modify a column which maps to a non key-preserved table
```

Nonupdatable Views

First of all, if you create a view with the WITH READ ONLY option (see Figure 10-1), data manipulation via that view is impossible by definition, regardless of how you defined the view.

The AVG_EVALUATIONS view definition (see Listing 10-11) contains a GROUP BY clause. This implies that there is no longer a one-to-one relationship between the rows of the view and the rows of the underlying base table. Therefore, data manipulation via the AVG_EVALUATIONS view is impossible.

If you use SELECT DISTINCT in your view definition, this has the same effect: it makes your view nonupdatable. You should try to avoid using SELECT DISTINCT in view definitions, because it has additional disadvantages; for example, each view access will force a sort to take place, whether or not you need it.

The set operators UNION, MINUS, and INTERSECT also result in nonupdatable views. For example, imagine that you are trying to insert a row via a view based on a UNION—in which underlying base table should the DBMS insert that row?

The Oracle documentation provides all of the details and rules with regard to view updatability. Most rules and exceptions are rather straightforward, and as noted earlier, most Oracle error messages clearly indicate the reason why certain data manipulation commands are forbidden.

The data dictionary offers a helpful view to find out which of your view columns are updatable: the USER_UPDATABLE_COLUMNS view. For example, Listing 10-14 shows that you cannot do much with the DESCRIPTION column of the CRS_OFFERINGS view. This is because it is based on a column from the COURSES table, which is a not a key-preserved table in this view.

Listing 10-14. *View Column Updatability Information from the Data Dictionary*

```
SQL> select column_name
  2  ,       updatable, insertable, deletable
  3  from    user_updatable_columns
  4  where   table_name = 'CRS_OFFERINGS';


COLUMN_NAME           UPD INS DEL
--------------------- --- --- ---
COURSE_CODE           YES YES YES
DESCRIPTION           NO  NO  NO
BEGINDATE             YES YES YES


SQL>
```

MAKING A VIEW UPDATABLE WITH INSTEAD-OF TRIGGERS

In a chapter about views, it's worth mentioning that PL/SQL (the standard procedural programming language for Oracle databases) provides a way to make any view updatable. With PL/SQL, you can define *instead-of triggers* on your views. These triggers take over control as soon as any data manipulation commands are executed against the view.

This means that you can make any view updatable, if you choose, by writing some procedural PL/SQL code. Obviously, it is your sole responsibility to make sure that those instead-of triggers do the "right things" to your database to maintain data consistency and integrity. Instead-of triggers should not be your first thought to solve data manipulation issues with views. However, they may solve your problems in some special cases, or they may allow you to implement a very specific application behavior.

The WITH CHECK OPTION Clause

If data manipulation is allowed via a certain view, there are two rather curious situations that deserve attention:

- You change rows with an UPDATE command against the view, and then the rows don't show up in the view anymore.

- You add rows with an INSERT command against the view; however, the rows don't show up when you query the view.

Disappearing Updated Rows

Do you still have the DEPT20_V view, created in Listing 10-1? Check out what happens in Listing 10-15: by updating four rows, they disappear from the view.

Listing 10-15. *UPDATE Makes Rows Disappear*

```
SQL> select * from dept20_v;

EMPNO ENAME    INIT  JOB       MGR BDATE        MSAL  COMM DEPTNO
----- -------- ----- -------- ----- ----------- ----- ----- ------
 7369 SMITH    N     TRAINER   7902 17-DEC-1965  800          20
 7566 JONES    JM    MANAGER   7839 02-APR-1967 2975          20
 7788 SCOTT    SCJ   TRAINER   7566 26-NOV-1959 3000          20
 7876 ADAMS    AA    TRAINER   7788 30-DEC-1966 1100          20
 7902 FORD     MG    TRAINER   7566 13-FEB-1959 3000          20

SQL> update dept20_v
  2  set     deptno = 30
  3  where   job    ='TRAINER';

4 rows updated.

SQL> select * from dept20_v;

EMPNO ENAME    INIT  JOB       MGR BDATE        MSAL  COMM DEPTNO
----- -------- ----- -------- ----- ----------- ----- ----- ------
 7566 JONES    JM    MANAGER   7839 02-APR-1967 2975          20

SQL> rollback;
Rollback complete.

SQL>
```

Apparently, the updates in Listing 10-15 are propagated to the underlying EMPLOYEES table. All trainers from department 20 don't show up anymore in the DEPT20_V view, because their DEPTNO column value is changed from 20 to 30.

Inserting Invisible Rows

The second curious scenario is shown in Listing 10-16. You insert a new row for employee 9999, and you get the message "1 row created." However, the new employee does not show up in the query.

Listing 10-16. *INSERT Rows Without Seeing Them in the View*

```
SQL> insert into dept20_v
  2  values ( 9999,'BOS','D', null, null
  3         , date '1939-01-01'
  4         , '10', null, 30);

1 row created.

SQL> select * from dept20_v;

EMPNO ENAME    INIT  JOB         MGR BDATE        MSAL  COMM DEPTNO
----- -------- ----- -------- ----- ----------- ----- ----- ------
 7369 SMITH    N     TRAINER   7902 17-DEC-1965   800          20
 7566 JONES    JM    MANAGER   7839 02-APR-1967  2975          20
 7788 SCOTT    SCJ   TRAINER   7566 26-NOV-1959  3000          20
 7876 ADAMS    AA    TRAINER   7788 30-DEC-1966  1100          20
 7902 FORD     MG    TRAINER   7566 13-FEB-1959  3000          20

5 rows selected.

SQL> rollback;
Rollback complete.

SQL>
```

Listing 10-16 shows that you can insert a new employee via the DEPT20_V view into the underlying EMPLOYEES table, without the new row showing up in the view itself.

Preventing These Two Scenarios

If the view behavior just described is undesirable, you can create your views with the WITH CHECK OPTION clause (see Figure 10-1). Actually, the syntax diagram in Figure 10-1 is not complete. You can assign a name to WITH CHECK OPTION constraints, as follows:

```
SQL> create [or replace] view ... with check option constraint <cons-name>;
```

If you don't provide a constraint name, the Oracle DBMS generates a rather cryptic one for you.

Listing 10-17 replaces the `DEPT20_V` view, using `WITH CHECK OPTION`, and shows that the `INSERT` statement that succeeded in Listing 10-16 now fails with an Oracle error message.

Listing 10-17. *Creating Views WITH CHECK OPTION*

```
SQL> create or replace view dept20_v as
  2  select * from employees where deptno = 20
  3  with check option constraint dept20_v_check;

View created.

SQL> insert into dept20_v
  2  values ( 9999,'BOS','D', null, null
  3         , date '1939-01-01'
  4         , '10', null, 30);
     , '10', null, 30)
     *
ERROR at line 4:
ORA-01402: view WITH CHECK OPTION where-clause violation

SQL>
```

Constraint Checking

In the old days, when the Oracle DBMS didn't yet support referential integrity constraints (which is a long time ago, before Oracle7), you were still able to implement certain integrity constraints by using `WITH CHECK OPTION` when creating views. For example, you could use subqueries in the view definition to check for row existence in other tables. Listing 10-18 gives an example of such a view. Nowadays, you don't need this technique anymore, of course.

Listing 10-18. *WITH CHECK OPTION and Constraint Checking*

```
SQL> create or replace view reg_view as
  2  select r.*
  3  from    registrations r
  4  where   r.attendee    in (select empno
  5                               from   employees)
  6  and     r.course      in (select code
  7                               from   courses)
  8  and     r.evaluation in (1,2,3,4,5)
  9  with check option;

View created.

SQL> select constraint_name, table_name
  2  from    user_constraints
  3  where   constraint_type = 'V';
```

```
CONSTRAINT_NAME        TABLE_NAME
-------------------    --------------------
SYS_C005979            REG_VIEW
DEPT20_V_CHECK         DEPT20_V

SQL>
```

Via the REG_VIEW view, you can insert registrations only for an existing employee and an existing course. Moreover, the EVALUATION value must be an integer between 1 and 5, or a null value. Any data manipulation command against the REG_VIEW view that violates one of the above three checks will result in an Oracle error message. CHECK OPTION constraints show up in the data dictionary with a CONSTRAINT_TYPE value V; notice the system-generated constraint name for the REG_VIEW view.

10.5 Data Manipulation via Inline Views

Inline views are subqueries assuming the role of a *table expression* in SQL commands. In other words, you specify a subquery (between parentheses) in places where you would normally specify a table or view name. We already discussed inline views in the previous chapter, but we considered inline views only in the FROM component of queries.

You can also use inline views for data manipulation purposes. Data manipulation via inline views is especially interesting in combination with updatable join views. Listing 10-19 shows an example of an UPDATE command against an inline updatable join view.

Listing 10-19. *UPDATE via an Inline Updatable Join View*

```
SQL> update ( select e.msal
  2            from    employees   e join
  3                    departments d using (deptno)
  4            where   location = 'DALLAS')
  5   set msal = msal + 1;

5 rows updated.

SQL> rollback;
Rollback complete.

SQL>
```

Listing 10-19 shows that you can execute UPDATE commands via an inline join view, giving all employees in Dallas a symbolic salary raise. Note that the UPDATE command does not contain a WHERE clause at all; the inline view filters the rows to be updated. This filtering would be rather complicated to achieve in a regular UPDATE command against the EMPLOYEES table. For that, you probably would need a correlated subquery in the WHERE clause.

At first sight, it may seem strange to perform data manipulation via inline views (or subqueries), but the number of possibilities is almost unlimited. The syntax is elegant and

readable, and the response time is at least the same (if not better) compared with the corresponding commands against the underlying base tables. Obviously, all restrictions regarding
data manipulation via updatable join views (as discussed earlier in this section) still apply.

10.6 Views and Performance

Normally, the Oracle DBMS processes queries against views in the following way:

1. The DBMS notices that views are involved in the query entered.

2. The DBMS retrieves the view definition from the data dictionary.

3. The DBMS merges the view definition with the query entered.

4. The optimizer chooses an appropriate execution plan for the result of the previous
   step: a command against base tables.

5. The DBMS executes the plan from the previous step.

In exceptional cases, the Oracle DBMS may decide to execute the view query from the
data dictionary, populate a temporary table with the results, and then use the temporary table
as a base table for the query entered. This happens only if the Oracle DBMS is not able to
merge the view definition with the query entered, or if the Oracle optimizer determines that
using a temporary table is a good idea.

In the regular approach, as outlined in the preceding five steps, steps 2 and 3 are the only
additional overhead. One of the main advantages of this approach is that you can benefit opti-
mally from indexes on the underlying base tables.

For example, suppose you enter the following query against the AVG_EVALUATIONS view:

```
SQL> select *
  2  from   avg_evaluations
  3  where  avg_eval >= 4
```

This query is transformed internally into the statement shown in Listing 10-20. Notice
that the WHERE clause is translated into a HAVING clause, and the asterisk (*) in the SELECT clause
is expanded to the appropriate list of column expressions.

Listing 10-20. *Rewritten Query Against the REGISTRATIONS Table*

```
SQL> select r.course
  2  ,        avg(r.evaluation) as avg_eval
  3  from     registrations r
  4  group by r.course
  5  having avg(r.evaluation) >= 4;

COURSE AVG_EVAL
------ --------
JAV       4.125
OAU        4.5
```

```
XML        4.5

SQL>
```

Especially when dealing with larger tables, the performance overhead of using views is normally negligible. If you start defining views on views on views, the performance overhead may become more significant. And, in case you don't trust the performance overhead, you can always use diagnostic tools such as SQL*Plus AUTOTRACE (see Chapter 7, Section 7.6) to check execution plans and statistics.

10.7 Materialized Views

A brief introduction of *materialized views* makes sense in this chapter about views. The intent of this section is to illustrate the concept of materialized views, using a simple example.

Normally, materialized views are mainly used in complex data warehousing environments, where the tables grow so big that the data volume causes unacceptable performance problems. An important property of data warehousing environments is that you don't change the data very often. Typically, there is a separate Extraction, Transformation, Loading (ETL) process that updates the data warehouse contents.

Materialized views are also often used with distributed databases. In such environments, accessing data over the network can become a performance bottleneck. You can use materialized views to replicate data in a distributed database.

To explore materialized views, let's revisit Listing 10-1 and add a third DDL command, as shown in Listing 10-21.

Listing 10-21. *Comparing Views, Tables, and Materialized Views*

```
SQL> create or replace VIEW dept20_v as
  2  select * from employees where deptno = 20;

View created.

SQL> create TABLE dept20_t as
  2  select * from employees where deptno = 20;

Table created.

SQL> create MATERIALIZED VIEW dept20_mv as
  2  select * from employees where deptno = 20;

Materialized view created.

SQL>
```

You already know the difference between a table and a view, but what is a materialized view? Well, as the name suggests, it's a view for which you store both its definition *and* the query results. In other words, a materialized view has its own rows. Materialized views imply redundant data storage.

The materialized view DEPT20_MV now contains all employees of department 20, and you can execute queries directly against DEPT20_MV, if you like. However, that's not the main purpose of creating materialized views, as you will learn from the remainder of this section.

Properties of Materialized Views

Materialized views have two important properties, in the areas of *maintenance* and *usage*:

- **Maintenance:** Materialized views are "snapshots." That is, they have a certain content at any point in time, based on "refreshment" from the underlying base tables. This implies that the contents of materialized views are not necessarily up-to-date all the time, because the underlying base tables can change. Fortunately, the Oracle DBMS offers various features to automate the refreshment of your materialized views completely, in an efficient way. In other words, yes, you have redundancy, but you can easily set up appropriate redundancy control.

- **Usage:** The Oracle optimizer (the component of the Oracle DBMS deciding about execution plans for SQL commands) is aware of the existence of materialized views. The optimizer also knows whether materialized views are up-to-date or stale. The optimizer can use this knowledge to replace queries written against regular base tables with corresponding queries against materialized views, if the optimizer thinks that approach may result in better response times. This is referred to as the *query rewrite* feature, which is explained in the next section.

■**Note** When you create materialized views, you normally specify whether you want to enable query rewrite, and how you want the Oracle DBMS to handle the refreshing of the materialized view. Those syntax details are omitted here. See *Oracle SQL Reference* for more information.

Query Rewrite

Let's continue with our simple materialized view, created in Listing 10-21. Assume you enter the following query, selecting all trainers from department 20:

```
SQL> select * from employees where deptno = 20 and job = 'TRAINER'
```

For this query, the optimizer may decide to execute the following query instead:

```
SQL> select * from dept20_mv where job = 'TRAINER'
```

In other words, the original query against the EMPLOYEES table is rewritten against the DEPT20_MV materialized view. Because the materialized view contains fewer rows than the EMPLOYEES table (and therefore fewer rows need to be scanned), the optimizer thinks it is a better starting point to produce the desired end result. Listing 10-22 shows query rewrite at work, using the SQL*Plus AUTOTRACE feature.

Listing 10-22. *Materialized Views and Query Rewrite at Work*

```
SQL> set autotrace on explain
SQL> select * from employees where deptno = 20 and job = 'TRAINER';

EMPNO ENAME    INIT JOB        MGR BDATE        MSAL COMM DEPTNO
------ -------- ---- -------- ----- ----------- ----- ---- ------
 7369 SMITH    N    TRAINER   7902 17-DEC-1965  800        20
 7788 SCOTT    SCJ  TRAINER   7566 26-NOV-1959 3000        20
 7876 ADAMS    AA   TRAINER   7788 30-DEC-1966 1100        20
 7902 FORD     MG   TRAINER   7566 13-FEB-1959 3000        20

Execution Plan
----------------------------------------------------------------------
  0   SELECT STATEMENT Optimizer=ALL_ROWS     (Cost=3 Card=4 Bytes=360)
  1 0   MAT_VIEW REWRITE ACCESS (FULL) OF 'DEPT20_MV' (MAT_VIEW REWRITE)
                                           (Cost=3 Card=4 Bytes=360)

SQL>
```

Although it is obvious from Listing 10-22 that you write a query against the EMPLOYEES table, the execution plan (produced with AUTOTRACE ON EXPLAIN) shows that the materialized view DEPT20_MV is accessed instead.

Materialized views normally provide better response times; however, there is a risk that the results are based on stale data because the materialized views are out of sync with the underlying base tables. You can specify whether you tolerate query rewrites in such cases, thus controlling the behavior of the optimizer. If you want precise results, the optimizer considers query rewrite only when the materialized views are guaranteed to be up-to-date.

Obviously, the materialized view example we used in this section is much too simple. Normally, you create materialized views with relatively "expensive" operations, such as aggregation (GROUP BY), joins over multiple tables, and set operators (UNION, MINUS, and INTERSECT)—operations that are too time-consuming to be repeated over and over again. For more details and examples of materialized views, see *Data Warehousing Guide*.

10.8 Exercises

As in the previous chapters, we end this chapter with some practical exercises. See Appendix D for the answers.

1. Look at the example discussed in Listings 10-7, 10-8, and 10-9. Rewrite the query in Listing 10-9 without using a view, by using the WITH operator.

2. Look at Listing 10-12. How is it possible that you can delete employee 7654 via this EMP view? There are rows in the HISTORY table, referring to that employee via a foreign key constraint.

3. Look at the view definition in Listing 10-18. Does this view implement the foreign key constraints from the REGISTRATIONS table to the EMPLOYEES and COURSES tables? Explain your answer.

4. Create a SAL_HISTORY view providing the following overview for all employees, based on the HISTORY table: For each employee, show the hire date, the review dates, and the salary changes as a consequence of those reviews.

Check your view against the following result:

```
SQL> select * from sal_history;

EMPNO HIREDATE    REVIEWDATE  SALARY_RAISE
----- ----------- ----------- ------------
 7369 01-JAN-2000 01-JAN-2000
 7369 01-JAN-2000 01-FEB-2000         -150
 7499 01-JUN-1988 01-JUN-1988
 7499 01-JUN-1988 01-JUL-1989          300
 7499 01-JUN-1988 01-DEC-1993          200
 7499 01-JUN-1988 01-OCT-1995          200
 7499 01-JUN-1988 01-NOV-1999         -100
 ...
 7934 01-FEB-1998 01-FEB-1998
 7934 01-FEB-1998 01-MAY-1998            5
 7934 01-FEB-1998 01-FEB-1999           10
 7934 01-FEB-1998 01-JAN-2000           10

79 rows selected.

SQL>
```

CHAPTER 11

■ ■ ■

SQL*Plus and *i*SQL*Plus

Chapter 2 introduced SQL*Plus and *i*SQL*Plus. In that chapter, we focused on the most essential commands required to get started with SQL, such as the SQL*Plus editor commands (LIST, INPUT, CHANGE, APPEND, DEL, and EDIT), file management (SAVE, GET, START, and SPOOL), and other commands (HOST, DESCRIBE, and HELP).

■**Note** SQL*Plus is the oldest Oracle tool still available. It was renamed from UFI (User Friendly Interface) in version 4 to SQL*Plus in Version 5.

This chapter covers some more advanced features of SQL*Plus and *i*SQL*Plus. Knowing how to use these features will enhance your skills in using these tools, thus increasing your satisfaction and productivity.

The first section introduces the various variable types supported by SQL*Plus: substitution variables, user variables, and system variables. When dealing with SQL*Plus variables, the most important commands are SET, SHOW, DEFINE, and ACCEPT.

The second section explains SQL bind variables. These bind variables are crucial when developing mission-critical database applications, if high performance and scalability are important goals.

In the previous chapters, you have used SQL*Plus in an *interactive* way—you enter the commands, hit the Enter key, and wait for the results to appear on your screen. Section 11.3 shows that you can also use SQL*Plus by using script files.

In Section 11.4, you will see how you can use SQL*Plus as a reporting tool, by enhancing the layout of the results with SQL*Plus commands such as the TTITLE, BTITLE, COLUMN, BREAK, and COMPUTE commands.

Section 11.5 focuses on various ways you can use SQL*Plus and *i*SQL*Plus as database tools in an HTML (browser) environment. The final section contains exercises.

11.1 SQL*Plus Variables

SQL*Plus supports the following three variable types:

- Substitution variables
- User-defined variables
- System variables

SQL*Plus Substitution Variables

Substitution variables appear in SQL or SQL*Plus commands. SQL*Plus prompts for a value when you execute those commands. We have used substitution variables in earlier examples in this book (Listing 5-14 and Listing 9-25), to test certain commands multiple times with different literal values.

Substitution variable values are volatile; that is, SQL*Plus doesn't remember them and doesn't store them anywhere. This is what distinguishes substitution variables from the other two types. If you execute the same SQL or SQL*Plus command again, SQL*Plus prompts for a value again. The default character that makes SQL*Plus prompt for a substitution variable value is the ampersand (&), also known as the DEFINE character. Check out what happens in Listing 11-1.

Listing 11-1. *Using the DEFINE Character (&)*

```
SQL> select * from departments
  2  where dname like upper('%&letter%');

Enter value for letter: a
old   2: where dname like upper('%&letter%')
new   2: where dname like upper('%a%')

  DEPTNO DNAME       LOCATION      MGR
-------- ---------- -------- --------
      10 ACCOUNTING NEW YORK     7782
      20 TRAINING    DALLAS       7566
      30 SALES       CHICAGO      7698

SQL>
```

Actually, if a substitution variable occurs twice within a single command, SQL*Plus also prompts twice for a value, as demonstrated in Listing 11-2.

Listing 11-2. *Prompting Twice for the Same Variable*

```
SQL> select ename from employees
  2  where  empno between &x and &x+100;
```

```
Enter value for x: 7500
Enter value for x: 7500
old   2: where  empno between &x and &x+100
new   2: where  empno between 7500 and 7500+100


ENAME
--------
WARD
JONES


SQL>
```

You can use the period character (.) to mark the end of the name of a substitution variable, as shown in Listing 11-3. The period (.) is also known as the CONCAT character in SQL*Plus.

Normally, you don't need the CONCAT character very often, because white space is good enough to delimit variable names; however, white space in strings can sometimes be undesirable. See Listing 11-3 for an example.

Listing 11-3. *Using the DEFINE and CONCAT Characters*

```
SQL> select '&drink.glass' as result from dual;

Enter value for drink: beer
old   1: select '&drink.glass' as result from dual
new   1: select 'beerglass' as result from dual

RESULT
---------
beerglass

SQL>
```

Note that you can display the current settings of the DEFINE and CONCAT characters with the SQL*Plus SHOW command, and you can change these settings with the SQL*Plus SET command, as shown in Listing 11-4. If you are using the GUI of SQL*Plus, you can also use the Options ➤ Environment menu option to display or manipulate these SQL*Plus settings.

Listing 11-4. *Displaying the DEFINE and CONCAT Character Settings*

```
SQL> show define
define "&" (hex 26)

SQL> show concat
concat "." (hex 2e)

SQL>
```

If you don't want SQL*Plus to display the explicit replacement of substitution variables by the values you entered (as in Listings 11-1, 11-2, and 11-3), you can suppress that with the SQL*Plus VERIFY setting, as shown in Listing 11-5.

Listing 11-5. *Switching the VERIFY Setting ON and OFF*

```
SQL> set  verify on
SQL> set  verify off
SQL> show verify
verify OFF

SQL>
```

For the SQL*Plus VERIFY setting, you can use the Options ➤ Environment menu option, just as you can for the DEFINE and CONCAT character settings.

If you change the VERIFY setting to OFF, as shown in Listing 11-5, and you execute the SQL command (still in the SQL buffer) with the SQL*Plus RUN command, you don't see the "old: ..." and "new: ..." lines anymore, as shown in Listing 11-6.

Listing 11-6. *The Effect of VERIFY OFF*

```
SQL> select ename from employees
  2  where  empno between &x and &x+100;

Enter value for x: 7500
Enter value for x: 7500

ENAME
--------
WARD
JONES

SQL>
```

SQL*Plus User-Defined Variables

If you want to store the value of a SQL*Plus variable (at least temporarily) so you can use it multiple times, you need the next category of SQL*Plus variables: *user-defined variables*.

You can use the SQL*Plus DEFINE command to declare user-defined variables and to assign values to them, as shown in Listing 11-7.

Listing 11-7. *Assigning Values to User-Defined Variables with DEFINE*

```
SQL> define x=7500

SQL> select ename from employees
  2  where  empno between &x and &x+100;
```

```
ENAME
--------
WARD
JONES

SQL>
```

The DEFINE command in Listing 11-7 stores the user-defined variable X with its value 7500.
That's why SQL*Plus doesn't prompt for a value for X anymore in Listing 11-7.

The SQL*Plus DEFINE command not only allows you to *assign* values to user-defined variables, but also to display current values. You can ask for the current value of a specific (named)
variable, or you can display a full overview of all user-defined variables by entering the DEFINE
command without any arguments. The SQL*Plus UNDEFINE command allows you to remove a
user-defined variable. Listing 11-8 shows examples of DEFINE and UNDEFINE.

Listing 11-8. *DEFINE and UNDEFINE Examples*

```
SQL> def x
DEFINE X              = "7500" (CHAR)

SQL> def
DEFINE _DATE          = "25-SEP-2004" (CHAR)
DEFINE _CONNECT_IDENTIFIER = "orcl" (CHAR)
DEFINE _USER          = "BOOK" (CHAR)
DEFINE _PRIVILEGE     = "" (CHAR)
DEFINE _SQLPLUS_RELEASE = "1001000200" (CHAR)
DEFINE _EDITOR        = "vim" (CHAR)
DEFINE _O_VERSION     = "Oracle Database 10g Enterprise Edition
Release 10.1.0.2.0 - Production
With the Partitioning, OLAP and Data Mining options" (CHAR)
DEFINE _O_RELEASE     = "1001000200" (CHAR)
DEFINE X              = "7500" (CHAR)

SQL> undefine x
SQL>
```

Implicit SQL*Plus User-Defined Variables

SQL*Plus also supports syntax allowing you to define variables implicitly. With this method,
you start with *substitution variables* in your SQL and SQL*Plus commands, and you end up
with *user-defined variables*; SQL*Plus prompts for a value only once. You can implement this
behavior by using double ampersands (&&). Look at the experiments in Listing 11-9, showing
that you start out without an ENR variable, you are prompted for a value only once, and then
an implicit DEFINE is executed.

Listing 11-9. *Using Double Ampersands (&&)*

```
SQL> define enr
SP2-0135: symbol enr is UNDEFINED

SQL> select * from employees
  2  where  empno between &&enr and &enr+100;

Enter value for enr: 7500

EMPNO ENAME    INIT JOB        MGR BDATE        MSAL  COMM DEPTNO
----- -------- ---- -------- ----- ----------- ----- ----- ------
 7521 WARD     TF   SALESREP  7698 22-FEB-1962  1250   500     30
 7566 JONES    JM   MANAGER   7839 02-APR-1967  2975           20

SQL> define enr
DEFINE ENR           = "7500" (CHAR)
SQL>
```

If you now reexecute the contents of the SQL buffer (with / or RUN), there is no prompting at all; the stored ENR value (7500) is used. So if you use this technique, make sure to end (or start) your scripts with the appropriate UNDEFINE commands.

User-Friendly Prompting

SQL*Plus provides a more user-friendly method to create user-defined variables and prompt for values, while offering some more control over the values as well. This method is especially useful with SQL*Plus scripts (discussed in Section 11.3). User-friendly prompting uses a combination of the three SQL*Plus commands: PROMPT, PAUSE, and ACCEPT. Listing 11-10 shows an example.

Listing 11-10. *Using PROMPT, PAUSE, and ACCEPT*

```
SQL> prompt This is a demonstration.
This is a demonstration.

SQL> pause Hit the [Enter] key...
Hit the [Enter] key...

SQL> accept x number -
> prompt "Enter a value for x: "
Enter a value for x: 42

SQL> define x
DEFINE X           =       42 (NUMBER)
SQL>
```

The PROMPT command allows you to write text to the screen, the PAUSE command allows you to suspend script execution, and the ACCEPT command gives you full control over the datatype of the user-defined variable and the screen text prompting for a value. Just try to enter a nonnumeric value for variable X in Listing 11-10. You will get the following SQL*Plus error message:

```
Enter a value for x: monkey
SP2-0425: "monkey" is not a valid NUMBER
```

By the way, note that you can split a SQL*Plus command over multiple lines, as shown in Listing 11-10 in the ACCEPT command example. Normally, the newline character is a SQL*Plus command delimiter, but you can "escape" from that special meaning of the newline character by ending your command lines with a minus sign (-).

■**Caution** Splitting commands over multiple lines by using the minus sign as an escape character is relevant only for SQL*Plus commands, *not* for SQL commands.

SQL*Plus System Variables

The third category of SQL*Plus variables is *system variables*. The values of these system-defined SQL*Plus variables control the overall behavior of SQL*Plus. You already saw various examples of these system variables, such as PAGESIZE and PAUSE, in Chapter 2.

In the previous section, you learned that you need the SQL*Plus commands DEFINE and UNDEFINE to manage *user-defined* variables. For *system* variables, you need the SQL*Plus commands SET and SHOW to assign or retrieve values, respectively. You can also manage SQL*Plus system variables via the Options ➤ Environment menu option.

Listing 11-11 shows some examples of system variables.

Listing 11-11. *Some SQL*Plus System Variable Examples*

```
SQL> show pagesize
pagesize 36

SQL> show pause
PAUSE is OFF

SQL> set  pause  '[Enter]... '
SQL> set  pause  on
SQL> set  pagesize 10

SQL> select * from employees;
[Enter]...

EMPNO ENAME    INIT  JOB          MGR BDATE         MSAL  COMM DEPTNO
----- -------- ----- -------- -------- ----------- ----- ----- ------
 7369 SMITH    N     TRAINER      7902 17-DEC-1965   800          20
 7499 ALLEN    JAM   SALESREP     7698 20-FEB-1961  1600   300    30
 7521 WARD     TF    SALESREP     7698 22-FEB-1962  1250   500    30
```

```
7566 JONES     JM    MANAGER    7839 02-APR-1967 2975        20
7654 MARTIN    P     SALESREP   7698 28-SEP-1956 1250  1400  30
7698 BLAKE     R     MANAGER    7839 01-NOV-1963 2850        30
7782 CLARK     AB    MANAGER    7839 09-JUN-1965 2450        10
[Enter]...

EMPNO ENAME     INIT  JOB        MGR  BDATE       MSAL COMM DEPTNO
----- --------- ----- --------- ----- ----------- ---- ---- ------
7788 SCOTT     SCJ   TRAINER    7566 26-NOV-1959 3000        20
7839 KING      CC    DIRECTOR        17-NOV-1952 5000        10
7844 TURNER    JJ    SALESREP   7698 28-SEP-1968 1500   0   30
7876 ADAMS     AA    TRAINER    7788 30-DEC-1966 1100        20
7900 JONES     R     ADMIN      7698 03-DEC-1969  800        30
7902 FORD      MG    TRAINER    7566 13-FEB-1959 3000        20
7934 MILLER    TJA   ADMIN      7782 23-JAN-1962 1300        10

14 rows selected.

SQL> set  pause off pagesize 42
SQL> show all
...
SQL>
```

If you execute the last command of Listing 11-11 (SHOW ALL), you will see that the number of SQL*Plus system variables is impressive. That's why the output in Listing 11-11 is suppressed.

Table 11-1 shows an overview of the SQL*Plus system variables, listing only the most commonly used SQL*Plus system variables. Where applicable, the third column shows the default values. In the first column, the brackets indicate abbreviations you may want to use.

Table 11-1. *Some Common SQL*Plus System Variables*

Variable	Description	Default
COLSEP	String to display between result columns	" " (space)
CON[CAT]	Character to mark the end of a variable name	. (period)
DEF[INE]	Character to refer to variable values	& (ampersand)
ECHO	Display or suppress commands (relevant only for scripts)	OFF
FEED[BACK]	Display "... rows selected" from a certain minimum result size	6
HEA[DING]	Display column names above results	ON
HEADS[EP]	Divide column headers over multiple lines	| (vertical bar)
LIN[ESIZE]	Line or screen width, in characters	80
LONG	Default width for LONG columns	80
NEWP[AGE]	Number of empty lines after every page break	1
NULL	Display of null values in the results	
NUMF[ORMAT]	Default format to display numbers	

Variable	Description	Default
NUM[WIDTH]	Default width for numeric columns	10
PAGES[IZE]	Number of lines per page	14
PAU[SE]	Display results per page	OFF
SQLP[ROMPT]	SQL*Plus prompt string	SQL>
SQLT[ERMINATOR]	SQL command delimiter (execute the command)	; (semicolon)
TIMI[NG]	Show elapsed time after each command	OFF
TRIMS[POOL]	Suppress trailing spaces in spool files	OFF
USER	Username for the current SQL*Plus session (cannot be set)	
VER[IFY]	Show command lines before/after variable substitution	ON

Let's look at some experiments with SQL*Plus system variables, beginning with the FEEDBACK variable. This variable is a switch (you can set it to ON or OFF) and also a threshold value, as shown in Listing 11-12 where we set it to 4.

■**Note** In order to save some trees, the listings don't repeat the query results each time. You can easily see the effects of the various system variable values yourself.

Listing 11-12. *Using the FEEDBACK System Variable*

```
SQL> select * from departments;

 DEPTNO DNAME      LOCATION     MGR
-------- ---------- -------- --------
     10 ACCOUNTING NEW YORK    7782
     20 TRAINING   DALLAS      7566
     30 SALES      CHICAGO     7698
     40 HR         BOSTON      7839

SQL> set feedback 4
SQL> /

 DEPTNO DNAME      LOCATION     MGR
-------- ---------- -------- --------
     10 ACCOUNTING NEW YORK    7782
     20 TRAINING   DALLAS      7566
     30 SALES      CHICAGO     7698
     40 HR         BOSTON      7839

4 rows selected.                <<<
```

```
SQL> select * from employees;
...
SQL> set  feedback off
SQL> show feedback
feedback OFF
SQL> /
...
SQL> set feedback 10
SQL>
```

Using COLSEP and NUMWIDTH, as shown in Listing 11-13, the default space separating
the result columns is replaced by a vertical line, and the GRADE and BONUS columns are now
10 columns wide.

Listing 11-13. *Using the COLSEP and NUMWIDTH System Variables*

```
SQL> select * from salgrades;

 GRADE LOWERLIMIT UPPERLIMIT  BONUS
------ ---------- ---------- ------
     1        700       1200      0
     2       1201       1400     50
     3       1401       2000    100
     4       2001       3000    200
     5       3001       9999    500

SQL> set colsep " | "
SQL> set numwidth 10
SQL> /

     GRADE | LOWERLIMIT | UPPERLIMIT |      BONUS
---------- | ---------- | ---------- | ----------
         1 |        700 |       1200 |          0
         2 |       1201 |       1400 |         50
         3 |       1401 |       2000 |        100
         4 |       2001 |       3000 |        200
         5 |       3001 |       9999 |        500

SQL>
```

Listing 11-14 shows examples of using NULL and NUMFORMAT. The NULL system variable
makes all null values more visible. The NUMFORMAT variable allows you to influence the layout
of all numeric columns. It supports the same formats as the SQL*Plus COLUMN command (see
Appendix A of this book or *SQL*Plus User's Guide and Reference* for details).

Listing 11-14. *Using the NULL and NUMFORMAT System Variables*

```
SQL> set numwidth 5
SQL> set null " [N/A]"

SQL> select ename, mgr, comm
  2  from    employees
  3  where   deptno = 10;

ENAME       MGR   COMM
--------  ------  ------
CLARK      7839   [N/A]
KING      [N/A]   [N/A]
MILLER     7782   [N/A]

SQL> set numformat 09999.99
SQL> select * from salgrades;

   GRADE LOWERLIMIT UPPERLIMIT    BONUS
--------- ---------- ---------- ---------
 00001.00   00700.00   01200.00 00000.00
 00002.00   01201.00   01400.00 00050.00
 00003.00   01401.00   02000.00 00100.00
 00004.00   02001.00   03000.00 00200.00
 00005.00   03001.00   09999.00 00500.00

SQL>
```

As Listing 11-15 shows, you can use the DEFINE system variable as a switch (ON or OFF) and you can also change the DEFINE character, if you need the ampersand character (&) without its special meaning.

Listing 11-15. *Using the DEFINE System Variable*

```
SQL> select 'Miracle&Co' as result from dual;
Enter value for co: Breweries

RESULT
----------------
MiracleBreweries

SQL> set define off
SQL> run
  1* select 'Miracle&Co' as result from dual
```

```
RESULT
----------
Miracle&Co

SQL> set define !
SQL> select 'Miracle&Co' as result from !table;
Enter value for table: dual

RESULT
----------
Miracle&Co

SQL> set define &
SQL>
```

■ **Tip** You have changed a lot of SQL*Plus settings in this section. In order to make a "clean" start, it is a good idea to exit SQL*Plus and to start a new session. This will reset all SQL*Plus variables to their default values.

11.2 Bind Variables

The previous section discussed SQL*Plus variables, which are variables maintained by the *tool* SQL*Plus. The SQL*Plus client-side program replaces all variables with actual values *before* the SQL commands are sent to the Oracle DBMS.

This section discusses *bind variables*, an important component of the SQL language. To be more precise, bind variables are a component of *dynamic* SQL, a PL/SQL interface that allows you to build and process SQL statements at runtime. Bind variables are tool-independent.

Bind variables are extremely important if you want to develop database applications for critical information systems. Suppose you have a database application to retrieve employee details. Application users just enter an employee number in a field on their screen, and then click the Execute button. For example, these SQL statements could be generated for two different database users, or for the same user using the same application twice:

```
SQL> select * from employees where empno = 7566;
SQL> select * from employees where empno = 7900;
```

These two SQL statements are obviously different, and the Oracle DBMS will also treat them as such. The optimizer will optimize them separately, and they will occupy their own memory structures (cursors). This approach can easily flood your internal memory, and it also forces the optimizer to produce execution plans over and over again. A much better approach would be to use a bind variable in the SQL command, instead of the literal employee number, and to provide values for the bind variable separately. In other words, all SQL commands coming from the application look like the following:

```
SQL> select * from employees where empno = :x;
```

Now, the Oracle DBMS is able to use cursor sharing, the optimizer can produce a single execution plan, and the SQL command can be executed many times for different values of the bind variable.

SQL*Plus offers support for bind variables with the VARIABLE and PRINT commands. You will also use the SQL*Plus EXECUTE command, allowing you to execute a single PL/SQL statement.

Bind Variable Declaration

You can declare bind variables with the SQL*Plus VARIABLE command, and you can display bind variable values with the SQL*Plus PRINT command. Because SQL doesn't support any syntax to assign values to bind variables, we use the SQL*Plus EXECUTE command to execute a single PL/SQL command from SQL*Plus. Listing 11-16 shows examples of using these commands.

Listing 11-16. *Declaring Bind Variables and Assigning Values*

```
SQL> variable x number
SQL> variable y varchar2(8)

SQL> execute :x := 7566
PL/SQL procedure successfully completed.

SQL> execute :y := 'ADMIN'
PL/SQL procedure successfully completed.

SQL> print x y

     X
------
  7566

Y
--------------------------------
ADMIN

SQL> variable
variable    x
datatype    NUMBER

variable    y
datatype    VARCHAR2(8)
SQL>
```

As you can see, we have created two variables, we have assigned values to them, and we can display those values. Note that := is the assignment operator in PL/SQL.

Bind Variables in SQL Statements

Now let's see whether we can retrieve the same two employees (7566 and 7900) using a bind variable. See Listing 11-17.

Listing 11-17. *Using Bind Variables in SQL Commands*

```
SQL> select * from employees where empno = :x;

 EMPNO ENAME   INIT JOB        MGR BDATE        MSAL  COMM DEPTNO
------ -------- ----- -------- ----- ----------- ------ ----- ------
  7566 JONES    JM    MANAGER  7839 02-APR-1967  2975          20

SQL> execute :x := 7900
PL/SQL procedure successfully completed.

SQL> run
  1* select * from employees where empno = :x

 EMPNO ENAME   INIT JOB        MGR BDATE        MSAL  COMM DEPTNO
------ -------- ----- -------- ----- ----------- ------ ----- ------
  7900 JONES    R     ADMIN    7698 03-DEC-1969   800          30

SQL>
```

Because EXECUTE is a SQL*Plus command, which means it is not stored in the SQL buffer, you can assign a new value and reexecute the query from the SQL buffer with the RUN command. If you want to see some evidence of the behavior of the Oracle DBMS, take a look at Listing 11-18.

Listing 11-18. *Querying V$SQLAREA to See the Differences*

```
SQL> select executions, sql_text
  2  from    v$sqlarea
  3  where   sql_text like 'select * from employees %';

EXECUTIONS SQL_TEXT
---------- -------------------------------------------
         2 select * from employees where empno = :x
         1 select * from employees where empno = 7566
         1 select * from employees where empno = 7900

SQL>
```

For more details about bind variables, refer to *PL/SQL User's Guide and Reference*.

11.3 SQL*Plus Scripts

In Chapter 2, you learned that you can save SQL commands with the SQL*Plus SAVE command. Until now, we have written only single SQL commands from the SQL buffer to a file. However, you can also create files with multiple SQL commands, optionally intermixed with SQL*Plus commands. This type of file is referred to as a SQL*Plus *script*.

Script Execution

You can execute SQL*Plus scripts with the SQL*Plus START command, or with its shortcut @. Listings 11-19 and 11-20 show examples of executing scripts.

Listing 11-19. *Creating and Running SQL*Plus Scripts*

```
SQL> select *
  2  from    employees
  3  where   deptno = &&dept_number
  4  and     job    = upper('&&job');
Enter value for dept_number: 10
Enter value for job: admin

EMPNO ENAME    INIT JOB       MGR BDATE        MSAL COMM DEPTNO
----- -------- ---- -------- ----- ----------- ----- ----- ------
 7934 MILLER   TJA  ADMIN     7782 23-JAN-1962 1300          10

SQL> save  testscript replace
Wrote file testscript.sql

SQL> clear buffer
SQL> start testscript
...
SQL> @testscript
...
SQL>
```

Listing 11-20. *Appending Commands to SQL*Plus Scripts*

```
SQL> select *
  2  from    departments
  3  where   deptno = &dept_number;

DEPTNO DNAME      LOCATION   MGR
-------- ---------- -------- --------
    10 ACCOUNTING NEW YORK   7782
```

```
SQL> save testscript append
Appended file to testscript.sql

SQL> @testscript
...
SQL>
```

Listing 11-21 shows what happens if you use the GET command and you try to execute the script from the SQL buffer. You get an Oracle error message, because the SQL buffer now contains multiple SQL commands (as a consequence of your GET command), which is a situation SQL*Plus cannot handle.

Listing 11-21. *What Happens If You Execute Scripts from the SQL Buffer*

```
SQL> get testscript
  1  select *
  2  from    employees
  3  where   deptno = &&dept_number
  4  and     job    = upper('&&job')
  5  /
  6  select *
  7  from    departments
  8* where   deptno = &dept_number
SQL> /
select *
*
ERROR at line 6:
ORA-00936: missing expression

SQL>
```

The SQL*Plus START command (or @) actually reads a script file *line by line*, as if those lines were entered interactively. At the end of the execution of a SQL*Plus script, you will see that only the SQL statement executed last is still in the SQL buffer.

This is also the reason why the SQL*Plus SAVE command always adds a slash (/) after the end of the contents of the SQL buffer. Check out what happens if you manually remove that slash, with an editor like Notepad. The script will wait for further input from the keyboard, as if the command were not finished yet.

By the way, you can also execute SQL*Plus scripts with a double at sign (@@) command. There is a subtle difference between the @ and @@ commands, which is relevant only if you invoke SQL*Plus scripts from other scripts. In such situations, @@ *always* searches for the (sub)script in the same folder (or directory) where the main (or calling) script is stored. This makes the syntax to call subscripts fully independent of any local environment settings, without the risk of launching wrong subscripts (with the same name, from other locations) by accident.

Script Parameters

The next feature to explore is the ability to specify parameters (values for variables) when calling scripts. You can specify up to nine command-line parameter values immediately after the SQL*Plus script name, and you can refer to these values in your script with &1, &2, ..., &9. To test this feature, open `testscript.sql` (the script you just generated in Listings 11-19 and 11-20) and make the changes shown in Listing 11-22.

Listing 11-22. *Contents of the* Changed *testscript.sql Script*

```
select *
from    employees
where   deptno = &&1        -- this was &&dept_number
and     job = upper('&2')   -- this was &&job
/
select *
from    departments
where   deptno = &1         -- this was &dept_number
/
undefine 1                  -- this line is added
```

Now you can call the script in two ways: with or without command-line arguments, as shown in Listings 11-23 and 11-24.

Listing 11-23. *Calling a Script Without Command-Line Arguments*

```
SQL> @testscript
Enter value for 1: 10
Enter value for 2: manager

EMPNO ENAME    INIT  JOB        MGR BDATE        MSAL  COMM DEPTNO
----- -------- ----- -------- ----- ----------- ----- ----- ------
 7782 CLARK    AB     MANAGER   7839 09-JUN-1965  2450          10

DEPTNO DNAME      LOCATION  MGR
------ ---------- --------- -----
    10 ACCOUNTING NEW YORK  7782

SQL>
```

As you can see in Listing 11-23, if you call the script without any arguments, SQL*Plus treats &1 and $2 just like any other substitution or user-defined variables, and prompts for their values—as long as earlier script executions didn't leave any variables defined. That's why we have added an UNDEFINE command to the end of our script, in Listing 11-22.

Listing 11-24 shows what happens if you specify two appropriate values (30 and salesrep) on the command line calling the script.

Listing 11-24. *Calling a Script with Command-Line Arguments*

```
SQL> @testscript 30 salesrep

EMPNO ENAME     INIT  JOB        MGR BDATE         MSAL  COMM DEPTNO
----- --------  ----  --------  ----- -----------  ----- ----- ------
 7499 ALLEN     JAM   SALESREP   7698 20-FEB-1961  1600   300    30
 7521 WARD      TF    SALESREP   7698 22-FEB-1962  1250   500    30
 7654 MARTIN    P     SALESREP   7698 28-SEP-1956  1250  1400    30
 7844 TURNER    JJ    SALESREP   7698 28-SEP-1968  1500     0    30

DEPTNO DNAME       LOCATION   MGR
------ ----------  --------  -----
    30 SALES       CHICAGO    7698

SQL>
```

SQL*Plus Commands in Scripts

SQL*Plus scripts may contain a mixture of SQL commands and SQL*Plus commands. This combination makes SQL*Plus a nice report-generating tool, as you will see in the next section of this chapter. One small problem is that SQL*Plus commands (entered interactively) don't go into the SQL buffer. Normally this is helpful, because it allows you to repeat your most recent SQL command from the SQL buffer, while executing SQL*Plus commands in between. However, this implies that you cannot add any SQL*Plus commands to your scripts with the SAVE ... APPEND command.

To get SQL*Plus commands into your scripts, you can use one of the following:

- An external editor

- A separate SQL*Plus buffer

Using an external editor is the most straightforward approach, in most cases. For example, you can use Notepad in a Microsoft Windows environment to maintain your SQL*Plus scripts. The charm of using a separate SQL*Plus buffer is that it is completely platform- and operating system-independent, and it is fully driven from the interactive SQL*Plus prompt. That's why we discuss using a separate buffer here.

Listing 11-25 shows an example of using a separate SQL*Plus buffer to generate scripts. To try this out, execute the CLEAR BUFFER and SET BUFFER BLAHBLAH commands, followed by the INPUT command, and enter the following 14 lines verbatim. Exit SQL*Plus input mode by entering another newline, so that you return to the SQL*Plus prompt.

Listing 11-25. *Using a Separate SQL*Plus Buffer to Generate Scripts*

```
SQL> clear buffer
SQL> set buffer blahblah
SQL> input
  1  clear screen
  2  set verify off
```

```
 3  set pause  off
 4  accept dept number -
 5        prompt "Enter a department number: "
 6  select *
 7  from    departments
 8  where   deptno = &dept;
 9  select ename, job, msal
10  from    employees
11  where   deptno = &dept;
12  undefine dept
13  set pause on
14  set verify on
15
SQL>
```

Now you can save the script and test it, as follows:

```
SQL> save testscript2
Created file testscript2.sql

SQL> @testscript2
Enter a department number: 20
...
```

The SET BUFFER command (choose any buffer name you like) creates a nondefault SQL*Plus buffer.

■Note According to the SQL*Plus documentation, using additional buffers is a deprecated feature since the early 1990s, from SQL*Plus version 3.0 onward. However, it seems to be the only way to prevent the SQL*Plus SAVE command from appending a slash (/) at the end of the script, which would execute the last SQL command twice if you have a SQL*Plus command at the end, as in Listing 11-25.

You can only *manipulate* the contents of nondefault SQL*Plus buffers with the SQL*Plus editor commands, and use SAVE and GET for file manipulation. You cannot *execute* the contents of those buffers with the START or @ command, because these commands operate only on the SQL buffer. That's why you must save the script with the SAVE command before you can use it.

SQL*Plus commands are normally entered on a single line. If that is impossible, or if you want to make your scripts more readable, you must explicitly "escape" the newline character with a minus sign (-), as we did before with the ACCEPT command in Listing 11-10, and again in Listing 11-25.

■Note The examples in the remainder of this chapter show only the contents of the SQL*Plus scripts. It is up to you to decide which method you want to use to create and maintain those scripts.

The login.sql Script

One special SQL*Plus script must be mentioned here: login.sql. SQL*Plus automatically executes this script when you start a SQL*Plus session, as long as the login.sql script is located in the folder (or directory) from where you start SQL*Plus, or if that script can be found via the SQLPATH environment variable (under Linux) or Registry setting (under Microsoft Windows).

Note that there is also a *global* SQL*Plus glogin.sql script. This script is executed for every user, and it allows you to have a mixture of global settings and personal settings in a multiuser environment. In a single-user Oracle environment, using both scripts is useless and can be confusing. The glogin.sql script is normally located in the sqlplus/admin directory under the Oracle installation directory.

■**Caution** In Oracle Database 10g, SQL*Plus also executes the glogin.sql and login.sql scripts if you execute a CONNECT command, without leaving SQL*Plus. This didn't happen with earlier releases of SQL*Plus.

You can use the glogin.sql and login.sql scripts to set various SQL*Plus system variables, user-defined variables, and column definitions. Listing 11-26 shows an example of a login.sql script, demonstrating that you can also execute SQL commands from this script. You can test it by saving this file to the right place and restarting SQL*Plus.

Listing 11-26. *Example of a login.sql Script*

```
--   ==========================================
--   LOGIN.SQL
--   ==========================================
set pause    "Enter... "
set pause    on
set numwidth 6
set pagesize 24
alter session set nls_date_format='dd-mm-yyyy';
-- define_editor=Notepad  /* for Windows */
-- define_editor=vi       /* for UNIX   */
clear screen
```

11.4 Report Generation with SQL*Plus

As you've learned in previous chapters, the SQL language enables you to write queries. Queries produce result tables. However, the default layout of those query results is often visually unappealing.

SQL*Plus offers many commands and features to enhance your query results into more readable reports. SQL*Plus is definitely the oldest "quick-and-dirty" Oracle report generator; the original name in the 1980s was UFI (User Friendly Interface), before they renamed it as

SQL*Plus. Several other Oracle reporting tools were developed and discarded over the years, but SQL*Plus is still here. Table 11-2 lists some of the SQL*Plus features you can use for enhancing your reports.

Table 11-2. *SQL*Plus Features to Enhance Reports*

Feature	Description
SET {LINESIZE|PAGESIZE|NEWPAGE}	Adjust the page setup
SET TRIMSPOOL ON	Suppress trailing spaces in SPOOL output
COLUMN	Adjust column layouts (header and contents)
TTITLE, BTITLE	Define top and bottom page titles
REPHEADER, REPFOOTER	Define report headers and footers
BREAK	Group rows (make sure the result is ordered appropriately)
COMPUTE	Add aggregate computations on BREAK definitions
SPOOL	Spool SQL*Plus output to a file

The SQL*Plus SET command was introduced in Section 11.1, in the discussion of SQL*Plus system variables. Now we'll look at the other SQL*Plus commands that are useful for producing reports.

The SQL*Plus COLUMN Command

You also already saw some examples of the COLUMN command. However, the SQL*Plus COLUMN command has many additional features, as you will learn in this section.

The general syntax of the SQL*Plus COLUMN command is as follows:

```
SQL> column [<col-name>|<expression>] [<option>...]
```

If you don't specify any arguments at all, the COLUMN command produces a complete overview of all current column settings. If you specify <col-name>, you get only the settings of that column. Note that <col-name> is mapped with column aliases in the SELECT clause; that is, with the column headings of the final query result. You can use <expression> to influence SELECT clause expressions; make sure to copy the expression verbatim from the query. For <option>, you can specify various ways to handle the column. Table 11-3 shows a selection of the valid options for the COLUMN command.

Table 11-3. *Some SQL*Plus COLUMN Command Options*

Option	Description
ALI[AS]	Column alias; useful in BREAK and COMPUTE commands
CLE[AR]	Reset all column settings
FOLD_A[FTER]	Insert a carriage return after the column
FOR[MAT]	Format display of column values
HEA[DING]	Define (different) column title
JUS[TIFY]	Justify column header: LEFT, CENTER or CENTRE, RIGHT

Continued

Table 11-3. *Continued*

Option	Description
LIKE	Copy settings over from another column
NEWL[INE]	Force a new line before this column
NEW_V[ALUE]	Variable to retain the last column value
NOPRI[NT]	Suppress display of specific columns
NUL[L]	Display of null values in specific columns
ON|OFF	Toggle to activate/deactivate column settings
WRA[PPED]	Wrap too-long column values to the following line
WOR[D_WRAPPED]	Wrap too-long column values to the following line, splitting the column value between words
TRU[NCATED]	Truncate too-long column values

The last three COLUMN options are mutually exclusive. In Table 11-3, the brackets indicate the abbreviations you can use. For example, you can abbreviate the first SQL*Plus command in Listing 11-27 as COL ENAME FOR A20 HEA LAST_NAME JUS C, if you like. If you do not specify a JUSTIFY value for a column, SQL*Plus uses the following alignment defaults:

- NUMBER column headings default to RIGHT.

- Other column headings default to LEFT.

Listings 11-27 through 11-29 show some examples of the SQL*Plus COLUMN command.

Listing 11-27. *Using COLUMN FORMAT, HEADING, JUSTIFY, and LIKE*

```
SQL> select empno, ename, bdate
  2  ,       msal        as salary
  3  ,       comm        as commission
  4  from    employees;

EMPNO ENAME     BDATE            SALARY COMMISSION
------ --------- ----------- -------- ----------
  7369 SMITH     17-DEC-1965     800
  7499 ALLEN     20-FEB-1961    1600        300
  7521 WARD      22-FEB-1962    1250        500
...
14 rows selected.

SQL> col ename      format  a20 heading last_name justify center
SQL> col salary     format  $9999.99
SQL> col commission like    salary
SQL> col salary     heading month|salary
SQL> /
                                        month
```

```
EMPNO      last_name        BDATE        salary COMMISSION
------ -------------------- ----------- --------- -----------
  7369 SMITH               17-DEC-1965    $800.00
  7499 ALLEN               20-FEB-1961   $1600.00     $300.00
  7521 WARD                22-FEB-1962   $1250.00     $500.00
...
14 rows selected.

SQL>
```

Note the effects of the vertical bar (|) in the COL SALARY command and the LIKE option for the COMMISSION column.

Listings 11-27 and 11-28 illustrate an important property of the COLUMN command: you must always specify the column *alias*, not the original column name, as its argument.

Listing 11-28. *Using COLUMN NOPRINT, ON, OFF*

```
SQL> col COMM NOPRINT                    -- Note the column name
SQL> select empno, ename, bdate
  2  ,       msal         as salary
  3  ,       comm         as commission  -- and the column alias
  4  from    employees;
                                  month
EMPNO      last_name        BDATE        salary COMMISSION
------ -------------------- ----------- --------- -----------
  7369 SMITH               17-DEC-1965    $800.00
  7499 ALLEN               20-FEB-1961   $1600.00     $300.00
  7521 WARD                22-FEB-1962   $1250.00     $500.00
...
14 rows selected.

SQL> col COMMISSION NOPRINT -- Now you use the column alias instead
SQL> /
                                  month
EMPNO      last_name        BDATE        salary
------ -------------------- ----------- ---------
  7369 SMITH               17-DEC-1965    $800.00
  7499 ALLEN               20-FEB-1961   $1600.00
  7521 WARD                22-FEB-1962   $1250.00
...
14 rows selected.

SQL> col commission off
SQL> /
                                  month
EMPNO      last_name        BDATE        salary COMMISSION
------ -------------------- ----------- --------- -----------
  7369 SMITH               17-DEC-1965    $800.00
```

```
 7499 ALLEN              20-FEB-1961  $1600.00           300
 7521 WARD               22-FEB-1962  $1250.00           500
...
SQL> col commission
COLUMN   commission OFF
FORMAT   $9999.99
NOPRINT
SQL> col commission on
SQL>
```

The NEW_VALUE feature of the COLUMN command is very nice, and you can use it for various tricks in SQL*Plus scripts. As you can see in Listing 11-29, the user-defined BLAH variable remembers the last EMPNO value for you.

Listing 11-29. *Using COLUMN NEW_VALUE*

```
SQL> col empno new_value BLAH
SQL> /
                                       month
EMPNO       last_name    BDATE         salary
------ -------------------- ----------- ---------
 7369 SMITH              17-DEC-1965    $800.00
 7499 ALLEN              20-FEB-1961   $1600.00
...
 7934 MILLER             23-JAN-1962   $1300.00

14 rows selected.

SQL> def BLAH
DEFINE BLAH          =    7934 (NUMBER)

SQL> I
  5  where   deptno = 30;
                                       month
EMPNO       last_name    BDATE         salary
------ -------------------- ----------- ---------
 7499 ALLEN              20-FEB-1961   $1600.00
 7521 WARD               22-FEB-1962   $1250.00
 7654 MARTIN             28-SEP-1956   $1250.00
 7698 BLAKE              01-NOV-1963   $2850.00
 7844 TURNER             28-SEP-1968   $1500.00
 7900 JONES              03-DEC-1969    $800.00

SQL> define BLAH
DEFINE BLAH          =    7900 (NUMBER)

SQL> undefine BLAH
SQL>
```

The SQL*Plus TTITLE and BTITLE Commands

As you have seen so far, the SQL*Plus COLUMN command allows you to influence the report layout at the column level, and you can influence the overall page layout with the SQL*Plus SET PAGESIZE and SET LINESIZE commands. You can further enhance your SQL*Plus reports with the SQL*Plus TTITLE and BTITLE commands, which allow you to add page headers and page footers to your report. The syntax is as follows:

```
SQL> ttitle [<print-spec> {<text>|<variable>}...] | [OFF|ON]
SQL> btitle [<print-spec> {<text>|<variable>}...] | [OFF|ON]
```

As Listing 11-30 shows, you can also use these commands to display their current settings (by specifying no arguments) or to enable/disable their behavior with ON and OFF.

Listing 11-30. *Using TTITLE and BTITLE*

```
SQL> set     pagesize 22
SQL> set     linesize 80
SQL> ttitle left        'SQL*Plus report'       -
  >         right       'Page: ' format 99 SQL.PNO -
  >         skip center 'OVERVIEW'               -
  >         skip center 'employees department 30' -
  >         skip 2
SQL> btitle col 20 'Confidential' tab 8 -
  >               'Created by: ' SQL.USER
SQL> /
SQL*Plus report                                                    Page:    1
                                OVERVIEW
                         employees department 30


                                    month
    EMPNO    last_name        BDATE         salary
    ------   --------------------  -----------  ---------
     7499 ALLEN             20-FEB-1961  $1600.00
     7521 WARD              22-FEB-1962  $1250.00
     7654 MARTIN            28-SEP-1956  $1250.00
     7698 BLAKE             01-NOV-1963  $2850.00
     7844 TURNER            28-SEP-1968  $1500.00
     7900 JONES             03-DEC-1969   $800.00

              Confidential        Created by: BOOK
SQL> btitle off
SQL> btitle
btitle OFF and is the following 66 characters:
col 20 'Confidential' tab 8                 'Created by: ' SQL.USER
SQL> ttitle off
SQL>
```

The output in Listing 11-30 shows the effects of the TTITLE and BTITLE commands. Note that we use two predefined variables: SQL.PNO for the page number and SQL.USER for the current username.

The TTITLE and BTITLE commands have several additional features. SQL*Plus also supports the REPHEADER and REPFOOTER commands, which allow you to add headers and footers at the report level, as opposed to the page level. See *SQL*Plus User's Guide and Reference* for more information about these commands.

The SQL*Plus BREAK Command

You can add "breaks" to the result of your reports with the SQL*Plus BREAK command. Breaks are locations in your report: between certain rows, between all rows, or at the end of the report. You can highlight breaks in your reports by suppressing repeating column values, by inserting additional lines, or by forcing a new page.

Breaks are also the positions within your reports where you can add subtotals or other data aggregations. You can use the SQL*Plus COMPUTE command for that purpose. Let's investigate the possibilities of the BREAK command first.

The syntax of the SQL*Plus BREAK command is shown in Figure 11-1.

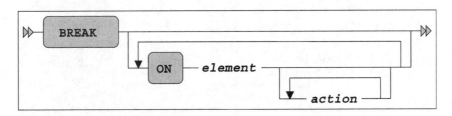

Figure 11-1. *BREAK command syntax diagram*

For *element*, you can specify a column name or a column expression, or a special report element, as discussed at the end of this section. The *action* values are listed in Table 11-4.

Table 11-4. *SQL*Plus BREAK Command Actions*

Action	Description
SKIP *n*	Skip *n* lines
SKIP PAGE	Insert a page break
[NO]DUPLICATES	Suppress or show duplicate values; NODUPLICATES is the default

Listing 11-31 shows an example of a BREAK command.

Listing 11-31. *Using the BREAK Command*

```
SQL> clear  columns

SQL> select deptno, job, empno, ename, msal, comm
  2  from    employees
```

```
  3  order  by deptno, job;

 DEPTNO JOB         EMPNO ENAME        MSAL      COMM
-------- -------- -------- -------- -------- --------
     10 ADMIN      7934 MILLER       1300
     10 DIRECTOR   7839 KING         5000
     10 MANAGER    7782 CLARK        2450
     20 MANAGER    7566 JONES        2975
     20 TRAINER    7369 SMITH         800
...
14 rows selected.

SQL> break on deptno skip 2
SQL> /
 DEPTNO JOB         EMPNO ENAME        MSAL      COMM
-------- -------- -------- -------- -------- --------
     10 ADMIN      7934 MILLER       1300
        DIRECTOR   7839 KING         5000
        MANAGER    7782 CLARK        2450

     20 MANAGER    7566 JONES        2975
        TRAINER    7369 SMITH         800
...
14 rows selected.

SQL> break
break on deptno skip 2 nodup

SQL> break on deptno page
SQL> set   pause on
SQL> /
[Enter]...

 DEPTNO JOB         EMPNO ENAME        MSAL      COMM
-------- -------- -------- -------- -------- --------
     10 ADMIN      7934 MILLER       1300
        DIRECTOR   7839 KING         5000
        MANAGER    7782 CLARK        2450
[Enter]...

 DEPTNO JOB         EMPNO ENAME        MSAL      COMM
-------- -------- -------- -------- -------- --------
     20 MANAGER    7566 JONES        2975
        TRAINER    7369 SMITH         800
...
14 rows selected.
SQL>
```

Note the ORDER BY clause in the query in Listing 11-31. You need this clause for the BREAK command to work properly. The BREAK command itself does not sort anything; it just processes the rows, one by one, as they appear in the result.

Note also that you can have only one break definition at any time. Each break definition implicitly overwrites any current break definition. This implies that if you want two breaks for your report, at different levels, you must define them in a single BREAK command; for example, see Listing 11-32.

Listing 11-32. *Multiple Breaks in a Single BREAK Command*

```
SQL> break on deptno skip page -
>         on job    skip 1
SQL> /
[Enter]...

  DEPTNO JOB        EMPNO ENAME        MSAL     COMM
-------- -------- -------- -------- -------- --------
      10 ADMIN       7934 MILLER       1300

         DIRECTOR    7839 KING         5000

         MANAGER     7782 CLARK        2450

[Enter]...

  DEPTNO JOB        EMPNO ENAME        MSAL     COMM
-------- -------- -------- -------- -------- --------
      20 MANAGER     7566 JONES        2975

         TRAINER     7369 SMITH         800
                     7902 FORD         3000
                     7788 SCOTT        3000
                     7876 ADAMS        1100
...
14 rows selected.

SQL> break
break on deptno page  nodup
         on job skip 1 nodup
SQL>
```

Note that you don't use any commas as break definition delimiters.

As you have seen so far, you can define breaks on columns or column expressions. However, you can also define breaks on two special report elements:

- ROW forces breaks on every row of the result.

- REPORT forces a break at the end of your report.

The SQL*Plus COMPUTE Command

The SQL*Plus COMPUTE command allows you to add aggregating computations on your break definitions. The syntax of the COMPUTE command is shown in Figure 11-2.

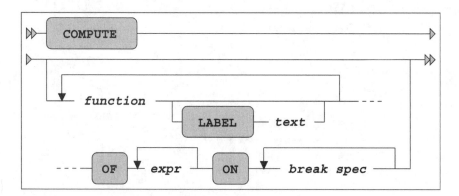

Figure 11-2. *COMPUTE command syntax diagram*

Table 11-5 lists the various functions supported by the SQL*Plus COMPUTE command.

Table 11-5. *SQL*Plus COMPUTE Functions*

Function	Description
AVG	The average
COUNT	The number of NOT NULL column values
MAX	The maximum
MIN	The minimum
NUMBER	The number of rows
STD	The standard deviation
SUM	The sum
VAR	The variance

The *expr* indicates on which column you want the *function* to be applied. The *break spec* indicates at which points in the report you want this computation to happen. The *break spec* must be a column, column expression, or a report element (ROW or REPORT) on which you previously defined a BREAK.

Listing 11-33 shows an example of using COMPUTE.

Listing 11-33. *Using COMPUTE for Aggregation*

```
SQL> set     pause off
SQL> break   on deptno skip page on job
SQL> compute sum label total of msal on deptno
SQL> compute count number    of comm on deptno
```

```
SQL> /
   DEPTNO JOB         EMPNO ENAME        MSAL     COMM
 -------- -------- -------- -------- -------- --------
       10 ADMIN        7934 MILLER       1300
          DIRECTOR     7839 KING         5000
          MANAGER      7782 CLARK        2450
********* ********                   -------- --------
count                                               0
number                                              3
total                                 8750


   DEPTNO JOB         EMPNO ENAME        MSAL     COMM
 -------- -------- -------- -------- -------- --------
       20 MANAGER      7566 JONES        2975
          TRAINER      7369 SMITH         800
                       7902 FORD         3000
                       7788 SCOTT        3000
                       7876 ADAMS        1100
********* ********                   -------- --------
count                                               0
number                                              5
total                                10875


   DEPTNO JOB         EMPNO ENAME        MSAL     COMM
 -------- -------- -------- -------- -------- --------
       30 ADMIN        7900 JONES         800
          MANAGER      7698 BLAKE        2850
          SALESREP     7499 ALLEN        1600      300
                       7654 MARTIN       1250     1400
                       7844 TURNER       1500        0
                       7521 WARD         1250      500
********* ********                   -------- --------
count                                               4
number                                              6
total                                 9250


14 rows selected.

SQL> compute
COMPUTE sum LABEL 'total' OF msal ON deptno
COMPUTE count LABEL 'count' number LABEL 'number' OF comm ON deptno
SQL> clear computes
SQL> clear breaks
SQL>
```

As Listing 11-33 shows, you can issue multiple COMPUTE commands, and you can have multiple COMPUTE definitions active at the same time. The CLEAR COMPUTES command erases all compute definitions, and the CLEAR BREAKS command clears the current break definition.

If you are happy with the final report results on screen, you can store all SQL and SQL*Plus commands in a script, and add commands to spool the output to a text file, as described in the next section.

The Finishing Touch: SPOOL

If you look at the results in Listing 11-33, you see that this mixture of SQL and SQL*Plus commands produces a rather complete report. Now you can use the SQL*Plus SPOOL command to save the report into a file; for example, to allow for printing. The syntax is as follows:

```
SQL> spool [<file-name>[.<ext>] [CREATE|REPLACE|APPEND] | OFF | OUT]
```

If you specify no arguments, the SPOOL command reports its current status. The default file name extension *<ext>* is LST or LIS on most platforms. SPOOL OFF stops the spooling. SPOOL OUT stops the spooling *and* sends the result to your default printer.

Suppose you have saved the example of Listing 11-33 in a script, containing all SQL*Plus commands and the SQL query. You can turn this script into a complete report by changing the contents as indicated in Listing 11-34. For readability, the three lines to be added are highlighted. The TRIMSPOOL setting suppresses trailing spaces in the result, and the REPLACE option of the SPOOL command ensures that an existing file (if any) will be overwritten.

Listing 11-34. *Using the SPOOL Command to Generate SQL*Plus Reports*

```
    set     pause off
    break   on deptno skip page on job
    compute sum label total of msal on deptno
    compute count number    of comm on deptno
>>> set trimspool on                        <<< added line
>>> spool report.txt replace                <<< added line
    -- The query
    select deptno, job, empno, ename, msal, comm
    from    employees
    order   by deptno, job;
>>> spool off                               <<< added line
    -- Cleanup section
    undefine dept
    clear computes
    clear breaks
    set pause on
```

If you execute this script, it generates a text file named report.txt in the current folder/directory.

11.5 HTML in SQL*Plus and *i*SQL*Plus

Both SQL*Plus and *i*SQL*Plus are perfect tools to generate reports in HTML format, allowing you to display the report results in a browser environment. *i*SQL*Plus has more features than SQL*Plus in this area, because it runs in a browser environment itself. Let's look at SQL*Plus first.

HTML in SQL*Plus

The SQL*Plus MARKUP setting is very important if you want to work with HTML. Listing 11-35 shows why this is so.

Listing 11-35. *The SQL*Plus MARKUP Setting*

```
SQL> show markup
markup HTML OFF HEAD "<style type='text/css'> body
{font:10pt Arial,Helvetica,sans-serif; color:black; background:White;} p {font:1F

SQL> set markup
SP2-0281: markup missing set option
Usage: SET MARKUP HTML [ON|OFF] [HEAD text] [BODY text]
 [TABLE text] [ENTMAP {ON|OFF}] [SPOOL {ON|OFF}] [PRE[FORMAT] {ON|OFF}]
SQL>
```

The SQL*Plus error message in Listing 11-35 (followed by the "Usage:" text) precisely indicates what you can do to fix the problem with the incomplete SET MARKUP command:

- SET MARKUP HTML is mandatory, followed by ON or OFF.

- HEAD allows you to specify text for the HTML <header> tag, BODY for the <body> tag, and TABLE for the <table> tag, respectively.

- ENTMAP allows you to indicate whether SQL*Plus should replace some special HTML characters (such as <, >, ', and &) by their corresponding HTML representations (<, >, ", and &).

- SPOOL lets you spool output to a file, without needing to use an additional SQL*Plus SPOOL command.

- PREFORMAT allows you to write output to a <pre> tag. The default value is OFF.

The HEADER option of the SET MARKUP command is particularly interesting, because it allows you to specify a *cascading style sheet*. Let's perform some experiments, as shown in Listing 11-36.

Listing 11-36. *Using the SQL*Plus SET MARKUP Command*

```
SQL> set markup html on head "<title>SQL*Plus demo</title>"
SQL&gt; select ename,init from employees where deptno = 10;
<br>
```

```
<p>
<table border='1' width='90%' align='center' summary='Script output'>
<tr>
<th scope="col">
last_name
</th>
<th scope="col">
INIT
</th>
</tr>
<tr>
<td>
CLARK
</td>
<td>
AB
</td>
</tr>
<tr>
<td>
KING
</td>
<td>
CC
</td>
</tr>
<tr>
<td>
MILLER
</td>
<td>
TJA
</td>
</tr>
</table>
<p>

SQL&gt; set markup html off
<br>
SQL>
```

As you can see in Listing 11-36, the screen output is in HTML format. Obviously, the MARKUP setting becomes truly useful in combination with the SQL*Plus SPOOL command, allowing you to open the result in a browser. The combination of the SQL*Plus MARKUP and SPOOL commands is so obvious that you are able to specify SPOOL ON as an option in the MARKUP setting (see Listing 11-35).

■**Tip** You can also specify the MARKUP setting as a command-line argument when you launch SQL*Plus. This is useful for certain reports, because SQL*Plus then processes the <html> and <body> tags *before* the first command is executed.

If you execute the SQL*Plus script in Listing 11-37, you will note what happens as a consequence of the SET ECHO OFF TERMOUT OFF command: the SQL*Plus screen remains empty. SQL*Plus only writes the results to a file.

Listing 11-37. *Contents of the htmldemoscript.sql Script*

```
-- ================================
-- htmldemoscript.sql
-- ================================
SET ECHO off TERMOUT OFF
set markup html on spool on                    -
    preformat off entmap on                    -
    head "<title>HTML Demo Report</title>      -
          <link rel='stylesheet' href='x.css'>"

spool htmldemo.htm replace

select empno, ename, init, msal
from    employees
where   deptno = 20;

spool off
set markup html off
set echo on
```

Figure 11-3 shows what happens if you open the result in a browser. The example assumes that you have an x.css cascading style sheet document in the current folder/directory.

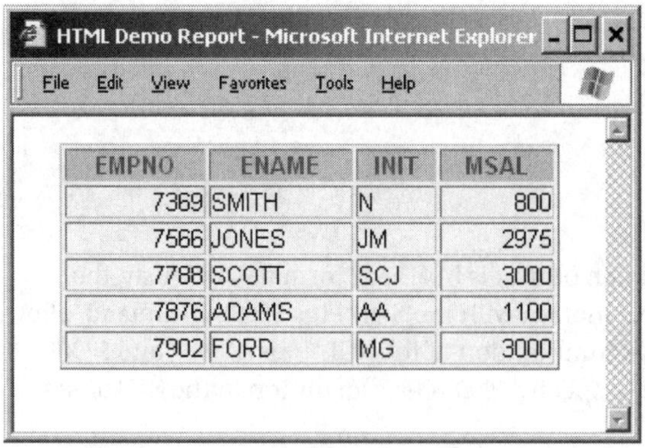

EMPNO	ENAME	INIT	MSAL
7369	SMITH	N	800
7566	JONES	JM	2975
7788	SCOTT	SCJ	3000
7876	ADAMS	AA	1100
7902	FORD	MG	3000

Figure 11-3. *Result of htmldemoscript.sql in a browser*

One more tip, before we continue with *i*SQL*Plus: you can achieve various "special effects" by selecting HTML fragments as alphanumerical literals in your queries. Listing 11-38 shows what happens if you add the following fragment to the `htmldemoscript.sql` script, just before the `SPOOL OFF` command.

Listing 11-38. *Addition to the htmldemoscript.sql Script*

```
set markup html entmap off preformat on
set heading off

select '<a href="http://www.naturaljoin.nl"> Visit this web site</a>'
from  dual;
```

HTML in *i*SQL*Plus

In *i*SQL*Plus, the possibilities of working with HTML are even more powerful than in SQL*Plus. This makes sense, since *i*SQL*Plus itself executes in a browser environment. For example, all *i*SQL*Plus results are by default in HTML format, based on a standard *i*SQL*Plus style sheet.

If you execute the query of Listing 11-37 in *i*SQL*Plus, you don't need to specify any SQL*Plus HTML settings (such as `MARKUP` or `SPOOL`), and you don't need to open the results in a browser, because this now happens implicitly.

Check out the HTML possibilities available through *i*SQL*Plus Preferences. To access the *i*SQL*Plus Preferences screen, click the Preferences link in the top-right corner of the Workspace screen. Then click the Script Formatting link under System Configuration (see Figure 2-7 in Chapter 2). See Figure 11-4 for a small sample of the options.

If you want to execute scripts in *i*SQL*Plus, you can do that in various ways. First of all, you can enter the script manually (or with copy and paste) into the Workspace area. However, if you click the Load Script button, you're offered two further possibilities, as shown in Figure 11-5. You can specify a local script in the File field, optionally using the Browse... button, or you can use the URL field to specify a script from the Internet. Then you can click the Load button, followed by the Execute button to run the script.

Just as you can start SQL*Plus with a single command line, including the SQL*Plus script that you want to execute, you can also use the *i*SQL*Plus address toolbar in several ways to specify additional information.

You must add the keyword `dynamic` if you want to specify additional information in the *i*SQL*Plus URL. For example, you can specify a name and a password, allowing you to skip the login dialog box, as shown here:

```
http://<IP address>:<port>/isqlplus/dynamic?userid=book/book
```

This example shows how you can specify a script to be executed:

```
http://<IP address>:<port>/isqlplus/dynamic?script=http://...
```

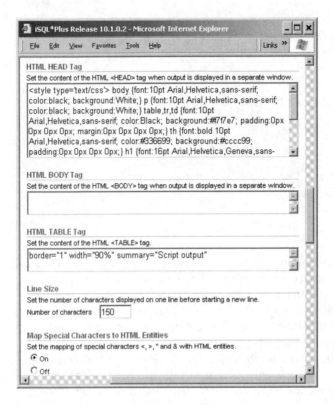

Figure 11-4. *iSQL*Plus Script Formatting Preferences*

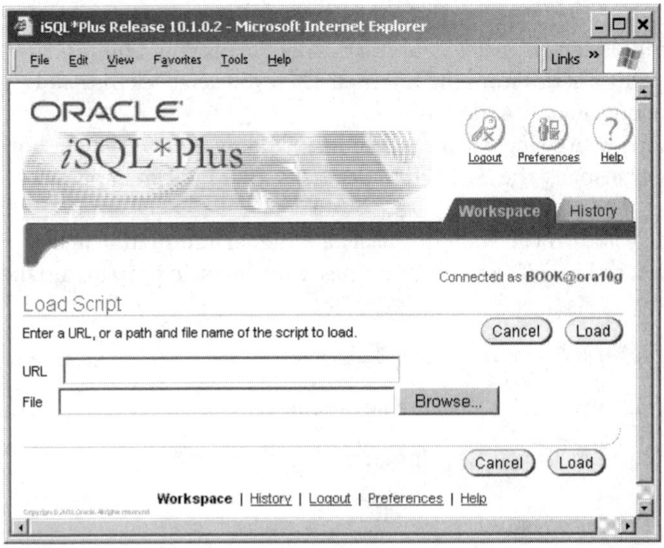

Figure 11-5. *Loading iSQL*Plus Scripts*

The following example is a combination of the first two examples. Note that the parameter section always starts with a question mark (?) and the individual parameters are separated using an ampersand (&).

```
http://<IP address>:<port>/isqlplus/dynamic?userid=book/book
                              &amp;script=http://...
```

Your URL can also contain an SQL command to be executed, including all other information needed to connect to the database. The following example loads the SQL command into the *i*SQL*Plus workspace and then waits for further commands.

```
http://<IP address>:<port>/isqlplus/dynamic?userid=book/book
                              &amp;script=select%20*%20from%20departments;
                              &amp;type=text
                              &amp;action=load
```

This example executes the SQL command and displays the results:

```
http://<IP address>:<port>/isqlplus/dynamic?userid=book/book
                              &amp;script=select%20*%20from%20departments;
                              &amp;type=text
                              &amp;action=execute
```

In this example (with `action=execute`), the browser displays only the results and suppresses the regular *i*SQL*Plus screen layout, just as in Figure 11-3.

Also, note that we replaced all spaces in the last two URL examples by `%20`, which is a commonly accepted browser standard. This is done because *i*SQL*Plus doesn't support spaces.

11.6 Exercises

The following exercises allow you to practice using the commands covered in this chapter. See Appendix D for the answers.

1. Look at Listings 11-26 and 11-37. Apart from aesthetics, there is another important reason why the lines surrounding the script headers in those two listings switch from minus signs to equal signs. Obviously, the first two minus signs are mandatory to turn the lines into comments. What would be wrong with using only minus signs?

2. Create a SQL*Plus script to create indexes. The script should prompt for a table name and a column name (or list of column names), and then *generate* the index name according to the following standard: `i_<tab-id>_<col-id>`.

3. Create a SQL*Plus script to produce an index overview. The script should prompt for a table name, allowing you to specify any leading part of a table name. That is, the script should automatically append a % wildcard to the value entered. Then it should produce a report of all indexes, showing the table name, index name, index type, and number of columns on which the index is based.

4. Create a script that disables all constraints in your schema.

CHAPTER 12

■■■

Object-Relational Features

As promised in the introduction of this book, this final chapter discusses some object-relational features of the Oracle DBMS. For a proper understanding and appreciation of object-relational database features in general, you should consider those features in the context of an object-oriented development environment. Because this book is devoted to Oracle SQL, this chapter focuses on the consequences of these object-relational features for the SQL language.

The first step in setting up an object-relational environment is the definition of the appropriate collection of *object types* and *methods*. Once you have defined your object types, you can use them to create *object tables*, thus creating a truly object-relational environment. You can also use *object views* to create an object-relational layer on top of standard relational environments. This chapter mainly uses object types as a starting point for creating user-defined datatypes, and then using those datatypes in relational table structures.

Along with "regular" user-defined datatypes, there are two special user-defined datatypes, also referred to as *collection types*, because they are multivalued: variable arrays and nested tables. The first four sections of this chapter cover collection types and user-defined datatypes.

Section 12.5 introduces the ANSI/ISO standard multiset operators, which allow you to perform various sophisticated operations with nested tables. The chapter ends with some exercises.

Note that the PL/SQL language normally plays an important role in creating an object-relational environment. PL/SQL is the programming language you need in the definition phase of such an environment. Because PL/SQL is not covered in this book, I assume some basic knowledge of this language.

■**Note** Instead of PL/SQL, you can also use the Java language to create an object-relational environment.

12.1 More Datatypes

So far in this book, we have used only the standard, built-in datatypes supported by Oracle, such as NUMBER, BINARY_FLOAT, BINARY_DOUBLE, DATE, TIMESTAMP [WITH [LOCAL] TIMEZONE], INTERVAL, [N]CHAR, and [N]VARCHAR2. This means that we haven't discussed the following two Oracle datatype categories:

- **Collection datatypes:** These are variable arrays (*varrays*) and *nested tables*. You are probably familiar with the concept of arrays from other programming languages, and nested tables are tables within a table.

- **User-defined datatypes:** These allow you (as the name indicates) to define your own complex datatypes.

Collection Datatypes

Collection datatypes are a special case of user-defined datatypes. Collection datatypes support attributes that can have multiple values. For example, you can store a list of phone numbers for each employee in a single column, or you can add a set of errata entries to every row in the COURSES table.

The first example (adding a list of phone numbers) is an obvious candidate for using a varray, because, in general, you know the maximum length of such a list of phone numbers in advance. Also, you probably want to assign some meaning to the order of the phone numbers in the list (office extension, home, mobile, fax, and so on).

It is probably better to implement the second example (maintaining course errata) with a nested table, because you don't have an idea beforehand about how many errata entries to expect. Also, the physical order of those errata is irrelevant, as long as you store enough errata attributes.

Note As you will see soon, you cannot create nested tables without using user-defined datatypes.

As a user-defined datatype, you might, for example, create an ADDRESS type, with STREET, NUMBER, POSTALCODE, and CITY components. You can create arrays of user-defined datatypes. For example, you could use the ADDRESS type to add an array of addresses to the OFFERINGS table. That would allow you to store multiple alternative location addresses for course offerings. If you want to store only a single location address, you obviously don't need an array—a regular user-defined address type would be sufficient.

Methods

You can add *methods* to user-defined datatypes. Methods are operations specifically developed to work with your user-defined datatypes; for example, to specify how you want to *compare* two address type values, or how you want to *sort* address values.

Methods add a lot of semantic power to your user-defined datatypes. Unfortunately we can't spend much time on methods in this book, because you need a great deal of PL/SQL programming to create methods. If you want to see some method examples, check out the CUSTOMERS table of the OE schema, one of the standard sample schemas that ships with the Oracle software.

As you will see in the next section, as soon as you create a user-defined datatype in Oracle, you implicitly get one method "for free"—a method with the same name as the datatype itself. That method is the *constructor method*, which allows you to create occurrences of the datatype.

⌐ OBJECT-RELATIONAL VS. STANDARD RELATIONAL TECHNIQUES

For the examples mentioned so far in this chapter, you could argue that you could implement them very well with standard relational techniques, as discussed in previous chapters of this book. You could separate various phone numbers into separate columns, you could create a separate ERRATA table with a foreign key constraint referring to the COURSES table, and so on.

So when should you choose an object-relational approach rather than a pure relational approach? It might be a matter of taste, and discussions about taste are probably a waste of time in a technical book like this one. As the Romans said, "*De gustibus non disputandum est...*" [1]

It might be the case that you have a powerful object-oriented design and development environment. You may find that Oracle's object-relational features enable you to maintain an intuitive and straightforward mapping between that development environment and the Oracle database structures.

In any case, this book does not speculate about when one approach is better than the other. The examples in this chapter have a single purpose: to illustrate the object-relational features of the Oracle DBMS.

As you read about the techniques described in this chapter, you may wonder whether they violate the first normal form as one of the foundations of the relational model. That is *not* the case. The relational model does not forbid in any way storing complex or set-valued attributes in your rows. Data "atomicity" is a rather slippery concept. For example, if you consider DATE values, aren't you looking at a compound datatype? A DATE value has meaningful subcomponents, such as year, month, and day. For a thorough treatment of this subject, see *An Introduction to Database Systems (8th Edition)*, by Chris Date.

12.2 Varrays

We will begin to explore varrays by implementing the phone list example introduced in the previous section. To keep our EMPLOYEES table unimpaired, we create a copy of the EMPLOYEES table for our experiments in this final chapter of the book. We also leave out some of the columns of the original EMPLOYEES table. See Listing 12-1.

Listing 12-1. *Creating a Copy of the EMPLOYEES Table*

```
SQL> create table e
  2  as
  3  select empno, ename, init, mgr, deptno
  4  from    employees;

Table created.
SQL>
```

Creating the Array

Before we can add a list of phone numbers for every employee in the E table, we must create a corresponding type first, as shown in Listing 12-2.

---

1. There is no disputing about tastes.

Listing 12-2. *Creating and Describing a Type*

```
SQL> create or replace type numberlist_t
  2  as varray(4) of varchar2(20);
  3  /

Type created.

SQL> describe numberlist_t
 numberlist_t VARRAY(4) OF VARCHAR2(20)

SQL> select type_name, typecode
  2  from   user_types;

TYPE_NAME                TYPECODE
------------------------ --------------------------------

NUMBERLIST_T             COLLECTION

SQL>
```

Note that you must end the CREATE TYPE command in Listing 12-2 with a slash (/) in the third line, although you ended the second line with a semicolon. The reason is that you are not entering an SQL or an SQL*Plus command; you're entering a PL/SQL command.

Note also that from now on, you can use this NUMBERLIST_T type as often as you like. It is known to the database, and its definition is stored in the data dictionary. You can query the USER_TYPES data dictionary view to see your own type definitions.

■**Note** To allow other database users to use your type definitions, you must grant them the EXECUTE privilege on those types.

In Listing 12-3, we add a column to the E table, using the NUMBERLIST_T type we created in Listing 12-2. Then, we execute a query.

Listing 12-3. *Adding a Column Based on the NUMBERLIST_T Type*

```
SQL> alter table e add (numlist numberlist_t);

Table altered.

SQL> describe e
Name                     Null?    Type
------------------------ -------- ---------------
 EMPNO                            NUMBER(4)
 ENAME                   NOT NULL VARCHAR2(8)
 INIT                    NOT NULL VARCHAR2(5)
```

```
MGR                               NUMBER(4)
DEPTNO                            NUMBER(2)
NUMLIST                           NUMBERLIST_T

SQL> select empno, numlist from e;

  EMPNO NUMLIST
------- ----------------------------------------
   7369
   7499
   7521
   7566
   7654
   7698
   7782
   7788
   7839
   7844
   7876
   7900
   7902
   7934

14 rows selected.

SQL>
```

The query results are not impressive. Obviously, the new NUMLIST column is still empty. So we have the following two problems to solve:

- How can we populate the NUMLIST column with phone numbers?

- After the column has these phone numbers, how can we retrieve them?

Populating the Array with Values

As mentioned earlier in the chapter, each user-defined object type implicitly has a function of the same name, allowing you to generate or construct values of that object type. This function is normally referred to as the *constructor method*. In other words, if you create a user-defined object type, you get a constructor method for free, with the same name as the object type.

Listing 12-4 shows how you can assign phone number lists to five employees in the E table. Note that you can skip elements, if you like, and you can also assign empty number lists.

Listing 12-4. *Assigning Values to the NUMLIST Column*

```
SQL> update e
  2  set    numlist = numberlist_t('1234','06-78765432','029-8765432')
  3  where  empno = 7839;
```

```
1 row updated.

SQL> update e
  2  set    numlist = numberlist_t('4231','06-12345678')
  3  where  empno = 7782;
1 row updated.

SQL> update e
  2  set    numlist = numberlist_t('2345')
  3  where  empno = 7934;
1 row updated.

SQL> update e
  2  set    numlist = numberlist_t('','06-23456789')
  3  where  empno = 7698;
1 row updated.

SQL> update e
  2  set numlist = numberlist_t()
  3  where  empno in (7566,7844);
2 rows updated.

SQL>
```

Querying Array Columns

Now let's see what happens if we select the NUMLIST column, without applying any functions or operators to that column. In that case, we simply get the values back the same way we inserted them, including the constructor method, as shown in Listing 12-5.

Listing 12-5. *Querying the NUMLIST Column*

```
SQL> select empno, numlist
  2  from   e
  3  where  empno in (7566,7698,77832,7839,7934);

   EMPNO NUMLIST
-------- ---------------------------------------------------
    7566 NUMBERLIST_T()
    7698 NUMBERLIST_T(NULL, '06-23456789')
    7839 NUMBERLIST_T('1234', '06-78765432', '029-8765432')
    7934 NUMBERLIST_T('2345')

SQL>
```

If you want to select individual phone numbers from the NUMLIST array, you need to "unnest" the phone numbers first. You can unnest arrays with the TABLE function. Listing 12-6 shows how you can use the TABLE function for that purpose. (For further details about the TABLE function, see *Oracle SQL Reference*.)

Listing 12-6. *Using the TABLE Function to Unnest the NUMLIST Array*

```
SQL> break on empno

SQL> select e.empno, n.*
  2  from   e
  3  ,      TABLE(e.numlist) n;

  EMPNO COLUMN_VALUE
-------- ------------------
   7698
         06-23456789
   7782 4231
         06-12345678
   7839 1234
         06-78765432
         029-8765432
   7934 2345

SQL>
```

Suppose that we want to go one step further and be able to select specific phone numbers from the array (for example, the second one). In that case, we need PL/SQL again, because the SQL language does not support a direct way to access array elements by their index value. It is not difficult to build a PL/SQL function to return a certain element from an array. Chapter 5 showed an example of a PL/SQL stored function to count the number of employees per department (Listing 5-31). Listing 12-7 shows how you can create a PL/SQL stored function to return the first phone number from the NUMLIST array, assuming that number represents the internal extension number.

Listing 12-7. *Creating a PL/SQL Function to Return Array Elements*

```
SQL> create or replace function ext
  2        (p_varray_in numberlist_t)
  3  return varchar2
  4  is
  5    v_ext varchar2(20);
  6  begin
  7    v_ext := p_varray_in(1);
  8    return v_ext;
  9  end;
 10 /
Function created.

SQL> select ename, init, ext(numlist)
```

```
  2  from   e
  3  where  deptno = 10;

ENAME    INIT  EXT(NUMLIST)
-------- ----- ------------
CLARK    AB    4231
KING     CC    1234
MILLER   TJA   2345

SQL>
```

The DEPTNO value (10) in the WHERE clause of this query is carefully chosen, in order to avoid error messages. Just change the DEPTNO value in Listing 12-7, and you will see the corresponding Oracle error messages.

■**Note** The EXT stored function is kept as simple as possible. For example, there is no code to handle situations where employees have no phone number list or an empty phone number list. It is relatively easy to enhance the EXT function definition with some proper exception handling. However, this is not a PL/SQL book, and the EXT function is meant only to illustrate the concept.

It is impossible to update specific elements of an array. You can only replace an entire array value by a new one.

12.3 Nested Tables

Nested tables offer you more flexibility than arrays. There are many similarities between arrays and nested tables. However, an important difference is that nested tables require one extra step. In the previous section, you saw that you create a type, and then use it to define arrays. For nested tables, you first create a type, then you create a table type based on that type, and then you create a nested table based on that table type.

Creating Table Types

To demonstrate how to use nested tables, we will implement the example of maintaining course errata, introduced in Section 12.1. Listing 12-8 shows how to create the two types we need for implementing the errata example as a nested table.

Listing 12-8. *Creating a Table Type for a Nested Table*

```
SQL> create or replace type erratum_t as object
  2  ( code varchar2(4)
  3  , ch   number(2)
  3  , pg   number(3)
  4  , txt  varchar2(40)
```

```
  5  );
  6  /

Type created.

SQL> create or replace type errata_tab_t as table of erratum_t;
  2  /

Type created.

SQL> describe errata_tab_t
 errata_tab_t TABLE OF ERRATUM_T
 Name                                Null?    Type
 ------------------------------- -------- ---------------
 CODE                                     VARCHAR2(4)
 CH                                       NUMBER(2)
 PG                                       NUMBER(3)
 TXT                                      VARCHAR2(40)

SQL>
```

Creating the Nested Table

Listing 12-9 shows the next step of creating the nested table based on the ERRATA_TAB_T type. Just as we did in the previous section with the EMPLOYEES table, we first create a copy C of the COURSES table, to keep that table unimpaired.

Listing 12-9. *Creating a Table with a Nested Table Column*

```
SQL> create table c
  2  as
  3  select * from courses;

Table created.

SQL> alter table c
  2  add (errata errata_tab_t)
  3  nested table errata store as errata_tab;

Table altered.

SQL> update c
  2  set    errata = errata_tab_t();

10 rows updated.

SQL>
```

In Listing 12-9, the ALTER TABLE command adds an ERRATA nested table column to the C table, and the UPDATE command assigns an empty nested table to the ERRATA column for every row. Note that we use the ERRATA_TAB_T table type constructor method for that purpose.

Populating the Nested Table

Now we can add rows to the nested table, as shown in Listing 12-10. Note that you can access nested tables *only* within the context of the table they are part of; it is *impossible* to access them as independent tables. Listing 12-10 uses the TABLE function again, just as we did before in Listing 12-6, to unnest the nested table.

Listing 12-10. *Inserting Rows into the Nested Table*

```
SQL> insert into table ( select errata
  2                       from   c
  3                       where  code = 'SQL')
  4  values ('SQL'
  5         , 3
  6         , 45
  7         , 'Typo in last line.');

1 row created.

SQL>
```

We inserted an erratum entry for the SQL course, Chapter 3, page 45. In a similar way, you can also delete rows from a nested table. As stated in the introduction to this section, nested tables offer more flexibility than arrays. For example, you can update individual column values of a nested table, whereas you can only replace arrays in their entirety.

Suppose we made a typo in Listing 12-10 while entering the chapter number: the erratum was not in Chapter 3, but rather in Chapter 7. Listing 12-11 shows how we can correct this mistake with an UPDATE command. Note that line 3 introduces tuple variable e ranging over the result of the TABLE function, allowing us to use that tuple variable on the fourth line to refer to its chapter (CH) column value.

Listing 12-11. *Updating Individual Columns of Nested Tables*

```
SQL> update table ( select errata
  2                  from   c
  3                  where  code = 'SQL') e
  4  set    e.ch  = 7;

1 row updated.

SQL>
```

Querying the Nested Table

If you want to retrieve all errata entries for the SQL course, you can join the courses table (C) with its nested table, as shown in Listing 12-12.

Listing 12-12. *Selecting Errata for the SQL Course*

```
SQL> select code
  2  ,       c.description
  3  ,       e.ch, e.pg, e.txt
  4  from    c
  5          join
  6          table(c.errata) e
  7          using (code);

CODE   DESCRIPTION
------ ----------------------------
 CH PG TXT
--- --- ----------------------------
SQL    Introduction to SQL
  7 45 Typo in last line.

SQL>
```

As Listing 12-12 shows, this nested table join syntax is very similar to the syntax you use for regular joins (discussed in Chapter 8). The TABLE function unnests its column-valued argument (c.ERRATA) into a table.

Note that you can only refer to c.ERRATA because you specify the C table first in the FROM clause. The FROM clause order is important in this case. If you swap the two table expressions, you get the following Oracle error message:

```
SQL> select code
  2  ,       c.description
  3  ,       e.ch, e.pg, e.txt
  4  from    table(c.errata) e
  5          join
  6          c
  7          using (code);
from   table(c.errata) e
              *
ERROR at line 4:
ORA-00904: "C"."ERRATA": invalid identifier

SQL>
```

Listing 12-12 shows only a single row, because we inserted only a single erratum into the nested table. The last section of this chapter revisits nested tables, showing how you can use *multiset operators* on nested tables. These multiset operators could be a reason to consider using nested tables instead of regular (relational) tables with primary key and foreign key constraints. The multiset operators allow you to write elegant SQL statements that would need quite complicated syntax without them.

12.4 User-Defined Types

Your application may require a special, complex datatype. In that case, you would create a user-defined type.

Creating User-Defined Types

The third example mentioned in Section 12.1 was the compound ADDRESS type, used to store addresses with meaningful subcomponents into a single column. Listing 12-13 shows how you can create such a type.

Listing 12-13. *Creating and Using User-Defined Types*

```
SQL> create type address_t as object
  2  ( street varchar2(20)
  3  , nr     varchar2(5)
  4  , pcode  varchar2(6)
  5  , city   varchar2(20)
  6  ) ;
  7  /

Type created.

SQL> describe address_t
 Name                                Null?    Type
 ----------------------------------- -------- ---------------
 STEET                                        VARCHAR2(20)
 NR                                           VARCHAR2(5)
 PCODE                                        VARCHAR2(6)
 CITY                                         VARCHAR2(20)

SQL> select type_name, typecode
  2  from   user_types;

TYPE_NAME                      TYPECODE
------------------------------ -------------------
NUMBERLIST_T                   COLLECTION
ERRATUM_T                      OBJECT
ERRATA_TAB_T                   COLLECTION
ADDRESS_T                      OBJECT

SQL> create table o
  2  as
```

```
  3  select course, begindate, trainer
  4  from   offerings;

Table created.

SQL> alter table o add (address address_t);

Table altered.

SQL> update o
  2  set    o.address =
  3         address_t('','','',
  4              (select initcap(x.location)
  5               from   offerings    x
  6               where  x.course    = o.course
  7               and    x.begindate = o.begindate)
  8         )
  9  ;

13 rows updated.

SQL>
```

Note that we now have four user-defined types, as shown by the query against the USER_TYPES data dictionary view. Then we create a copy O of the OFFERINGS table (again, to keep the original table unimpaired) and add an ADDRESS column to the O table. As a last step, Listing 12-13 updates the O table with some address values. The last command uses the ADDRESS_T function to generate address values, leaving the first three address fields empty and selecting the city name from the original OFFERINGS table with a subquery.

Showing More Information with DESCRIBE

If you use user-defined datatypes, you can change the behavior of the SQL*Plus DESCRIBE command to show more information, by setting its DEPTH attribute to a value higher than 1 or to ALL. See Listing 12-14 for an example.

Listing 12-14. *Setting the DEPTH Attribute of the DESCRIBE Command*

```
SQL> describe o
Name                Null?    Type
------------------- -------- ------------
COURSE              NOT NULL VARCHAR2(4)
BEGINDATE           NOT NULL DATE
TRAINER                      NUMBER(4)
ADDRESS                      ADDRESS_T

SQL> set describe depth 2
SQL> describe o
```

```
Name                  Null?     Type
-----------------     --------  ----------------
COURSE                NOT NULL  VARCHAR2(4)
BEGINDATE             NOT NULL  DATE
TRAINER                         NUMBER(4)
ADDRESS                         ADDRESS_T
   STREET                       VARCHAR2(20)
   NR                           VARCHAR2(5)
   PCODE                        VARCHAR2(6)
   CITY                         VARCHAR2(20)

SQL>
```

The DESCRIBE command now also shows the subcomponents of your user-defined types. If your object-relational tables have additional method functions, they are shown as well.

12.5 Multiset Operators

This section discusses the ANSI/ISO standard multiset operators of the SQL language. We will first look at a complete list of all SQL multiset operators with a brief description. You can use these operators *only* on nested tables. Therefore, to allow for some multiset operator examples in this section, we will enter some more nested table entries in the ERRATA nested table. You will also see how you can convert arrays into nested tables "on the fly," using the CAST and COLLECT functions.

Which SQL Multiset Operators Are Available?

If you are using nested tables in your table design, you can apply various SQL *multiset operators* against those tables. Multiset operators allow you to compare nested tables, check certain nested table properties, or derive new nested tables from existing ones.

Note The SQL language refers to *multisets* to indicate a rather important difference between these sets and "regular" sets. In mathematics, duplicate elements in sets are meaningless. In SQL, multisets may have meaningful duplicates; that is, you cannot ignore duplicates in multisets.

Table 12-1 shows an overview of the Oracle multiset operators. Note that these multiset operators are also part of the ANSI/ISO SQL standard. For completeness, Table 12-1 not only shows the SQL multiset operators, but also some other operations you can apply to nested tables.

Table 12-1. *SQL Multiset Operators and Functions*

Multiset Operator or Function	Description
nt1 MULTISET EXCEPT [DISTINCT] *nt2*	The difference of *nt1* and *nt2* (equivalent with the MINUS set operator)
nt1 MULTISET INTERSECT [DISTINCT] *nt2*	The intersection of *nt1* and *nt2*
nt1 MULTISET UNION [DISTINCT] *nt2*	The union of *nt1* and *nt2*
CARDINALITY(*nt*)	The number of rows in *nt*
nt IS [NOT] EMPTY	Boolean function to check whether *nt* is empty
nt IS [NOT] A SET	Boolean function to check whether *nt* contains duplicates
SET(*nt*)	Remove duplicates from *nt*
nt1 = *nt2*	Check whether *nt1* and *nt2* are equal
nt1 IN (*nt2*, *nt3*, ...)	Check whether *nt1* occurs in a list of nested tables
nt1 [NOT] SUBMULTISET OF *nt2*	Is *nt1* a subset of *nt2*?
r [NOT] MEMBER OF *nt*	Does row *r* occur in table *nt*?
CAST(COLLECT(*col*))	Produce a nested table based on column *col*
POWERMULTISET(*nt*)	The set of all nonempty subsets of *nt*
POWERMULTISET_BY_CARDINALITY(*nt*,*c*)	The set of all nonempty subsets of *nt* with cardinality *c*

The following sections show a few typical examples of using multiset operators and functions. See the *Oracle SQL Reference* documentation for examples of all these operators and functions.

Preparing for the Examples

In Section 12.3 of this chapter, you learned how you can store errata entries for courses in a nested table. In Listing 12-10, we inserted only a single erratum. In Listing 12-15, we insert some more rows into the ERRATA nested table.

Listing 12-15. *Inserting Some More Errata Rows*

```
SQL> insert into table ( select errata
  2                       from   c
  3                       where  code = 'SQL' )
  4  values ('SQL'
  5         , 3
  6         , 46
  7         ,'Layout illustration' );
1 row created.

SQL> insert into table ( select errata
  2                       from   c
  3                       where  code = 'SQL' )
  4  values ('SQL'
```

```
    5            , 5
    6            , 1
    7            ,'Introduction missing.' );
1 row created.

SQL> insert into table ( select errata
  2                        from    c
  3                        where   code = 'XML')
  4  values ('XML'
  5            , 5
  6            , 1
  7            , 'Introduction missing.' );
1 row created.

SQL> insert into table ( select errata
  2                        from    c
  3                        where   code = 'XML' )
  4  values ('XML'
  5            , 7
  6            , 3
  7            ,'Line 5: "succeeds" should read "fails"' );
1 row created.

SQL>
```

Now we have five errata entries in total: three for the SQL course and two for the XML course. If you execute a "regular" query against the C table and select its ERRATA column without using any modifying functions, the structure of the ERRATA column (with the nested table) becomes clear from the query result, as shown in Listing 12-16.

Listing 12-16. *Querying a Nested Table Without Using Modifying Functions*

```
SQL> col errata format a80 word

SQL> select errata
  2  from    c
  3  where   code = 'SQL';

ERRATA(CODE, CH, PG, TXT)
-----------------------------------------------------------------------
ERRATA_TAB_T(ERRATUM_T('SQL', 7, 45, 'Typo in last line.'),
            ERRATUM_T('SQL', 3, 46, 'Layout illustration'),
            ERRATUM_T('SQL', 5,  1, 'Introduction missing.'))

SQL>
```

■Note The query output in Listing 12-16 is formatted for readability.

The query result in Listing 12-16 consists of only a single row with a single column. In other words, you are looking at a complicated but *single* value. If you interpret that single value "inside out," you see that the ERRATUM_T constructor function (or method) appears three times to build individual erratum entries. These three erratum entries, in turn, are elements in a comma-separated list. The ERRATA_TAB_T constructor function takes that comma-separated errata list as an argument to convert it into a nested table.

Using IS NOT EMPTY and CARDINALITY

Listing 12-17 uses the IS NOT EMPTY operator to select only those courses that have at least one erratum entry, and it uses the CARDINALITY function to show the number of errata for those courses.

Listing 12-17. *IS NOT EMPTY and CARDINALITY Example*

```
SQL> select code, cardinality(errata)
  2  from   c
  3  where  errata is not empty;

CODE    CARDINALITY(ERRATA)
------- -------------------
SQL                       3
XML                       2

SQL>
```

A corresponding query against a "regular" relational errata table would need a COUNT(*), a GROUP BY, and a HAVING clause.

Using POWERMULTISET

Listing 12-18 shows how you can produce the *powermultiset* of the ERRATA column for the SQL course. To increase the readability of the results in Listing 12-18, we issue a SQL*Plus BREAK command, which highlights the fact that the query result contains seven rows. Every row is a subset of the ERRATA nested table for the SQL course.

■Note In mathematics, the *powerset* of a set X is the set consisting of all possible subsets of X.

Listing 12-18. *POWERMULTISET Example*

```
SQL> break on row page

SQL> select *
  2  from   table ( select powermultiset(errata)
  3                 from   c
  4                 where  code = 'SQL' );

COLUMN_VALUE(CODE, CH, PG, TXT)
-----------------------------------------------------------------------
ERRATA_TAB_T(ERRATUM_T('SQL', 7, 45, 'Typo in last line.'))

COLUMN_VALUE(CODE, CH, PG, TXT)
-----------------------------------------------------------------------
ERRATA_TAB_T(ERRATUM_T('SQL', 3, 46, 'Layout illustration'))

COLUMN_VALUE(CODE, CH, PG, TXT)
-----------------------------------------------------------------------
ERRATA_TAB_T(ERRATUM_T('SQL', 7, 45, 'Typo in last line.'),
             ERRATUM_T('SQL', 3, 46, 'Layout illustration'))

COLUMN_VALUE(CODE, CH, PG, TXT)
-----------------------------------------------------------------------
ERRATA_TAB_T(ERRATUM_T('SQL', 5,  1, 'Introduction missing.'))

COLUMN_VALUE(CODE, CH, PG, TXT)
-----------------------------------------------------------------------
ERRATA_TAB_T(ERRATUM_T('SQL', 7, 45, 'Typo in last line.'),
             ERRATUM_T('SQL', 5,  1, 'Introduction missing.'))

COLUMN_VALUE(CODE, CH, PG, TXT)
-----------------------------------------------------------------------
ERRATA_TAB_T(ERRATUM_T('SQL', 3, 46, 'Layout illustration'),
             ERRATUM_T('SQL', 5,  1, 'Introduction missing.'))

COLUMN_VALUE(CODE, CH, PG, TXT)
-----------------------------------------------------------------------
ERRATA_TAB_T(ERRATUM_T('SQL', 7, 45, 'Typo in last line.'),
             ERRATUM_T('SQL', 3, 46, 'Layout illustration'),
             ERRATUM_T('SQL', 5,  1, 'Introduction missing.'))

7 rows selected.

SQL>
```

The result contains seven rows because we have three SQL errata; see also Listing 12-17. Why seven rows for three errata? Well, there are the following possible subsets:

- Three possible subsets with cardinality 1 (rows 1, 2, and 4)

- Three possible subsets with cardinality 2 (rows 3, 5, and 6)

- One possible subset with cardinality 3 (row 7; that is, the nested table itself)

In mathematics, we would also expect the empty set to show up as an element of the powerset. However, the definition of the POWERMULTISET operator (see Table 12-1) explicitly excludes that subset, by stating that only *nonempty* subsets are considered.

Using MULTISET UNION

Listing 12-19 shows how you can use the MULTISET UNION operator to merge two nested tables into a single one. The query result is manually formatted to enhance readability, allowing you to see that the result is a single nested table, containing five errata entries. Without manual formatting, the query result will show up as one unstructured string.

Listing 12-19. *MULTISET UNION Example*

```
SQL> select c1.errata
  2         MULTISET UNION
  3         c2.errata
  4         as result
  5  from   c c1,
  6         c c2
  7  where  c1.code = 'SQL'
  8  and    c2.code = 'XML';

RESULT(CODE, CH, PG, TXT)
--------------------------------------------------------------------------
ERRATA_TAB_T( ERRATUM_T('SQL', 7, 45, 'Typo in last line.')
            , ERRATUM_T('SQL', 3, 46, 'Layout illustration')
            , ERRATUM_T('SQL', 5, 1, 'Introduction missing.')
            , ERRATUM_T('XML', 5, 1, 'Introduction missing.')
            , ERRATUM_T('XML', 7, 3, 'Line 5: "succeeds" should read "fails"')
            )

SQL>
```

Converting Arrays into Nested Tables

For the last example, we revisit the E table with the phone number array (see Listings 12-1 through 12-6). Listing 12-20 shows how you can use the COLLECT and CAST operators to convert an array into a nested table. To be able to capture the result, we first create a new NUMBER_TAB_T type using the existing NUMBERLIST_T type.

Listing 12-20. *CAST and COLLECT Example to Convert an Array into a Nested Table*

```
SQL> create type number_tab_t
  2  as table of numberlist_t;
  3  /

Type created.

SQL> select cast(collect(numlist) as number_tab_t) as result
  2  from   e
  3  where  empno in (7839, 7782);

RESULT
------------------------------------------------------------------------
NUMBER_TAB_T(NUMBERLIST_T('4231', '06-12345678'),
            NUMBERLIST_T('1234', '06-78765432', '029-8765432'))

SQL>
```

This final chapter gave you a high-level introduction to the object-relational features of the Oracle DBMS, focusing on the way you can use those features in SQL. You learned how you can create object types, and how you can use those types as user-defined datatypes. You also learned about the Oracle collection types: variable arrays and nested tables. If your tables contain nested tables, you can use SQL multiset operators on those tables.

If you want to learn more about the object-relational features of Oracle, refer to the Oracle documentation. *Application Developer's Guide: Object-Relational Features* is an excellent starting point for further study in this area.

12.6 Exercises

You can do the following exercises to practice using the object-relational techniques covered in this chapter. The answers are in Appendix D.

1. The SALGRADES table has two columns to indicate salary ranges: LOWERLIMIT and UPPERLIMIT. Define your own SALRANGE_T type, based on a varray of two NUMBER(6,2) values, and use it to create an alternative SALGRADES2 table.

2. Fill the new SALGRADES2 table with a single INSERT statement, using the existing SALGRADES table.

3. Create a table TESTNEST with two columns: column X and column MX. Column X is NUMBER(1,0) with values 2, 3, 4, ..., 9. Column MX is a nested table, based on a MX_TAB_T type, containing all multiples of X less than or equal to 20.

4. Use multiset operators to solve the following problems, using the TESTNEST table you created and populated in the previous exercise:

   a. Which rows have a nested table containing value 12?

   b. Which nested tables are *not* a subset of any other subset?

   c. Which nested tables have more than 42 different nonempty subsets?

■ ■ ■

Quick Reference to SQL and SQL*Plus

This appendix offers quick references for SQL*Plus and the SQL language. It is far from a complete reference, but it should still prove useful. The Oracle documentation contains (besides the comprehensive and complete references) an *SQL Quick Reference* and a *SQL*Plus Quick Reference*, but this appendix is much more concise than those two Oracle quick references.

You may abbreviate most SQL*Plus commands and their components, as long as you don't introduce ambiguity. This appendix does not show all SQL*Plus command abbreviation possibilities explicitly, in order to enhance its readability. For example, where this appendix lists the COMPUTE command, it should show it as COMP[UTE], because you can abbreviate the SQL*Plus COMPUTE command to COMP. Abbreviation is available only for SQL*Plus commands; you must always enter SQL commands completely. Refer to *SQL*Plus User's Guide and Reference* for all of the abbreviations for SQL*Plus commands and their components.

Tip When writing SQL*Plus *scripts*, use the full SQL*Plus commands and the full command component names instead of their abbreviations. This will enhance the readability of your scripts. When you are using SQL*Plus *interactively*, you may want to use the abbreviations.

There are some differences between SQL*Plus and *i*SQL*Plus; however, this appendix does not list those differences. Refer to *SQL*Plus User's Guide and Reference* for more details. The Oracle documentation also explicitly shows all abbreviations for SQL*Plus commands and their components.

After a section about the syntax conventions used in this appendix, the commands are organized as follows:

- Starting and stopping; entering and executing commands

- Working with the SQL*Plus editor, manipulating SQL*Plus scripts, and SQL*Plus interactivity commands

- Variables and parameters

- Formatting query results

- SQL: data manipulation (DML), transactions, and queries

- SQL: data definition (DDL)

- SQL: other commands

- SQL: operators, functions, and regular expressions

- Rules for naming Oracle database objects; SQL reserved words

Note that this appendix also shows constructs, operators, and commands that are *not* covered in the chapters of this book.

Syntax Conventions Used in This Appendix

Table A-1 shows the general syntax conventions used in this appendix. Table A-2 identifies the characters and formatting that have special meaning in this appendix.

Table A-1. *General Syntax Conventions*

Element	Meaning
CREATE	Command name or keyword, to be entered exactly as spelled (not necessarily in uppercase)
str	Alphanumeric literal between quotes (string)
cond	Boolean expression (condition)
d, d1, d2	Expressions of datatype DATE
expr, e1, e2	Arbitrary expressions
m, n	Numeric expressions
query	Query embedded within a command (subquery)
txt	Alphanumeric expression (with or without quotes)

Table A-2. *Characters and Formatting with Special Meaning*

Element	Example	Meaning
[ ]	[NOWAIT]	Brackets enclose one or more optional items. Options are separated by vertical bars.
Underlining	[ASC|DESC]	Underscored value is the default used if you don't make a choice yourself.
{ }	{expr1|expr2}	Braces enclose two or more items, separated by vertical bars. Choose *precisely one* of them.
...	expr[,...]	Horizontal ellipsis indicates that you may repeat the preceding item as many times as you like, or that irrelevant parts of the code are omitted.

You should *not* enter the characters of Table A-2 with a special meaning (square brackets, braces, vertical lines, and ellipsis) themselves. Regular parentheses (like the ones surrounding this text), commas, periods, single and double quotation marks (' and "), at signs (@), ampersands (&), and any other "exotic" characters have no special meaning in the syntax descriptions in this appendix; therefore, you should enter them verbatim.

Starting and Stopping

```
SQLPLUS {-HELP|-VERSION}
SQLPLUS [-COMPATIBILITY x.y.z] [/NOLOG|name[/passwd]] [@script]
[-MARKUP "options"] [-RESTRICT {1|2|3}] [-SILENT]

script ::= {file[.ext]|url} [arg1 arg2 ...]}
```

Start a SQL*Plus session or display help/version information.

CONNECT name[/passwd][@database-spec]

Create a new SQL*Plus session from the SQL*Plus prompt with the given name/password.

DISCONNECT

Commit transaction and close database session, but do *not* exit SQL*Plus.

{EXIT|QUIT} [SUCCESS|FAILURE|WARNING|n|var] [COMMIT|ROLLBACK]

Close database session and leave SQL*Plus; by default, with a COMMIT and a SUCCESS exit code for the calling environment.

PASSWORD [user]

Change your password (screen echo suppressed) or change the password for a specific user.

SHUTDOWN [ABORT|IMMEDIATE|NORMAL|TRANSACTIONAL [LOCAL]]

Shut down the Oracle instance.

STARTUP [FORCE] [RESTRICT] [QUIET] [OPEN [READ ONLY]] ...

Start up the Oracle instance. There are several additional options for this command.

Entering and Executing Commands

/

Entering a forward slash executes the SQL command in the SQL buffer, without listing the command.

DESCRIBE [schema.]obj-name

Display the definition/structure of the specified object. Use the SET DESCRIBE command to influence the DESCRIBE command.

EXECUTE plsql-statement

Execute a single PL/SQL statement.

HOST [os-command]

Execute a single operating system command and return to the SQL*Plus prompt. Without an argument, the HOST command starts a subsession at the operating system level.

RUN

Display and execute the SQL command in the SQL buffer.

TIMING [START txt|SHOW|STOP]

Record timing data, list current timer's name and timing data, or list the number of active timers.

Working With the SQL*Plus Editor

These commands are not available in *i*SQL*Plus. Note that this section explicitly shows the SQL*Plus command abbreviations (as opposed to the other sections of this appendix) because these commands are used often.

A[PPEND] txt

Add txt at the end of the current line in the buffer. Use *two* spaces to enter a space before txt.

C[HANGE] /old[/[new[/]]]

Change old on the current line into new. Any nonalphanumeric character is allowed as the separator instead of the slash (/). The third separator is optional; you need it only when new ends with one or more spaces.

DEL [n [m]]

Delete one or more lines from the buffer. The default is to delete only the current line. Instead of line numbers (n, m), you can also use the following expressions: LAST (last line) or * (current line).

I[NPUT] [txt]

Add lines to the SQL buffer under the current line.

L[IST] [n [m]]

Display one or more buffer lines. Without arguments, LIST displays all lines in the buffer. Instead of line numbers, you can use the same special expressions as with the DEL command: * and LAST.

Manipulating SQL*Plus Scripts

Note that most commands listed in this section are not available in *i*SQL*Plus.

EDIT `[file[.ext]]`

Start an external editor and open `file.ext`. Without an argument, EDIT edits the SQL buffer.

GET `file[.ext] [LIST|NOLIST]`

Load the contents of a file into the SQL buffer.

REMARK `[txt]`

Enter comments. Oracle ignores `txt` until the end of the current line.

SAVE `file[.ext] [CREATE|REPLACE|APPEND]`

Save the content of the SQL buffer in `file.ext`.

STORE SET `file[.ext] [CREATE|REPLACE|APPEND]`

Save the current SQL*Plus settings in `file.ext`.

`{`**START**`|@|@@} {url|script[.ext]} [arg1 arg2 ...]`

Execute `script` (default file extension `SQL`). Oracle substitutes arguments for variables &1, &2, and so on.

WHENEVER OSERROR
`{EXIT [SUCCESS|FAILURE|n] [COMMIT|ROLLBACK]`
`|CONTINUE [COMMIT|ROLLBACK|NONE]}`

Indicate what SQL*Plus should do in case of operating system error conditions.

WHENEVER SQLERROR
`{EXIT [SUCCESS|FAILURE|WARNING|n] [COMMIT|ROLLBACK]`
`|CONTINUE [COMMIT|ROLLBACK|NONE]}`

Indicate what SQL*Plus should do when SQL commands create error situations.

SQL*Plus Interactivity Commands

ACCEPT `var [NUMBER|CHAR|DATE|BINARY_FLOAT|BINARY_DOUBLE]`
`[FORMAT fmt] [DEFAULT dflt] [PROMPT txt|NOPROMPT] [HIDE]`

Prompt with `txt` and assign entered value to variable `var`.

DEFINE `[x[=txt]]`

Assign value txt to variable x; show current value for x, or show all defined variables.

PAUSE [txt]

Display txt (or an empty line) and wait for an Enter keypress.

PROMPT [txt]

Write txt (or an empty line) to the screen.

UNDEFINE x

Undefine variable x.

Variables and Parameters

&n

Refer to a command-line parameter in a SQL*Plus script: &1 for the first argument, &2 for the second, and so on. Actually, the ampersand (&) is the default setting for the DEFINE character. See the SQL*Plus SET command.

&var, &&var

Refer to the value of variable var. If var is undefined, SQL*Plus prompts for a value; with & this happens each time, and with && only once (&& is an implicit DEFINE).

.

A period is the separator between variable names and following text (the CONCAT character).

PRINT [var]

Display the value of bind variable var, or all current bind variable values.

SET sys-var value

Assign values to SQL*Plus system variables. The following are common SQL*Plus system variables:

APPINFO {ON|OFF|txt]   PAGESIZE {14|n}

ARRAYSIZE {15|n}   PAUSE {ON|OFF|txt}

AUTOCOMMIT {ON|OFF|IMMEDIATE|n}   RECSEP {WRAPPED|EACH|OFF}

AUTOTRACE {ON|OFF|TRACEONLY} [EXPLAIN] RECSEPCHAR {_|c}
[STATISTICS]

CMDSEP {;|c|ON|OFF}   SERVEROUTPUT {ON|OFF} [SIZE n]
                                        [FORMAT {WRAPPED|WORD_WRAPPED|TRUNC}]

COLSEP { |txt}   SHOWMODE {ON|OFF}

CONCAT {.|c|ON|OFF}

DEFINE {&|c|ON|OFF}

DESCRIBE [DEPTH{1|n|ALL}]
[LINENUM {ON|OFF}] [INDENT {ON|OFF}]

ECHO {ON|OFF}

EDITFILE name[.ext]

ESCAPE {\|c|ON|OFF}

FEEDBACK {6|n|ON|OFF}

HEADING {ON|OFF}

HEADSEP {||c|ON|OFF}

INSTANCE [path|LOCAL]

LINESIZE {80|n}

LONG {80|n}

MARKUP HTML [ON|OFF] [HEAD txt]
[BODY txt] [TABLE txt] [ENTMAP {ON|OFF}]
[SPOOL {ON|OFF}] [PREFORMAT {ON|OFF}]

NEWPAGE {1|n|NONE}

NULL txt

NUMFORMAT fmt

NUMWIDTH {10|n}

SQLBLANKLINES {ON|OFF}

SQLCASE {MIXED|LOWER|UPPER}

SQLCONTINUE {>|txt}

SQLNUMBER {ON|OFF}

SQLPREFIX {#|c}

SQLPROMPT {SQL>|txt}

SQLTERMINATOR {;|c|ON|OFF}

SUFFIX {SQL|txt}

TAB {ON|OFF}

TERMOUT {ON|OFF}

TIME {ON|OFF}

TIMING {ON|OFF}

TRIMOUT {ON|OFF}

TRIMSPOOL {ON|OFF}

UNDERLINE {-|c|ON|OFF}

VERIFY {ON|OFF}

WRAP {ON|OFF}

SHOW [sys-var|USER|TTITLE|BTITLE|ERRORS|SPOOL|ALL]

Display the specified value/setting, or display all settings (ALL).

VARIABLE [var {NUMBER|CHAR[(n)]|VARCHAR2(n)| ...}

Declare bind variable var, or display all declared bind variables. You can specify many more Oracle datatypes.

Formatting Query Results

BREAK [ON element [action [action]]] ...

element ::= {col-name|expr|ROW|REPORT}
action ::= [SKIP n|PAGE] [NODUPLICATES|DUPLICATES]

Specify where and how you want to change query result formatting; for example, skip lines when column values change. BREAK without arguments shows the current break definition. The BREAK command always overwrites the current break definition.

BTITLE [print-spec [txt|var] ...] | [OFF|ON]

Define a footer (bottom title) for each page, or show the current BTITLE setting. See TTITLE for more details.

CLEAR {BREAKS|BUFFER|COLUMNS|COMPUTES|SCREEN|SQL|TIMING}

Reset the corresponding option.

COLUMN [{col-name|expr} [option ...]]

Display or change column display settings. COLUMN without arguments shows all current column settings. col-name (or expr) shows settings for that column. option ... changes column settings. The following are common COLUMN command options:

ENTMAP {ON|OFF}	LIKE {expr|alias}	NULL str
FOLD_AFTER	NEWLINE	OLD_VALUE var
ALIAS alias	HEADING txt	{ON|OFF}
CLEAR	JUSTIFY {L|C|R}	{WRAP|WORD_WRAP|TRUNC}
FOLD_BEFORE	NEW_VALUE var	
FORMAT fmt (see Table A-3)	{NOPRINT|PRINT}	

Table A-3. *Common FORMAT Formatting Elements*

Element	Example	Description
An	A10	Display alphanumeric column with width n
9	9999	Number width without leading zeros
0	0999	Number width with leading zeros
	9990	Replace spaces with zeros
$	$9999	Prefix numbers with dollar signs
B	B9999	Display zero with a space
MI	9999MI	Minus sign following negative numbers
PR	9999PR	Negative numbers between <brackets>
S	S9999	+ for positive, - for negative numbers
D	99D99	Position for decimal character
G	9G999	Position for number separator
C	C999	ISO currency symbol
L	L999	Local currency symbol (NLS)
,	9,999	Position for decimal comma
.	99.99	Position for decimal period

Element	Example	Description
V	999V99	Multiply number with 10^n; exponent n is the number of nines after the V
EEEE	9.999EEEE	Scientific notation
RN,rn	RN	Roman numbers (uppercase or lowercase)
DATE	DATE	Date in *MM/DD/YY* format

```
COMPUTE [function [LABEL txt] ... OF col-spec [...] ON location [...] ]

col-spec ::= {expr|col-name|c-alias}
location ::= {break-spec|REPORT|ROW}
```

Add aggregated computations, or display current COMPUTE settings. All functions (except NUMBER) ignore null values. Table A-4 shows COMPUTE functions.

Table A-4. *COMPUTE Functions*

Function	Computes	Supported Datatypes
AVG	Average value	Numeric
COUNT	Number of values	All types
MAXIMUM	Maximum value	Numeric, alphanumeric
MINIMUM	Minimum value	Numeric, alphanumeric
NUMBER	Number of rows	All types
STD	Standard deviation	Numeric
SUM	Sum of all values	Numeric
VARIANCE	Statistical variance	Numeric

```
REPFOOTER [PAGE] [print-spec [txt|var]...]|[OFF|ON]
REPHEADER [PAGE] [print-spec [txt|var]...]|[OFF|ON]

print-spec ::= {COL n|SKIP [n]|TAB n|FORMAT txt|BOLD|LEFT|CENTER|RIGHT}
```

Add a footer or a header to your report, or list the current definitions. PAGE begins a new page after printing the specified header or before printing the specified footer.

```
SPOOL [file[.ext][CREATE|REPLACE|APPEND]|OFF|OUT]
```

Save screen output to a file. SPOOL without arguments shows the current status. OFF means stop spooling. OUT means stop spooling and print the file to default printer.

```
TTITLE [spec [txt|var]...] | [OFF|ON]

spec ::= {COL n|BOLD|TAB n|SKIP [n]|LEFT|RIGHT|CENTER|FORMAT txt}
```

Specify a page header (top title) or show current setting.

SQL: Data Manipulation (DML), Transactions, and Queries

COMMIT [WORK]

Confirm pending changes and close current transaction.

DELETE FROM {tab-name|(tab-expr)} [WHERE cond]

Delete rows for which cond evaluates to TRUE. Delete *all* rows if there is no WHERE clause.

INSERT INTO {tab-name|(tab-expr)}[(col-name, ...)] {VALUES(expr, ...)|query}

Insert new rows, using literal expressions or a subquery.

```
MERGE INTO destination USING delta-source ON (cond)
WHEN MATCHED THEN UPDATE SET col=...[,...]
    [WHERE ...] [DELETE WHERE ...]
WHEN NOT MATCHED THEN INSERT [(col-name-list)] VALUES (...)
    [WHERE ...]
```

Perform a mixture of inserts, updates, and deletes on a destination table based on a delta-source. This can be a table, view, or the result of a subquery.

ROLLBACK [TO SAVEPOINT sp-name]

Cancel all pending changes made since savepoint sp-name, or cancel all pending changes and close current transaction.

SAVEPOINT sp-name

Mark savepoints in a transaction. You can use savepoints in ROLLBACK commands.

```
[WITH name AS subquery [, name AS subquery] ...]
SELECT [DISTINCT] sel-expr[, ...]
FROM tab-expr [AS OF {SCN|TIMESTAMP}...|VERSIONS BETWEEN ... AND ...][, ...]
[WHERE cond]
[[START WITH cond] CONNECT BY [NOCYCLE] cond
[GROUP BY [CUBE|ROLLUP|GROUPING SETS] expr[, ...]]
[HAVING cond]
[{UNION [ALL]|INTERSECT|MINUS} query]
[ORDER [SIBLINGS] BY sort-expr[, ...]]

sel-expr  ::= {*|t-alias.*|expr|scalar-subquery [[AS] c-alias]}
tab-expr  ::= {[schema.]table|(subquery)|join-expr} [t-alias]
join-expr ::= [t1 JOIN t2 {USING (col-list)|ON (cond)}
              |t1 {NATURAL|CROSS} JOIN t2
              |t1 [LEFT|FULL|RIGHT] OUTER JOIN t2 {USING...|ON...}
              ]
sort-expr ::= {expr|c-alias} [ASC|DESC] [NULLS {FIRST|LAST}]
```

Query one or more tables or views; returns rows and columns. Can be used as subquery within other SQL commands, where appropriate.

```
UPDATE {tab-name|(tab-expr)} [t-alias]
SET    {col-name = expr[, ...] | (col-name[, ...]) = (subquery)}
       [WHERE cond]
```

Change column values in rows for which cond evaluates to TRUE. Changes all rows if you have no WHERE clause.

SQL: Data Definition (DDL)

```
ALTER SEQUENCE seq-name [INCREMENT BY n]
[MAXVALUE n|NOMAXVALUE] [MINVALUE n|NOMINVALUE]
[ORDER|NOORDER] [CYCLE|NOCYCLE]
```

Change the definition of an existing sequence.

```
ALTER TABLE [schema.]tab-name
[RENAME TO new-name]
[RENAME COLUMN old-name TO new-name]
[ADD ({col-def|ool-constr}[, ...])]
[MODIFY (col-def[, ...])]
[DROP COLUMN col-name [CASCADE CONSTRAINTS]]
[{DROP|DISABLE|ENABLE} constr] ...
[SHRINK SPACE [CASCADE]]
```

Change the structure of an existing table. See CREATE TABLE for more details.

```
COMMENT ON {TABLE tab-name|COLUMN col-name} IS 'txt'
```

Add clarifying text about tables, views, and columns to the data dictionary.

```
CREATE [UNIQUE|BITMAP] INDEX idx-name
ON tab-name(col-expr {ASC|DESC}[, ...]) [NOSORT]
```

Create an index on the specified column(s) of a table. There are several different index types; this syntax is far from complete.

```
CREATE [PUBLIC] SYNONYM syn-name FOR [schema.]obj-name[@db-link]
```

Create a synonym for a table or a view. Public synonyms are available for all database users.

```
CREATE SEQUENCE seq-name [START WITH n] [INCREMENT BY n]
[MAXVALUE n|NOMAXVALUE] [MINVALUE n|NOMINVALUE]
[ORDER|NOORDER] [CYCLE|NOCYCLE]
```

Create a sequence to generate sequence numbers.

```
CREATE TABLE tab-name ({col-def|ool-constr}[,...])[AS query]

col-def ::=   col-name datatype [DEFAULT expr] [inl-constr]
```

Create a table; define columns and constraints. inl-constr stands for inline constraints, ool-constr stands for out-of-line constraints, and DEFAULT specifies the default value for a column. See Table A-5 for Oracle datatypes.

Table A-5. *Oracle Datatypes*

Datatype	Description
CHAR[(n)]	Fixed-length string (max n=2000; default n = 1)
VARCHAR[2](n[BYTE|CHAR])	Variable-length string (max n = 4000), expressed in bytes or in characters
CLOB	Character large object; max (4GB - 1) * database block size
BLOB	Binary large object; max (4GB - 1) * database block size
BFILE	Locator to external binary file; max 4GB
DATE	Date between 01-JAN-4712 BC and 31-DEC-9999 AD
TIMESTAMP(sp) [WITH [LOCAL] TIMEZONE]	Timestamp with sp fractional digits for the seconds
INTERVAL YEAR(jp) TO MONTH	Time interval; jp digits for the years
INTERVAL DAY(dp) TO SECOND(sp)	Time interval; dp digits for the days and sp fractional digits for the seconds
LONG	Variable-length string (max 2GB) (deprecated datatype; don't use it)
RAW(n)	Binary data up to n bytes (max n = 2000)
LONG RAW	Binary LONG data (deprecated datatype)
NUMBER(p[,s])	Number with max p digits in total, max s of them to the right of the decimal period
	(max p = 38; -84 <= s <= 127; default s = 0)
NUMBER(*,s)	Same as NUMBER(38,s)
BINARY_FLOAT	32-bit floating-point number
BINARY_DOUBLE	64-bit floating-point number

```
CREATE [OR REPLACE] [FORCE] VIEW v-name [(c-alias[, ...])]
AS query [WITH CHECK OPTION [CONSTRAINT cons-name]|WITH READ ONLY]
```

Create or replace a view. FORCE creates the view regardless of whether the referenced database objects exist or you have enough privileges.

```
DROP INDEX idx-name
```

```
DROP SEQUENCE seq-name
```

```
DROP [PUBLIC] SYNONYM syn-name
```

```
DROP TABLE tab-name [PURGE] [CASCADE CONSTRAINTS]
```

```
DROP VIEW v-name
```

```
GRANT {obj-priv[, ...]|ALL [PRIVILEGES]} ON obj-name
TO {user[, ...]|role[, ...]|PUBLIC}
[WITH GRANT OPTION]
```

Grant object privileges to database users or roles.

```
PURGE {{TABLE|INDEX} obj-name|{[DBA_]RECYCLEBIN}|TABLESPACE ts [USER user]}
```

Purge objects from the recycle bin.

```
RENAME old TO new
```

Rename tables, views, or synonyms.

```
REVOKE {obj-priv[, ...]|ALL [PRIVILEGES]}
ON obj-name
FROM {user[, ...]|role[, ...]|PUBLIC}
```

Revoke object privileges from database users or roles.

```
TRUNCATE TABLE tab-name [{DROP|REUSE} STORAGE]
```

Efficiently empty a table, and optionally keep or reclaim table storage.

SQL: Other Commands

```
ALTER SESSION SET parameter=value
```

Change session-level parameters, such as NLS (National Language Support) settings.

```
ALTER SYSTEM SET parameter=value
```

Change parameters, such as NLS settings, for all sessions.

```
SET CONSTRAINTS {ALL|constr-name[, …]} {IMMEDIATE|DEFERRED}
```

Indicate when deferrable constraints should be checked.

```
SET TRANSACTION {READ ONLY|READ WRITE|
ISOLATION LEVEL {SERIALIZABLE|READ COMMITTED}}
```

Specify the desired level of read consistency and transaction isolation.

```
/* free text */
-- free text
```

Comment; you can use this anywhere in your SQL commands. -- works until the end of the line.

SQL: Operators

Tables A-6 through A-11 list the Oracle SQL operators in decreasing precedence. Use parentheses, ( ), in expressions to influence operator precedence.

Table A-6. *Arithmetic Operators*

Operator	Description
+ -	Prefix positive/negative expression (unary operators)
* /	Multiplication and division
+ -	Addition and subtraction

Table A-7. *Alphanumeric Operators*

Operator	Description
||	Concatenate strings

Table A-8. *Comparison Operators*

Operator	Description
=	Equal to
!= ^= <>	Not equal to
> >=	Greater than; greater than or equal to]
< <=	Less than; less than or equal to
IN	Equals a value from a set (or subquery)
NOT IN	Equals no value from a set (or subquery)
ANY	For at least one value from ...
ALL	For all values from ...
BETWEEN x AND y	Between x and y, including boundaries
EXISTS	True if the subquery returns at least one row
LIKE [ESCAPE 'x']	Check alphanumeric values using wildcards; % represents 0, 1, or more arbitrary characters; _ represents precisely one arbitrary character; x disables wildcard character meanings
IS NULL	Contains a null value

Table A-9. *Logical Operators (in Precedence Order)*

Operator	Description
NOT	Negation of a logical expression
AND	Returns TRUE if both operands return TRUE
OR	Returns TRUE if at least one operand returns TRUE

Table A-10. *Set Operators (Combining Two Query Expressions)*

Operator	Description
UNION [ALL]	Merges rows from both query results; ALL keeps duplicate rows
INTERSECT	Rows that occur in both query results
MINUS	Rows from the first query result that don't occur in the second query result

Table A-11. *Other SQL Operators*

Operator	Description
(+)	Indicator for outer join columns (deprecated syntax)
*	Select all columns of a table or view
DISTINCT	Eliminate duplicate rows from a query result
CASE expr WHEN v1 THEN r1 WHEN v2 THEN r2 ... [ELSE rn] END	Simple CASE expression; if expr = v1 then return r1, ...; otherwise rn (or a null value)
CASE WHEN c1 THEN r1 WHEN c2 THEN r2 ... [ELSE rn] END	Searched CASE expression; if c1 is TRUE then return r1, ...; otherwise rn (or a null value)

SQL: Functions

Tables A-12 through A-19 list the Oracle SQL functions.

Table A-12. *Numeric Functions*

Numeric Function	Description
ABS(n)	Absolute value of n
BITAND(n,m)	Logical AND over binary representations of n and m
CEIL(n)	Smallest integer greater than or equal to n
COS(n), COSH(n), ACOS(n)	Cosine, hyperbolic cosine, arccosine
EXP(n)	e (2.71828183...) raised to the nth power
FLOOR(n)	Largest integer less than or equal to n
LN(n), LOG(m,n)	Natural logarithm of n, or logarithm base m
MOD(m,n)	Remainder of m divided by n (returns m if n is 0; result rounded with FLOOR)
POWER(m,n)	m raised to the nth power
REMAINDER(m,n)	Remainder of m divided by n (n = 0 returns an error; result rounded with ROUND)
ROUND(n[,m])	n rounded to m positions (default m = 0)
SIGN(n)	If n < 0, n = 0, n > 0: respectively, -1, 0, and 1

Continued

Table A-12. *Continued*

Numeric Function	Description
SIN(n), SINH(n), ASIN(n)	Sine, hyperbolic sine, arcsine
SQRT(n)	Square root of n (n < 0 returns a null value)
TAN(n), TANH(n), ATAN(n), ATAN2(n,m)	Tangent, hyperbolic tangent, arctangent
TRUNC(n[,m])	n truncated to m positions (default m = 0)
WIDTH_BUCKET(e,min,max,nb)	Histogram; bucket to which e belongs if you divide the interval from min to max into nb buckets

Table A-13. *Alphanumeric Functions Returning Alphanumeric Results*

Alphanumeric Function	Description
CHR(n)	Character with ASCII value n
CONCAT(c1,c2)	Concatenate c1 and c2
INITCAP(txt)	Each word in txt starts uppercase; remainder lowercase
LOWER(txt)	All characters in txt converted to lowercase
LPAD(c1,n,c2)	c1 left-padded to length n with characters from c2 (default c2 is a space)
LTRIM(txt[,set])	Trim characters from the left of txt until the first character not in set (default set is a space)
REGEXP_REPLACE(c1,p[,...])	Search c1 for regular expression p; return the position
REGEXP_SUBSTR(c1,p[,...])	Search c1 for regular expression p; return substring
REPLACE(txt,s,r)	Replace all occurrences of s in txt with r; without r, remove all occurrences
RPAD(c1,n,c2)	c1 right-padded to length n with characters from c2 (default c2 is a space)
RTRIM(txt[,set])	Trim characters from the right of txt until the first character not in set (default set is a space)
SUBSTR(txt,m,n)	Substring of txt from position m, length n (without n: until the end of txt)
TRANSLATE(txt,from,to)	txt, translated from character set from to to
TRIM([... FROM] txt)	Trim characters from the left and/or right of txt
UPPER(txt)	txt converted to uppercase

Table A-14. *Alphanumeric Functions Returning Numeric Values*

Alphanumeric Function	Description
ASCII(txt)	ASCII value first character of txt
INSTR(c1,c2,[,n[,m]])	Position mth occurrence of c2 in c1; search from position n (defaults: m = 1, n = 1)
LENGTH(txt)	Length of txt (expressed in characters)
REGEXP_INSTR(txt,p,[,...])	Position of regular expression p in txt

Table A-15. *Group Functions*

Group Function	Description
AVG(n)	Average value
CORR(expr1,expr2)	Correlation coefficient
COUNT({*|expr})	Number of rows where expr is not NULL (* counts all rows)
MAX(expr)	Maximum value
MEDIAN(expr)	Middle value
MIN(expr)	Minimum value
SUM(n)	Sum of all values
STATS_MODE(expr)	Most frequent value (mode)
STDDEV(n)	Standard deviation
VARIANCE(n)	Variance
[DISTINCT]	All group functions support this option; count different values only once

Table A-16. *Date Functions*

Date Function	Description
ADD_MONTHS(d,n)	Date d plus n months
CURRENT_DATE	Current date with time zone information
CURRENT_TIMESTAMP[(p)]	Current timestamp (precision p) with time zone information
EXTRACT(c FROM d)	Extract component c from date or interval d
LAST_DAY(d)	The last day of the month containing d
LOCALTIMESTAMP[(p)]	Current timestamp (precision p) without time zone information
MONTHS_BETWEEN(d1,d2)	Difference in months between dates d1 and d2
NEXT_DAY(d,str)	The first weekday named by str, later than date d
NUMTODSINTERVAL(n,unit)	Convert n to INTERVAL DAY TO SECOND
ROUND(d[,fmt])	Date d, rounded on unit fmt (default fmt = 'DD')
SESSIONTIMEZONE	Time zone current session
SYS_EXTRACT_UTC(dwtz)	Convert date and time with time zone dwtz to UTC
SYSDATE	Current system date and time
SYSTIMESTAMP	Current system timestamp with time zone
TRUNC(d[,fmt])	Date d truncated on unit fmt (default fmt = 'DD')

Table A-17. *Conversion Functions*

Conversion Function	Description
ASCIISTR(txt)	Convert non-ASCII characters in txt to \XXXX format
BIN_TO_NUM(e1[,e2,...])	Convert expressions from binary to decimal
CAST(expr AS type)	Convert expr to datatype type
COMPOSE('txt')	Convert txt to Unicode to produce composite characters
CONVERT(txt,dks[,bks])	Convert txt from character set bks to dks
DECOMPOSE(str)	Convert str (in Unicode) to decompose composite characters
TO_BINARY_DOUBLE(e[,fmt])	Convert e to double-precision, floating-point number
TO_BINARY_FLOAT(e[,fmt])	Convert e to floating-point number
TO_CHAR(expr[,fmt])	Convert expr to CHAR using format fmt (there is a default date format, and by default, numbers are displayed wide enough to show all significant digits; see Tables A-20 and A-22)
TO_CLOB(txt)	Convert txt to CLOB (Character Large Object)
TO_DATE(str[,fmt])	Convert str to DATE using format fmt (fmt is optional if str is specified in default date format); see Table A-20
TO_DSINTERVAL(str)	Convert str to INTERVAL DAY TO SECOND
TO_LOB(lc)	Convert lc from LONG [RAW] to a LOB type
TO_NUMBER(txt)	Convert txt to NUMBER
TO_TIMESTAMP(str[,fmt])	Convert str to TIMESTAMP
TO_TIMESTAMP_TZ(str[,fmt])	Convert str to TIMESTAMP WITH TIME ZONE
TO_YMINTERVAL(str)	Convert str to INTERVAL YEAR TO MONTH

Table A-18. *Collection Functions*

Collection Function	Description
CARDINALITY(nt)	Return the number of elements in a nested table nt
COLLECT(col)	Create a nested table out of col values from the rows selected
POWERMULTISET(nt)	Return a nested table containing all nonempty subsets of a nested table nt
POWERMULTISET_BY_CARDINALITY(nt,n)	Return a nested table containing all subsets of a nested table nt with cardinality n
SET(nt)	Convert a nested table into a set by eliminating duplicates

Table A-19. *Other SQL Functions and Pseudo Columns*

Function	Description
COALESCE(a,b,c,...)	Return the first not-null argument
DECODE(x,s1,r1[,s2,r2,]... [dflt])	Return r1 if x = s1, r2 if x = s2, ...; otherwise dflt
DUMP(expr[,fmt[,startpos[,len]]])	Dump datatype code, length in bytes, and internal representation of expr

Function	Description
GREATEST(expr[,...])	Return expr with the largest value
LEAST(expr[,...])	Return expr with the smallest value
LEVEL	Level in the tree (for hierarchical queries only)
LNNVL(cond)	Return TRUE if cond returns FALSE or UNKNOWN; otherwise FALSE
NULLIF(expr1,expr2)	Return NULL if expr1 = expr2; otherwise expr1
NVL(expr1,expr2)	Return expr2 if expr1 is NULL; otherwise expr1
NVL2(expr1,expr2,expr3)	Return expr2 if expr1 is not NULL; otherwise expr3
ORA_HASH(expr[,nb[,s]])	Hash value for expr, using nb buckets and seed value s
SYS_CONNECT_BY_PATH(...)	Path to the root value (for hierarchical queries only)
SYS_CONTEXT('ns','sp')	Value of system parameter sp of the ns (namespace) context (a common namespace is USERENV with 42 pre-defined parameters; see *Oracle SQL Reference* for details)
UID	Number of the current database user
USER	Name of the current database user
VSIZE(expr)	Number of bytes occupied by expr

Date Format Models

You can use any combination of the elements listed in Table A-20 as the fmt argument for the TO_CHAR and TO_DATE functions. Table A-21 lists optional date format modifiers.

Table A-20. *TO_CHAR and TO_DATE Format Elements*

Format Element	Description
[S]CC	Century; S displays BC dates with a minus sign
[S]YYYY	Year; S as in SCC
YYY, YY, Y	Last three, two, or one digits of the year
RR	Last two digits of the year (with interpretation for 20th century)
IYYY, IYY, IY, I	ISO year; last three, two, or one digits of the ISO year
[S]YEAR	Year, spelled out; S as in SCC
BC, AD	BC/AD indicator (B.C. and A.D. also allowed)
Q	Quarter number (1, 2, 3, 4)
MM	Month number (01–12)
MONTH	Month name; padded with spaces to length 9
MON	Month name; three-character abbreviation
RM	Month in Roman numerals
WW, IW	(ISO) week number (01–53)

Continued

Table A-20. *Continued*

Format Element	Description
W	Week number within the month (1–5)
DDD, DD, D	Day number within the year (1–366), month (1–31), and week (1–7)
DAY	Day name, padded with spaces to length 9
DY	Day name abbreviation (three characters)
DS, DL	Date in short (S) or long (L) representation; reacts on NLS_TERRITORY and NLS_LANGUAGE settings
J	Julian date; day number since 01-JAN-4712 BC
TS	Time of the day; reacts NLS_TERRITORY and NLS_LANGUAGE settings
AM, PM	AM/PM indicator (A.M. and P.M. also allowed)
HH[12], HH24	Hour of the day (1–12 or 0–23)
MI	Minutes (0–59)
SS,SSSSS	Seconds (0–59); seconds since midnight (0–86399)
FF[n]	Fractional seconds; n digits behind the decimal point
TZD,TZH,TZM,TZR	Time zone information: daylight saving time, hours, minutes, and time zone
- / . , ; :	Display characters as specified
"text"	Display text as specified

Table A-21. *Optional Date Format Modifiers*

Element	Type	Description
FM	Prefix	Fill mode toggle to suppress padding with spaces
FX	Prefix	The input argument and format model must match exactly
TH	Suffix	Ordinal number (e.g., 4th)
SP	Suffix	Spelled-out number (e.g., four)
SPTH, THSP	Suffix	Spelled-ordinal number (e.g., fourth)

Number Format Models

You can use any combination of the elements listed in Table A-22 as fmt argument for the TO_CHAR function.

Table A-22. *TO_CHAR Number Format Elements*

Element	Examples	Description
,	'9,999'	Display group separator comma in this position
.	'99.99'	Display decimal point in this position
9	'9999'	Control number display length

Element	Examples	Description
0	'0999', '9990'	Display numbers with leading or trailing zeros
$	'$9999'	Display dollar sign before a number
B	'B9999'	Display zero with spaces
C	'C9999'	Display ISO currency symbol before a number
D	'99D99'	Display decimal character in this position (depends on NLS_NUMERIC_CHARACTER setting)
EEEE	'9.99EEEE'	Scientific notation
G	'9G999'	Display group separator in this position (depends on NLS_NUMERIC_CHARACTER setting)
L	'L9999'	Display local currency symbol before a number
MI	'9999MI'	Display minus sign after negative values
PR	'9999PR'	Display negative values between brackets (< and >)
RN, rn	'RN'	Roman numerals (uppercase or lowercase)
S	'S999', '999S'	Display plus/minus sign before or after a number (only allowed at the beginning or end of a number)
TM	'TM'	Shortest notation; switches to scientific notation with 64 characters
U	'U9999'	Display euro (or other dual currency) symbol before a number
V	'999V99'	Multiply with 10^n; n is the number of nines after the V
X	'XXXX'	Hexadecimal representation
DATE	'DATE'	Convert Julian day number to *MM*/*DD*/*YY*

SQL: Regular Expressions

Table A-23 lists common SQL regular expression operators and metasymbols. Table A-24 lists regular expression character classes.

Table A-23. *Common Regular Expression Operators and Metasymbols*

Operator	Description
*	Matches zero or more occurrences
+	Matches one or more occurrences
?	Matches zero or one occurrence
|	Alternation operator for specifying alternative matches
^	Matches the beginning-of-line character
$	Matches the end-of-line character
.	Matches any character in the supported character set except NULL

Continued

Table A-23. *Continued*

Operator	Description
[ ]	Bracket expression for specifying a matching list that should match any one of the expressions represented in the list; a leading circumflex (^) specifies a list that matches any character except for the expressions represented in the list
( )	Grouping expression, treated as a single subexpression
{m}	Matches exactly m times
{m,}	Matches at least m times
{m,n}	Matches at least m times but no more than n times
\n	Back reference (n is a digit between 1 and 9) matching the nth subexpression enclosed between (and) preceding the \n
[..]	Collation element; can be a multicharacter element (e.g., [.ch.] in Spanish)
[::]	Matches any character within a character class; see Table A-24
[==]	Matches all characters having the same equivalence class. For example, [=a=] matches all characters having base letter *a*.

Table A-24. *Regular Expression Character Classes*

Class	Meaning
[:alnum:]	Alphanumeric character
[:alpha:]	Alphabetic character
[:blank:]	Blank space character
[:cntrl:]	Control character (nonprinting)
[:digit:]	Numeric digit
[:graph:]	[:punct:], [:upper:], [:lower:], or [:digit:] character
[:lower:]	Lowercase alphabetic character
[:print:]	Printable character
[:punct:]	Punctuation character
[:space:]	Space character (nonprinting)
[:upper:]	Uppercase alphabetic character
[:xdigit:]	Hexadecimal character

Rules for Naming Oracle Database Objects

Names for database objects (such as tables, views, indexes, synonyms, and columns) must obey the following rules:

- Names cannot exceed a maximum length of 30 characters.

- Names cannot contain quotation marks.

- Names must be unique in their namespace; normally within a schema, sometimes within the entire database.

- Names must start with a letter (*A* through *Z*).

- There is no distinction between uppercase and lowercase characters.

- You can use the characters *A* through *Z*, 0 through 9, $, #, and _ (underscore); however, Oracle discourages the use of the $ and # characters.

- Reserved words (see the next section) are not allowed.

If you put object names between double quotation marks, the fourth and remaining items listed no longer apply. For example, within double quotation marks, uppercase and lowercase characters make a difference, and you can use spaces if you like. Note, however, that this is *not* a recommended practice.

SQL: Reserved Words

The words listed in Table A-25 have special meanings in the SQL language. Therefore, you cannot use them as names for database objects.

Note In addition to the reserved words listed in Table A-25, Oracle uses system-generated names beginning with "SYS_" for implicitly generated schema objects and subobjects. Don't use this prefix in your object names.

Table A-25. *SQL Reserved Words*

ACCESS ADD* ALL* ALTER* AND* ANY* AS* ASC* AUDIT BETWEEN* BY* CHAR* CHECK* CLUSTER COLUMN COMMENT COMPRESS CONNECT* CREATE* CURRENT* DATE* DECIMAL* DEFAULT* DELETE* DESC* DISTINCT* DROP* ELSE* EXCLUSIVE EXISTS* FILE FLOAT* FOR* FROM* GRANT* GROUP* HAVING* IDENTIFIED IF* IMMEDIATE* IN* INCREMENT INDEX INITIAL INSERT* INTEGER* INTERSECT* INTO* IS* LEVEL* LIKE* LOCK LONG MAXEXTENTS MINUS MLSLABEL MODE MODIFY NOAUDIT NOCOMPRESS NOT* NOWAIT NULL* NUMBER OF* OFFLINE ON* ONLINE OPTION* OR* ORDER* PCTFREE PRIOR* PRIVILEGES* PUBLIC* RAW RENAME RESOURCE REVOKE* ROW ROWID ROWLABEL ROWNUM ROWS* SELECT* SESSION* SET* SHARE SIZE* SMALLINT* START SUCCESSFUL SYNONYM SYSDATE TABLE* THEN* TO* TRIGGER UID UNION* UNIQUE* UPDATE* USER* VALIDATE VALUES* VARCHAR* VARCHAR2 VIEW* WHENEVER* WHERE* WITH*

Also ANSI/ISO SQL reserved words.

■ ■ ■

Data Dictionary Overview

This appendix provides a concise overview of the Oracle data dictionary. In order to reduce its size and increase its usefulness, it is far from complete.

The base tables of the Oracle data dictionary are stored in the SYS schema; in other words, user SYS is owner of the data dictionary. When you create a new database (with the CREATE DATABASE command) the Oracle DBMS creates and populates the SYS schema automatically. You should *never* directly manipulate the tables of the SYS schema. These tables are maintained by the Oracle DBMS.

■**Note** Although the Oracle data dictionary consists of public synonyms, based on views, based on underlying (undocumented) tables, we sometimes just refer to *data dictionary tables* for convenience.

This appendix starts with some commonly used data dictionary views, and then lists views organized by the four separate view categories, which you can recognize by their prefix:

- ALL views have information about all *accessible* data. Regular database users have access to these views.

- USER views have information about *your own* data. Regular database users have access to these views.

- DBA views have database-wide information. You need DBA privileges (or some specific system privileges) to access these views.

- V$ views are dynamic performance views. You need DBA privileges (or some specific system privileges) to access these views.

The first three categories are commonly referred to as "static" to distinguish them from the fourth category, the dynamic performance views.

This appendix lists the names of the data dictionary views, without any column descriptions. For column details, you can use the SQL*Plus DESCRIBE command or query the DICT_COLUMNS data dictionary view (see Listing 3-11 in Chapter 3 of this book). The view descriptions themselves are also very concise, and they may refer to concepts or terms not covered anywhere in this book. See *Oracle Reference* for further data dictionary details and explanations.

General Data Dictionary Views

Table B-1 lists some commonly used data dictionary views.

Table B-1. *Commonly Used Data Dictionary Views*

View Name	Description
DICTIONARY (or DICT)	Description of all data dictionary tables
DICT_COLUMNS	Description of all data dictionary table columns
DUAL	Dummy table with a single row and a single column
FLASHBACK_TRANSACTION_QUERY	All flashback transaction queries in the database
NLS_DATABASE_PARAMETERS	NLS (National Language Support) parameter settings for the database
NLS_INSTANCE_PARAMETERS	NLS parameter settings for the instance
NLS_SESSION_PARAMETERS	NLS parameter settings for your current session
PUBLICSYN	All public synonyms in the database
ROLE_ROLE_PRIVS	Roles granted to roles
ROLE_SYS_PRIVS	System privileges granted to roles
ROLE_TAB_PRIVS	Table privileges granted to roles
SESSION_PRIVS	Active session privileges
SESSION_ROLES	Active session roles

ALL Views: Information About Accessible Objects

Table B-2 lists views that have information about all accessible data and can be used by regular database users.

Table B-2. *ALL Data Dictionary Views*

View Name	Description
ALL_CATALOG	All accessible database objects (three columns)
ALL_COL_COMMENTS	Comments for all accessible columns
ALL_COL_PRIVS	Column privileges where you are involved
ALL_COL_PRIVS_MADE	Column privileges where you are the grantor
ALL_COL_PRIVS_RECD	Column privileges where you are the grantee
ALL_CONS_COLUMNS	All accessible constraint columns
ALL_CONSTRAINTS	All accessible constraint definitions
ALL_INDEXES	Descriptions of all accessible indexes

View Name	Description
ALL_IND_COLUMNS	Column descriptions of all accessible indexes
ALL_IND_EXPRESSIONS	Expressions of all accessible function-based indexes
ALL_MVIEWS	Descriptions for all accessible materialized views
ALL_NESTED_TABLE_COLS	All accessible columns of nested tables
ALL_NESTED_TABLES	All accessible nested tables
ALL_OBJECTS	All accessible database objects (13 columns)
ALL_SEQUENCES	All accessible sequences
ALL_SYNONYMS	Synonyms you can use
ALL_TABLES	All accessible tables
ALL_TAB_COLS	Column descriptions for all accessible tables
ALL_TAB_COLUMNS	Column descriptions for all accessible tables, without hidden columns
ALL_TAB_COMMENTS	All comments for accessible tables
ALL_TAB_PRIVS	Table privileges where you are involved
ALL_TAB_PRIVS_MADE	Table privileges where you are object owner or grantor
ALL_TAB_PRIVS_RECD	Table privileges where you are the privilege grantee
ALL_UPDATABLE_COLUMNS	Accessible updatable join view columns
ALL_USERS	Information about all database users (no full details)
ALL_VIEWS	Information about all accessible views

USER Views: Information About Your Own Data

The USER views have information about your own data and are accessible to regular database users. First, Table B-3 shows some useful shorthand names for these views. Table B-4 lists the USER views.

Table B-3. *Some Useful Shorthand Names for USER Views*

View Name	Synonym For
CAT	USER_CATALOG
COLS	USER_TAB_COLUMNS
IND	USER_INDEXES
OBJ	USER_OBJECTS
RECYCLEBIN	USER_RECYCLEBIN
SEQ	USER_SEQUENCES
SYN	USER_SYNONYMS
TABS	USER_TABLES

Table B-4. *USER Data Dictionary Views*

View Name	Description
USER_AUDIT_TRAIL	Audit trail entries where you are involved
USER_CATALOG	Indexes, tables, views, clusters, synonyms, and sequences
USER_COL_COMMENTS	Comments on your columns
USER_COL_PRIVS	Column privileges where you are involved
USER_COL_PRIVS_MADE	Column privileges where you are the object owner or grantor
USER_COL_PRIVS_RECD	Column privileges where you are the grantee
USER_CONS_COLUMNS	Columns involved in constraints
USER_CONSTRAINTS	All your constraints
USER_EXTENTS	All extents (allocation units for database objects)
USER_FREE_SPACE	Available free space for creating objects
USER_INDEXES	Description of all your indexes
USER_IND_COLUMNS	Description of all your index columns
USER_IND_EXPRESSIONS	Description of all your function-based index expressions
USER_MVIEWS	All your materialized views
USER_NESTED_TABLE_COLS	All columns of your nested tables
USER_NESTED_TABLES	All your nested tables
USER_OBJECTS	All your object descriptions
USER_RECYCLEBIN	Your recycle bin
USER_ROLE_PRIVS	Roles granted to you
USER_SEGMENTS	Storage-related information about your objects
USER_SEQUENCES	All your sequences
USER_SYNONYMS	All your synonym definitions
USER_SYS_PRIVS	System privileges granted to you
USER_TABLES	Description of your tables
USER_TAB_COLS	Description of your table columns
USER_TAB_COLUMNS	Description of your table columns, without hidden columns
USER_TAB_COMMENTS	Comments on your tables
USER_TAB_PRIVS	Table privileges where you are involved
USER_TAB_PRIVS_MADE	Table privileges where you are the object owner or grantor
USER_TAB_PRIVS_RECD	Table privileges where you are the grantee
USER_TABLESPACES	Accessible tablespaces
USER_TS_QUOTAS	Quota for accessible tablespaces
USER_UPDATABLE_COLUMNS	Columns of updatable join views
USER_USERS	Information about yourself
USER_VIEWS	Description of all your views

DBA Views: Full Database Information

The views listed in Table B-5 have database-wide information and are accessible only to those with DBA privileges.

Table B-5. *DBA Data Dictionary Views*

View Name	Description
DBA_AUDIT_TRAIL	All entries of the audit trail
DBA_CATALOG	All indexes, tables, views, clusters, synonyms, and sequences
DBA_COL_COMMENTS	All column comments in the database
DBA_COL_PRIVS	All column privileges in the database
DBA_CONSTRAINTS	All constraints in the database
DBA_DATA_FILES	All data files belonging to the database
DBA_DB_LINKS	All database links
DBA_EXTENTS	All extents (allocation units for database objects)
DBA_FREE_SPACE	Summary of all free space in the database
DBA_INDEXES	Description of all indexes
DBA_IND_COLUMNS	Description of all index columns
DBA_IND_EXPRESSIONS	Expressions of all function-based indexes
DBA_LOCKS	All locks (and latches) in the database
DBA_MVIEWS	All materialized views
DBA_NESTED_TABLE_COLS	All columns of nested tables
DBA_NESTED_TABLES	All nested tables
DBA_OBJECTS	All database objects
DBA_RECYCLEBIN	All dropped objects in the recycle bin
DBA_ROLE_PRIVS	All roles, granted to users or other roles
DBA_ROLES	All roles in the database
DBA_SEGMENTS	All segments (e.g., tables and indexes) in the database
DBA_SEQUENCES	All sequences in the database
DBA_SYNONYMS	All synonyms in the database
DBA_SYS_PRIVS	All system privileges granted to users or roles
DBA_TABLES	Description of all tables
DBA_TABLESPACES	All tablespaces in the database
DBA_TAB_COLS	Description of all columns
DBA_TAB_COLUMNS	Description of all columns, without hidden columns
DBA_TAB_COMMENTS	All table comments in the database
DBA_TAB_PRIVS	All table privileges in the database
DBA_TS_QUOTAS	All user quota, per tablespace

Continued

Table B-5. *Continued*

View Name	Description
DBA_UPDATABLE_COLUMNS	All columns of updatable join views
DBA_USERS	Information about all users
DBA_VIEWS	Description of all views
DBA_WAITERS	All sessions waiting for something (locks)

V$ Views: Dynamic Performance Views

Table B-6 lists the dynamic performance views. You need DBA privileges (or some specific system privileges) to access these views.

Table B-6. *V$ Data Dictionary Views*

View Name	Description
V$BGPROCESS	The Oracle background processes
V$CONTROLFILE	The names of the control files
V$DATABASE	Information about the database from the control file
V$DATAFILE	Information about the data files from the control file
V$ENABLEDPRIVS	Enabled privileges
V$FILESTAT	I/O activity per data file
V$FIXED_TABLE	Displays all dynamic performance tables, views, and derived tables
V$FIXED_VIEW_DEFINITION	Displays the definitions of all the fixed views
V$INSTANCE	Status information about the instance
V$LICENSE	Information about license limits
V$LOCK	Information about active locks
V$MYSTAT	Statistics for the current session
V$NLS_PARAMETERS	Current NLS parameter values
V$NLS_VALID_VALUES	All valid values for NLS parameters
V$OPTION	The installed Oracle options
V$PARAMETER	Current initialization parameter values for the session
V$PROCESS	Information about all active processes
V$RESERVED_WORDS	All keywords used by the PL/SQL compiler (a superset of the SQL reserved words)
V$SESS_IO	I/O statistics for all active sessions
V$SESSION	Information about all active sessions
V$SESSION_EVENT	Information about waits for an event by a session
V$SESSION_LONGOPS	Status of operations that run for longer than 6 seconds
V$SESSION_WAIT	Resources or events for which active sessions are waiting

View Name	Description
V$SESSTAT	User session statistics
V$SGA	Information about the shared global area (SGA)
V$SGASTAT	Detailed information about the SGA components
V$SPPARAMETER	Information about the contents of the server parameter file
V$SQL	Detailed information about SQL statements in memory
V$SQLAREA	Aggregated information about SQL statements in memory
V$SQL_PLAN	Execution plan information for SQL statements in memory
V$SQL_PLAN_STATISTICS	Execution statistics of SQL statements in memory
V$SQLTEXT	The text of SQL statements in memory
V$SQLTEXT_WITH_NEWLINES	Same as V$SQLTEXT, with improved legibility
V$SYSSTAT	All system statistics
V$SYSTEM_PARAMETER	Information about the initialization parameters in effect
V$TABLESPACE	Information about all tablespaces
V$TIMER	Internal clock, in hundredths of a second
V$TIMEZONE_NAMES	List of names and abbreviations of time zones
V$TRANSACTION	Information about all active transactions
V$VERSION	Version information about installed Oracle products
V$WAITSTAT	Block contention statistics

APPENDIX C

■ ■ ■

The Seven Case Tables

This appendix offers an overview of the seven case tables used throughout this book, in various formats. Its main purpose is to help you in writing SQL commands and checking your results.

The first section shows an Entity Relationship Modeling (ERM) diagram, indicating the entities of the underlying data model, including their unique identifiers and their relationships. Then you can find descriptions of the seven case tables, with names and datatypes of all their columns and short explanations, when necessary. The next section shows a table diagram, focusing on all primary key and foreign key constraints. This diagram may be especially helpful when you are writing joins.

The biggest component of this appendix (with the highest level of detail) is a complete listing of the seven case tables with all their rows. This overview may be useful to check your query results for correctness.

At the end of this appendix, you will find two alternative representations of the case table data, showing the table rows in a compact format. The first diagram shows an overview of the 14 employees. It clearly shows the department populations and the hierarchical (manager/subordinate) relationships. The second illustration shows a matrix overview of all course offerings, with starting dates, locations, attendees (A), and trainers (T). Again, these representations may be useful to check your query results for correctness.

You can also find information about the case tables within this book, as follows:

Location	Comments
1.9 Case Tables	First introduction
3.4 Creating the Case Tables	Simple CREATE TABLE commands (without constraints)
7.4 Constraints	Full CREATE TABLE commands (with constraints)

ERM Diagram

The ERM diagram, shown in Figure C-1, shows the seven entities (the rounded-corner boxes) with their unique identifiers and their mutual relationships.

The ten crow's feet indicate one-to-many relationships. The diagram shows two types of one-to-many relationships: three relationships are *completely* optional (indicated by all dashed lines) and the remaining ones are mandatory in one direction (indicated by the solid part of the line).

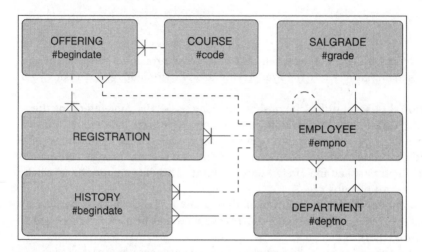

Figure C-1. *ERM diagram of the case entities*

Hash signs (#) in front of an attribute mean that the attribute is part of the unique identifier; relationship cross-lines indicate that the relationship is part of the unique identifier. Note that the diagram shows only attributes that are part of unique identifiers, for enhanced readability.

You can interpret the relationships in this diagram as follows:

- Every employee has *at most one* manager (and employees may have multiple subordinates).

- Every employee belongs to *precisely one* salary grade and is employed by *at most one* department (employees without a department are allowed).

- Each department has *precisely one* manager (and employees may be manager of multiple departments).

- Each course offering refers to *precisely one* existing course, with *at most one* employee as trainer.

- Each registration is for *precisely one* employee and for *precisely one* course offering.

- Each history record refers to *precisely one* employee and *precisely one* department.

Table Structure Descriptions

This section presents descriptions of the table structures. In the listings, * means NOT NULL and P means primary key.

```
EMPLOYEES:      EMPNO       N(4)      P   Unique employee number
                ENAME       VC(8)     *   Last name
                INIT        VC(5)     *   Initials (without punctuation)
                JOB         VC(8)         Job description
                MGR         N(4)          Manager (references EMPLOYEES)
                BDATE       DATE      *   Date of birth
                MSAL        N(6,2)    *   Monthly salary (excluding net bonus)
                COMM        N(6,2)        Commission (per year, for sales reps)
                DEPTNO      N(2)          Department (references DEPARTMENTS)

DEPARTMENTS:    DEPTNO      N(2)      P   Unique department number
                DNAME       VC(10)    *   Name of the department
                LOCATION    VC(8)     *   Location (city)
                MGR         N(4)          Manager (references EMPLOYEES)

SALGRADES:      GRADE       N(2)      P   Unique salary grade number
                LOWERLIMIT  N(6,2)    *   Minimum salary for this grade
                UPPERLIMIT  N(6,2)    *   Maximum salary for this grade
                BONUS       N(6,2)    *   Net bonus on top of monthly salary

COURSES:        CODE        VC(6)     P   Unique course code
                DESCRIPTION VC(30)    *   Course description (title)
                CATEGORY    C(3)      *   Course category (GEN,BLD, or DSG)
                DURATION    N(2)      *   Course duration (in days)

OFFERINGS:      COURSE      VC(6)     P   Course code      (references COURSES)
                BEGINDATE   DATE      P   First course day
                TRAINER     N(4)          Instructor       (references EMPLOYEES)
                LOCATION    VC(8)         Location of the course offering

REGISTRATIONS:  ATTENDEE    N(4)      P   Attendee         (references EMPLOYEES)
                COURSE      VC(6)     P   Course code      (references OFFERINGS)
                BEGINDATE   DATE      P   First course day (references OFFERINGS)
                EVALUATION  N(1)          Attendee's opinion (scale 1 - 5)

HISTORY:        EMPNO       N(4)      P   Employee         (references EMPLOYEES)
                BEGINYEAR   N(4)      *   Year component of BEGINDATE
                BEGINDATE   DATE      P   Begin date interval
                ENDDATE     DATE          End date interval
                DEPTNO      N(2)      *   Department       (references DEPARTMENTS)
                MSAL        N(6,2)    *   Monthly salary during the interval
                COMMENTS    VC(60)        Free text space
```

Columns and Foreign Key Constraints

Figure C-2 shows the columns and foreign key constraints in the case tables. The primary key components have a dark-gray background, and all arrows point from the foreign keys to the corresponding primary keys. Boxes surrounding multiple columns indicate composite keys.

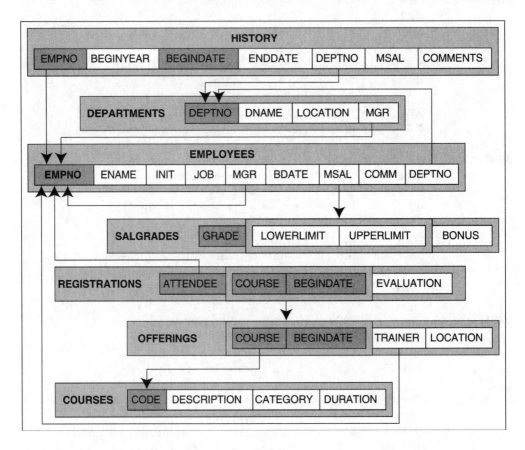

Figure C-2. *Columns and foreign key constraints*

Contents of the Seven Tables

This section lists the contents of each of the seven case tables.

EMPLOYEES

EMPNO	ENAME	INIT	JOB	MGR	BDATE	MSAL	COMM	DEPTNO
7369	SMITH	N	TRAINER	7902	17-12-1965	800		20
7499	ALLEN	JAM	SALESREP	7698	20-02-1961	1600	300	30
7521	WARD	TF	SALESREP	7698	22-02-1962	1250	500	30
7566	JONES	JM	MANAGER	7839	02-04-1967	2975		20
7654	MARTIN	P	SALESREP	7698	28-09-1956	1250	1400	30
7698	BLAKE	R	MANAGER	7839	01-11-1963	2850		30
7782	CLARK	AB	MANAGER	7839	09-06-1965	2450		10
7788	SCOTT	SCJ	TRAINER	7566	26-11-1959	3000		20
7839	KING	CC	DIRECTOR		17-11-1952	5000		10
7844	TURNER	JJ	SALESREP	7698	28-09-1968	1500	0	30
7876	ADAMS	AA	TRAINER	7788	30-12-1966	1100		20
7900	JONES	R	ADMIN	7698	03-12-1969	800		30
7902	FORD	MG	TRAINER	7566	13-02-1959	3000		20
7934	MILLER	TJA	ADMIN	7782	23-01-1962	1300		10

14 rows selected.

DEPARTMENTS

DEPTNO	DNAME	LOCATION	MGR
10	ACCOUNTING	NEW YORK	7782
20	TRAINING	DALLAS	7566
30	SALES	CHICAGO	7698
40	HR	BOSTON	7839

SALGRADES

GRADE	LOWERLIMIT	UPPERLIMIT	BONUS
1	700	1200	0
2	1201	1400	50
3	1401	2000	100
4	2001	3000	200
5	3001	9999	500

COURSES

CODE	DESCRIPTION	CATEGORY	DURATION
JAV	Java for Oracle developers	BLD	4
PLS	Introduction to PL/SQL	BLD	1
XML	XML for Oracle developers	BLD	2
ERM	Data modeling with ERM	DSG	3
GEN	System generation	DSG	4
PMT	Process modeling techniques	DSG	1
PRO	Prototyping	DSG	5
RSD	Relational system design	DSG	2
OAU	Oracle for application users	GEN	1
SQL	Introduction to SQL	GEN	4

10 rows selected.

OFFERINGS

COURSE	BEGINDATE	TRAINER	LOCATION
SQL	12-04-1999	7902	DALLAS
OAU	10-08-1999	7566	CHICAGO
SQL	04-10-1999	7369	SEATTLE
SQL	13-12-1999	7369	DALLAS
JAV	13-12-1999	7566	SEATTLE
JAV	01-02-2000	7876	DALLAS
XML	03-02-2000	7369	DALLAS
PLS	11-09-2000	7788	DALLAS
XML	18-09-2000		SEATTLE
OAU	27-09-2000	7902	DALLAS
ERM	15-01-2001		
PRO	19-02-2001		DALLAS
RSD	24-02-2001	7788	CHICAGO

13 rows selected.

REGISTRATIONS

ATTENDEE	COURSE	BEGINDATE	EVALUATION
7499	SQL	12-04-1999	4
	JAV	13-12-1999	2
	XML	03-02-2000	5
	PLS	11-09-2000	
7521	OAU	10-08-1999	4
7566	JAV	01-02-2000	3

```
       PLS    11-09-2000
7698  SQL    12-04-1999       4
       SQL    13-12-1999
       JAV    01-02-2000       5
7782  JAV    13-12-1999       5
7788  SQL    04-10-1999
       JAV    13-12-1999       5
       JAV    01-02-2000       4
7839  SQL    04-10-1999       3
       JAV    13-12-1999       4
7844  OAU    27-09-2000       5
7876  SQL    12-04-1999       2
       JAV    13-12-1999       5
       PLS    11-09-2000
7900  OAU    10-08-1999       4
       XML    03-02-2000       4
7902  OAU    10-08-1999       5
       SQL    04-10-1999       4
       SQL    13-12-1999
7934  SQL    12-04-1999       5
```

26 rows selected.

HISTORY (formatted, and without COMMENTS column values)

EMPNO	BEGINYEAR	BEGINDATE	ENDDATE	DEPTNO	MSAL
7369	2000	01-01-2000	01-02-2000	40	950
	2000	01-02-2000		20	800
7499	1988	01-06-1988	01-07-1989	30	1000
	1989	01-07-1989	01-12-1993	30	1300
	1993	01-12-1993	01-10-1995	30	1500
	1995	01-10-1995	01-11-1999	30	1700
	1999	01-11-1999		30	1600
7521	1986	01-10-1986	01-08-1987	20	1000
	1987	01-08-1987	01-01-1989	30	1000
	1989	01-01-1989	15-12-1992	30	1150
	1992	15-12-1992	01-10-1994	30	1250
	1994	01-10-1994	01-10-1997	20	1250
	1997	01-10-1997	01-02-2000	30	1300
	2000	01-02-2000		30	1250
7566	1982	01-01-1982	01-12-1982	20	900
	1982	01-12-1982	15-08-1984	20	950
	1984	15-08-1984	01-01-1986	30	1000

	1986	01-01-1986	01-07-1986	30	1175
	1986	01-07-1986	15-03-1987	10	1175
	1987	15-03-1987	01-04-1987	10	2200
	1987	01-04-1987	01-06-1989	10	2300
	1989	01-06-1989	01-07-1992	40	2300
	1992	01-07-1992	01-11-1992	40	2450
	1992	01-11-1992	01-09-1994	20	2600
	1994	01-09-1994	01-03-1995	20	2550
	1995	01-03-1995	15-10-1999	20	2750
	1999	15-10-1999		20	2975
7654	1999	01-01-1999	15-10-1999	30	1100
	1999	15-10-1999		30	1250
7698	1982	01-06-1982	01-01-1983	30	900
	1983	01-01-1983	01-01-1984	30	1275
	1984	01-01-1984	15-04-1985	30	1500
	1985	15-04-1985	01-01-1986	30	2100
	1986	01-01-1986	15-10-1989	30	2200
	1989	15-10-1989		30	2850
7782	1988	01-07-1988		10	2450
7788	1982	01-07-1982	01-01-1983	20	900
	1983	01-01-1983	15-04-1985	20	950
	1985	15-04-1985	01-06-1985	40	950
	1985	01-06-1985	15-04-1986	40	1100
	1986	15-04-1986	01-05-1986	20	1100
	1986	01-05-1986	15-02-1987	20	1800
	1987	15-02-1987	01-12-1989	20	1250
	1989	01-12-1989	15-10-1992	20	1350
	1992	15-10-1992	01-01-1998	20	1400
	1998	01-01-1998	01-01-1999	20	1700
	1999	01-01-1999	01-07-1999	20	1800
	1999	01-07-1999	01-06-2000	20	1800
	2000	01-06-2000		20	3000
7839	1982	01-01-1982	01-08-1982	30	1000
	1982	01-08-1982	15-05-1984	30	1200
	1984	15-05-1984	01-01-1985	30	1500
	1985	01-01-1985	01-07-1985	30	1750
	1985	01-07-1985	01-11-1985	10	2000
	1985	01-11-1985	01-02-1986	10	2200
	1986	01-02-1986	15-06-1989	10	2500
	1989	15-06-1989	01-12-1993	10	2900
	1993	01-12-1993	01-09-1995	10	3400
	1995	01-09-1995	01-10-1997	10	4200

	1997	01-10-1997	01-10-1998	10	4500
	1998	01-10-1998	01-11-1999	10	4800
	1999	01-11-1999	15-02-2000	10	4900
	2000	15-02-2000		10	5000
7844	1995	01-05-1995	01-01-1997	30	900
	1998	15-10-1998	01-11-1998	10	1200
	1998	01-11-1998	01-01-2000	30	1400
	2000	01-01-2000		30	1500
7876	2000	01-01-2000	01-02-2000	20	950
	2000	01-02-2000		20	1100
7900	2000	01-07-2000		30	800
7902	1998	01-09-1998	01-10-1998	40	1400
	1998	01-10-1998	15-03-1999	30	1650
	1999	15-03-1999	01-01-2000	30	2500
	2000	01-01-2000	01-08-2000	30	3000
	2000	01-08-2000		20	3000
7934	1998	01-02-1998	01-05-1998	10	1275
	1998	01-05-1998	01-02-1999	10	1280
	1999	01-02-1999	01-01-2000	10	1290
	2000	01-01-2000		10	1300

79 rows selected.

Hierarchical Employees Overview

Figure C-3 illustrates an overview of the employees and management structure. Note that department 40 has no employees.

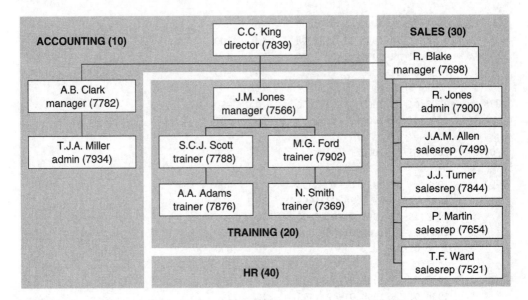

Figure C-3. *Employee overview with management structure*

Course Offerings Overview

This section shows an overview of the course offerings. In the listing A stands for Attendee and T stands for Trainer.

Course code:		SQL	OAU	SQL	JAV	SQL	JAV
Begindate:		12/04/99	10/08/99	04/10/99	13/12/99	13/12/99	01/02/00
Location:		Dallas	Chicago	Seattle	Seattle	Dallas	Dallas
Smith, N	7369	.	.	T	.	T	.
Allen, JAM	7499	A	.	.	A	.	.
Ward, TF	7521	.	A	.	.	.	.
Jones, JM	7566	.	T	.	T	.	A
Martin, P	7654	.	.	.	.	.	.
Blake, R	7698	A	.	.	.	A	A
Clark, AB	7782	.	.	.	A	.	.
Scott, SCJ	7788	.	.	A	A	.	A
King, CC	7839	.	.	A	A	.	.
Turner, JJ	7844	.	.	.	.	.	.
Adams, AA	7876	A	.	.	A	.	T
Jones, R	7900	.	A	.	.	.	.
Ford, MG	7902	T	A	A	.	A	.
Miller, TJA	7934	A	.	.	.	.	.

Course code:		XML	PLS	...	OAU	...	RSD
Begindate:		03/02/00	11/09/00	...	27/09/00	...	24/02/01
Location:		Dallas	Dallas	...	Dallas	...	Chicago
Smith, N	7369	T	.	...	.	...	.
Allen, JAM	7499	A	A	...	.	...	.
Ward, TF	7521	.	.	...	.	...	.
Jones, JM	7566	.	A	...	.	...	.
Martin, P	7654	.	.	...	.	...	.
Blake, R	7698	.	.	...	.	...	.
Clark, AB	7782	.	.	...	.	...	.
Scott, SCJ	7788	.	T	...	.	...	T
King, CC	7839	.	.	...	.	...	.
Turner, JJ	7844	.	.	...	A	...	.
Adams, AA	7876	.	A	...	.	...	.
Jones, R	7900	A	.	...	.	...	.
Ford, MG	7902	.	.	...	T	...	.
Miller, TJA	7934	.	.	...	.	...	.

Course code:	XML	ERM	PRO	Scheduled; however:
Begindate:	18/09/00	15/01/01	19/02/01	- No trainer assigned
Location:	Seattle		Dallas	- No registrations yet

■ ■ ■

Answers to the Exercises

This appendix provides answers and solutions to the exercises in Chapters 4, 5, 7, 8, 9, 10, 11, and 12. In some cases, I have presented multiple (alternative) solutions for a single exercise. Sometimes you will see warnings for possible *incorrect* solutions, in case of known pitfalls.

Of course, it is impossible to list all correct solutions for each exercise; the SQL language is too rich (or redundant?) for such an attempt. This implies that it is perfectly possible for you to approach and solve certain exercises in a completely different way. In that case, you can compare your results with the results listed in this appendix. However, always keep the following warning in mind.

■**Caution** Although a query may produce the correct result, this doesn't imply that you wrote the right query. Incorrect SQL statements sometimes produce the correct results by accident. These are the most treacherous queries, because they can start producing wrong results at any point in the future, based on the actual contents of the tables involved.

Some exercises in this book are quite tough. For some of them, it may be challenging to fully appreciate and understand the given solutions. The reasoning behind including such exercises is the following: to test your SQL knowledge, you can look at the abundance of relatively simple examples in *Oracle SQL Reference*, and you can easily come up with simple SQL experiments yourself.

Chapter 4 Exercises

1. Provide the code and description of all courses with an exact duration of four days.

Solution 4-1.

```
SQL> select code, description
  2  from    courses
  3  where   duration = 4;

CODE DESCRIPTION
---- ------------------------------
SQL  Introduction to SQL
JAV  Java for Oracle developers
GEN  System generation

SQL>
```

2. List all employees, sorted by job, and per job by age (from young to old).

Solution 4-2.

```
SQL> select *
  2  from    employees
  3  order   by job, bdate desc;

EMPNO ENAME     INIT  JOB        MGR  BDATE        MSAL  COMM  DEPTNO
----- --------  ----- --------   ---- -----------  ----- ----- -------
 7900 JONES     R     ADMIN      7698 03-DEC-1969   800           30
 7934 MILLER    TJA   ADMIN      7782 23-JAN-1962  1300           10
 7839 KING      CC    DIRECTOR        17-NOV-1952  5000           10
 7566 JONES     JM    MANAGER    7839 02-APR-1967  2975           20
 7782 CLARK     AB    MANAGER    7839 09-JUN-1965  2450           10
 7698 BLAKE     R     MANAGER    7839 01-NOV-1963  2850           30
 7844 TURNER    JJ    SALESREP   7698 28-SEP-1968  1500     0     30
 7521 WARD      TF    SALESREP   7698 22-FEB-1962  1250   500     30
 7499 ALLEN     JAM   SALESREP   7698 20-FEB-1961  1600   300     30
 7654 MARTIN    P     SALESREP   7698 28-SEP-1956  1250  1400     30
 7876 ADAMS     AA    TRAINER    7788 30-DEC-1966  1100           20
 7369 SMITH     N     TRAINER    7902 17-DEC-1965   800           20
 7788 SCOTT     SCJ   TRAINER    7566 26-NOV-1959  3000           20
 7902 FORD      MG    TRAINER    7566 13-FEB-1959  3000           20

14 rows selected.

SQL>
```

3. Which courses have been held in Chicago and/or in Seattle?

Solution 4-3.

```
SQL> select distinct course
  2  from    offerings
  3  where   location in ('CHICAGO','SEATTLE');

COURSE
------
JAV
OAU
RSD
SQL
XML

SQL>
```

Notice the DISTINCT keyword in the SELECT clause, to ensure that a course code doesn't show up more than once. This way, you get the correct answer to the question.

4. Which employees attended both the Java course and the XML course? (Provide their employee numbers.)

Solution 4-4.

```
SQL> select attendee
  2  from    registrations
  3  where   course   = 'JAV'
  4  and     attendee in (select attendee
  5                       from    registrations
  6                       where   course = 'XML');

ATTENDEE
--------
    7499

SQL>
```

You might want to add the DISTINCT keyword to the SELECT clause here, too, just as you did in the previous exercise; otherwise, what happens if someone attends the XML course once and attends the Java course twice?

This fourth exercise has many different solutions. For example, you can also use two subqueries instead of one. Obviously, the following solutions with AND or OR at the row level are wrong:

```
where course = 'JAV' and course = 'XML'  -- Wrong: Gives "no rows selected."
where course = 'JAV' or  course = 'XML'  -- Wrong: Gives too many results.
```

5. List the names and initials of all employees, except for R. Jones.

Solution 4-5a. *Using Parentheses*

```
SQL> select ename, init
  2  from    employees
  3  where   not (ename = 'JONES' and init = 'R');

ENAME     INIT
--------  -----
SMITH     N
ALLEN     JAM
WARD      TF
JONES     JM
MARTIN    P
BLAKE     R
CLARK     AB
SCOTT     SCJ
KING      CC
TURNER    JJ
ADAMS     AA
FORD      MG
MILLER    TJA

13 rows selected.

SQL>
```

Solution 4-5b. *Without Parentheses (Note the OR)*

```
SQL> select ename, init
  2  from    employees
  3  where   ename <> 'JONES' OR init <> 'R';
```

6. Find the number, job, and date of birth of all trainers and sales representatives born before 1960.

Solution 4-6a. *First Solution*

```
SQL> select empno, job, bdate
  2  from    employees
  3  where   bdate < date '1960-01-01'
  4  and     job in ('TRAINER','SALESREP');
```

```
   EMPNO JOB       BDATE
-------- -------- -----------
    7654 SALESREP 28-SEP-1956
    7788 TRAINER  26-NOV-1959
    7902 TRAINER  13-FEB-1959

SQL>
```

Here is an alternative solution; note the parentheses to force operator precedence.

Solution 4-6b. *Second Solution*

```
SQL> select empno, job, bdate
  2  from   employees
  3  where  bdate < date '1960-01-01'
  4  and    (job = 'TRAINER' or job = 'SALESREP');
```

7. List the numbers of all employees who do not work for the training department.

Solution 4-7.

```
SQL> select empno
  2  from   employees
  3  where  deptno <> (select deptno
  4                    from   departments
  5                    where  dname = 'TRAINING');

   EMPNO
--------
    7499
    7521
    7654
    7698
    7782
    7839
    7844
    7900
    7934

SQL>
```

■**Note** This solution assumes that there is only one training department. You could also use
NOT IN instead of <>.

8. List the numbers of all employees who did not attend the Java course.

Solution 4-8a. *Correct Solution*

```
SQL> select empno
  2  from    employees
  3  where   empno not in (select attendee
  4                        from    registrations
  5                        where   course = 'JAV');

   EMPNO
--------
    7369
    7521
    7654
    7844
    7900
    7902
    7934

SQL>
```

The following two solutions are *wrong*.

Solution 4-8b. *Wrong Solution 1*

```
SQL> select distinct attendee
  2  from    registrations
  3  where   attendee not in (select attendee
  4                           from    registrations
  5                           where   course = 'JAV');

ATTENDEE
--------
    7521
    7844
    7900
    7902
    7934

SQL>
```

This result shows only five employees because employees 7369 and 7654 never attended any course; therefore, their employee numbers do not occur in the REGISTRATIONS table.

Solution 4-8c. *Wrong Solution 2*

```
SQL> select distinct attendee attendee
  2  from    registrations
  3  where   course <> 'JAV';

ATTENDEE
--------
    7499
    7521
    7566
    7698
    7788
    7839
    7844
    7876
    7900
    7902
    7934

11 rows selected.

SQL>
```

This result shows too many results, because it also shows employees who attended the Java course *and* at least one non-Java course; for example, employee 7566 attended the Java and the PL/SQL courses.

9a. Which employees have subordinates?

Solution 4-9a. *Employees with Subordinates*

```
SQL> select empno, ename, init
  2  from    employees
  3  where   empno in (select mgr
  4                    from    employees);

  EMPNO ENAME     INIT
-------- --------- -----
    7566 JONES     JM
    7698 BLAKE     R
    7782 CLARK     AB
    7788 SCOTT     SCJ
    7839 KING      CC
    7902 FORD      MG

SQL>
```

9b. Which employees *don't* have subordinates?

Solution 4-9b. *Employees Without Subordinates*

```
SQL> select empno, ename, init
  2  from    employees
  3  where   empno not in (select mgr
  4                        from    employees
  5                        where   mgr is not null);

   EMPNO ENAME     INIT
-------- --------- -----
    7369 SMITH     N
    7499 ALLEN     JAM
    7521 WARD      TF
    7654 MARTIN    P
    7844 TURNER    JJ
    7876 ADAMS     AA
    7900 JONES     R
    7934 MILLER    TJA

SQL>
```

Note The WHERE clause on the fifth line of Solution 4-9b is necessary for a correct result, assuming that null values in the MGR column always mean "not applicable." See also Solution 4-12.

10. Produce an overview of all general course offerings (course category GEN) in 1999.

Solution 4-10.

```
SQL> select *
  2  from    offerings
  3  where   begindate between date '1999-01-01'
  4                        and date '1999-12-31'
  5  and     course in (select code
  6                     from    courses
  7                     where   category = 'GEN');

COURSE BEGINDATE    TRAINER LOCATION
------ ------------ ------- --------
OAU    10-AUG-1999     7566 CHICAGO
SQL    12-APR-1999     7902 DALLAS
SQL    04-OCT-1999     7369 SEATTLE
SQL    13-DEC-1999     7369 DALLAS

SQL>
```

You can solve the "1999 condition" in many ways by using SQL functions (see Chapter 5). Here are three valid alternatives for lines 3 and 4:

```
where to_char(begindate,'YYYY') = '1999'
where extract(year from begindate) = 1999
where begindate between to_date('01-JAN-1999','DD-MON-YYYY')
                    and to_date('31-DEC-1999','DD-MON-YYYY')
```

■**Caution** Avoid using column names as function arguments if it is possible to express the same functional result without having to do that, because it may have a negative impact on performance. In this case, Solution 4-10 and the last alternative are fine; the first two alternatives should be avoided.

---

11. Provide the name and initials of all employees who have ever attended a course taught by N. Smith. Hint: Use subqueries, and work "inside out" toward the result; that is, retrieve the employee number of N. Smith, search for the codes of all courses he ever taught, and so on.

Solution 4-11.

```
SQL> select ename, init
  2  from     employees
  3  where    empno in
  4        (select attendee
  5         from    registrations
  6         where (course, begindate) in
  7               (select course, begindate
  8                from    offerings
  9                where  trainer =
 10                      (select empno
 11                       from    employees
 12                       where   ename = 'SMITH'
 13                       and     init  = 'N'
 14                      )
 15               )
 16        );

ENAME    INIT
-------- -----
ALLEN    JAM
BLAKE    R
SCOTT    SCJ
KING     CC
JONES    R
FORD     MG

SQL>
```

12. How could you redesign the EMPLOYEES table to avoid the problem that the COMM column contains null values meaning *not applicable*?

Answer: By dropping that column from the EMPLOYEES table and by creating a separate SALESREPS table, with the following rows:

```
EMPNO     COMM
--------  --------
    7499       300
    7521       500
    7654      1400
    7844         0
```

In this table, the EMPNO column is not only the primary key, but it is also a foreign key referring to the EMPLOYEES table.

13. In Section 4.9, you saw the following statement: In SQL, NOT is not "not." What is this statement trying to say?

Answer: In three-valued logic, the NOT operator is not the complement operator anymore:

```
NOT TRUE is equivalent with FALSE
not TRUE is equivalent with FALSE OR UNKNOWN
```

14. Referring to the brain-twister at the end of Section 4.9, what is the explanation of the result "no rows selected" in Listing 4-44?

Answer: The following WHERE clause:

```
2  where evaluation not in (1,2,3,NULL)
```

is logically equivalent with the following "iterated AND" condition:

```
2  where evaluation <> 1
3  AND    evaluation <> 2
4  AND    evaluation <> 3
5  AND    evaluation <> NULL
```

If you consider a row with an EVALUATION value of 1, 2, or 3, it is obvious that out of the first three conditions, one of them returns FALSE and the other two return TRUE. Therefore, the complete WHERE clause returns FALSE.

If the EVALUATION value is NULL, all four conditions return UNKNOWN. Therefore, the end result is also UNKNOWN. So far, there are no surprises.

If the EVALUATION value is 4 or 5 (the remaining two allowed values), the first three conditions all return TRUE, but the last condition returns UNKNOWN. So you have the following expression:

```
(TRUE) and (TRUE) and (TRUE) and (UNKNOWN)
```

This is logically equivalent with UNKNOWN, so the complete WHERE clause returns UNKNOWN.

15. At the end of Section 4.5, you saw the following statement.

The following two queries are logically equivalent:

```
select * from employees where NOT (ename = 'BLAKE' AND init = 'R')
select * from employees where      ename <> 'BLAKE' OR init <> 'R'
```

Prove this, using a truth table.

Answer: First, we assign names to the two WHERE clause components.

- Let's represent ename = 'BLAKE' with P.

- Let's represent init = 'R' with Q.

Then we must show that NOT(P AND Q) and NOT(P) OR NOT(Q) are logically equivalent. The truth tables for both expressions look as follows:

P	Q	P AND Q	NOT(P AND Q)
TRUE	TRUE	TRUE	FALSE
TRUE	FALSE	FALSE	TRUE
TRUE	UNK	UNK	UNK
FALSE	TRUE	FALSE	TRUE
FALSE	FALSE	FALSE	TRUE
FALSE	UNK	FALSE	TRUE
UNK	TRUE	UNK	UNK
UNK	FALSE	FALSE	TRUE
UNK	UNK	UNK	UNK

P	Q	NOT(P)	NOT(Q)	NOT(P) OR NOT(Q)
TRUE	TRUE	FALSE	FALSE	FALSE
TRUE	FALSE	FALSE	TRUE	TRUE
TRUE	UNK	FALSE	UNK	UNK
FALSE	TRUE	TRUE	FALSE	TRUE
FALSE	FALSE	TRUE	TRUE	TRUE
FALSE	UNK	TRUE	UNK	TRUE
UNK	TRUE	UNK	FALSE	UNK
UNK	FALSE	UNK	TRUE	TRUE
UNK	UNK	UNK	UNK	UNK

As you can see, the last columns in the two truth tables are identical. This proves that the two expressions are logically equivalent.

Chapter 5 Exercises

1. For all employees, provide their last name, a comma, followed by their initials.

Solution 5-1.

```
SQL> select ename ||', '||init
  2          as full_name
  3  from   employees;

FULL_NAME
---------------
SMITH, N
ALLEN, JAM
WARD, TF
JONES, JM
MARTIN, P
BLAKE, R
CLARK, AB
SCOTT, SCJ
KING, CC
TURNER, JJ
ADAMS, AA
JONES, R
FORD, MG
MILLER, TJA

14 rows selected.

SQL>
```

2. For all employees, list their last name and date of birth, in a format such as April 2nd, 1967.

Solution 5-2.

```
SQL> select ename
  2  ,      to_char(bdate,'fmMonth ddth, yyyy')
  3  from   employees;

ENAME     TO_CHAR(BDATE,'FMMON
--------  --------------------
SMITH     December 17th, 1965
ALLEN     February 20th, 1961
WARD      February 22nd, 1962
JONES     April 2nd, 1967
MARTIN    September 28th, 1956
```

```
BLAKE     November 1st, 1963
CLARK     June 9th, 1965
SCOTT     November 26th, 1959
KING      November 17th, 1952
TURNER    September 28th, 1968
ADAMS     December 30th, 1966
JONES     December 3rd, 1969
FORD      February 13th, 1959
MILLER    January 23rd, 1962

14 rows selected.

SQL>
```

Note You can change the language to display the month names in this result with the NLS_LANGUAGE parameter setting, as in this example:

```
SQL> alter session set nls_language=dutch;
Sessie is gewijzigd.

SQL>
```

3a. On which day are (or were) you exactly 10,000 days old?

Solution 5-3a.

```
SQL> select date '1954-08-11' + 10000
  2         as "10,000 days"
  3  from   dual;

10,000 days
-----------
27-DEC-1981

SQL>
```

3b. On which day of the week is (was) this?

Solution 5-3b.

```
SQL> select to_char(date '1954-08-11' + 10000,'Day')
  2         as "On a:"
  3  from   dual;
```

```
On a:
---------
Sunday

SQL>
```

4. Rewrite the example in Listing 5-23 using the NVL2 function.

Solution 5-4.

```
SQL> select ename, msal, comm
  2  ,       nvl2(comm,12*msal+comm,12*msal) as yearsal
  3  from    employees
  4  where   ename like '%T%';

ENAME        MSAL     COMM  YEARSAL
--------  --------  -------- --------
SMITH         800             9600
MARTIN       1250     1400   16400
SCOTT        3000            36000
TURNER       1500        0   18000

SQL>
```

5. Rewrite the example in Listing 5-24 to remove the DECODE functions using CASE expressions, both in the SELECT clause and in the ORDER BY clause.

Solution 5-5.

```
SQL> select job, ename
  2  ,       case
  3            when msal <= 2500
  4            then 'cheap'
  5            else 'expensive'
  6          end          as class
  7  from    employees
  8  where   bdate < date '1964-01-01'
  9  order   by case job
 10              when 'DIRECTOR' then 1
 11              when 'MANAGER'  then 2
 12                              else 3
 13          end;
```

```
JOB       ENAME    CLASS
--------  -------- ---------
DIRECTOR  KING     expensive
MANAGER   BLAKE    expensive
SALESREP  ALLEN    cheap
SALESREP  WARD     cheap
ADMIN     MILLER   cheap
TRAINER   FORD     expensive
TRAINER   SCOTT    expensive
SALESREP  MARTIN   cheap

SQL>
```

■**Note** The TO_DATE function expression is also replaced by a DATE literal.

---

6. Rewrite the example in Listing 5-20 using DATE and INTERVAL constants, in such a way that they become independent of the NLS_DATE_FORMAT setting.

Solution 5-6.

```
SQL> select date '1996-01-29' + interval '1' month as col_1
  2  ,       date '1997-01-29' + interval '1' month as col_2
  3  ,       date '1997-08-11' - interval '3' month as col_3
  4  from    dual;
,       date '1997-01-29' + interval '1' month as col_2
                *
ERROR at line 2:
ORA-01839: date not valid for month specified

SQL> select date '1996-01-29' + interval '1' month as col_1
  2  ,       date '1997-01-28' + interval '1' month as col_2
  3  ,       date '1997-08-11' - interval '3' month as col_3
  4  from    dual;


COL_1       COL_2       COL_3
----------- ----------- ---------
29-FEB-1996 28-FEB-1997 11-MAY-1997

SQL>
```

As you can see, January 29 plus a month causes problems for 1997, which is not a leap year. If you change 1997-01-29 to 1997-01-28 on the second line, there is no longer a problem.

7. Investigate the difference between the date formats WW and IW (week number and ISO week number) using an arbitrary date, and explain your findings.

Solution 5-7.

```
SQL>  1  select date '2005-01-01' as input_date
  2  ,       to_char(date '2005-01-01', 'ww') as ww
  3  ,       to_char(date '2005-01-01', 'iw') as iw
  4* from   dual

INPUT_DATE  WW IW
----------- -- --
01-JAN-2005 06 07

SQL>
```

If you don't get different results, try different dates within the same week. The difference between WW and IW has to do with the different definitions of week numbers. The WW format starts week number 1 on January 1, regardless of which day of the week that is. The ISO standard uses different rules: an ISO week *always* starts on a Monday. The rules around the new year are as follows: if January 1 is a Friday, a Saturday, or a Sunday, the week belongs to the previous year; otherwise, the week fully belongs to the new year. Similar rules apply for the ISO year numbering.

8. Look at Listing 5-15, where we use the REGEXP_INSTR function to search for words. Rewrite this query using REGEXP_LIKE. Hint: You can use {n,} to express "at least n times."

Solution 5-8a. *First Solution*

```
SQL> select comments
  2  from   history
  3  where  regexp_like(comments, '([^ ]+ ){8,}');

COMMENTS
----------------------------------------------------------------
Not a great trainer; let's try the sales department!
Sales also turns out to be not a success...
Hired as the new manager for the accounting department
Junior sales rep -- has lots to learn... :-)

SQL>
```

You could make your solution more readable by using character classes.

Solution 5-8b. *Second Solution, Using Character Classes*

```
SQL> select  comments
  2  from    history
  3  where   regexp_like(comments, '([[:alnum:]+[:punct:]]+[[:space:]]+){8,}');

COMMENTS
-------------------------------------------------------------
Not a great trainer; let's try the sales department!
Sales also turns out to be not a success...
Hired as the new manager for the accounting department
Junior sales rep -- has lots to learn... :-)

SQL>
```

■**Note** See Appendix C or *Oracle SQL Reference* for more details about character classes.

Chapter 7 Exercises

1. Listing 7-5 defines the constraint E_SALES_CHK in a rather cryptic way. Formulate the same constraint without using DECODE and NVL2.

   Solution 7-1a. *Solution 1*

   ```
   check ((job = 'SALESREP' and comm is not null) or
          (job <>'SALESREP' and comm is null)           )
   ```

   Solution 7-1b. *Solution 2*

   ```
   check ((job = 'SALESREP' or  comm is null) and not
          (job = 'SALESREP' and comm is null)           )
   ```

2. Why do you think the constraint E_DEPT_FK (in Listing 7-7) is created with a separate ALTER TABLE command?

   Answer: You must define this constraint with an ALTER TABLE command because you have a "chicken/egg" problem. A foreign key constraint can refer to only an *existing* table, and you have two tables (EMPLOYEES and DEPARTMENTS) referring to each other.

3. Although this is not covered in this chapter, try to come up with an explanation of the following phenomenon: when using sequences, you cannot use the pseudo column CURRVAL in your session without first calling the pseudo column NEXTVAL.

Answer: In a multiuser environment, multiple database users can use the same sequence generator at the same time. Therefore, they will be using *different* CURRVAL values at the same time; that is, there is no database-wide "current" CURRVAL value. On the other hand, NEXTVAL is always defined as the next available sequence value.

4. Why is it better to use sequences in a multiuser environment, as opposed to maintaining a secondary table with the last/current sequence values?

Answer: A secondary table will become a performance bottleneck. Each update to a sequence value will lock the corresponding row. The next update can take place only after the first transaction has committed. In other words, all transactions needing a sequence value will be serialized. Sequences are better because they don't have this problem. With sequences, multiple transactions can be served simultaneously and independently.

5. How is it possible that the EVALUATION column of the REGISTRATIONS table accepts null values, in spite of the constraint R_EVAL_CHK (see Listing 7-11)?

Answer: This is caused by three-valued logic. A CHECK constraint condition can result in TRUE, FALSE, or UNKNOWN. Moreover, a CHECK constraint reports a violation *only* if its corresponding condition returns FALSE.

■**Note** This implies that you always need an explicit NOT NULL constraint if you want your columns to be mandatory; a CHECK constraint as shown in Listing 7-11 is not enough.

---

6. If you define a PRIMARY KEY or UNIQUE constraint, the Oracle DBMS normally creates a unique index under the covers (if none of the existing indexes can be used) to check the constraint. Investigate and explain what happens if you define such a constraint as DEFERRABLE.

Answer: If you define PRIMARY KEY or UNIQUE constraints as DEFERRABLE, the Oracle DBMS creates nonunique indexes. This is because indexes must be maintained immediately. Therefore, indexes for deferrable constraints must allow for temporary duplicate values until the end of your transactions.

7. You can use function-based indexes to implement "conditional uniqueness" constraints. Create a unique function-based index on the REGISTRATIONS table to check the following constraint: employees are allowed to attend the OAU course only once. They may attend other courses as many times as they like. Test your solution with the following command (it should fail):

```
SQL> insert into registrations values (7900,'OAU',trunc(sysdate),null);
```

Hint: You can use a CASE expression in the index expression.

Solution 7-7.

```
SQL> create unique index oau_reg on registrations
  2  ( case course when 'OAU' then attendee else null end
  3  , case course when 'OAU' then course   else null end );

Index created.

SQL>
```

The trick is to create a function-based index on (ATTENDEE, COURSE) combinations, while ignoring all non-OAU course registrations.

Here's the test:

```
SQL> insert into registrations values (7900,'OAU',sysdate,null);
insert into registrations values (7900,'OAU',sysdate,null)
*
ERROR at line 1:
ORA-00001: unique constraint (BOOK.OAU_REG) violated

SQL>
```

■**Note** Notice the Oracle error message number for the unique constraint violation: 00001. This must have been one of the first error messages implemented in Oracle!

Chapter 8 Exercises

1. Produce an overview of all course offerings. Provide the course code, begin date, course duration, and name of the trainer.

Solution 8-1a. *First Solution*

```
SQL> select c.code
  2  ,      o.begindate
  3  ,      c.duration
  4  ,      e.ename   as   trainer
  5  from   employees e
  6  ,      courses   c
  7  ,      offerings o
  8  where  o.trainer = e.empno
  9  and    o.course  = c.code;
```

```
CODE BEGINDATE    DURATION TRAINER
---- -----------  -------- --------
XML  03-FEB-2000         2 SMITH
SQL  13-DEC-1999         4 SMITH
SQL  04-OCT-1999         4 SMITH
OAU  10-AUG-1999         1 JONES
JAV  13-DEC-1999         4 JONES
RSD  24-FEB-2001         2 SCOTT
PLS  11-SEP-2000         1 SCOTT
JAV  01-FEB-2000         4 ADAMS
SQL  12-APR-1999         4 FORD
OAU  27-SEP-2000         1 FORD

10 rows selected.

SQL>
```

If you also want to see all course offerings with an unknown trainer, you can change the solution as follows:

Solution 8-1b. *Second Solution, Also Showing Course Offerings with Unknown Trainers*

```
SQL> select DISTINCT c.code
  2 ,        o.begindate
  3 ,        c.duration
  4 ,        case when o.trainer is not null
  5               then e.ename
  6               else null
  7          end  as trainer
  8  from    employees e
  9 ,        courses   c
 10 ,        offerings o
 11  where   coalesce(o.trainer,-1) in (e.empno,-1)
 12  and     o.course = c.code;

CODE BEGINDATE    DURATION TRAINER
---- -----------  -------- --------
ERM  15-JAN-2001         3
JAV  13-DEC-1999         4 JONES
JAV  01-FEB-2000         4 ADAMS
OAU  10-AUG-1999         1 JONES
OAU  27-SEP-2000         1 FORD
PLS  11-SEP-2000         1 SCOTT
PRO  19-FEB-2001         5
RSD  24-FEB-2001         2 SCOTT
SQL  12-APR-1999         4 FORD
SQL  04-OCT-1999         4 SMITH
```

```
SQL  13-DEC-1999    4 SMITH
XML  03-FEB-2000    2 SMITH
XML  18-SEP-2000    2

13 rows selected.

SQL>
```

Line 11 might look curious at first sight. It "relaxes" the join between OFFERINGS and EMPLOYEES a bit. Instead of –1, you can use any other arbitrary numeric value, as long as it could not be an existing employee number. Note also that this trick makes the addition of DISTINCT necessary.

2. Provide an overview, in two columns, showing the names of all employees who ever attended an SQL course, with the name of the trainer.

Solution 8-2.

```
SQL> select  a.ename    as attendee
  2  ,        t.ename    as trainer
  3  from     employees    t
  4           join
  5           offerings    o on  (o.trainer = t.empno)
  6           join
  7           registrations r using (course, begindate)
  8           join
  9           employees    a on (r.attendee = a.empno)
 10  where    course = 'SQL';

ATTENDEE TRAINER
-------- --------
ALLEN    FORD
BLAKE    FORD
ADAMS    FORD
MILLER   FORD
SCOTT    SMITH
KING     SMITH
FORD     SMITH
BLAKE    SMITH
FORD     SMITH

SQL>
```

This solution uses the new ANSI/ISO join syntax, just for a change.

3. For all employees, list their name, initials, and yearly salary (including bonus and commission).

Solution 8-3.

```
SQL> select e.ename, e.init
  2  ,       12 * (e.msal + s.bonus)
  3          + nvl(e.comm,0) as yearsal
  4  from    employees e
  5          join
  6          salgrades s
  7          on (e.msal between s.lowerlimit
  8                         and s.upperlimit);

ENAME     INIT  YEARSAL
--------  ----- --------
SMITH     N        9600
JONES     R        9600
ADAMS     AA      13200
WARD      TF      16100
MARTIN    P       17000
MILLER    TJA     16200
TURNER    JJ      19200
ALLEN     JAM     20700
CLARK     AB      31800
BLAKE     R       36600
JONES     JM      38100
SCOTT     SCJ     38400
FORD      MG      38400
KING      CC      66000

14 rows selected.

SQL>
```

4. For all course offerings, list the course code, begin date, and number of registrations. Sort your results on the number of registrations, from high to low.

Solution 8-4.

```
SQL> select  course
  2  ,        begindate
  3  ,        count(r.attendee) as reg_count
  4  from     offerings    o
  5           left outer join
  6           registrations r
  7           using (course, begindate)
  8  group by course
  9  ,        begindate
 10  order by reg_count desc;
```

```
COURSE BEGINDATE    REG_COUNT
------ ----------- ---------
JAV    13-DEC-1999         5
SQL    12-APR-1999         4
JAV    01-FEB-2000         3
OAU    10-AUG-1999         3
PLS    11-SEP-2000         3
SQL    04-OCT-1999         3
SQL    13-DEC-1999         2
XML    03-FEB-2000         2
OAU    27-SEP-2000         1
ERM    15-JAN-2001         0
XML    18-SEP-2000         0
PRO    19-FEB-2001         0
RSD    24-FEB-2001         0

13 rows selected.

SQL>
```

You need an outer join here, to see all courses without registrations in the result as well. Note also that COUNT(*) in the third line would give you wrong results.

5. List the course code, begin date, and the number of registrations for all course offerings in 1999 with at least three registrations.

Solution 8-5.

```
SQL> select    course
  2 ,          begindate
  3 ,          count(*)
  4 from       registrations
  5 where      extract(year from begindate) = 1999
  6 group by course
  7 ,          begindate
  8 having    count(*) >= 3;

COURSE BEGINDATE    COUNT(*)
------ ----------- --------
JAV    13-DEC-1999         5
OAU    10-AUG-1999         3
SQL    12-APR-1999         4
SQL    04-OCT-1999         3

SQL>
```

In this case, accessing the REGISTRATIONS table is enough, because you are not interested in offerings without registrations. The solution would have been more complicated if the question were "... with *fewer than* three registrations," because zero is also less than three.

6. Provide the employee numbers of all employees who ever taught a course as a trainer, but never attended a course as an attendee.

Solution 8-6a. *First Solution*

```
SQL> select trainer  from offerings
  2  minus
  3  select attendee from registrations;

 TRAINER
--------
    7369


SQL>
```

This solution looks good; however, if you look very carefully, the solution is suspect. You don't see it immediately, but this result doesn't contain a single row, but two rows, as becomes apparent if you set FEEDBACK to 1:

```
SQL> set feedback 1
SQL> /

 TRAINER
--------
    7369


2 rows selected.

SQL>
```

Because a null value obviously doesn't represent a valid trainer, you need to exclude null values in the TRAINER column explicitly.

Solution 8-6b. *Second Solution, Excluding Null Values*

```
SQL> select trainer  from offerings
  2  where  trainer  is not null
  3  minus
  4  select attendee from registrations;
```

```
 TRAINER
--------
    7369

1 row selected.

SQL>
```

7. Which employees attended a specific course more than once?

Solution 8-7.

```
SQL> select   attendee,course
  2  from      registrations
  3  group by attendee,course
  4  having    count(*) > 1 ;

ATTENDEE COURSE
-------- ------
    7698 SQL
    7788 JAV
    7902 SQL

SQL>
```

8. For all trainers, provide their name and initials, the number of courses they taught, the total number of students they had in their classes, and the average evaluation rating. Round the evaluation ratings to one decimal.

Solution 8-8.

```
SQL> select   t.init, t.ename
  2  ,         count(distinct begindate) courses
  3  ,         count(*)                  attendees
  4  ,         round(avg(evaluation),1)  evaluation
  5  from      employees    t
  6  ,         registrations r
  7            join
  8            offerings     o
  9            using (course, begindate)
 10  where     t.empno = o.trainer
 11  group by t.init, t.ename;
```

```
INIT   ENAME    COURSES ATTENDEES EVALUATION
-----  -------- ------- --------- ----------
N      SMITH       3        7         4
AA     ADAMS       1        3         4
JM     JONES       2        8        4.3
MG     FORD        2        5         4
SCJ    SCOTT       1        3

SQL>
```

■**Note** While counting courses, this solution assumes that trainers cannot teach more than one course on the same day.

9. List the name and initials of all trainers who ever had their own manager as a student in a general course (category GEN).

Solution 8-9.

```
SQL> select distinct e.ename, e.init
  2  from    employees    e
  3  ,       courses      c
  4  ,       offerings    o
  5  ,       registrations r
  6  where   e.empno     = o.trainer
  7  and     e.mgr       = r.attendee
  8  and     c.code      = o.course
  9  and     o.course    = r.course
 10  and     o.begindate = r.begindate
 11  and     c.category  = 'GEN';

ENAME    INIT
-------- -----
SMITH    N

SQL>
```

10. Did we ever use two classrooms at the same time in the same course location?

Solution 8-10.

```
SQL> select o1.location
  2  ,       o1.begindate, o1.course, c1.duration
  3  ,       o2.begindate, o2.course
```

```
 4  from    offerings   o1
 5  ,        offerings   o2
 6  ,        courses     c1
 7  where   o1.location  = o2.location
 8  and     (o1.begindate < o2.begindate or
 9           o1.course   <> o2.course       )
10  and     o1.course    = c1.code
11  and     o2.begindate between o1.begindate
12                            and o1.begindate + c1.duration;


LOCATION BEGINDATE    COUR DURATION BEGINDATE    COURSE
-------- -----------  ---- -------- -----------  ------
DALLAS   01-FEB-2000  JAV         4 03-FEB-2000  XML

SQL>
```

The solution searches for two *different* course offerings (see lines 8 and 9) at the same location (see line 7) overlapping each other (see lines 11 and 12). Apparently, the Java course starting February 1, 2000, in Dallas overlaps with the XML course starting two days later (note that the Java course takes four days).

11. Produce a matrix report (one column per department, one row for each job) where each cell shows the number of employees for a specific department and a specific job. In a single SQL statement, it is impossible to dynamically derive the number of columns needed, so you may assume you have three departments only: 10, 20, and 30.

Solution 8-11.

```
SQL> select  job
  2  ,        count(case
  3                  when deptno <> 10
  4                  then null
  5                  else deptno
  6                  end                    ) as dept_10
  7  ,        sum(case deptno
  8               when 20
  9               then 1
 10               else 0
 11               end                       ) as dept_20
 12  ,        sum(decode(deptno,30,1,0)) as dept_30
 13  from     employees
 14  group by job;


JOB        DEPT_10  DEPT_20  DEPT_30
--------   -------- -------- --------
ADMIN            1        0        1
DIRECTOR         1        0        0
```

```
MANAGER          1          1          1
SALESREP         0          0          4
TRAINER          0          4          0

SQL>
```

This solution shows three different valid methods to count the employees: for department 10, it uses a searched CASE expression; for department 20, it uses a simple CASE expression and a SUM function; and for department 30, it uses the Oracle DECODE function, which is essentially the same solution as for department 20.

12. Listing 8-26 produces information about all departments with *more* than four employees. How can you change the query to show information about all departments with *fewer* than four employees?

Solution 8-12a. *Incorrect Solution*

```
SQL> select deptno, count(empno)
  2  from    employees
  3  group  by deptno
  4  having count(*) < 4;

 DEPTNO COUNT(EMPNO)
-------- ------------
     10            3

SQL>
```

This solution is *not* correct, because it does not show departments with zero employees. You can fix this in several ways; for example, by using an outer join.

Solution 8-12b. *Correct Solution*

```
SQL> select deptno, count(empno)
  2  from    departments
  3          left outer join
  4          employees
  5          using (deptno)
  6  group  by deptno
  7  having count(*) < 4;

 DEPTNO COUNT(EMPNO)
-------- ------------
     10            3
     40            0

SQL>
```

13. Look at Listings 8-44 and 8-45. Are those two queries logically equivalent? Investigate the two queries and explain the differences, if any.

Solution 8-13. *Making the Difference Visible with FEEDBACK*

```
SQL> set feedback 1

SQL> select o.location from offerings   o
  2  MINUS
  3  select d.location from departments d;

LOCATION
--------
SEATTLE


2 rows selected.

SQL> select DISTINCT o.location
  2  from    offerings o
  3  where   o.location not in
  4          (select d.location
  5           from    departments d);

LOCATION
--------
SEATTLE

1 row selected.

SQL>
```

If you change the SQL*Plus FEEDBACK setting to 1, the difference becomes apparent.

We have one course offering with unknown location, and (as you know by now) you cannot be too careful with null values. The first query produces two rows. The null value appears in the result because the MINUS operator does not remove the null value. However, if the second query checks the ERM course offering (with the null value) the WHERE clause becomes

```
... where NULL not in ('NEW YORK','DALLAS','CHICAGO','BOSTON');
```

This WHERE clause returns UNKNOWN. Therefore, the row does not pass the WHERE clause filter, and as a consequence the result contains only one row.

Chapter 9 Exercises

1. It is normal practice that (junior) trainers always attend a course taught by a senior colleague before teaching that course themselves. For which trainer/course combinations did this happen?

   Solution 9-1.

   ```
   SQL> select o.course, o.trainer
     2  from    offerings o
     3  where   exists
     4          (select r.*
     5           from    registrations r
     6           where   r.attendee  = o.trainer
     7           and     r.course    = o.course
     8           and     r.begindate < o.begindate)
     9  and     not exists
    10          (select fo.*
    11           from    offerings fo
    12           where   fo.course    = o.course
    13           and     fo.trainer   = o.trainer
    14           and     fo.begindate < o.begindate);


   COURSE  TRAINER
   ------  --------
   JAV        7876
   OAU        7902

   SQL>
   ```

   This exercise is not an easy one. You can solve it in many ways. The solution shown here uses the EXISTS and the NOT EXISTS operators. You can read it as follows:

   "Search course offerings for which (1) the trainer attended an *earlier* offering of the same course as a student, and for which (2) the trainer is teaching that course for the first time."

   Note The second condition is necessary, because otherwise you would also get "teach/attend/teach" combinations.

   ---

2. Actually, if the junior trainer teaches a course for the first time, that senior colleague (see the previous exercise) sits in the back of the classroom in a supporting role. Try to find these course/junior/senior combinations.

Solution 9-2.

```
SQL> select o1.course
  2  ,        o1.trainer    as senior
  3  ,        o2.trainer    as junior
  4  from     offerings     o1
  5  ,        registrations r1
  6  ,        offerings     o2
  7  ,        registrations r2
  8  where    o1.course    = r1.course    -- join r1 with o1
  9  and      o1.begindate = r1.begindate
 10  and      o2.course    = r2.course    -- join r2 with o2
 11  and      o2.begindate = r2.begindate
 12  and      o1.course    = o2.course    -- o1 and o2 same course
 13  and      o1.begindate < o2.begindate -- o1 earlier than o2
 14  and      o1.trainer   = r2.attendee  -- trainer o1 attends o2
 15  and      o2.trainer   = r1.attendee  -- trainer o2 attends o1
 16  ;

COURSE  SENIOR   JUNIOR
------- -------- --------
JAV        7566     7876

SQL>
```

This solution uses a join, for a change.

3. Which employees never taught a course?

Solution 9-3a. *Using NOT IN*

```
SQL> select e.*
  2  from    employees e
  3  where   e.empno not in (select o.trainer
  4                          from   offerings o);

no rows selected

SQL>
```

Solution 9-3b. *Using NOT EXISTS*

```
SQL> select e.*
  2  from    employees e
  3  where   not exists (select o.trainer
  4                      from   offerings o
  5                      where  o.trainer = e.empno);
```

```
EMPNO ENAME     INIT  JOB         MGR BDATE         MSAL  COMM DEPTNO
----- --------  ----- --------    ----- ----------- ----- ----- ------
 7499 ALLEN     JAM   SALESREP   7698 20-FEB-1961   1600   300     30
 7521 WARD      TF    SALESREP   7698 22-FEB-1962   1250   500     30
 7654 MARTIN    P     SALESREP   7698 28-SEP-1956   1250  1400     30
 7698 BLAKE     R     MANAGER    7839 01-NOV-1963   2850           30
 7782 CLARK     AB    MANAGER    7839 09-JUN-1965   2450           10
 7839 KING      CC    DIRECTOR        17-NOV-1952   5000           10
 7844 TURNER    JJ    SALESREP   7698 28-SEP-1968   1500     0     30
 7900 JONES     R     ADMIN      7698 03-DEC-1969    800           30
 7934 MILLER    TJA   ADMIN      7782 23-JAN-1962   1300           10

9 rows selected.

SQL>
```

At first sight, you might think that both of these solutions are correct. However, the results are different. Now, which one is the correct solution?

You can come up with convincing arguments for both solutions. Note that you have three course offerings with a null value in the TRAINER column.

- If you interpret these null values as "trainer unknown," you can never say *with certainty* that an employee never taught a course.

- The second query obviously treats the null values differently. Its result (with nine employees) is what you probably expected.

The different results are *not* caused by an SQL bug. You simply have two SQL statements with different results, so they must have a different meaning. In such cases, you must revisit the query in natural language and try to formulate it more precisely in order to eliminate any ambiguities.

Last but not least, our OFFERINGS table happens to contain only data from the past. If you want a correct answer to this exercise under all circumstances, you should also add a condition to check the course dates against SYSDATE.

4. Which employees attended all build courses (category BLD)? They are entitled to get a discount on the next course they attend.

Solution 9-4a. *Using NOT EXISTS Twice*

```
SQL> select   e.empno, e.ename, e.init
  2  from     employees e
  3  where    not exists
  4           (select c.*
  5            from   courses c
  6            where  c.category = 'BLD'
  7            and    not exists
  8                   (select r.*
```

```
 9                 from    registrations r
10                 where   r.course    = c.code
11                 and     r.attendee = e.empno
12                 )
13          );

  EMPNO ENAME     INIT
-------- -------- -----
   7499 ALLEN     JAM

SQL>
```

Solution 9-4b. *Using GROUP BY*

```
SQL> select    e.empno, e.ename, e.init
  2  from       registrations r
  3             join
  4             courses   c on (r.course = c.code)
  5             join
  6             employees e on (r.attendee = e.empno)
  7  where      c.category = 'BLD'
  8  group by e.empno, e.ename, e.init
  9  having     count(distinct r.course)
 10          = (select count(*)
 11             from    courses
 12             where   category = 'BLD');

  EMPNO ENAME     INIT
-------- -------- -----
   7499 ALLEN     JAM

SQL>
```

This is not an easy exercise. Both of these solutions are correct.

5. Provide a list of all employees having the same monthly salary and commission as (at least) one employee of department 30. You are interested in only employees from other departments.

Solution 9-5.

```
SQL> select e.ename
  2  ,       e.msal
  3  ,       e.comm
  4  from    employees e
  5  where   e.deptno <> 30
  6  and     (       e.msal,coalesce(e.comm,-1) ) in
  7          (select x.msal,coalesce(x.comm,-1)
```

```
 8          from    employees x
 9          where   x.deptno = 30              );


ENAME          MSAL      COMM
--------    --------  --------
SMITH           800


SQL>
```

Note that this solution uses the COALESCE function, which you need to make comparisons with null values evaluate to true, in this case. The solution uses the value –1 based on the reasonable assumption that the commission column never contains negative values. However, if you check the definition of the EMPLOYEES table, you will see that there actually is *no* constraint to allow only nonnegative commission values. It looks like you found a possible data model enhancement here. Such a constraint would make your solution—using the negative value in the COALESCE function—correct under all circumstances.

6. Look again at Listings 9-4 and 9-5. Are they really logically equivalent? Just for testing purposes, search on a nonexisting job and execute both queries again. Explain the results.

Solution 9-6.

```
SQL> select e.empno, e.ename, e.job, e.msal
  2  from    employees e
  3  where   e.msal > ALL (select b.msal
  4                         from    employees b
  5                         where   b.job = 'BARTENDER');

  EMPNO ENAME     JOB          MSAL
-------- --------  --------  --------
   7369 SMITH     TRAINER       800
   7499 ALLEN     SALESREP     1600
   7521 WARD      SALESREP     1250
   7566 JONES     MANAGER      2975
   7654 MARTIN    SALESREP     1250
   7698 BLAKE     MANAGER      2850
   7782 CLARK     MANAGER      2450
   7788 SCOTT     TRAINER      3000
   7839 KING      DIRECTOR     5000
   7844 TURNER    SALESREP     1500
   7876 ADAMS     TRAINER      1100
   7900 JONES     ADMIN         800
   7902 FORD      TRAINER      3000
   7934 MILLER    ADMIN        1300

14 rows selected.
```

```
SQL> select e.empno, e.ename, e.job, e.msal
  2  from    employees e
  3  where   e.msal >      (select MAX(b.msal)
  4                         from    employees b
  5                         where   b.job = 'BARTENDER');

no rows selected

SQL>
```

This example searches for BARTENDER. The subquery returns an empty set, because the EMPLOYEES table contains no bartenders. Therefore, the > ALL condition of the first query is *true* for every row of the EMPLOYEES table. This outcome complies with an important law derived from mathematical logic. The following statement is always true, regardless of the expression you specify following the colon:

- For all elements x of the empty set: …

This explains why you see all 14 employees in the result of the first query.

The second query uses a different approach, using the MAX function in the subquery. The maximum of an empty set results in a null value, so the WHERE clause becomes WHERE E.MSAL > NULL, which returns *unknown* for every row. This explains why the second query returns no rows.

7. You saw a series of examples in this chapter about all employees that ever taught an SQL course (in Listings 9-9 through 9-11). How can you adapt these queries in such a way that they answer the negation of the same question (… all employees that *never* …)?

Solution 9-7a. *Negation of Listing 9-9*

```
SQL> select e.*
  2  from    employees e
  3  where   NOT exists (select o.*
  4                      from    offerings o
  5                      where   o.course = 'SQL'
  6                      and     o.trainer = e.empno);
```

EMPNO	ENAME	INIT	JOB	MGR	BDATE	MSAL	COMM	DEPTNO
7499	ALLEN	JAM	SALESREP	7698	20-FEB-1961	1600	300	30
7521	WARD	TF	SALESREP	7698	22-FEB-1962	1250	500	30
7566	JONES	JM	MANAGER	7839	02-APR-1967	2975		20
7654	MARTIN	P	SALESREP	7698	28-SEP-1956	1250	1400	30
7698	BLAKE	R	MANAGER	7839	01-NOV-1963	2850		30
7782	CLARK	AB	MANAGER	7839	09-JUN-1965	2450		10
7788	SCOTT	SCJ	TRAINER	7566	26-NOV-1959	3000		20
7839	KING	CC	DIRECTOR		17-NOV-1952	5000		10

```
7844 TURNER   JJ    SALESREP  7698 28-SEP-1968  1500    0    30
7876 ADAMS    AA    TRAINER   7788 30-DEC-1966  1100         20
7900 JONES    R     ADMIN     7698 03-DEC-1969   800         30
7934 MILLER   TJA   ADMIN     7782 23-JAN-1962  1300         10

12 rows selected.

SQL>
```

Solution 9-7b. *Negation of Listing 9-10*

```
SQL> select e.*
  2  from    employees e
  3  where   e.empno NOT in (select o.trainer
  4                          from    offerings o
  5                          where   o.course = 'SQL');

EMPNO ENAME    INIT  JOB       MGR  BDATE        MSAL  COMM DEPTNO
----- -------- ----- --------- ---- ----------- ----- ----- ------
 7499 ALLEN    JAM   SALESREP  7698 20-FEB-1961  1600   300    30
 7521 WARD     TF    SALESREP  7698 22-FEB-1962  1250   500    30
...
 7934 MILLER   TJA   ADMIN     7782 23-JAN-1962  1300          10

12 rows selected.

SQL>
```

This looks good—you get back the same 12 employees. However, you were lucky, because all SQL course offerings happen to have a trainer assigned. If you use the NOT IN and NOT EXISTS operators, you should *always* investigate whether your subquery could possibly produce null values and how they are handled.

The following negation for Listing 9-11 is *wrong*.

Solution 9-7c. *Wrong Negation for Listing 9-11*

```
SQL> select DISTINCT e.*
  2  from    employees e
  3         join
  4         offerings o
  5         on e.empno = o.trainer
  6  where   o.course <> 'SQL';

EMPNO ENAME    INIT  JOB       MGR  BDATE        MSAL  COMM DEPTNO
----- -------- ----- --------- ---- ----------- ----- ----- ------
 7369 SMITH    N     TRAINER   7902 17-DEC-1965   800          20
 7566 JONES    JM    MANAGER   7839 02-APR-1967  2975          20
```

```
7788 SCOTT    SCJ    TRAINER    7566 26-NOV-1959  3000           20
7876 ADAMS    AA     TRAINER    7788 30-DEC-1966  1100           20
7902 FORD     MG     TRAINER    7566 13-FEB-1959  3000           20

SQL>
```

It is not an easy task to transform this join solution into its negation.

8. Check out your solution for exercise 4 in Chapter 8: "For all course offerings, list the course code, begin date, and number of registrations. Sort your results on the number of registrations, from high to low." Can you come up with a more elegant solution now, without using an outer join?

Solution 9-8. *A More Elegant Solution for Exercise 4 in Chapter 8*

```
SQL> select    course
  2  ,          begindate
  3  ,         (select count(*)
  4            from   registrations r
  5            where  r.course = o.course
  6            and    r.begindate = o.begindate)
  7            as     registrations
  8  from      offerings o
  9  order by registrations;

COURSE BEGINDATE    REGISTRATIONS
------ -----------  -------------
ERM    15-JAN-2001              0
PRO    19-FEB-2001              0
XML    18-SEP-2000              0
RSD    24-FEB-2001              0
OAU    27-SEP-2000              1
SQL    13-DEC-1999              2
XML    03-FEB-2000              2
JAV    01-FEB-2000              3
SQL    04-OCT-1999              3
PLS    11-SEP-2000              3
OAU    10-AUG-1999              3
SQL    12-APR-1999              4
JAV    13-DEC-1999              5

13 rows selected.

SQL>
```

9. Who attended (at least) the same courses as employee 7788?

Solution 9-9.

```
SQL> select e.ename, e.init
  2  from    employees e
  3  where   e.empno <> 7788
  4  and     not exists
  5          (select r1.course
  6           from    registrations r1
  7           where   r1.attendee = 7788
  8           MINUS
  9           select r2.course
 10           from    registrations r2
 11           where   r2.attendee = e.empno);

ENAME     INIT
--------  -----
ALLEN     JAM
BLAKE     R
KING      CC
ADAMS     AA

SQL>
```

This is not an easy exercise. The elegant solution shown here uses the MINUS set operator and a correlated subquery. Note the correct position of the negation on the fourth line. You can read the solution as follows:

"List all employees (except employee 7788 himself/herself) for which you cannot find a course attended by employee 7788 and not attended by those employees."

The first subquery (see lines 5 through 7) is not correlated, and it results in all courses attended by employee 7788. The second subquery (see lines 9 through 11) is correlated, and it produces all courses attended by employee e.

■**Note** This exercise is similar to exercise 4 in this chapter. Both exercises belong to the same category of "subset problems." This means that the solutions of Chapter 9's exercises 4 and 9 are interchangeable (not verbatim, of course, because the exercises are different; however, they can be solved with the same approach).

---

10. Give the name and initials of all employees at the bottom of the management hierarchy, with a third column showing the number of management levels above them.

Solution 9-10.

```
SQL> select      ename, init
  2  ,            (level - 1) as levels_above
  3  from         employees
  4  where        connect_by_isleaf = 1
  5  start with mgr is null
  6  connect by prior empno = mgr;

ENAME    INIT  LEVELS_ABOVE
-------- ----- ------------
ADAMS    AA               3
SMITH    N                3
ALLEN    JAM              2
WARD     TF               2
MARTIN   P                2
TURNER   JJ               2
JONES    R                2
MILLER   TJA              2

8 rows selected.

SQL>
```

11. Look at the query result in Listing 9-22. The last two rows are:

7902	SMITH	800	800
	KING	5000	5000

Looking at the other rows in Listing 9-22, you might expect the following results instead:

7902	SMITH	800	800
	KING	5000	5800

What is the correct result, and why?

Answer: The SQL*Plus BREAK setting is confusing in this result. The empty space under 7902 is *not* caused by the BREAK setting suppressing a repeating column value; instead, it is a null value. Therefore, the PARTITION BY MGR clause starts a new group for all employees with a null value in the MGR column, and starts from zero again to sum the salaries in that group. By coincidence, this group contains only a single employee.

12. Why don't you get any result from the following query?

```
SQL> select * from employees where rownum = 2;

no rows selected

SQL>
```

Answer: The ROWNUM pseudo column value gets its values when rows arrive in the result set. The first candidate row is rejected by the WHERE clause, because it is not the second one; therefore, the query result stays empty. This means that you should always use the ROWNUM pseudo column with the comparison operator < or <= to get results.

Chapter 10 Exercises

1. Look at the example discussed in Listings 10-7, 10-8, and 10-9. Rewrite the query in Listing 10-9 without using a view, by using the WITH operator.

   Solution 10-1. *Listing 10-9 Rewritten to Use the WITH Operator*

```
SQL> with    course_days as
  2          (select   e.empno, e.ename
  3          ,         sum(c.duration) as days
  4          from      registrations r
  5          ,         courses        c
  6          ,         employees      e
  7          where     e.empno  = r.attendee
  8          and       c.code   = r.course
  9          group by e.empno, e.ename)
 10  select *
 11  from    course_days
 12  where   days > (select avg(days)
 13                  from    course_days);

  EMPNO ENAME       DAYS
-------- -------- --------
    7499 ALLEN         11
    7698 BLAKE         12
    7788 SCOTT         12
    7839 KING           8
    7876 ADAMS          9
    7902 FORD           9

SQL>
```

2. Look at Listing 10-12. How is it possible that you can delete employee 7654 via this EMP view? There are rows in the HISTORY table, referring to that employee via a foreign key constraint.

   Answer: You can delete that employee because you created the foreign key constraint with the CASCADE DELETE option, so all corresponding HISTORY rows are deleted implicitly.

3. Look at the view definition in Listing 10-18. Does this view implement the foreign key constraints from the REGISTRATIONS table to the EMPLOYEES and COURSES tables? Explain your answer.

   Answer: No, it doesn't. The view checks insertions and updates, but it doesn't prevent you from deleting any rows from the EMPLOYEES and COURSES tables; that is, the view implements only one side of those foreign key constraints.

■**Tip** Don't try to program your own referential integrity constraint checking. Your solution will probably overlook something, and it will always be less efficient than the declarative constraints of the Oracle DBMS.

---

4. Create a SAL_HISTORY view providing the following overview for all employees, based on the HISTORY table: For each employee, show the hire date, the review dates, and the salary changes as a consequence of those reviews.

   Solution 10-4. *The SAL_HISTORY View*

```
SQL> create or replace view sal_history as
  2  select empno
  3  ,      min(begindate) over
  4         (partition by empno)
  5         as hiredate
  6  ,      begindate as reviewdate
  7  ,      msal - lag(msal) over
  8         (partition by empno
  9             order by empno, begindate)
 10         as salary_raise
 11  from   history;

View created.

SQL> break on empno on hiredate
SQL> select * from sal_history;

EMPNO HIREDATE    REVIEWDATE   SALARY_RAISE
----- ----------- ------------ ------------
 7369 01-JAN-2000 01-JAN-2000
                  01-FEB-2000          -150
 7499 01-JUN-1988 01-JUN-1988
                  01-JUL-1989           300
                  01-DEC-1993           200
```

```
                        01-OCT-1995              200
                        01-NOV-1999             -100
    7521 01-OCT-1986 01-OCT-1986
    ...
    7934 01-FEB-1998 01-FEB-1998
                        01-MAY-1998                5
                        01-FEB-1999               10
                        01-JAN-2000               10

79 rows selected.

SQL>
```

Chapter 11 Exercises

1. Look at Listings 11-26 and 11-37. Apart from aesthetics, there is another important reason why the lines surrounding the script headers in those two listings switch from minus signs to equal signs. Obviously, the first two minus signs are mandatory to turn the lines into comments. What would be wrong with using only minus signs?

   Answer: It is the last minus sign that causes trouble. It will make SQL*Plus interpret the next line as a continuation of the current line. Since the current line is a comment, the next line will be considered a continuation of that comment. Therefore, the SQL or SQL*Plus command on the next line will be *ignored* by SQL*Plus.

2. Create a SQL*Plus script to create indexes. The script should prompt for a table name and a column name (or list of column names), and then *generate* the index name according to the following standard: i_<tab-id>_<col-id>.

   Solution 11-2. *SQL*Plus Script to Create Indexes*

```
accept table_name            -
      default &&table_name -
      prompt 'Create index on table [&table_name]: '
accept column_name           -
      default &&column_name -
      prompt 'on column(s) [&column_name]: '
set    termout off
store  set sqlplus_settings replace
save   buffer.sql replace
column dummy new_value index_name
set    heading off feedback off verify off
set    termout on

select 'Creating index'
,      upper(substr( 'i_'                          ||
```

```
                       substr('&table_name',1,3) ||
                       ' '                         ||
                       translate
                       ( replace
                         ( '&column_name'
                         , ' ', '')
                         , ',', '_')
                       , 1, 30)
        ) as dummy
,       '...'
from    dual;

create index &index_name
on &table_name(&column_name);

get     buffer.sql nolist
@sqlplus_settings
set     termout on
```

The following are some comments on this solution:

- The script "remembers" table names and column names, and offers them as default values on consecutive executions. This may save you some time when creating multiple indexes.

- The script saves all current SQL*Plus settings before changing the SQL*Plus environment. This enables the script to restore the original SQL*Plus environment at the end of the script.

- The script saves the current contents of the SQL buffer, and then restores the contents at the end with the GET ... NOLIST command. This way, you can resume working on that SQL statement.

- The COLUMN DUMMY NEW_VALUE INDEX_NAME command captures the result of the query against the DUAL table, which generates the index name.

- The index name generation contains many SQL functions. It takes the first three characters of the table name as the table identifier. The script removes all spaces from the column name list, and then replaces the commas with underscores. To avoid error messages for too-long index names, the script truncates the result to a maximum length of 30.

3. Create a SQL*Plus script to produce an index overview. The script should prompt for a table name, allowing you to specify any leading part of a table name. That is, the script should automatically append a % wildcard to the value entered. Then it should produce a report of all indexes, showing the table name, index name, index type, and number of columns on which the index is based.

Solution 11-3. *SQL*Plus Script to Produce an Index Overview*

```
set       termout off
store     set sqlplus_settings.sql replace
save      buffer.sql replace
set       verify off feedback off
set       termout on
break     on table_name skip 1 on index_type

accept    table_name default &&table_name -
          prompt 'List indexes on table [&table_name.%]: '

select    ui.table_name
,         decode(ui.index_type
                  ,'NORMAL', ui.uniqueness
                  ,ui.index_type) as index_type
,         ui.index_name
,       (select count(*)
          from    user_ind_columns uic
          where   uic.table_name = ui.table_name
          and     uic.index_name = ui.index_name) as col_count
from      user_indexes  ui
where     ui.table_name like upper('&table_name.%')
order by ui.table_name
,         ui.uniqueness desc;

get       buffer.sql nolist
@sqlplus_settings
set       termout on
```

Many SQL*Plus tricks in this script are similar to the ones used in the script for the previous exercise. Here are some additional comments on this solution:

- The BREAK command enhances the readability.

- You use the same default value trick for the table name.

- You need the period character in the ACCEPT command as a separator between the TABLE_NAME variable and the percent sign.

4. Create a script that disables all constraints in your schema.

Answer: First, you must find out which SQL statement allows you to disable constraints, because your script is going to generate that statement. The following SQL command is the most obvious choice:

```
SQL> ALTER TABLE <table-name> DISABLE CONSTRAINT <constraint-name> [CASCADE]
```

As the next step, you must figure out how to retrieve relevant information about your constraints. The SQL*Plus DESCRIBE command is useful:

```
SQL> describe user_constraints
Name                                   Null?     Type
-------------------------------------- -------- ------------
OWNER                                  NOT NULL VARCHAR2(30)
CONSTRAINT_NAME                        NOT NULL VARCHAR2(30)
CONSTRAINT_TYPE                                 VARCHAR2(1)
TABLE_NAME                             NOT NULL VARCHAR2(30)
SEARCH_CONDITION                                LONG
R_OWNER                                         VARCHAR2(30)
R_CONSTRAINT_NAME                               VARCHAR2(30)
DELETE_RULE                                     VARCHAR2(9)
STATUS                                          VARCHAR2(8)
DEFERRABLE                                      VARCHAR2(14)
DEFERRED                                        VARCHAR2(9)
VALIDATED                                       VARCHAR2(13)
GENERATED                                       VARCHAR2(14)
BAD                                             VARCHAR2(3)
RELY                                            VARCHAR2(4)
LAST_CHANGE                                     DATE
INDEX_OWNER                                     VARCHAR2(30)
INDEX_NAME                                      VARCHAR2(30)
INVALID                                         VARCHAR2(7)
VIEW_RELATED                                    VARCHAR2(14)

SQL>
```

By executing some test queries, it becomes apparent which columns of the
USER_CONSTRAINTS view you need. Let's look at a first attempt to generate the
ALTER TABLE commands.

Solution 11-4a. *First Attempt to Generate the Correct SQL*

```
SQL> select 'ALTER TABLE '||table_name||' DISABLE CONSTRAINT
  2          '||constraint_name||';'
  3  from    user_constraints;
```

However, if you capture the output from this query in a script file and execute it, you
will discover that there is room for improvement. Some ALTER TABLE commands may
fail with the following message:

```
ORA-02297: cannot disable constraint (BOOK.xxx) - dependencies exist
```

You can fix this problem in two ways:

- Add the CASCADE keyword to the generated ALTER TABLE commands.

- Sort the ALTER TABLE commands in such a way that all primary keys are disabled
  before the foreign key constraints.

Let's implement both fixes. Also, let's add a WHERE clause to the query to avoid generating ALTER TABLE commands for constraints that are disabled already.

Solution 11-4b. *Second Attempt to Generate the Correct SQL*

```
SQL> select 'ALTER TABLE '||table_name
  2         ||' DISABLE CONSTRAINT '||constraint_name
  3         ||' CASCADE;'
  4  from   user_constraints
  5  where  status <> 'DISABLED'
  6  order  by case constraint_type
  7            when 'P' then 1 else 2 end;
```

Finally, now that you are satisfied with the result of the query, you add the appropriate SQL*Plus commands to capture and execute the query result. The final script looks like the following.

Solution 11-4c. *SQL*Plus Script to Disable All Constraints of a Schema*

```
set    pagesize 0 verify off feedback off trimspool on
spool  doit.sql replace
select 'ALTER TABLE '||table_name||
       ' DISABLE CONSTRAINT '||constraint_name||' CASCADE;'
from   user_constraints
where  status <> 'DISABLED'
order  by case constraint_type when 'P' then 1 else 2 end;
spool off
@doit
exit
```

You can build many useful SQL*Plus scripts, once you have discovered how you can use SQL*Plus as a command generator.

Chapter 12 Exercises

1. The SALGRADES table has two columns to indicate salary ranges: LOWERLIMIT and UPPERLIMIT. Define your own SALRANGE_T type, based on a varray of two NUMBER(6,2) values, and use it to create an alternative SALGRADES2 table.

Solution 12-1.

```
SQL> create or replace type salrange_t
  2  as varray(2) of number(6,2);
  3  /

Type created.
```

```
SQL> create table salgrades2
  2  ( grade        number(2)   constraint S2_PK
  3                             primary key
  4  , salrange     salrange_t  constraint S2_RANGE_NN
  5                             not null
  6  , bonus        NUMBER(6,2) constraint S2_BONUS_NN
  7                             not null
  8  ) ;

Table created.

SQL>
```

2. Fill the new SALGRADES2 table with a single INSERT statement, using the existing SALGRADES table.

Solution 12-2.

```
SQL> insert into salgrades2
  2  select grade
  3  ,      salrange_t(lowerlimit,upperlimit)
  4  ,      bonus
  5  from   salgrades;

5 rows created.

SQL> col salrange format a25
SQL> select * from salgrades2;

    GRADE SALRANGE                     BONUS
--------- ------------------------- --------
        1 SALRANGE_T(700, 1200)           0
        2 SALRANGE_T(1201, 1400)         50
        3 SALRANGE_T(1401, 2000)        100
        4 SALRANGE_T(2001, 3000)        200
        5 SALRANGE_T(3001, 9999)        500

5 rows selected.

SQL>
```

3. Create a table TESTNEST with two columns: column X and column MX. Column X is NUMBER(1,0) with values 2, 3, 4, ..., 9. Column MX is a nested table, based on a MX_TAB_T type, containing all multiples of X less than or equal to 20.

Solution 12-3a. *Table TESTNEST Creation*

```
SQL> create or replace type mx_tab_t
  2  as table of number(2);
  3  /

Type created.

SQL> create table testnest
  2  ( x     number(1,0)
  3  , mx    mx_tab_t
  4  ) nested table mx store as mx_tab;

Table created.

SQL>
```

You can use pure INSERT statements to populate the TESTNEST table. The following solution uses PL/SQL to insert all rows in an efficient way. The PL/SQL syntax is straightforward.

Solution 12-3b. *Table TESTNEST Population*

```
SQL> declare
  2    i number;
  3    j number;
  4  begin
  5    for i in 2..9 loop
  6      insert into testnest (x, mx)
  7                    values (i, mx_tab_t());
  8      for j in 1..20 loop
  9        exit when i*j > 20;
 10        insert into table (select mx from testnest where x=i)
 11                   values (i*j);
 12      end loop;
 13    end loop;
 14  end;
 15  /

PL/SQL procedure successfully completed.

SQL>
```

Now, let's check the contents of the TESTNEST table.

Solution 12-3c. *Table TESTNEST Query*

```
SQL> col x  format 9
SQL> col mx format a80
SQL> select * from testnest;

 X  MX
 -- ----------------------------------------------
  2  MX_TAB_T(2, 4, 6, 8, 10 ,12, 14, 16, 18, 20)
  3  MX_TAB_T(3, 6, 9, 12, 15, 18)
  4  MX_TAB_T(4, 8, 12, 16, 20)
  5  MX_TAB_T(5, 10, 15, 20)
  6  MX_TAB_T(6, 12, 18)
  7  MX_TAB_T(7, 14)
  8  MX_TAB_T(8, 16)
  9  MX_TAB_T(9, 18)

8 rows selected.

SQL>
```

4. Use multiset operators to solve the following problems, using the TESTNEST table you created and populated in the previous exercise:

   a. Which rows have a nested table containing value 12?

   Answer: 2, 3, 4, 6

Solution 12-4a.

```
SQL> select *
  2  from    testnest
  3  where   12 member of mx;

 X MX
 -- ----------------------------------------------
  2 MX_TAB_T(2, 4, 6, 8, 10, 12, 14, 16, 18, 20)
  3 MX_TAB_T(3, 6, 9, 12, 15, 18)
  4 MX_TAB_T(4, 8, 12, 16, 20)
  6 MX_TAB_T(6, 12, 18)

SQL>
```

   b. Which nested tables are *not* a subset of any other subset?

   Answer: 2, 3, 5, 7

Solution 12-4b.

```
SQL> select t1.*
  2  from    testnest t1
  3  where   not exists
  4          (select t2.*
  5           from    testnest t2
  6           where   t2.x <> t1.x
  7           and     t1.mx submultiset of t2.mx);

 X MX
-- ---------------------------------------------
 2 MX_TAB_T(2, 4, 6, 8, 10, 12, 14, 16, 18, 20)
 3 MX_TAB_T(3, 6, 9, 12, 15, 18)
 5 MX_TAB_T(5, 10, 15, 20)
 7 MX_TAB_T(7, 14)

SQL>
```

c. Which nested tables have more than 42 different nonempty subsets?

Answer: 2, 3

Solution 12-4c.

```
SQL> select x
  2  ,       cardinality(powermultiset(mx))
  3  from    testnest
  4  where   cardinality(powermultiset(mx)) > 42;

 X CARDINALITY(POWERMULTISET(MX))
-- ------------------------------
 2                           1023
 3                             63

SQL>
```

APPENDIX E

■ ■ ■

Oracle Documentation, Web Sites, and Bibliography

As the title indicates, this appendix offers an overview of the Oracle documentation, a list of useful web sites, and a short bibliography.

Oracle Documentation

The complete Oracle documentation is accessible online, both in PDF and HTML format, via Oracle Technology Network (OTN). Scroll down to the Resources section and select "Database" from the "Select Documentation" dropdown list. This brings you to the page shown in Figure E-1.

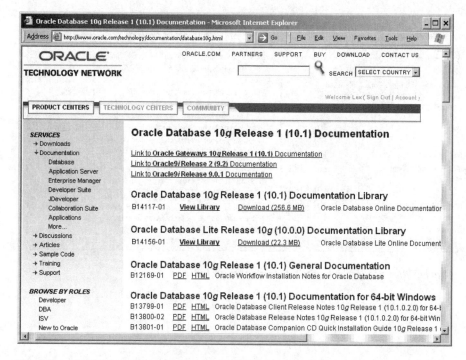

Figure E-1. *OTN Documentation home page*

The Oracle documentation consists of two title types: *generic* documentation and *platform-specific* documentation. You can navigate to the platform-specific documentation from the OTN Documentation home page (Figure E-1). At the bottom of the screen shown in the figure, you can see the link to the documentation for 64-bit Windows. If you scroll down further, you will see links for all other operating systems.

To navigate to the generic (platform-independent) Oracle Database 10g documentation from the OTN Documentation home page, click the View Library link next to B14117-01. If you like, you can also download the complete generic documentation by clicking the Download link next to B14117-01. If you click the View Library link, you'll see the screen shown in Figure E-2.

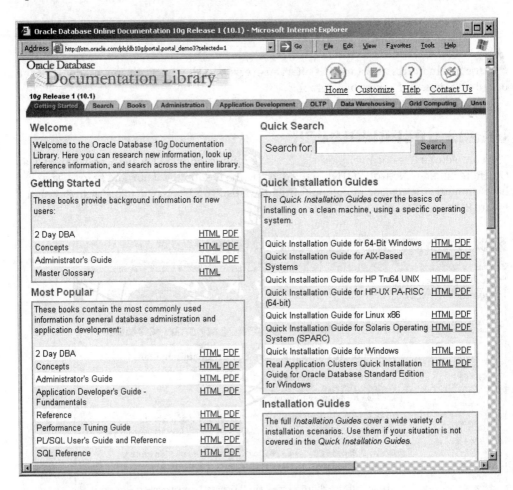

Figure E-2. *Oracle Database 10g Release 1 Documentation Library*

Figure E-2 shows a useful portal to the most popular documentation titles. As you can see, there are various tabs allowing you to drill down into specific areas of interest, such as administration, application development, or data warehousing. Via the Books tab, you can navigate to a complete overview of all documentation titles, as shown in Figure E-3.

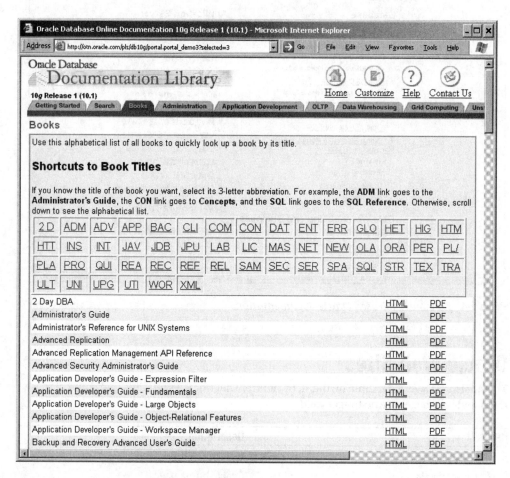

Figure E-3. *List of shortcuts to all book titles*

If you know the documentation title abbreviations, you can navigate quickly within this screen by clicking the appropriate shortcut at the top of the screen. For example, click the SQL shortcut to navigate to the point where all book titles start with "SQL."

If you are working with previous releases of the Oracle DBMS, you can search the corresponding documentation as well, as shown in Figure E-4. You can navigate to this page by selecting SERVICES ➤ Documentation ➤ More. . . in the navigation pane on the left side of Figure E-1.

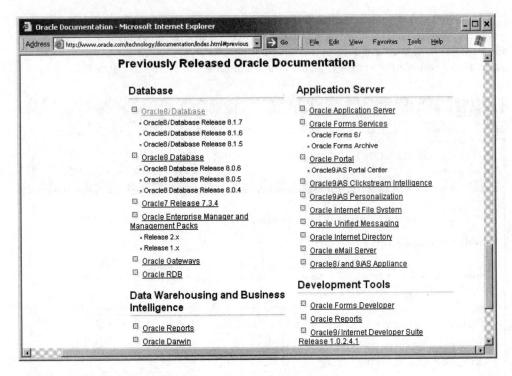

Figure E-4. *Previously released Oracle documentation*

Oracle Web Sites

The Internet is a very dynamic medium, by nature. Therefore, it's possible that some of these URLs and web pages are no longer valid.

URL	Description
http://www.naturaljoin.nl	Web site of the author
http://www.oracle.com	Oracle home page
http://www.oracle.com/database	Oracle database home page
http://metalink.oracle.com	Information about bugs, patches, etc.
http://www.oracle.com/technology/obe/start	Oracle By Example series
http://www.oracle.com/oramag	Oracle Magazines
http://shop.osborne.com/cgi-bin/oraclepress	Oracle Press series
http://www.dbazine.com/oracle.shtml	Various Oracle articles
http://www.orablogs.com	Blogs for Oracle developers
http://www.dbdebunk.com	Fabian Pascal, Chris Date
http://www.oracle-home.com	Online Oracle bibliography
http://www.ioug.org	International Oracle Users Group

URL	Description
http://www.oaktable.net	Oak Table Network
http://asktom.oracle.com	Tom Kyte's Q&A web site
http://www.hotsos.com	Hotsos (Cary Millsap et al.)
http://www.ixora.com.au	Ixora (Steve Adams)
http://www.jlcomp.demon.co.uk	JL Computer Consultancy (Jonathan Lewis)
http://www.scaleabilities.com	Scale Abilities (James Morle, Jeff Needham)

Bibliography

The references are listed in order of publication date.

E.F. Codd: *Derivability, Redundancy, and Consistency of Relations Stored in Large Data Banks* (IBM Research Report RJ599, August 1969)

E.F. Codd: *A Relational Model of Data for Large Shared Data Banks* (CACM 13, No. 6, June 1970)

E.F. Codd: *The Relational Model for Database Management Version 2* (Addison-Wesley, 1990)

C.J. Date: *Relational Database Writings 1985-1989* (Addison-Wesley, 1990)

C.J. Date, Hugh Darwen: *Relational Database Writings 1989-1991* (Addison-Wesley, 1992)

C.J. Date: *Relational Database Writings 1991-1994* (Addison-Wesley, 1995)

C.J. Date, Hugh Darwen: *A Guide to the SQL Standard* (Addison-Wesley, 1997)

C.J. Date (et al.): *Relational Database Writings 1994-1997* (Addison-Wesley, 1998)

C.J. Date, Hugh Darwen: *The Third Manifesto: Foundation for Future Database Systems* (Addison-Wesley, 2000)

Thomas Kyte: *Expert One-on-One Oracle* (Apress, 2001)

C.J. Date: *The Database Relational Model: A Retrospective Review and Analysis* (Addison-Wesley, 2001)

J. Melton and A.R. Simon: *SQL:1999 – Understanding Relational Language Components* (Morgan Kaufmann Publishers, 2002)

J. Melton: *Advanced SQL:1999 – Understanding Object-Relational and Other Advanced Features* (Morgan Kaufmann Publishers, 2003)

C.J. Date, Hugh Darwen, Nikos A. Lorentzos: *Temporal Data and the Relational Model* (Morgan Kaufmann Publishers, 2003)

Thomas Kyte: *Effective Oracle by Design* (Oracle Press/Osborne, 2003)

C.J. Date: *An Introduction to Database Systems (8th edition)* (Addison-Wesley, 2004)

Connor McDonald (et al.): *Mastering Oracle PL/SQL* (Apress, 2004)

Kevin Loney: *Oracle Database 10g The Complete Reference* (Oracle Press/Osborne, 2004)

Mogens Nørgaard (et al.): *Oracle Insights: Tales of the Oak Table* (Apress, 2004)

Index